Administering Apache

Mark Arnold

McGraw-Hill
New York   San Francisco   Washington, D.C.
Auckland   Bogotá   Caracas   Lisbon   London   Madrid
Mexico City   Milan   Montreal   New Delhi   San Juan
Singapore   Sydney   Tokyo   Toronto

McGraw-Hill

A Division of The McGraw·Hill Companies

Copyright © 2000 by The McGraw-Hill Companies, Inc. All rights reserved. Printed in the United States of America. Except as permitted under the United States Copyright Act of 1976, no part of this publication may be reproduced or distributed in any form or by any means, or stored in a data base or retrieval system, without the prior written permission of the publisher.

1 2 3 4 5 6 7 8 9 0   AGM/AGM   0 5 4 3 2 1 0

ISBN 0-07-212291-9

The sponsoring editor for this book was Michael Sprague and the production manager was Clare Stanley. It was set in Esprit by Patricia Wallenburg.

Printed and bound by Quebecor/Martinsburg.

Throughout this book, trademarked names are used. Rather than put a trademark symbol after every occurrence of a trademarked name, we use names in an editorial fashion only, and to the benefit of the trademark owner, with no intention of infringement of the trademark. Where such designations appear in this book, they have been printed with initial caps.

 This book is printed on recycled, acid-free paper containing a minimum of 50% recycled, de-inked fiber.

Contents

Contents

Contents

Preface

"I'm an Internet Service Provider and I want to provide more services—safely."

Here's how.

"I'm a web developer and I want to create interactive and adaptive web sites."

Apache provides full featured content manipulation services.

"I'm an applications programmer and it's time to web-enable my product. If I could just get the web server to _____."

Guess what. You can.

"I'm a corporate system administrator. The VP of marketing just breezed past my stack of outstanding service requests and proclaimed, 'We need a Web server for free by yesterday on an OS you don't know.'"

Let's get it done.

Acknowledgments

Mark Arnold would like to thank: Gwen Rhine for her contributions to the Appendix (and constant expresso); Michael at theplanet.com for reviewing Chapter 5; the other authors for getting their parts done; my family, my current clients (Kintetsu World Enterprises and BrightStar), the editor (Michael Sprague), the agent (Margot Maley), and the typesetter (Patty Wallenburg) for their patience while I juggled several projects. I would like to thank Arthur Griffith (author of *COBOL for Dummies*) for referring me to Margot.

Jeff Almeida would like to thank: Clint, for suggesting me to Mark, and Mark for involving me; mom, without whom I wouldn't be around in the first place; my wife Steph and our puppy Berg, for putting up with me not being around as much last winter while writing this; my father-in-law Kurt, for his encouragement and that sanity-saving trip to Disneyland; my longtime best friend Bart Whitmore, who got the "book bug" to bite me initially, about a year ago; Brennan Stehling, for hosting my websites and email, teaching me the trick involving sendmail domains in Chapter 8, and just being an all-around good guy; Siyuan Chen, for teaching me everything I know about DNS and laying out UNIX filesystems; Jack Siemsen, for suggesting many years ago that I have a talent for doing this sort of thing; Paul Albitz and Cricket Liu, for writing the Bible of DNS; whoever it was that wrote that little, wire-o-bound quick reference from which I learned vi; Doug MacEachern, Vivek Khera, Dean Gaudet, Ralf Engelschall, Randy Terbush, Rasmus Lerdorf, et al. for being "giants with easily accessible shoulders;" you've made it really easy to accomplish great things with Apache; Steve Kann, for "formally" releasing his gold nugget of a module that I dug up in a mailing-list archive, and for his words of encouragement; Ryan Lindsay of Covalent, for his words of encouragement on the show floor of LinuxWorld; Kevin, Chris, Dale, Steve, Bob and the rest of the Hartford Perl Mongers, for listening to me rant occasionally; some of the people who helped fan the early flames of my 'net addiction in grad school: Tony Rosati, Nelson Daniel, Ken Meerdink, John Cowgill, Mike Smith, Sean Wilson, Scott Wimer, J. Richard Rock, Gena Minden, Wendi Smit, Jay Rambo, Brandy Lennert, Jon Nelson, et al; Billy

Schwartz, Ray Rocker, Simon Marsh, the people running Quartz at Rutgers, and everyone on Usenet back then, for providing things to do while I was online; and Scott Yanoff, for writing the guide to how to find them. Lastly, I'd like to thank ESR, for his inspired talks and essays, and particularly for teaching me the hows and whys of thanking people profusely in this community.

Planning Ahead

Don't Skip This Chapter

All right, go to Chapter 2: "Creating the Web Server" and play with your new toy. But come back here and figure out what you really want to do with this server.

Introduction

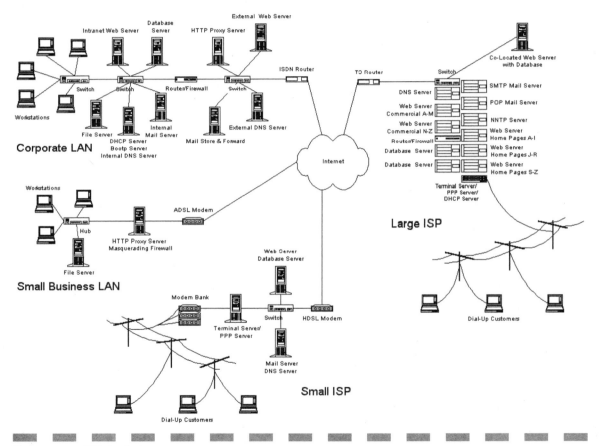

Figure 1.1   *This is the Internet.*

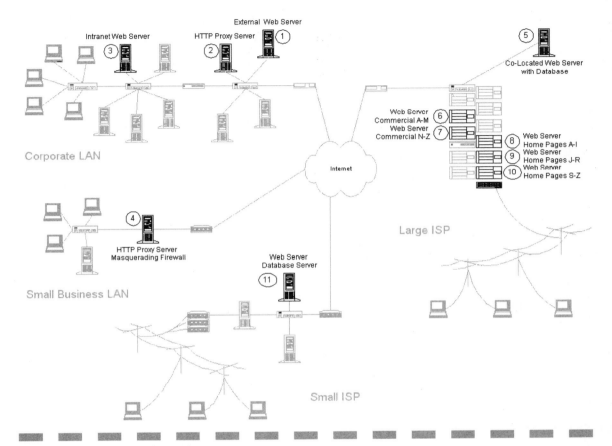

Figure 1.2 *This is Apache on the Internet.*

Any questions?

Know what's expected. Your web server's behavior depends greatly upon whom it serves. Your Apache server's configuration depends on which server you are implementing, what services it must provide, and who will be using it. All these things determine how you will read this book. This chapter will help you determine your server's capabilities. It will also help you define your policies regarding your web site's content and development. After you make your policy decisions, this chapter will direct you to the chapters and sections of this book that will guide you through the implementation of those capabilities and policies.

Strategies for the Corporation

(1) External Web Server

The external web server can publish advertising, product announcements, product documentation, the company's public directory, stock information, etc. It may gather qualified leads and customer input through e-mail links. When tied to a database, the external web server may provide online sales, secure customer account and billing inquiry, customer support and support tracking. It could gather qualified leads and customer input, through sweepstakes, giveaways, surveys, and the like.

More often than not, the system administrator and the content author are different people. The implementation of the more sophisticated services, however, will require changes to the Apache server configuration—which requires root user privileges. The system administrator is probably too busy with network administration to be continually making configuration changes and restarting the server at the behest of the webmaster. It would be easiest for the system administrator to build a web server for the web development team and then let the web development team administer it. Since everyone is working for the same company, accountability is high. You will still need to delineate exactly what each person is trusted to do. The system administrator could be responsible for the server's hardware, OS configuration, network interfaces, and start-up scripts. The managerial head of the web development team could then be responsible for user login accounts, FTP and telnet configurations, the Apache server configuration, and starting and stopping the Apache server. Beware; sharing the root password can get out of hand fairly quickly. You will need to change the root password often. Alternatively, you could supply the web development team with a server that they can tear up. Then, once a week or so, the system administrator could update the production web server with the development server's new configuration and content. On the production web server, the system administrator maintains tight security. The production server has very few user accounts: notably the root user, the Apache server daemon account (and any other necessary daemon accounts), and one webmaster user account. The production server's Internet services are locked down. FTP and telnet are allowed only from the system administrator's account on the development server. In contrast, security on the development server is more relaxed. Those on the web team who have the root user password to the development server are free to experiment with different configurations of Apache and its support of content manipulation. FTP and telnet to the development server are allowed from several (if not all) workstations on the LAN, and possibly from outside the LAN for those working from home or for contractors hired by the web team. The web team *must*, however, become security conscious for the configuration and content ported to the production server. Your development server may be loose, but your code had better not be. If your public site provides online sales, you will want to secure transactions with the Secure Sockets Layer. If your web site deals in high dollar volumes or sensitive information, you may wish to require additional physical authentication by issuing certificates to your customers or even a SecurID[1] or SecurCard[2].

Most likely, the system administrator will build both machines and then turn the development server over to the web team.

System Administrator

The system administrator should read the following (what the web team should read is discussed below).

Chapter 2: Creating the Web Server

SYSTEM REQUIREMENTS

REMOVING ANY PRE-EXISTING WEB SERVERS

DOWNLOADING THE APACHE SERVER

DOWNLOADING AND COMPILING THE SOURCE CODE
A full-featured corporate web server will require adding modules and frequent recompiling of the server. You will want to provide the development team with the Apache source code.

CONFIGURING THE INSTALLED SERVER
As fare as, *Basic Directives* are concerned (those configurations that refer to the OS configuration, like the hostname).

---

1 SecurID systems are available from Security Dynamics (RSA Security) at **http://www.rsasecurity.com/products/securid/authenticators.html**. You will also need the server, which you will find at **http://www.rsasecurity.com/products/securid/dsaceserver.html**. SecurID systems are also available from Intel Network Systems at **http://www.shiva.com/prod/docs/nilibrary/bi0406.html**. An Apache module for authenticating through the SecurID ACE server is available at **http://persoweb.francenet.fr/ ~ pasty/mod_securid/**.

2 SecurCard systems are available from Imaging Automation at **http://www.imagingauto.com/securcr.htm**.

STARTING, STOPPING, AND RESTARTING THE SERVER

Autolaunching the Server at Boot time. This subsection configures OS startup scripts.

Chapter 3: Creating the Web Site

STRATEGY
Your strategy is to lock down the production server.

CREATING THE DAEMON ACCOUNT
Set this up on both the production and the development machines.

CREATING THE WEBMASTER ACCOUNT
On the production server, there is just one webmaster user account.

ACCEPTING CONTENT
On the production server, you will want to open up FTP and telnet only as much as necessary to perform the updates from the development server.

Chapter 5: Using Logs

LOGGING ERRORS
The error log on the production server will optimally contain only startup and shutdown messages. The web team should have sufficiently debugged content and CGI scripts before porting it up to the production server. Any errors that do appear in the production server's error log will then be OS related and the responsibility of the system administrator. Reality check. You will need to give the web team access to the error log. The safest thing to do would be to e-mail it to them on a regular basis or copy it down to a file on the development server.

LOGGING DOCUMENT TRANSFERS
Logging every transfer degrades performance. If the web team needs to observe document transfers, they can develop a custom log and configure the server to log only transfers of interest. On the other hand, logging every transfer may be handy in settling customer disputes. Base your decision on the liability created by the content being published. You may want to log every transfer on secure servers providing e-commerce services.

ROTATING LOG FILES
Traffic, disk capacity, and archival backup systems determine how often you rotate the log files and how many archival copies you keep online.

Chapter 6: Securing the Server, the Content, and the Connection

SECURING THE SERVER

Configuring a Firewall

Configuring a Corporate Firewall. When updating the production server, you will need to connect to it through your corporate firewall. Also, the external web server may need to connect to servers inside the firewall (e.g. a database server or an intranet web server). If you have a separate development server inside the firewall, you may need to open ports through the firewall for web team members working from home and for contractors hired by the web team.

Configuring a Small Business Firewall. If your corporate firewall happens to be a Linux box running ipchains, you will find an example configuration in this subsection (but note the differences between the port rules for the small business versus the port rules you'll need for the corporate firewall).

Locking Down Internet Services. On the production server, the only non-HTTP connections you want to allow are telnet and FTP from the system administrator account on the development server.

Configuring Apache's Self-Defenses. The Apache configuration directives described in this subsection protect Apache from particular kinds of hacker attacks. Watch the Apache error log and the system error and system message logs for indications of a hacker attack: such things as exceeding the maximum number of connections, exceeding process time limits, overflow of buffers, or overflow of the process id table. When under attack, you can reduce the limits imposed by these directives. If you need to make these limits permanent, coordinate with the web team on getting these changes into the configuration file on the development server that updates the production server.

SECURING THE CONTENT

Allowing/Blocking Content Access

Requiring Authentication to Access Content. You can restrict access to administrative areas (e.g. log viewing scripts).

Preventing/Allowing Search Engine Site Inspection. You might read this section if you discover that a misbehaving robot is inundating your production server.

SECURING THE SERVER-BROWSER CONNECTIONS WITH SECURE SOCKETS LAYER

Understanding SSL. The web team will have the largest hand in implementing SSL. As the system administrator, though, you may have to make the purchase of the server certificate from a certificate authority (since the sys admin is usually in charge of network assets).

Chapter 10: Troubleshooting

GETTING THE STATUS OF THE SERVER

If you set up the extended status module, you can check in on the production server remotely.

RESPONDING TO ERROR MESSAGES

TUNING APACHE FOR PERFORMANCE

Watch the load on the production server.

LOAD BALANCING

Let's hope you have this problem.

WEB DEVELOPMENT TEAM

The web development team should read the following:

Chapter 2: Creating the Web Server

DOWNLOADING AND COMPILING THE SOURCE CODE

You will be doing this a lot.

SELECTING APACHE MODULES

You should have a project plan in which you have made all your decisions regarding what services you are going to code for. This section will help you decide what Apache modules you need to implement those services.

COMPILING THE SERVER MANUALLY

Read this section if you will be writing your own Apache modules.

CONFIGURING THE INSTALLED SERVER

Pay particular attention to the subsection *Directive Scopes.* This affects many of the directives you will use in delivering content. In *Basic Directives,* you will need to read about the activation and loading of modules that you've compiled into your server.

STARTING, STOPPING, AND RESTARTING THE SERVER
You will be doing this a lot, too.

Chapter 3: Creating the Web Site

STRATEGY
On the development server, your strategy is to allow developer freedom without everyone stepping on one another.

CREATING THE DAEMON ACCOUNT
The system administrator should already have set this up for you when the server was built. The only time you need to be concerned with the daemon account is when you are tying the web server to a database; in this case, you will need to coordinate with the system administrator anyway.

CREATING THE WEBMASTER ACCOUNT
How you set up this account is determined by how you coordinate your development effort. You could set up one webmaster account and several developer accounts—the webmaster account acting as the source code librarian for the development team. That is the safest way. But developers are going to want to interactively develop and test their code. You could give everyone write permissions to the document directory tree. Alternatively you could setup two web servers on the same machine. A staging server, maintained by the librarian/webmaster, would contain the content ready to go to production. A test server, which listens to a different TCP port and publishes a different document directory tree, displays content currently under construction. You could then grant to all the developers write permissions to the test document directory tree.

ACCEPTING CONTENT
In a librarian scenario, developers either telnet in and develop content in their home directories; or they develop content on their local workstations and FTP the code up to their home directories on the development server. The webmaster account then copies the staged code out of the developer home directories and into the web server document directory tree.

Chapter 4: Manipulating Content

Read the entire chapter.

Chapter 5: Using Logs

LOGGING ERRORS

On the development server, this log will be full of access denied errors, file not found errors, CGI script errors, and other content-related errors. All the developers will need permission to read this log on the development server.

LOGGING DOCUMENT TRANSFERS

This log may be useful during development and debugging, but it will dog a production server. Be sure to disable this log before porting the configuration and content to the production server. If you need to log transfers, create a custom log to log transfers of interest selectively. This won't hit server performance so hard.

CREATING CUSTOM LOGS

TRACKING USER HABITS—THE CLICKSTREAM LOG

Custom logs and the clickstream log can help you see your site through the eyes of your site visitors.

LOGGING REFERRING SITES

The referer log helps you gauge the effectiveness of your search engine keywords and the effectiveness of your advertising.

PAYING REFERRING SITES—THE PAID REFERER LOG

You can generate traffic to your site by paying sites that display your banner ads.

LOGGING USER AGENTS

You're the looser in the browser wars. Logging user agents helps you decide what browsers to code for.

ROTATING LOG FILES

This is really a system administrator's responsibility. You probably don't need to read this section; but be sure that the system administrator gives you copies of the log archives before they go to tape.

Chapter 6: Securing the Server, the Content, and the Connection

SECURING THE SERVER

Configuring a Firewall. Know the basics of packet filtering, so you know how to ask the system administrator to open up ports to telecommuters and outside contractors.

Locking Down Internet Services. On the development server, you probably want to restrict FTP and telnet access to web team members.

SECURING THE CONTENT

Allowing/Blocking Content Access.

Requiring Authentication to Access Content. The content on the development server is not ready for public consumption. You probably want to restrict web site access to the web team. Be sure to remove these access and authentication directives before porting the development site to the production site. On the production server, you may have administrative areas that should be secured by both access and authentication restrictions (e.g. scripts that display customer information from the database).

Authenticating PUT Requests. On your development server, you might implement a PUT request handler in a CGI script, if your web-authoring tools use the PUT method to upload content. You might not want to allow this on the production server. You could put all your developer tools and scripts in a restricted directory; just don't port that directory to the production server.

Preventing/Allowing Search Engine Site Inspection. You should use a robots.txt file to keep search engines out of your dynamic content (e.g. CGI scripts).

Securing the Server-Browser Connections with Secure Sockets Layer. If you are providing secure customer logins (for account queries, online sales, etc.), then you need to read this section, which offers two different implementations of SSL.

SECURITY CONSIDERATIONS FOR CGI

Good Programming Habits. Don't leave yourself open.

Non-Script Aliased vs. Script-Aliased. A corporate web server will have many custom features and CGI scripts. You may wish to organize your site into functionally modular directories; this would mean allowing CGI scripts to be run from different directories. Non-Script Aliased CGI will allow you to do that. After all, this is not a web-hosting ISP server, so you don't have the security considerations that would require Script-Aliased CGI.

Security Considerations for Front Page Extensions

If your development tools require it, you could enable Front Page Server Extensions on your development server. The Front Page site-management facilities might be handy; but, you probably don't want to use the Front Page pre-canned CGI scripts. Porting them to your production server would open up a large security hole. If you really need the Front Page CGI scripts for your production server, then you'll find Front Page Server Extensions much easier to implement on Microsoft's web server (rather than on Apache).

Chapter 7: Creating Homepage Web Sites

You can create a homepage for each developer to develop and test their incremental part of the Web site.

Chapter 8: Creating Virtual Domain Web Sites

If you are implementing SSL, you may need to split your server into two virtual hosts: one handling insecure HTTP requests and the other handling secure HTTPS requests. If there are subdivisions within your company that have their own internet domain, you may want to host their domains on this web server. More than likely, though, a company subdivision would have its own web server at another location.

Chapter 10: Troubleshooting

GETTING THE RAW HTTP WITH TELNET
Use this to verify the response headers that your are sending out.

RESPONDING TO ERROR MESSAGES

Chapter 12: Programming the Apache Server

If you cannot find a module to do what you need, then write one.

Appendix

WHERE IN THE WEB
You might be able to find modules already written to provide the services you want to implement. You will also find references to the RFCs that define the protocols you are writing to.

(2) HTTP Proxy Server

The proxy server provides the LAN's connection to the web. It increases throughput by caching. It logs the browsing habits of the LAN workstations, and it can be used, to some extent, to censure requested content.

There are only a few policy decisions required for the proxy server: How much disk space are you willing to dedicate to caching? How many requests are you going to log? How much censoring will the proxy perform? How many archival logs will you keep on the server?

Relevant chapters are noted here.

Chapter 2: Creating the Web Server

DOWNLOADING AND COMPILING THE SOURCE CODE

SELECTING APACHE MODULES

The `mod_proxy` module is not a default module. You need to compile it explicitly.

CONFIGURING THE INSTALLED SERVER

Be sure that `mod_proxy` is activated and loaded in the configuration file.

STARTING, STOPPING, AND RESTARTING THE SERVER

Autolaunching the Server at Boottime

Chapter 5: Using Logs

LOGGING ERRORS

LOGGING DOCUMENT TRANSFERS

You could use the transfer log to log all transfers. Performance will be affected if you do this.

CREATING CUSTOM LOGS

Create a custom log that conditionally logs only transfers of interest. This will not affect performance as much. How much you log depends on how closely you want to keep on eye on employee use of the Internet.

ROTATING LOG FILES

You may wish to rotate log files and store archival logs to tape (if you think you might need it for future litigation).

Chapter 9: Proxying with Apache

This is the main course for the Apache proxy server.

(3) Intranet Web Server

The intranet web server publishes internal documents: project specifications, product manuals, company policy, an event calendar, a personnel directory, etc. When tied to a database, it could collect employee input, suggestions, tax form data, insurance data, and the like.

The intranet server presents many of the same policy considerations as the external web server: the administrator and the content author(s) are likely to be different people and the implementation of the more sophisticated services requires Apache configuration changes (which requires root privileges). The major difference between the intranet web server and the external web server is that the content on the intranet server is almost all private to the company. You may wish to place both access and authentication restrictions on most (if not all) of the document directory tree. This would effectively transfer responsibility for the maintenance of web site login accounts from the web development team to the system administrator, since a web site login will need to be created every time a network login is created. For the more sensitive information (trade secrets, marketing strategies, and the like), you may wish to require some kind of physical authentication in addition to the password login—such as browser certificates or even a SecurID or SecurCard system. Another consideration for the intranet server is whether it publishes any public data. It may be more productive to develop just one web site, the intranet site, and then publish portions thereof to the Internet. A reverse proxy server on the external web server may allow you to do so securely.

The system administrator and the web development team need to read the same chapters and sections as prescribed above for the external web server. The system administrator will also need to additionally read the following.

Chapter 6: Securing the Server, the Content, and the Connection

SECURING THE SERVER-BROWSER CONNECTION WITH SECURE SOCKETS LAYER

If you will be issuing browser certificates, you then you should read this entire section.

The web development team may also wish to read:

Chapter 9: Proxying with Apache

If your intranet server publishes portions of the site to the web, read this chapter to implement a reverse proxy server on the external web server.

Strategies for the Small Business

(4) HTTP Proxy Server/Masquerading Firewall

This server provides to the small business its connection to the Internet. Its masquerading firewall protects the LAN and provides workstation-to-web connectivity at minimum cost. The proxy server increases throughput, logs requested content, and performs some censoring functions.

For this box, the same considerations as those of the HTTP proxy server (noted above) are relevant. How much disk space are you willing to dedicate to caching? How many requests are you going to log? How much censoring will the proxy perform? How many archival logs will you keep on the server? Since this machine is also a firewall, additional considerations apply. What traffic will you allow in and out of the LAN? What Internet services are LAN users allowed to use at work?

Relevant reading includes the following material:

Chapter 2: Creating the Web Server

DOWNLOADING AND COMPILING THE SOURCE CODE

SELECTING APACHE MODULES

The mod_proxy module is not a default module. You need to compile it explicitly.

Configuring the Installed Server

Be sure that mod_proxy is activated and loaded in the configuration file.

STARTING, STOPPING, AND RESTARTING THE SERVER

Autolaunching the Server at Boottime

Chapter 5: Using Logs

LOGGING ERRORS

LOGGING DOCUMENT TRANSFERS

You could use the transfer log to log all transfers. Performance will be affected if you do this.

CREATING CUSTOM LOGS

Create a custom log that conditionally logs only transfers of interest. This will not affect performance as much.

ROTATING LOG FILES

You many wish to rotate log files and store archival logs to tape, if you need proof of an employee's browsing habits.

Chapter 6: Securing the Server, the Content, and the Connection

CONFIGURING A FIREWALL

CONFIGURING A SMALL BUSINESS FIREWALL

LOCKING DOWN INTERNET SERVICES

Chapter 9: Proxying with Apache

(5) Co-Located Web Server with Database

Typically, a small business with web presence uses the web-hosting services of an ISP. There may come a time in your business needs or business growth where co-location becomes the best option. In co-location you move your web site off the ISP's web-hosting server and put it on your own server located at the ISP—attached to the ISP's big-bandwidth pipe. You maintain your server and the ISP leases you bandwidth. There are two reasons to co-locate: you need more control over your web site and/or increased traffic to your site demands better performance. Regarding the former: your ISP's web-hosting server may not allow you to develop all the services you require. Your ISP's server may not allow you to write your own CGI scripts or to write them in your favorite programming language. Or your ISP might not be providing you with database services or may be charging a lot for database space. Regarding the second reason for co-location: traffic to your site demands a dedicated server; but you're not quite ready to buy a big-bandwidth pipe to your office. This is a nice problem to have. One or more dedicated servers can provide the demanded connections and the necessary disk space for a large database.

Co-located servers are wonderful for consultants. You can provide secure customer access to time/billing information. You can provide FTP download of your software products and custom development. You can use the server for proof-of-concept demonstrations.

Do you maintain this server or does the ISP provide the machine? Both situations are available from various ISPs. You can reduce costs if you provide and maintain the server, and all you rent is bandwidth. You will need to configure FTP to receive content and telnet for remote maintenance. You might want to restrict these connections to specifically authorized machines.

It is nice to have complete control of your own machine. You can use your favorite language and database. You can take full advantage of all the Apache content manipulation directives: directory displays, MIME types, customized HTTP headers, CGI and SSI processing, and image maps. You can optimize your web server for your kind of content.

Relevant reading is noted below.

Chapter 2: Creating the Web Server

DOWNLOADING THE APACHE SERVER

DOWNLOADING AND COMPILING THE SOURCE CODE
You'll want the source code, especially if you are compiling in a language module (like `php3` or `mod_perl`).

SELECTING APACHE MODULES
Initially, you might compile in most of the Apache modules so that you can experiment with the development of different kinds of content. If you are co-locating for performance reasons, then you will want to compile in only the modules necessary to provide your specific content.

COMPILING THE SERVER MANUALLY
Read this section if you will be writing your own Apache modules.

CONFIGURING THE INSTALLED SERVER

STARTING, STOPPING, AND RESTARTING THE SERVER

AUTOLAUNCHING THE SERVER AT BOOTTIME

Chapter 3: Creating the Web Site

STRATEGY
For the co-located server, the system administrator and the content author are likely to be the same person; there need not be such a division of responsibility as is illustrated in the strategy section.

CREATING THE DAEMON ACCOUNT

CREATING THE WEBMASTER ACCOUNT

ACCEPTING CONTENT

Chapter 4: Manipulating Content

Read this whole chapter.

Chapter 5: Using Logs

LOGGING ERRORS

The error log not only helps you maintain your server; it helps you debug your code as well.

ROTATING LOG FILES

When the log files are rotated, you may wish to have the oldest archive file e-mailed to you before being overwritten.

Chapter 6: Securing the Server, the Content, and the Connection

The good thing about co-location is that your server is more accessible to the world. The bad thing is that your server is more accessible to the world. This server hangs in the breeze. It sits on one of the most public portions of the Internet. Security by obscurity is no longer an option. Unfortunately, co-location increases the probability that you will get hacked.

SECURING THE SERVER

Locking Down Internet Services. Make sure that you are the only one who can administer this server.

Configuring Apache's Self-Defenses. This section helps you defend yourself from specific hacks.

SECURING THE CONTENT

Allowing/Blocking Content Access

Requiring Authentication to Access Content. If you publish customer billing information, you will want to apply access and authentication restrictions so that only customers can access their information—and only their own information.

Preventing/Allowing Search Engine Site Inspection. Getting indexed brings traffic to your site; but don't let the search engine robots overpower your server. You should also keep them out of your dynamically generated content. If you provide this web server only for the benefit of your authenticated customers, then you may wish to prohibit search engine site inspection altogether.

SECURING THE SERVER-BROWSER CONNECTION WITH SECURE SOCKETS LAYER
Transmission of customer information and online sales require this level of security.

SECURITY CONSIDERATIONS FOR CGI

Good Programming Habits. This is especially necessary, given your very public location.

NonScript Aliased vs. Script Aliased. It's your server. You can organize it how you like. This means that you don't have to restrict CGI to one `/cgi-bin/` directory, but be careful.

Chapter 10: Troubleshooting

GETTING THE STATUS OF THE SERVER
This will let you check in on your server remotely.

GETTING THE RAW HTTP WITH TELNET
This will help you debug your custom response headers.

TUNING APACHE FOR PERFORMANCE
If performance is your reason for co-location, you will want to maximize the server's capabilities.

LOAD BALANCING
This is a nice problem to have. Here is how you solve it.

Chapter 12: Programming the Apache Server

This is something your ISP won't let you do on their web-hosting server. You can do this on your co-located server.

Strategies for the Large ISP

(6) (7) Web Server—Commercial

"Commercial" may be too specific a word for these servers, which host the sites of any ISP web-hosting customer with its own Internet domain name. This includes organizations and individuals. These are the virtual-host servers, each domain served being virtually its own web server. The largest number of virtual-host customers, however, are likely to be small and medium-size companies who do not want to maintain their own web servers and Internet pipes. These customers want to maintain their own web sites on your virtual-host server. Generally, commercial web sites require more services than the home page web sites (as discussed below). Also, the content authors are more likely to be professional developers. Most will want to write their own CGI scripts and most will want to collect data to a database. Some may want to compile binaries. Some may want specific interpreters installed (e.g. php3 or mod_perl). Some will want to transact online sales, which requires a secure connection and credit card verification. Your differentiator in the ISP market will be how many of these services you can provide.

Plan up front what services you want to provide. Temper this with a truthful assessment of what services you *can* provide (that is, what services you are willing and able to provide and maintain and front the cost for). Then, factor in extra time for maintenance given the following vital consideration. How do you keep a thousand different development teams safe from each other on the same server? Basic user account security and directory and file permissions will need to be tight. That is easy enough. You can keep the various content authors out of each other's directories, but those permissions become a little harder to enforce under the running web server. All the virtual-host web sites are served by the same server daemon. Each content author must give the same server daemon permission to access a site. This poses no problem for read-only HTML documents in read-only directories. It becomes a concern when running CGI scripts and when executing scripts from within a server-parsed file. A problem arises when the script (or binary) needs to save data to disk. If a content author gives the server daemon user account permission to write to a directory, then any content author of any of the other virtual-host site can write a malicious script to exploit those permissions to write bogus data into the writeable directory. The suexec utility offers a solution. When this is used, the content author does not grant write permissions to the web-server daemon. Instead, he gives himself the necessary permissions and the `suexec` utility becomes the content author to run the CGI script. That is, `suexec` switches the effective user ID to that of the owner of the CGI script before executing the script. In this way, the CGI script has write permissions only to the files and directories owned by the content author who wrote the script. The content author should beware that this opens up the content author's home directory to targeted hacker attacks. The `suexec` utility does come with a performance price, but it is the price of peace when you allow a thousand virtual-host customers to write their own CGI scripts. You must balance necessity with security.

You also have to balance customization against administration. Apache allows you to create a default web-server configuration for all the virtual hosts. Apache also allows you to create custom configurations for selected virtual hosts. If you have a thousand virtual hosts, maintaining custom configurations for each would become overwhelming. This forces you to categorize your service offerings into those services that everyone gets and services that require a custom configuration. You might allow everyone things like fancy index generation, server-sided image map processing, metafile headers, server-side-includes, and CGI scripting. To select customers, you might provide: database services, telnet access for compiling binaries, secure connections with SSL, online sales, and credit card verification. As ISPs compete for commercial customers, the trend has been to provide more of the higher-ended services generically to everyone. Additionally, many ISPs provide value-added applications like online catalogs, customer account maintenance, and shopping carts.

Any service you add to the web server must be scrutinized for security. Customers may ask you to add things to your server: a particular shopping cart, a particular script interpreter or language compiler, a development environment server (à la MS Front Page Server Extensions), or an Apache module found on the web. At some point, you will want to draw the line and suggest the customer use your co-location service.

Any service you add to the web server must be optimized for performance. Commercial sites strive for traffic, live for traffic. As traffic increases, you can add more servers to handle the load. The example in Figure 1.2 divides the commercial sites by domain name across two servers. Higher-ended services require longer connection times, which bottlenecks traffic. This requires you to spread your commercial sites across more and more servers, which increases your capital costs.

These costs are exponential. Each service you provide incurs capital and labor costs. Each service you provide must be deployed on a massive scale. Each customer will be pressing you to add another service.

Relevant reading includes the following material.

Chapter 2: Creating the Web Server

SYSTEM REQUIREMENTS

DOWNLOADING THE APACHE SERVER

DOWNLOADING AND COMPILING THE SOURCE CODE

SELECTING APACHE MODULES
For premium performance, you will want to compile in only those modules providing the services that you, by policy, provide.

CONFIGURING THE INSTALLED SERVER

STARTING, STOPPING, AND RESTARTING THE SERVER

AUTOLAUNCHING THE SERVER AT BOOTTIME

Chapter 3: Creating the Web Site

STRATEGY

CREATING THE DAEMON ACCOUNT

CREATING THE WEBMASTER ACCOUNT
Use the account described here as a template for new customers. Then write a script to create new accounts, copy the template home directory, set permissions, and provide the initial virtual-host configuration.

ACCEPTING CONTENT
You will be accepting content from just about anywhere. You won't be able to restrict connections.

Chapter 4: Manipulating Content

Read this chapter to learn the configurations required for providing specific services.

Chapter 5: Using Logs

LOGGING ERRORS

LOGGING DOCUMENT TRANSFERS

CREATING CUSTOM LOGS
Every customer will want his own logs. The Apache User's Guide suggests, for performance reasons, that you create one error log (and maybe

one transfer log), then provide scripts for customers to extract their records. Such logs must be created as custom logs. You must add fields to the log for filtering by host. The extraction process must be strictly controlled. You don't want one customer to be able to view the log entries of another. Instead of supplying this extraction on demand, you might run it in batch as a nighttime process or as part of the log rotation schedule. The batch extraction could write to files in the content authors' home directories—outside the content author's public document directory tree. If you write to a file within the host's document directory tree, you should secure the file with authentication. The downside of the one-log batch method is that content authors can't see their error-log entries while they are interactively developing and testing their content. However, to give each virtual host its own error and transfer logs requires more file handles from the server. This might require you to spread your virtual-host sites across more server machines.

ROTATING LOG FILES

For the large ISP, this actually becomes an ethical and a privacy issue. The thought police love it when you keep archives and backups of the log files rotated off the system—especially if you proxy and log the web habits of your dial-up customers. Privacy has become such an issue that some ISPs even advertise that they keep no logs at all. For your virtual-host customers, you might extract each customer's log entries and e-mail them to the virtual-host content author, then delete the log—keeping no backups.

Chapter 6: Securing the Server, the Content, and the Connection

SECURING THE SERVER

Configuring a Firewall. You might configure a firewall between the web servers and database servers so that only the web servers can access the databases. This puts the databases one more step removed from the hackers. The downside is that content authors will have to be telnetted into the web server in order to use command line SQL.

Locking Down Internet Services. You can turn off ports the web server is not serving; but as an ISP, you can't really lock down services like the private servers can (e.g. the corporate or co-located servers). You have to accept content from anywhere. You could restrict telnet to the web server administrators, unless you provide telnet services to your virtual-host customers.

Configuring Apache's Self-Defenses. Read this section if you think you are under attack.

SECURING THE CONTENT

Allowing/Blocking Content Access. You won't be setting any access restrictions, but your web-host customers may want to. The content authors may want to restrict particular directories by IP or client hostname. You will have to modify the Apache configuration to allow them to do so.

Requiring Authentication to Access Content Web. sites supporting authenticated customer services will want to configure their own authentication. You will have to configure the Apache configuration file to allow them to do so. If you write logs to the virtual-host document directory tree, then you will want to require the content author's authentication for viewing those logs.

Authenticating PUT Requests. More and more web authoring tools are using PUT requests to transmit content to the web server.

Preventing/Allowing Search Engine Site Inspection. Individual content authors will be more interested in this, but you may have to get involved if a misbehaved robot is bogging down your servers.

SECURING THE SERVER-BROWSER CONNECTION WITH SECURE SOCKETS LAYER

Secure connections allow commercial sites to interact more freely with their customers. SSL is the starting point for all sorts of other services (online sales, shopping carts, customer account maintenance, etc.).

SECURITY CONSIDERATIONS FOR CGI

Setting Policy

Good Programming Habits. Tell your content authors about this.

NonScript Aliased vs. Script Aliased. Script aliased CGI is more controlled than non-script aliased CGI, but you will have to set up a /cgi-bin/ directory for each virtual host.

Using CGI Wrappers. This is a necessary evil.

Chapter 8: Creating Multiple Domain Web Sites On One Server

This chapter is the main course for the virtual-host web server.

Chapter 10: Troubleshooting

TUNING APACHE FOR PERFORMANCE

This is a high-performance site.

Appendix

WHERE IN THE WEB

This section will help you find products to increase your service offerings.

(8) (9) (10) Web Server—Home Pages

These servers host the home pages of web-host customers who do not have their own registered domains. These are mostly publish-only sites which do not interact much with site visitors. What interaction the sites provide usually goes through CGI scripts written and maintained by the ISP. The content authors are less likely to be professional developers and are less inclined to write their own CGI scripts. All this is changing as home page authors are getting more savvy.

Users are discovering more of what is possible and will expect you to provide more precanned scripts and applications (support for guest books, discussion groups, mail lists, form input, etc.). At the same time, home-page authors are becoming more technically proficient. Many ISPs are allowing home-page customers to develop their own CGI scripts. This blurs the line between the commercial web servers and the home-page web servers. One day, the only difference may be the registration of a domain name. This creates a unique problem. You are supporting a user base with growing technical skill; but the users have not all achieved proficiency. Every service you provide generates additional support calls. You could turn this investment into opportunity. As proficiencies grow, you can "graduate" each user to your more lucrative commercial site service.

Relevant reading includes the following material.

Chapter 2: Creating the Web Server

SYSTEM REQUIREMENTS

REMOVING ANY PRE-EXISTING WEB SERVERS

DOWNLOADING THE APACHE SERVER

DOWNLOADING AND COMPILING THE SOURCE CODE

SELECTING APACHE MODULES

Like the commercial web servers, the home-page servers must be performance driven. Compile only in those modules that support the services that you, by policy, provide to your home-page customers.

CONFIGURING THE INSTALLED SERVER

STARTING, STOPPING, AND RESTARTING THE SERVER

AUTOLAUNCHING THE SERVER AT BOOTTIME

Chapter 3: Creating the Web Site

STRATEGY

CREATING THE DAEMON ACCOUNT

CREATING THE WEBMASTER ACCOUNT
Configure a webmaster account and use it as a template for creating accounts for the home page content-authors.

ACCEPTING CONTENT

Chapter 4: Manipulating Content

Most of the services described herein may be granted to the home-page content author. Give some thought, however, to the implementation of CGI and SSI.

Chapter 5: Using Logs

LOGGING ERRORS

LOGGING DOCUMENT TRANSFERS

CREATING CUSTOM LOGS
Most home-page authors want to know their site statistics, but you probably have far too many home-page sites to provide individual log files or even batch-extracted logs. You can create a custom log and then provide a CGI script to calculate and display statistics on demand for each home page. You might want to require authentication of the content author before granting access to the viewing script.

ROTATING LOG FILES
As with the commercial sites, this is a matter of privacy. You might not want to keep backups of log files rotated off the system.

Chapter 6: Securing the Server, the Content, and the Connection

SECURING THE SERVER

Locking Down Internet Services. You can turn off ports the server is not serving; but FTP connections must be accepted from anywhere. Allowing telnet to home page authors is a matter of policy.

Configuring Apache's Self-Defenses. Read this if you are under attack.

SECURING THE CONTENT

Allowing/Blocking Content Access

Requiring Authentication to Access Content. It is a matter of policy and user proficiency how much control you give the home-page author over access and authentication. If a user wants to control authentication, you might sell the user a domain name and a commercial site. You may wish to implement authentication for home authors to view their site statistics.

Authenticating PUT Requests. Many home-page authors use web-authoring tools that publish content to the server through PUT requests.

Preventing/Allowing Search Engine Site Inspection. Read this if your servers are getting overwhelmed by a misbehaved search engine robot.

SECURITY CONSIDERATIONS FOR CGI

Setting Policy

Good Programming Habits

NonScript Aliased vs. Script Aliased. If you, the ISP, maintain the CGI scripts, one /cgi-bin/ script aliased directory is fine. If you allow home-page authors to write CGI, you can use either script aliased or non-script aliased CGI. See Chapter 7.

Using CGI Wrappers. The suexec wrapper is an even more necessary evil if you allow home-page authors to write CGI scripts. It is more likely on home-page servers than commercial servers that you will get a young, wannabe hacker trying to exploit CGI to get into other people's sites.

SECURITY CONSIDERATIONS FOR FRONT PAGE EXTENSIONS
Microsoft, again, brings computing to the masses. Front Page removes much of the technical know-how from site development. Many home-page customers will want you to install the Front Page Server Extensions (probably more so than the commercial site customers). If you want to support Front Page, it would be better to move the sites requiring it to an NT server running Microsoft's web server.

Chapter 7: Creating Multiple User Web Sites On One Server

This is the main course for the home-page servers.

Chapter 10: Troubleshooting

TUNING APACHE FOR PERFORMANCE
This is a high-performance site.

Appendix

WHERE IN THE WEB
This section will help you find products to increase your service offerings.

Strategies for the Small ISP

(11) Web Server—Database Server

This server hosts commercial sites and others with domain names. It also hosts home-page sites. You are competing with all the services that the large ISPs provide. You have one advantage: personal service. You know your customers personally and can provide for their individual needs. You have fewer customers than the large ISPs and you can provide custom configurations.

However, you still have all the policy and security considerations applicable to both the commercial servers and the homepage servers of the large ISP.

I know you are thinking, "If I could just get a few more customers, I can quit my day job and sleep at night." Sorry, you are running the "everything" server. You need to read this book cover to cover.

Creating the Web Server

System Requirements

Operating System

Linux, SunOS, UnixWare, FreeBSD, Solaris, AIX, OpenBSD, IRIX, SCO, NetBSD, HPUX, BSDI, Digital UNIX, Win32 (Windows NT and 98), or almost any other operating system with an ANSI C compiler.

Win32 Warning

The InstallShield script used to install the Win32 release of the Apache source code and binaries provides this warning:

> WARNING: The Win32 release of Apache should still be considered beta quality code. It does not meet the normal standards of stability and security that UNIX releases do. There are numerous known bugs and inconsistencies. There is also a much greater chance of security holes being present in the Win32 version of Apache.

In this book, all discussions regarding the Win32 release may be found in Chapter 11: "Using Apache on Windows 95/NT." All other chapters presume the environment to be UNIX.

Disk Space

The requirement is 12 megabytes for the Apache source code and executables. Add 5 to 10 megabytes for each Web site that this Apache server will be hosting. If this Web server will be hosting sites with attached databases (e.g. e-commerce Web sites) and those databases will be hosted on the same hard drive as the Web server, then account for the size of the databases as well. An average-sized database might consume 100 megabytes. Larger commercial Web sites might require over 500 megabytes per database.

Removing Any Pre-Existing Web Servers

Stop the Running Server

Before installing the Apache Web server, make sure that a Web server is not already running. If the Web server has an administration utility, use

that utility to shut down the running server. Servers lacking an administration utility may be shutdown manually. Log in as root and look for any
processes named httpd and kill them. At the UNIX shell prompt, type

```
ps ax | grep httpd
```

to list those processes. The ps command lists the processes and the
grep command looks for httpd in that list. Note that the parameters used
in the above ps command work in Linux and may be different for your
flavor of UNIX. The parameters should tell the ps command to list the
processes of all users (not just your own) and to list processes not
attached to a controlling terminal (i.e. daemons). Consult your system's
MAN pages for the appropriate ps command parameters. If a Web server
is running, the above command will display a list similar to this:

```
769   ?   S     0:00 /usr/sbin/httpd
770   ?   S     0:00 /usr/sbin/httpd
771   ?   S     0:00 /usr/sbin/httpd
```

The first column displays the process ID you will use to kill the
process. Kill the first process by typing

```
kill 769
```

(replacing 769 with the appropriate process ID in your display). Shutting down the first httpd process may very well kill the other httpd
processes. Retype the ps command to see if the others are still running. If
so, kill them individually. If any of the daemons refuse to die, you could
use extreme prejudice with:

```
kill -9 769
```

Prevent Autolaunch of the Existing Server

It is also necessary to make sure that the pre-existing Web server will not
automatically launch next time the operating system boots up. UNIX variants have a variety of methods for auto-launching processes. In Linux,
processes launched at boot time are listed in files and scripts under the
/etc/rc.d/ directory tree. Specifically, look for and remove the file
named httpd in the /etc/rc.d/init.d/ directory and any links with
HTTP in their names in the /etc/rc.d/rc?d directories.

You must also make sure that the UNIX Internet daemon does not
launch the pre-existing Web server. The Internet daemon, inetd, listens to

all of the Internet ports for service requests. When a request comes in on a given port, the Internet daemon launches the appropriate program to handle the request. The ports to which `inetd` listens are listed in the file `/etc/services`. Use an ASCII text editor (such as `vi`) to edit this file. Look for a line beginning with `http`, such as

```
http   80/tcp
```

This line gives the name "http" to service requests hitting port 80 with the TCP protocol. Insert a pound sign at the beginning of this line and save the file. This will comment out the line so that the Internet daemon will quit listening for TCP requests on port 80. Once `inetd` has a name for a service request, it launches the appropriate handler program listed in the file `/etc/inetd.conf`. Use an ASCII text editor to edit this file. Look for a line beginning with `http`, such as

```
http   stream   tcp   nowait   root   /usr/sbin/httpd
```

This line tells `inetd` to launch the program `/usr/sbin/httpd` whenever a service request named http is received. Insert a pound sign at the beginning of this line and save the file. This will comment out the line so that the Internet daemon will not launch the `/usr/sbin/httpd` Web server when an `http` service request is received.

Once the Internet daemon's configuration files have been modified, the Internet daemon must be told to reread those configuration files. Send a hang-up signal (a HUP signal) to the `inetd` process. Linux offers a shortcut for this. Type

```
killall -HUP inetd
```

If your flavor of UNIX does not offer such a shortcut, then first find the `inetd` process. Type

```
ps ax | grep inetd
```

If `inetd` is running, the above command will display a line similar to

```
330  ?  S    0:00 inetd
```

The first column displays the process ID used to HUP the daemon. Send the HUP signal by typing

```
kill -HUP 330
```

(replacing `330` with the appropriate process ID on your display).

Removing the Pre-Existing Web Server

To permanently remove the pre-existing Web server, remove all its files. Many UNIX systems have package managers for installing and uninstalling software (e.g. the `rpm` command in Linux). If your pre-existing Web server is not registered with a package manager, the files must be removed manually. Look for and remove files and directories named `http` or `httpd`. The `httpd` server binary might be in `/bin/`, `/usr/bin/`, `/sbin/`, or `/usr/sbin/`. There might be a configuration directory named `/etc/httpd/`. There might be a pre-existing Web server and/or Web site under a user directory named httpd (e.g. `/home/httpd/`). There might be manual pages for the old server—under `/var/catman/` or `/usr/lib/man/`. A quick way to find all of them would be:

```
find / -name \*http\* -exec ls -ld {} \;
```

The above `find` command starts at the root directory (`/`) and, from there on down, looks for anything whose name contains `http` (`\*http\*`). When it finds a matching file or directory, it displays a line of detail describing what was found (`-exec ls -ld {} \;`). The results of this command will read like this:

```
drwxr-xr-x     2    root    root    1024    Jul 27   20:46    /etc/httpd
-r—rw-r—       1    root    man     1857    Jul 27   20:29    /var/catman/cat8/httpd.8.gz
etceteras…
```

Delete what you can; save what you will.

Downloading the Apache Server

The Apache Web server is free and can be downloaded from the Apache Software Foundation's Web site. Point your browser[1] to **http://www.apache.org**. On the Apache Software Foundation's home page, click the Apache Server link. From the Apache HTTP Server Pro-

---

1 If you prefer to use FTP to download these files, the Apache Software Foundation lists both browser and anonymous FTP mirror sites at: **http://www.apache.org/dyn/closer.cgi**. The Apache Software Foundation discourages public use of its own FTP site, which is intended for use by their mirror sites. It is possible to connect to their FTP site at **ftp.apache.org**—where you can log in an anonymous (using your valid e-mail address as the password) and can retrieve these files from the `/dist/` and `/dist/binaries/` directories. Anonymous FTP may not long be offered at that site.

ject page, click the Download! link. (The URL directly linked to this page is **http://www.apache.org/dist/**). You should arrive at the Web page shown in Figure 2.1.

Figure 2.1

Apache download site.

From the Web page shown in Figure 2.1, download the Apache server source code or proceed to the `binaries/` subdirectory to download a precompiled Apache server. If you download the source code, you can tailor an Apache server to meet your needs, but you will have to compile the source code. If you download a precompiled binary, you won't have to compile the source code, but you also won't be able to add modules that you might need. The following section is for those who opt to download the precompiled binaries. If you opt to download and compile the source code, skip to the section "Downloading the Source Code."

Downloading and Installing the Pre-Compiled Binaries

To install an Apache precompiled binary, we will perform the following tasks: **download** the appropriate compressed archive file, **uncompress** the archive file, **extract** the files in the archive to a source directory, and **install** certain files from the source directory to an installation directory.

Download

First, create a source directory in which to download the appropriate archive. I suggest the directory `/usr/local/src/apache/`. Downloading the archive and extracting it will create a new subdirectory named `apache_1.3.6/`. When you download and extract future upgrades and releases of the server, a subdirectory for each version will be created.

Next, find the archive containing the binaries compiled for your platform. From the Web page shown in Figure 2.1, click on the link to the `binaries/` subdirectory (directly, this is **http://www.apache.org/dist/binaries/**). There you will find a subdirectory for each supported platform. Each platform subdirectory contains compressed archive files, each of which contains both the precompiled binary and the source code for a specific version of the Apache server. The name of each archive file prescribes the version of the Apache server contained therein, the hardware platform for which the binary was compiled, and the operating system version with which the precompiled binary is compatible. For example, one of the archives in the `aix/` subdirectory is named

```
apache_1.3.6-rs6000-ibm-aix4.2.tar.gz
```

which is a tar ball archive (compressed with gzip) containing the precompiled binary of the Apache server version 1.3.6, compiled on the IBM RS600, for the AIX operating system version 4.2.

The latest version of the Apache server is 1.3.6. Look for and download the archive file whose name contains that version number. Not all platform subdirectories have caught up to the latest version of Apache. If you cannot find an archive for your platform or if you prefer a later version than is available for your platform, then you must resort to downloading the source code and compiling the server (proceed to the section titled "Downloading the Source Code").

Uncompress

Most of the compressed archives are UNIX tar balls compressed with the GNU gzip utility (*.tar.gz). To decompress such a file, go to a UNIX shell prompt and (in the directory in which you downloaded the archive) type

```
gunzip <file name>
```

replacing `<file name>` with the name of the compressed archive file that you downloaded. This in-place decompression will replace the file named *.tar.gz with the uncompressed file named *.tar.

The following platform subdirectories do not contain gzipped tar balls (these are the exceptions):

- os2/—The OS2 archive is a PkWare pkzip archive. After unzipping the archive, you will find a file named OS2.README in the apache_1.3.6\ directory. This file will tell you how to run the pre-compiled server program (httpd.exe in the apache_1.3.6\src\ subdirectory).
- win32/—The Win32 archive is an InstallShield program. When you run the apache_1_3_6_win32.exe program, the InstallShield script will extract everything to the C:\Program Files\Apache Group\ Apache directory (unless you tell it otherwise). The InstallShield script also adds icons to your Windows Start bar for launching the server.
- reliantunix/—The ReliantUNIX archive is a package file compressed with the GNU gzip utility—which may be decompressed in the same manner as discussed above. After decompression, return your browser to the reliantunix/ subdirectory. The index page displayed there contains instructions for installing the package file.

All discussion of the BS2000/OSD mainframe version of the Apache server is deferred to Siemens Computer Systems at **http://www.siemens.com/servers/apache_osd/apache_us.htm**.

Extract

The UNIX tar ball may be extracted by typing

```
tar xvf <tar ball>
```

replacing <tar ball> with the file name of the uncompressed tar ball archive. Note: The parameters used in the above tar command work in Linux and may be different for your flavor of UNIX. The parameters should tell the tar command to extract the files from the archive and maintain relative directory paths. Consult your UNIX's MAN pages for the appropriate tar command parameters. This tar extraction will create and populate a new directory named apache_1.3.6/. Since I downloaded my tar ball into /usr/local/src/apache, the full path to this directory on my machine is /usr/local/src/apache/apache_1.3.6/.

This tar extraction does not remove the original apache_1.3.6.tar file. Now that the files have been extracted, save disk space by recompressing the tar ball. Keep this tar ball around. You can compress the tar ball by typing

```
gzip <file name>
```

replacing `<file name>` with the name of the tar ball archive file. This in-place compression will replace the original file (*.tar) with the smaller file (*.tar.gz).

The tar extraction has created a new directory—`apache_1.3.6/`—containing several new subdirectories. The `apache_1.3.6/bindist/` subdirectory contains the precompiled binaries (and other files) that will be copied to the installation directory. The other subdirectories contain files pertinent to compiling the source code and installing the compiled server (discussed in the section "Downloading the Source Code").

Install

The extracted archive contains both the source code and the precompiled binaries. The `apache_1.3.6/` directory contains all the README and INSTALL files pertaining both. The file to read is named INSTALL.bindist. Use the `more` command or the `vi` command to read this file. The INSTALL.bindist file will give you a terse rendition of the following procedure: At a UNIX shell prompt, in the `apache_1.3.6/` directory, type

```
./install-bindist.sh <install dir>
```

replacing `<install dir>` with the name of the directory in which you wish to install the Apache server. Do not install the Apache tree in your `/bin/`, `/usr/bin/`, `/sbin/`, or `/usr/sbin/` directories. The Apache installation is an entire system comprised of several subdirectories. You should give the Apache installation its own, new installation directory. The default installation directory is `/usr/local/apache`.

You now have an installed Apache server. Proceed to the section titled "Configuring the Installed Server."

Downloading and Compiling the Source Code

First, make sure you have the appropriate compiler. Many UNIX systems already have an ANSI C compiler. If yours does not, download the GNU gcc compiler from **http://gnu.internexus.net/software/gcc/gcc.html**.

To compile and install an Apache server from the source code, we will perform the following tasks: **download** the appropriate compressed archive file, **uncompress** the archive file, **extract** the files in the archive to a source directory, **configure** the Makefile for compiling, **compile** the server binary, and **install** certain files from the source directory to an installation directory.

Download

First, create a directory in which to download the source code archive. I suggest the directory /usr/local/src/apache/. The UNIX source code bundle that you download will create a new subdirectory named apache_1.3.6/ in which it will extract its files. When you download future upgrades and releases of the server, you will have a subdirectory for each version.

From the Web page shown in Figure 2.1 (directly, this is **http://www.apache.org/dist/**) download the compressed archive file appropriate to your platform. The Apache Software Foundation has bundled the current release (version 1.3.6) of the Apache Web server source code into these archive files:

- apache_1.3.6.tar.gz—UNIX gzip tar ball. This tar archive has been compressed with the GNU gzip utility. If your UNIX system has the GNU gzip and gunzip utilities, download this file.
- apache_1.3.6.tar.Z—UNIX compress tar ball. This tar archive has been compressed with the UNIX compress utility. If your UNIX system has the compress utility, download this file.
- apache_1_3_6_win32.exe—Windows NT/98 InstallShield archive. This self-extracting archive contains both the Apache server source code and a precompiled Windows 32-bit server program. Downloading and installing this file is discussed in Chapter 11: "Using Apache on Windows 95/NT."

Uncompress

Go to a UNIX shell prompt and go to the same directory in which you downloaded the compressed archive file. If you downloaded the gzip tar ball, uncompress it by typing

```
gunzip apache_1.3.6.tar.gz
```

This in-place decompression replaces the original file named apache_1.3.6.tar.gz with the uncompressed file named apache_1.3.6.tar. If you downloaded the compressed tar ball, uncompress it by typing

```
uncompress apache_1.3.6.tar.Z
```

This in-place decompression replaces the original file named apache_1.3.6.tar.Z file with the file named apache_1.3.6.tar.

Extract

Extract the files from the tar ball by typing

```
tar xvf apache_1.3.6.tar
```

Note that the parameters used in the above tar command work in Linux and may be different for your flavor of UNIX. The parameters should tell the tar command to extract the files from the archive and maintain relative directory paths. Consult your UNIX's MAN pages for the appropriate tar command parameters. This tar extraction will create and populate a new directory named apache_1.3.6/. Since I downloaded my tar ball into /usr/local/src/apache, the full path to this directory on my machine is /usr/local/src/apache/apache_1.3.6/.

This tar extraction does not remove the original apache_1.3.6.tar file. Now that the files have been extracted, save disk space by recompressing the tar ball. Keep this tar ball around. If you uncompressed the tar ball using the gunzip utility, then you can recompress the tar ball by typing

```
gzip apache_1.3.6.tar
```

This in-place compression will replace the original file, apache_1.3.6.tar, with the smaller file, apache_1.3.6.tar.gz. If you had uncompressed the tar ball using the uncompress utility, you can recompress the tar ball by typing

```
compress apache_1.3.6.tar
```

This in-place compression will replace the original file, apache_1.3.6.tar, with the smaller file, apache_1.3.6.tar.Z.

The tar extraction has created a new directory: apache_1.3.6/— containing several new subdirectories:

- cgi-bin/—scripts for testing CGI. Later, the installation process will copy these files to the server's cgi-bin directory. If you enable Apache's Common Gateway Interface facilities, these scripts may be used to test those facilities.
- conf/—configuration files. These distribution configurations should not be edited. The installation process copies these files to the server's configuration directory. Those copies will be edited extensively.
- htdocs/—first Web site. The installation process copies these files to the server's document root directory. Your browser's first test of the server will display these pages.
- icons/—directory index icons. These image files will become the icons used by the Web server for fancy directory indexing.
- logs/—logging facilities. This directory is empty. The installation process will create a logs directory for the installed server.
- src/—source code. This directory (and its subdirectories) contain the C language source files that you will compile to create the Apache Web server.

This new apache_1.3.6/ directory also contains a configure-compile-install utility and two important files, README and INSTALL. Use the more command or the vi command to read through these two files. You are now ready to compile and install the Apache Web server.

Configure the Makefile

The Apache Web server comes with a very handy utility called APACI to help you configure, compile, and install the Apache server. The APACI command file named configure resides in the newly created apache_1.3.6/ directory. The configure command accepts various command line arguments describing the Web server you wish to create. At a bare minimum, specify the name of the directory in which you will want the Apache server's run-time system installed. Type

```
./configure --prefix=/usr/local/apache
```

The ./ in front of the configure command is necessary because the apache_1.3.6/ directory is not in your PATH. The -prefix= argument defines the server installation directory, which is /usr/local/apache in our example. When you press the < **Enter** > key, this command does a lot of work. It creates a Makefile that will be used to compile and install the server. The configure command customizes this Makefile for your system. It detects which compiler you have. It finds your C compiler's header files and library files. It determines what flags need to be passed to your compiler and linker. It creates Makefiles for compiling the various Apache modules that you have chosen to include in your server. We have not chosen any modules. This first example does not specify any modules. The `configure` command has included all the default Apache modules. Module selection is discussed in the section "Selecting Apache Modules."

Compile

At a UNIX shell prompt in the new `apache_1.3.6/` directory, compile the Apache server by typing

```
make
```

The `make` command (which comes with probably all UNIX variants) reads a file named Makefile in the current directory and performs the commands therein. The `configure` command has created the `apache_1.3.6/Makefile` so that `make` will compile all of the necessary source code in the `apache_1.3.6/src/` directory tree. The result will be the Web server executable named `httpd` in the `apache_1.3.6/src/` subdirectory.

Install

The `configure` command has created the `apache_1.3.6/Makefile` such that passing the `install` argument will cause the `make` command to copy the compiled server (and all its associated run-time files) to the installation directory—the directory you specified to the configure command with the `-prefix=` argument. To perform the installation, type

```
make install
```

In our example, we named `/usr/local/apache` as the installation directory. The above command will have populated that directory with a number of subdirectories:

- `bin/`—binary files. This directory contains the executables for the Web server system. It includes the Web server (httpd), a start-stop utility (apachectl), and a number of other helper programs.
- `cgi-bin/`—CGI files. This directory initially contains two shell scripts that you can use to test Apache's Common Gateway Interface facili-

ties. When you begin supporting CGI on this Web site, Web developers will place their CGI scripts and binaries in this directory.

- `conf/`—configuration files. The distribution configuration files from `apache_1.3.6/conf` have been copied to this location. These files will be edited extensively throughout this book.

- `htdocs/`—DocumentRoot. This is the root directory for the Web site hosted by this server. It is initially populated by a Web page congratulating you on successfully installing the server. We will soon see this page in a browser. More important, the `htdocs/manual/` directory contains the Apache HTTP Server User's Guide.

- `icons/`—image files. Apache's fancy indexing facility will use these files to display icons next to file and directory names.

- `include/`—C language header files. These header files are required by the server binary when loading dynamically loaded modules. They also describe the constants, variables, and functions available in the Apache Application Programmer's Interface (the Apache API). You will need these when you write your own Apache modules.

- `libexec/`—dynamically loaded modules. This directory stores the object files of modules that are loaded at run-time. In this example, this directory is empty. No modules were compiled as shared. Dynamically loaded modules are discussed in the section "Selecting Apache Modules," below.

- `logs/`—log files. When the Apache server starts up, it writes its process ID to the file named `httpd.pid` in this `logs/` directory. As browsers access pages in the Web site hosted by this server, the server adds a line to the file named `access_log` in this directory. When run-time errors are encountered, the server writes a message to the file named `error_log` in this directory.

- `man/`—nroff formatted MAN page files. These are the MAN pages for the commands newly installed in the `bin/` directory. The easiest way to install these MAN pages to your system's man command is to add this `man/` directory to your `man` command's directory search path. On Linux, edit the file `man.config` in the `/etc/` directory. Find the section containing `MANPATH` statements and add the line

```
MANPATH /usr/local/apache/man
```

(replacing `/usr/local/apache/` with the installation directory you prescribed to the APACI utility with the `-prefix=` argument).

Alternately, the MAN pages in this directory tree may be individually added to the system MAN pages by copying them to the appropriate directory (e.g. copy the files from `/usr/local/apache/man/man1/` to `/usr/local/man/man1/`).

If you wish to view these pages before installing them, use `nroff` to display them. For example, to display the MAN page for the newly installed `dbmmanage` command, go to the `/usr/local/apache/man/man1/` directory and type

```
cat dbmmanage.1 | nroff -Tascii -mandoc | less -is
```

- `proxy/`—cache directory for the Apache proxy server. In our example, this directory is empty. If the Apache server is configured to be a proxy server, and caching is enabled for it, then the proxy server uses this directory to cache the Web content it relays.

You now have an installed Apache server. If the default Apache modules are all you need, proceed to the section "Configuring the Installed Server." If, on the other hand, you would like to specify the Apache modules to be included in your server, continue with the next section, "Selecting Apache Modules."

Selecting Apache Modules

Herein lies the beauty of compiling the Apache server (versus downloading the precompiled binaries). Apache's web-server functions are grouped into modules. Customize your Apache server by selecting which Apache modules are compiled into your Apache server binary (httpd). The more modules you add, the more the server can do—but the larger the server will be. Some available modules may even have a noticeable impact on server performance. The table in Figure 2.2 gives a description for each Apache module.

In Figure 2.2, a check appears in the Default column for each module that is automatically compiled by the APACI utility. If you want the functionality of a *non*-default module, you must explicitly enable it to get it included in the compile. If you wish to exclude a *default* module from the compile, you must explicitly disable it.

The Enable/Disable column is for your use. Pencil in a plus sign next to each *non*-default module you wish to explicitly include. Pencil in a minus sign next to each *default* module you wish to explicitly exclude.

Figure 2.2
A description of each Apache model.

Enable/ Disable	Shared	Default	Module	Description[2]
			Environment Creation	
		✔	mod_env	Set environment variables for CGI/SSI scripts
		✔	mod_setenvif	Set environment variables based on HTTP headers
			mod_unique_id	Generate unique identifiers for request
			Content Type Decisions	
		✔	mod_mime	Content type/encoding determination (configured)
			mod_mime_magic	Content type/encoding determination (automatic)
		✔	mod_negotiation	Content selection based on the HTTP Accept* headers
			URL Mapping	
		✔	mod_alias	Simple URL translation and redirection
			mod_rewrite	Advanced URL translation and redirection
		✔	mod_userdir	Selection of resource directories by username
			mod_speling	Correction of misspelled URLs
			Directory Handling	
		✔	mod_dir	Directory and directory default file handling
		✔	mod_autoindex	Automated directory index file generation
			Access Control	
		✔	mod_access	Access Control (user, host, network)
		✔	mod_auth	HTTP Basic Authentication (user, passwd)
			mod_auth_dbm	HTTP Basic Authentication via UNIX NDBM files
			mod_auth_db	HTTP Basic Authentication via Berkeley-DB files

continued on next page

Figure 2.2 *continued*	Enable/ Disable	Shared	Default	Module	Description[2]
				mod_auth_anon	HTTP Basic Authentication for Anonymous-style users
				mod_digest	HTTP Digest Authentication
			HTTP Response		
				mod_headers	Arbitrary HTTP response headers (configured)
				mod_cern_meta	Arbitrary HTTP response headers (CERN-style files)
				mod_expires	Expires HTTP responses
		✔		mod_asis	Raw HTTP responses
			Scripting		
		✔		mod_include	Server Side Includes (SSI) support
		✔		mod_cgi	Common Gateway Interface (CGI) support
		✔		mod_actions	Map CGI scripts to act as internal "handlers"
			Internal Content Handlers		
		✔		mod_status	Content handler for server run-time status
				mod_info	Content handler for server configuration summary
			Request Logging		
		✔		mod_log_config mod_log_agent	Customizable logging of requests Specialized HTTP User-Agent logging (deprecated)
				mod_log_refer	Specialized HTTP Referrer logging (deprecated)
				mod_usertrack	Logging of user click-trails via HTTP Cookies
			Miscellaneous		
		✔		mod_imap	Server-side Image Map support
				mod_proxy	Caching Proxy Module (HTTP, HTTPS, FTP)
	Cannot be shared			mod_so	Dynamic Shared Object (DSO) bootstrapping

continued on next page

Figure 2.2
continued

Enable/ Disable	Shared	Default	Module	Description[2]
			Experimental	
			mod_mmap_static	Caching of frequently served pages via mmap()
			Development	
			mod_example	Apache API demonstration (developers only)

2 These module descriptions are quoted from the INSTALL file in the apache_1.3.6/ directory. A more detailed description of each module is available in HTML format in the *Apache User's Guide* (**< install directory > /htdocs/manual/mod/index.html**).

The Shared column is also for your use. Pencil in a plus sign next to each module you wish to load dynamically. Dynamically loaded modules are compiled, but not linked. When a module is compiled as shared, the module source is compiled to an object file. The object file is installed in the libexec/ subdirectory of the installation directory. When the httpd server binary starts up, it loads the shared modules from the libexec/ directory. The advantage of shared modules is that you can put off decisions about which modules to include. You can compile (almost) all the modules as shared, then decide at run-time which modules are loaded. Looking ahead, when the httpd program starts up, it reads a configuration file.[3] In this configuration file, you specify which shared modules httpd is to load. To add a Web server service, add a line to this configuration file and restart the server. You won't have to come back and recompile the Apache server binary.

Dynamic loading offers the additional advantage of adding products on to your already-compiled server. Various add-on modules are available for the Apache server: Perl and PHP interpreters, authentication modules, etc.[4]

The disadvantage of dynamic loading is that it takes the server longer to start up and, on some platforms, there is an operational performance hit. Furthermore, dynamic loading is not available on all platforms. Apache implements dynamic loading through the underlying UNIX system's Dynamic Shared Object support. The APACI utility knows how to compile DSO objects on the following platforms: Linux, SunOS, UNIXWare, FreeB-

3 These configuration files are discussed in the section "Configuring the Installed Server."
4 See the section "Where in the Web" in the Appendix.

SD, Solaris, AIX, OpenBSD, IRIX, SCO, NetBSD, HPUX, BSDI, and Digital UNIX. If you do not find your platform in this list and you are determined to enable DSO support, you must manually set certain compiler flags and linker flags. See the section "Compiling the Server Manually." DSO on the ULTRIX platform is explicitly *not* supported.

Use the APACI utility to explicitly enable and disable modules and to specify which modules are to be shared. Among the many arguments accepted by the APACI utility's `configure` command (in the `apache_1.3.6/` directory), the following relate to module specifications. Replace ⟨module name⟩ with the name of the module you wish to enable, disable, or share. When replacing ⟨module name⟩, do not include the "mod_" prefix (e.g. to explicitly enable `mod_info`, specify `--enable-module=info`):

- `--enable-module=`⟨module name⟩—specifies that ⟨module name⟩ be included in the compile. Only *non*-default modules need be enabled with this argument. *Default* modules are enabled automatically. Add an `--enable-module=` argument to the `configure` command line for each module that you marked with a plus sign in the Enable/Disable column of the table in Figure 2.2. ⟨module name⟩ may be replaced with the keyword "all" to specify that all Apache modules are to be enabled (i.e. `--enable-module=all`). Some modules are experimental or system specific. A more prudent shortcut would be to replace ⟨module name⟩ with the keyword "most" (i.e. `--enable-module=most`). The "most" keyword compiles all modules except: `mod_auth_db`, `mod_mmap_static`, `mod_so`, `mod_example`, `mod_log_agent`, and `mod_log_referer`.
- `--disable-module=`⟨module name⟩—specifies that ⟨module name⟩ is to be excluded from the compile. Only *default* modules need be disabled with this argument. *Non*-default modules are excluded automatically. Add a `--disabled-module=` argument to the configure command line for each module you marked with a minus sign in the Enable/Disable column of the table in Figure 2.2.
- `--enable-shared=`⟨module name⟩—specifies that ⟨module name⟩ is to be compiled as a dynamically loaded module. Any module (except for `mod_so`) may be shared. Add an `--enable-shared=` argument to the configure command line for each module you marked with a plus sign in the Shared column of the table in Figure 2.2. Replace ⟨module name⟩ with the keyword "max" (i.e. `--enable-shared=max`) to compile as many modules as possible as shared.

The following `configure` command enables most of the Apache modules as shared. Note that you must always specify the installation directory with the `--prefix=` argument

```
./configure --prefix=/usr/local/apache --enable-module=most
--enable-shared=max
```

The following example disables the module named `mod_cgi` (a default module), enables the module named `mod_info` (a non-default module), and compiles `mod_info` as a shared module

```
./configure --prefix=/usr/local/apache --disable-module=cgi
--enable-module=info --enable-shared=info
```

Note that when you compile at least one module as shared, the `configure` command automatically enables the `mod_so` module (which bootstraps the dynamic loading of modules).

After you have made your module specifications with the `configure` command, the server may be compiled and installed in the same way as described in the previous section, "Downloading the Source Code" section. That is, you compile the server with the `make` command and you install the server with the `make install` command.

You now have a custom compiled and installed Apache server. If you want to look under the hood, continue with the next section, "Compiling the Server Manually;" otherwise, proceed to the section "Configuring the Installed Server."

Compiling the Server Manually

You are reading this section because you like getting greasy.

Before proceeding with the manual compile, it would be best to get the APACI utility to work just once (maybe by changing some arguments to the `Configure` command). The APACI utility's `make install` command does a lot of work for you. If you can get through it, by whatever means necessary, then the Apache server system (and all its support files) will have been installed and configured. Then you can proceed with the manual compile and all you need to do is copy the server binary (`httpd`) into place. Otherwise, after the manual compile, you will need to do manual installation of the whole Apache server system.

Go to a UNIX shell prompt and go to the `src/` subdirectory of the new `apache_1.3.6` directory. In this subdirectory, there is a file named

`Configuration.tmpl` describing the compile. Later, this file will be used by a command named `Configure` to create a `Makefile` that will be used to compile the server. Do not edit this `Configuration.tmpl` file directly. Copy it, instead, to another file by typing

```
cp Configuration.tmpl Configuration.<host name>
```

replacing `<host name>` with the host name of the machine for which you are compiling this server. Edit the copy with an ASCII editor, such as the `vi` command. In this file, the pound sign begins a comment that continues to the end of the line. All other (non-blank) lines in this file issue directives to the `Configure` command.

This `Configuration.<host name>` file offers options for adding extra flags to the compiler and linker flags. Add flags specific to your compiler with the `EXTRA_CFLAGS=` option. Add flags specific to your linker with the `EXTRA_LDFLAGS=` option. You may add extra include and library search directories to the `EXTRA_LIBS=` and `EXTRA_INCLUDES=` options, respectively. You may specify the full path to your compiler in the `CC=` option.

Usually, the `Configure` command will autodetect your compiler's manner of creating shared objects. If you must to tell the compiler how to create shared objects for the DSO modules, then to set the `CFLAGS_SHLIB=`, `LD_SHLIB=`, `LDFLAGS_SHLIB=`, and `LDFLAGS_SHLIB_EXPORT=` options. Read the comments in the `Configuration.<host name>` file carefully. Also read the page regarding DSO modules in the *Apache HTTP Server User's Guide*. This HTML-formatted page is contained in the file named `dso.html` in the `apache_1.3.6/htdocds/manual/` subdirectory.

The `Configuration.<host name>` file provides rules for turning on certain functions. Set a rule to "yes" to turn on that function (e.g. `SOCKS5=yes`). You may set a rule to "default" to let the `Configure` command make its best guess about whether or not that function is available on your platform. Set a rule to "no" (or any other value) specifically to disable that function. The `SOCKS4` and `SOCKS5` rules allow you to integrate your Apache server with the `SOCKS` proxy. Read the comments within the `Configuration.<host name>` file. You will be directed to add extra linker flags. Also read the answer to the question "Can I use the Apache proxy module with my SOCKS proxy?" That answer is at the `#socks` anchor of the *Apache HTTP Server User's Guide*'s Apache module `mod_proxy` page (`apache_1.3.6/htdocs/manual/mod/mod_proxy.html#socks`). IRIX users may need to enable the `IRIXNIS` or the `IRIXN32` rules. Again, read `Configure.<host name>`'s internal comments. The `WANTHSREGEX` rule enables Henry Spencer's POSIX-compliant regular expression processor. The default for WANTHSREGEX is "yes." If your system's regex library is better than Spencer's, then set this rule to "no." The Configure command will try to locate and link your regex library. If the Configure command cannot find it, you will need to add it to the EXTRA_LIBS= option or the EXTRA_LDFLAGS= option.

The Configuration.<host name> file also provides module directives for enabling/disabling specific modules and for compiling specific modules as shared. The AddModule directive enables the specified module. The syntax of the AddModule directive is

```
AddModule <module object>
```

where <module object> is the relative path and file name of the module's object file (relative to the apache_1.3.6/src/ directory). For example, the line

```
AddModule modules/standard/mod_mime.o
```

enables the mod_mime module. The Configuration.<host name> file contains an AddModule directive for every available Apache module. The AddModule directives for *non*-default modules are commented out with a pound sign. If you wish to enable a *non*-default module, remove the pound sign. If you wish to disable a *default* module, add a pound sign to the beginning of its AddModule directive. If you wish to compile a module as a shared module (DSO), then replace its AddModule directive with a SharedModule directive and change the .o file name extension to .so. For example, the following directive enables the mod_info module and compiles it as a shared module

```
SharedModule modules/standard/mod_info.so
```

Don't forget to change the .o extension to .so. If you compile any module as shared, you must also enable the mod_so module (which is not a default module). The mod_so module bootstraps the dynamic loading of the shared modules. The mod_so module must be enabled, but it cannot be shared. Find this line in the Configuration.<host name> file

```
# AddModule modules/standard/mod_so.o
```

and remove the pound sign from it.

After you have made and saved your changes to the Configuration.<host name> file, you are ready to create a Makefile. Type

```
./Configure -file Configuration.<host name>
```

replacing <host name> with the host name of the machine for which you are compiling this server. Note that capital C in the Configure command, which differentiates this Configure command from the APACI utility's configure command in the apache_1.3.6/ directory. This Configure command reads the specified Configuration.<host name> configuration file and uses it to create a Makefile in this src/ subdiretory. If you feel the need, take this opportunity to edit the Makefile. If you know Makefile syntax, you can add dependencies and modify options. If you do make changes to the Makefile, you may wish to make a copy of the modified Makefile. The next time Configure runs, your modified Makefile will be overwritten. Now, compile the server by typing

```
make
```

The make command reads the Makefile and performs the instructions prescribed therein to compile the Apache server. The result is the server program executable named httpd in the apache_1.3.6/src/ subdirectory.

The server is now compiled, but you must manually install the compiled server. If, before this manual compile, you have previously run the APACI utility to a successful completion, then all you need to do is copy the newly compiled server program (httpd) to its proper place in the installation directory. From a UNIX shell prompt, then apache_1.3.6 directory, type

```
cp src/httpd /usr/local/apache/bin/
```

replacing /usr/local/apache with the installation directory you previously specified with the --prefix= argument to the APACI utility's configure command. If you have not been able to run the APACI utility to completion, then you will need to install the entire Apache server system by hand.

The Makefile in the apache_1.3.6/src/ subdirectory (created by the manual compile's Configure command) does not support an "install" argument (as does the Makefile created by the APACI utility's configure command). You may be tempted to custom compile your server here in the apache_1.3.6/src/ subdirectory and then go to the apache_1.3.6/ directory and run the make install command to install it. Don't. The Makefile in the apache_1.3.6/ directory will recreate the Makefile in the src/ subdirectory and it will recompile your server according to the last parameters passed to the APACI utility's configure command. Thus you will lose all the work you have done in manually compiling the server. You must manually install your custom-compiled server.

Create an installation directory for the Apache server. I suggest the default, which is to type

```
mkdir /usr/local/apache
```

Make a `bin/` subdirectory under the installation directory (e.g. `mkdir /usr/local/apache/bin`). Copy the binary files and script files from the source directory tree into the installation directory's `bin/` subdirectory. At a UNIX shell prompt in the `apache_1.3.6/` subdirectory, type the following commands

```
cp src/httpd /usr/local/apache/bin/
cp src/support/ab /usr/local/apache/bin/
cp src/support/apxs /usr/local/apache/bin/
cp src/support/rotatelogs /usr/local/apache/bin/
cp src/support/apachectl /usr/local/apache/bin/
cp src/support/dbmmanage /usr/local/apache/bin/
cp src/support/htpasswd /usr/local/apache/bin/
cp src/support/logresolve /usr/local/apache/bin/
cp src/support/htdigest /usr/local/apache/bin/
```

Two of the files copied by the above commands are script files that need a little touching up. The first is a Perl script named `apxs`. This script can be used to compile DSO modules outside of the Apache source code directory tree. The `Makefile` has inserted, into this Perl script, the Apache C language header files and the platform-dependant compiler flags and linker flags necessary to build a DSO module. When you are building a DSO module not delivered with Apache (e.g. a third-party product), you can use `apxs` to compile the module without integrating the module source code into the Apache source code directory tree. The `Makefile` left some work unfinished—work normally done by the APACI utility we did not use in this manual compile. Edit the copy of `apxs` now residing in the installation directory's `bin/` directory (with an ASCII editor, such as the `vi` command). Find the lines that read

```
my $CFG_PREFIX     = '@prefix@';
my $CFG_SBINDIR    = '@sbindir@';
my $CFG_INCLUDEDIR = '@includedir@';
my $CFG_LIBEXECDIR = '@libexecdir@';
my $CFG_SYSCONFDIR = '@sysconfdir@';
```

In these lines, the @whatever@ values must be replaced with the appropriate directory names (without a final backslash). Replace @prefix@ with the name of the installation directory (/usr/local/apache, in our example). Replace @sbindir@ with the full path to the installation directory's bin/ subdirectory (e.g., /usr/local/apache/bin). Replace @includedir@ with the full path to the installation directory's include/ subdirectory (e.g., /usr/local/apache/include). Replace @libexecdir@ with the installation directory's libexec/ subdirectory (e.g., /usr/local/apache/libexec). Replace @sysconfigdir@ with the installation directory's conf/ subdirectory (e.g. /usr/local/apache/conf). Save the apxs file.

The second script file that must be edited is the shell script named apachectl. This script is used to start and stop the Web server program (httpd). When this script starts the httpd daemon, it writes the process ID of the daemon to a text file. When this script stops the daemon, it reads the text file to obtain the process ID of the process that must killed. The full path and file name of this text file is defined in the variable named PIDFILE. Look for the line reading

```
PIDFILE='/usr/local/apache/logs/httpd.pid'
```

and replace /usr/local/apache/logs with the full path to your installation directory's logs/ directory. Leave the httpd.pid file name unchanged. In our example (since we used the default installation directory of /usr/local/apache), this line is fine the way it is and needs no correction. Now find the variable named HTTPD. This variable stores the full path and file name of the Apache server program. Look for the line reading

```
HTTPD='/usr/local/apache/src/httpd'
```

and replace /usr/local/apache/src with the full path to your installation directory's bin/ directory. Leave the httpd file name unchanged. In our example, the full path and file name would be /usr/local/apache/bin/httpd.

Make a man/ subdirectory under the installation directory (e.g. mkdir /usr/local/apache/libexec/). Some files in the src/support/ subdirectory have numbers for their file name extension. These files are nroff formatted MAN pages describing the new commands we just installed in the installation directory's bin/ subdirectory. Each MAN page must be copied to its appropriate categorical subdirectory under the man/ subdirectory we just created. At a UNIX shell prompt, in the apache_1.3.6/ subdirectory, type the following commands:

```
mkdir /usr/local/apache/man/man1
cp src/support/*.1 /usr/local/apache/man/man1/
mkdir /usr/local/apache/man/man8
cp src/support/*.8 /usr/local/apache/man/man8/
```

The easiest way to install these MAN pages to your system's man command is to add the /usr/local/apache/man/ directory to your MAN command's directory search path. On Linux, edit the file man.config in the /etc/ directory. Find the section containing MANPATH statements and add the line

```
MANPATH /usr/local/apache/man
```

(replacing /usr/local/apache/ with the installation directory you created). Alternately, these MAN pages may be individually added to the system MAN pages by copying them to the appropriate directory (e.g. copy the files from /usr/local/apache/man/man1/ to /usr/local/man/man1/).

Make a libexec/ subdirectory under the installation directory (e.g. mkdir /usr/local/apache/libexec/). If you compiled any module as shared, then you must find all the shared object files compiled and copy them to the installation directory's new libexec/ subdirectory. The find command can make this easy for you. At a UNIX shell prompt in the apache_1.3.6/ subdirectory, type

```
find src -name \*.so -exec cp {} /usr/local/apache/libexec \;
```

Make a conf/ subdirectory under the installation directory (e.g. mkdir /usr/local/apache/conf). Copy the run-time configuration files appropriate to your platform from the apache_1.3.6/conf/ subdirectory to the installation's conf/ subdirectory. For those configuration files named with a -dist suffix, replace the -dist suffix in the source file with a .default file name extension in the destination file. For those configuration files named without a -dist suffix, add a .default file name extension in the destination file. Specifically, from a UNIX shell prompt in the apache_1.3.6/ subdirectory, type the following commands

```
cp conf/access.conf-dist /usr/local/apache/conf/access.conf.default
cp conf/httpd.conf-dist /usr/local/apache/conf/httpd.conf.default
cp conf/mime.types /usr/local/apache/conf/mime.types.default
cp conf/magic /usr/local/apache/conf/magic.default
cp conf/srm.conf-dist /usr/local/apache/conf/srm.conf.default
```

Copy these same distribution configuration files again; but, this time, leave off the .default file name extension in the destination file. Type

```
cp conf/access.conf-dist /usr/local/apache/conf/access.conf
cp conf/httpd.conf-dist /usr/llocal/apache/conf/httpd.conf
cp conf/mime.types /usr/local/apache/conf/mime.types
cp conf/magic /usr/local/apache/conf/magic
cp conf/srm.conf-dist /usr/local/apache/conf/srm.conf
```

Now the installation's new conf/ subdirectory contains two copies of each configuration file: one the server will use (the one without the .default file name extension) and one to revert to (the one with the .default file name extension) after you mangle the one the server uses.

Several of the subdirectories of the apache_1.3.6/ directory need to be copied in their entirety to the installation directory: icons/, man/, cgi-bin/, htdocs/, and src/include/. From a UNIX shell prompt, in the apache_1.3.6/ directory, type the following commands

```
cp -R icons/ /usr/local/apache
cp -R cgi-bin/ /usr/local/apache
cp -R htdocs/ /usr/local/apache
cp -R src/include/ /usr/local/apache
```

The -R flag in the above commands instructs the cp command to copy directories recursively. The recursive copy flag may be different for the cp command in your flavor of UNIX. Consult the cp command's MAN page on your system.

Finally, a couple of platform-specific files need to be copied to the installation directory's include/ subdirectory. From a UNIX shell prompt in the apache_1.3.6/ directory, type the following commands

```
cp src/os/unix/os.h /usr/local/apache/include/
cp src/os/unix/os-inline.c /usr/local/apache/include/
```

Your Apache server is now compiled and installed. Proceed to the next section, "Configuring the Installed Server."

Configuring the Installed Server

Configuration Files

At this point, you have a fully installed Apache Web server—whether you got here by installing a precompiled binary, by compiling the source code with the APACI utility, or by compiling the source code manually. All paths converge here. The task before us is to get the Apache server to run on this machine on this network. We must tailor Apache's run-time configuration files for this environment. There are five such files and they all live in the installation directory's `conf/` subdirectory:

- `httpd.conf`—the main Apache server configuration file
- `srm.conf`—server resource configuration
- `access.conf`—directory and file access restrictions
- `mime.types`—relates media types to file name extensions
- `magic`—lists recognizable byte sequences used by the `mod_mime_magic` module (if enabled) to determine a file's media type by examining the first few bytes of the file.

For each of these files, there should be a copy of the distribution original having a `.default` file name extension (i.e. `httpd.conf.default`, `srm.conf.default`, etc.) also residing in the `conf/` subdirectory. If there is not, then copy each of these files to a file with the same name, but with the added `.default` extension (e.g. `cp httpd.conf httpd.conf.default`). The `.default` files give us a safety net—a backup of the original versions of these files. When we irrevocably destroy the working copy of one of these files (the one without the `.default` extension), then we can restore the working copy from the `.default` backup.

The only file of concern here is `httpd.conf`. The `srm.conf` file and the `access.conf` file exist for backward compatibility. All the configurations previously kept in those files may now be kept in the `httpd.conf` file—making maintenance easier by keeping all of those configurations in the same file. The `mime.types` file and the `magic` file are discussed in Chapter 4 "Manipulating Content."

Syntax

In the `httpd.conf` file, a pound sign begins a comment that continues to the end of the line. All other (non-blank) lines contain configuration directives used by the server. There are two kinds of directives: 1) variable assignments, and 2) block directives. The syntax for the variable assignments is `<variable name><white space><value>`. For example, the `ServerRoot` variable is assigned the full path to installation directory by the line

```
ServerRoot "/usr/local/apache"
```

Values that may contain white space must be surrounded by double quotations.

The second type of configuration directive, the block directive, uses syntax resembling HTML matched tags. There is a starting tag, followed by variable assignments, followed by an ending tag. For example, a Directory directive, such as

```
<Directory "/usr/local/apache/htdocs">
    Options Indexes FollowSymLinks
    AllowOverride None
    Order allow,deny
    Allow from all
</Directory>
```

begins with the <Directory "/usr/local/apache/htdocs"> tag and ends with the </Directory> tag. The variable assignments between the two tags apply only to the directory named in the <Directory ...> start tag.

Basic Directives

Of the many configuration directives in httpd.conf, the only ones of concern here are those directly related to the server program and the environment in which it runs. Here, we modify those directives necessary to get the server up and running. Other configuration directives are discussed in other (more functionally appropriate) chapters.

ServerType

This specifies how the Apache server daemon is launched. Given the default setting of

```
ServerType standlone
```

the Apache server listens on the TCP/IP HTTP port for Web requests. The server daemon is initially launched manually or at boot time by the system startup scripts in /etc/rc.d/init.d (see the section "Starting, Testing, and Stopping the Server," below). Once launched, the daemon listens for HTTP requests and launches one or more instances of itself to service these requests.

On the other hand, given a value of

```
ServerType inetd
```

the Apache server waits to be called by the `inetd` Internet daemon. The `inetd` daemon listens to all of the TCP/IP ports for service requests. When inetd receives a request on the HTTP port, it launches an instance of the Apache Web server to service the request. The `ServerType inetd` directive tells the Apache server to service the request and exit—leaving `inetd` to listen to the HTTP port for more service requests. This method of invocation is computationally expensive. A new server process must be started up and shut down for each browser request. Furthermore, the *Apache User's Guide* warns

> "Inetd mode is no longer recommended and does not always work properly. Avoid it if at all possible."[5]

If you do choose to set `ServerType` to `inetd`, you must also tell the `inetd` daemon how to call the new Apache server. Edit the file `/etc/services` with an ACSII text editor (such as `vi`). Make sure the following line is not commented out with a pound sign

```
http 80/tcp
```

This line gives the name "http" to service requests hitting port 80 with the TCP protocol. Save your changes to `/etc/services`, then edit the file `/etc/inetd.conf`. Look for a line beginning with `http`, such as

```
http stream  tcp  nowait  root  /usr/sbin/httpd  in.httpd
```

This line tells `inetd` to launch the program `/usr/sbin/httpd` whenever a service request named `http` is received. Make sure that the line is not commented out with a pound sign. Change the `/usr/sbin/httpd` path to point to your new server (`/usr/local/apache/bin/httpd`, in our example).

Once you have modified the Internet daemon's configuration files, you must tell the Internet daemon to reread those configuration files. Send a hang-up signal (a HUP signal) to the `inetd` process. HUPping the `inetd` daemon is discussed in detail in the section "Removing Any Pre-Existing Web Servers," above.

ServerRoot

This specifies the Apache installation directory (`/usr/local/apache/`, in our example). The directive should read

---

5 /usr/local/apache/htdocs//manual/mod/core.html#servertype

```
ServerRoot "/usr/local/apache"
```

If you used the APACI utility to compile and install the server, then this configuration directive will have already been set to the appropriate directory (the directory you supplied to the `configure` command with the `--prefix` argument). If you compiled and installed the server manually, then this line will read

```
ServerRoot "@@ServerRoot@@"
```

You must replace @@ServerRoot@@ with the correct full path to the Apache installation directory. Be sure not to add a final backslash to your directory specification.

LockFile

This specifies the path and file name of the lock file used by the server when running in a serialized mode. The default value of

```
LockFile logs/accept.lock
```

should suffice. The only reason to change this directive is if the logs directory is NFS mounted. The lock file must live on a local file system.

PidFile

This specifies the path and file name of the text file in which the Apache server records its process ID number. This is used for stopping the running server. The default value of

```
PidFile logs/httpd.pid
```

should suffice. I would suggest that this file reside on a local filesystem. The shutdown daemons for the `ServerType` standalone Apache server will need this file to shut down the running server.

ScoreBoardFile

This specifies the path and file name of the file in which the Apache server stores some of its own process information. The default value of

```
ScoreBoardFile logs/apache_runtime_status
```

should suffice. Not all systems require this file. If your system requires this file, the file named in the above directive will be created when you run the server. If you are running more than one server (on different TCP ports, for instance), make sure that each has its own ScoreBoardFile (e.g. run each instance with a different httpd.conf file).

ResourceConfig

This specifies the path and file name of the resource configuration file to use. The default value of

```
#ResourceConfig conf/srm.conf
```

is commented out by the pound sign. Apache's default action is to process first httpd.conf, then srm.conf, and then access.conf. Directives encountered in later files override the directives in earlier files. Maintenance will be easier if you leave the srm.conf file empty and keep all your configurations in the httpd.conf file.

AccessConfig

This specifies the path and file name of the access security configuration file to use. The default value of

```
#AccessConfig conf/access.conf
```

is commented out by the pound sign. Apache's default action is to process first httpd.conf, then srm.conf, and then access.conf. Directives encountered in later files override the directives in earlier files. Maintenance will be easier if you leave the access.conf file empty and keep all your configurations in the httpd.conf file.

LoadModule

This specifies that Apache is to load the specified module in the specified shared object file. There should be one such LoadModule directive for each module compiled as a DSO. If you used the APACI utility to compile and install the server, there will already be one such LoadModule directive for each --enable-shared= argument that you passed to the configure command. If you compiled the server manually or if you are adding a module compiled outside the Apache source code tree, then you will need to add a LoadModule directive for each module compiled as a shared object. Some modules have dependencies on other modules, so the order in which they are loaded is very important. The following list was generated by the APACI utility with --enabled-shared=max argument passed to the configure command. Refer to this list to know where to insert the shared module you are adding. If you are adding a third-party product, you will probably insert its LoadModule directive at the end of this list.

```
LoadModule env_module  libexec/mod_env.so
LoadModule config_log_module libexec/mod_log_config.so
LoadModule mime_magic_module libexec/mod_mime_magic.so
LoadModule mime_module libexec/mod_mime.so
LoadModule negotiation_module libexec/mod_negotiation.so
LoadModule status_module libexec/mod_status.so
LoadModule info_module libexec/mod_info.so
LoadModule includes_module libexec/mod_include.so
LoadModule autoindex_module libexec/mod_autoindex.so
LoadModule dir_module  libexec/mod_dir.so
LoadModule cgi_module  libexec/mod_cgi.so
LoadModule asis_module libexec/mod_asis.so
LoadModule imap_module libexec/mod_imap.so
LoadModule action_module libexec/mod_actions.so
LoadModule speling_module libexec/mod_speling.so
LoadModule userdir_module libexec/mod_userdir.so
LoadModule proxy_module libexec/libproxy.so
LoadModule alias_module libexec/mod_alias.so
LoadModule rewrite_module libexec/mod_rewrite.so
LoadModule access_module libexec/mod_access.so
LoadModule auth_module libexec/mod_auth.so
LoadModule anon_auth_module libexec/mod_auth_anon.so
LoadModule dbm_auth_module libexec/mod_auth_dbm.so
LoadModule digest_module libexec/mod_digest.so
LoadModule cern_meta_module libexec/mod_cern_meta.so
LoadModule expires_module libexec/mod_expires.so
LoadModule headers_module libexec/mod_headers.so
LoadModule usertrack_module libexec/mod_usertrack.so
```

AddModule

This specifies that Apache is to load the specified module. A list of AddModule directives specifies the order in which Apache is to load the modules. This directive is used for both shared object modules and statically linked modules. After all, modules dependent one upon the other remain so whether or not either one of them is loaded dynamically. If you used the APACI utility to compile and install the server, then the AddModule list will already have been generated for you. If you do have to make a change to the LoadModule list (described above), be sure to make the corresponding change in the AddModule list. The following list was generated by the APACI utility when passed the --enable-module=most argument. Refer to this list to know where you should insert the module you are adding. If you are adding a third-party product, you will probably insert its `AddModule` directive at the end of this list. The `ClearModule` directive at the head of this list empties out any module list that the Apache server program may have built in memory before arriving at this section of the `httpd.conf` configuration file.

```
ClearModuleList
AddModule mod_env.c
AddModule mod_log_config.c
AddModule mod_mime_magic.c
AddModule mod_mime.c
AddModule mod_negotiation.c
AddModule mod_status.c
AddModule mod_info.c
AddModule mod_include.c
AddModule mod_autoindex.c
AddModule mod_dir.c
AddModule mod_cgi.c
AddModule mod_asis.c
AddModule mod_imap.c
AddModule mod_actions.c
AddModule mod_speling.c
AddModule mod_userdir.c
AddModule mod_proxy.c
AddModule mod_alias.c
AddModule mod_rewrite.c
AddModule mod_access.c
AddModule mod_auth.c
AddModule mod_auth_anon.c
AddModule mod_auth_dbm.c
AddModule mod_digest.c
AddModule mod_cern_meta.c
AddModule mod_expires.c
AddModule mod_headers.c
AddModule mod_usertrack.c
AddModule mod_unique_id.c
AddModule mod_so.c
AddModule mod_setenvif.c
```

Port

This specifies the TCP port to which a `ServerType standalone` server is to listen. This setting has no effect if the Apache server is being launched by the `inetd` daemon. The international standard port for HTTP is port 80. So the default setting of

```
Port 80
```

configures a public server to serve anyone in the Word Wide Web community. Note that if the specified port number is less than 1023, the Apache Web server will need to be launched by the root user. Ports below 1024 are standardized to service certain protocols (e.g. port 80 for HTTP, 21 for FTP, 25 for SMTP, etc.). Non-root users are not allowed access to these ports. Standards are not imposed on ports 1023 and above, which are thus known as "ethereal" ports. You would bind the Apache server to an ethereal port for a server that must be started and stopped by normal users, such as an experimental server that is stopped or restarted (often) by a software developer. Furthermore, binding Apache to an ethereal port removes the server from the mainstream. When using Apache as a corporate internal or intranet server, an ethereal port may gain you a little more privacy. Note that the browser clients making requests to such a server must enter the non-standard port number in the URL in order to access this server's content.

ServerAdmin

This specifies the e-mail address to which error messages may be sent. The APACI utility will have already set this value to

```
ServerAdmin root@<host>.<domain>
```

where `<host>.<domain>` will have been replaced with the hostname of the machine on which the server is installed. APACI obtained this value by running the `hostname` command. Some error messages sent back to the browser may display this address. Expect root to receive e-mail from complete strangers.

ServerName

This specifies the hostname name of the machine on which this Apache server is running. The default value of

```
#ServerName new.host.name
```

is commented out, in which case the output of the `hostname` command is used. If you want your Apache server to answer to a different name, uncomment the `ServerName` directive and replace `new.host.name` with the desired hostname. Oftentimes, the Apache server is installed on an existing server whose existing hostname is already known to other machines and services. If you would like your Apache server also to answer to the standard WWW machine name (without changing the machine's real hostname), then you may specify www in the ServerName directive. Be sure that the name servers for the domain in which the Apache server is running know how to redirect requests to the new hostname. If this machine is unknown to the name servers, you may use the machine's IP address to connect to the Apache server; in which case you will need to replace new.host.name with that IP address.

DocumentRoot

This specifies the top of the directory tree containing this server's content. The browsers connecting to this server will see this as the root directory. They will not be able to see "above" this directory. The APACI utility will have set this directive to the htdocs/ subdirectory of the installation directory you specified with the --prefix= argument to the configure command:

```
DocumentRoot "/usr/local/apache/htdocs"
```

This directory is initially populated with an index.html congratulating you on getting the server running. There will also be a manual/ subdirectory containing the *Apache User's Guide* in HTML format. It spells out quite a few implementation specifics, caveats, and watch-out-fors. You may well want to move or remove the manual/ subdirectory when you put your Apache server into production. All this manual (plus a search engine) is available at the **www.apache.org** homepage. I keep mine near at hand.

You may have good reasons for pointing the DocumentRoot directive to another directory. Continuing development makes the content volatile. If you back up the user home directories more often than the system directories, you may wish to locate the DocumentRoot directory among the home directories (e.g. /home/httpd/). You may be running more than one Apache server on a given machine, each with its own content directory tree (each of which must also have its own httpd.conf specifying each its own Port, PidFile, ScoreBoardFile, and DocumentRoot directives).

<Directory>

This is a block tag with a matching </Directory> end tag. The opening tag specifies a directory path. The directives between the opening and end tags specify what files are visible and what services are available in the specified path. Such access permissions are inherited. That is, a subdirectory inherits the access permissions of its parent directory; unless a

`<Directory>` directive for the subdirectory specifically overrides the access permissions defined in the parent directory's `<Directory>` directive. Note that the directories specified in the opening tag are absolute filesystem directories. They are *not* relative to the DocumentRoot directory (the `<Location>` block directive provides access control by URL). The first `<Directory>` directive in the httpd.conf file specifies restrictive access for the root directory. These permissions become the default permission set:

```
<Directory />
    Options FollowSymLinks
    AllowOverride None
    </Directory>
```

The DocumentRoot directory requires less restrictive permissions. The http.conf file *must* contain a `<Directory>` directive for the directory specified in the DocumentRoot directive:

```
<Directory "/usr/local/apache/htdocs">
    Options Indexes FollowSymLinks
    AllowOverride None
    Order allow,deny
    Allow from all
</Directory>
```

The values set in the above `<Directory>` blocks should be sufficient for getting your server up. The `<Directory>` block and its directives are discussed in more detail as they are used in other chapters to implement specific features (especially those chapters devoted to content and to security). Suffice it to say that you must have a default `<Directory>` block and a DocumentRoot `<Directory>` block.

Testing the Configuration

Once you have made and saved your modifications, you may test your configuration with the apachectl utility. This resides in the bin/ subdirectory of your Apache server's installation directory (e.g. /usr/local/apache/bin/). At a UNIX shell prompt in that directory, type

```
./apachectl configtest
```

The server should respond with

```
Syntax OK
```

otherwise, the `apachectl` command will issue an error message detailing the problem and the file name and line number where the problem was found.

Given the `configtest` stamp of approval, your Apache server is now configured and ready to run. Proceed to the next section, "Starting, Testing, and Stopping the Server."

Starting, Stopping, and Restarting the Server

Starting the Server

If you configured the `ServerType` directive as `inetd`, then you need not manually start the server. The server will be started as needed by the `inetd` daemon. If your `ServerType` is set to `standalone`, then use the `apachectl` utility manually to start and stop the Apache Web server. This utility resides in the `bin/` subdirectory of your Apache server's installation directory (e.g. `/usr/local/apache/bin/`). At a UNIX shell prompt in that directory, type

```
./apachectl start
```

The server should respond with

```
./apachectl start: httpd started
```

To see the running server processes, type

```
ps ax | grep httpd
```

replacing `ax` with the appropriate arguments for the `ps` command on your system. You should see output similar to

```
15317  ?  S    0:00 /usr/local/apache/bin/httpd
15318  ?  S    0:00 /usr/local/apache/bin/httpd
15319  ?  S    0:00 /usr/local/apache/bin/httpd
15320  ?  S    0:00 /usr/local/apache/bin/httpd
15321  ?  S    0:00 /usr/local/apache/bin/httpd
15322  ?  S    0:00 /usr/local/apache/bin/httpd
```

The Apache server system dynamically launches enough server daemons to handle the current load of browser requests.

The Moment of Truth

Hit your server with a browser. Point your browser to the same server name that you specified in the `ServerName` directive of the `httpd.conf` configuration file. Your browser should display the Web page shown in Figure 2.3.

Figure 2.3

It worked!

Stopping the Server

If you configured the `ServerType` directive as `inetd`, then you need not manually stop the server. When called by the `inetd` daemon, the Apache server services the one request for which it was called and then exits. If your `ServerType` is set to `standalone`, then use the `apachectl` utility to manually stop the server. At a UNIX shell prompt, in the `bin/` subdirectory of the Apache installation directory (e.g. `/usr/local/apache/bin/`), type

```
./apachectl stop
```

The server should respond with

```
./apachectl stop: httpd stopped
```

Restarting the Server

Whenever you make a change to one of the configuration files, you must restart the Apache server for those changes to take effect. (This is, of course, not necessary if your `ServerType` is set to `inetd`.) The `apachectl` utility provides two methods for restarting the server. Passing an argument of `graceful` to the `apachectl` command signals the server to stop serving browser requests and—when it is finished serving the outstanding requests—stop and restart the server. At a shell prompt in the `bin/` subdirectory of the Apache installation directory (e.g. `/usr/local/apache/bin/`), type

```
./apachectl graceful
```

The server should respond with

```
./apachectl graceful: httpd gracefully restarted
```

If you want Apache to restart right away you can use the more Bolshevik argument

```
./apachectl restart
```

The server will immediately stop, without finishing the outstanding requests, and then restart, responding with

```
./apachectl restart: httpd restarted
```

Autolaunching the Server at Boot Time

You can configure your UNIX system to start the standalone Apache server automatically when the UNIX system boots up. Different UNIX systems have different system initialization procedures. Worse yet, different packages of the same UNIX flavor may have different startup procedures. The procedures discussed below use the System V style initialization procedures—specifically the RedHat Linux implementation. Other packages of Linux and other System V UNIX variants use similar procedures, but the directory naming conventions are different. Refer to your system's MAN page on the `init` command.

The system boot procedures invoke the `init` command to bring the system up into a particular runlevel. Runlevel 0 is for shutting the system down. Runlevel 1 brings the system up in single-user mode. Runlevel 6 is reserved. Runlevels 2 through 5 bring up system services and allow multi-user login. We need to tell the `init` command to start the Apache server up at runlevels 2 through 5 and to shut the Apache server down at runlevels 0, 1, and 6. The `init` command reads the configuration file named `/etc/inittab` to determine what scripts and programs are to be run at each runlevel. The `/etc/inittab` file tells `init` to run the script named `/etc/rc.d/rc` at each runlevel, passing it the runlevel as an argument. The `rc` command looks for scripts in a directory named after the runlevel. At runlevel 0, for instance, the `rc` command runs the scripts in the `/etc/rc.d/rc0.d/` directory. At runlevel 1, the `rc` command calls the scripts in the `/etc/rc.d/rc1.d/` directory. The `rc` command first runs all the kill scripts in the appropriate directory, then runs all the startup scripts in that directory. *Kill scripts* are scripts whose names begin with a capital K and are expected to receive the word `stop` as an argument. Start-up scripts begin with a capital S and are expected to receive the word `start` as an argument. These scripts also have numbers in their names specifying the order in which the scripts are to be executed. For example, the script named `S10network` is run before the script named `S60nfs`. This makes sense given that network services must be available before starting the NFS services that use them. Network services must be available before starting our new Apache server, too. To determine the number to use for our Apache startup script, at a UNIX shell prompt, go to the `/etc/rc.d/rc3.d/` directory and get a directory listing. It will look somewhat like this:

```
K05innd        K30mcserv     S01kerneld  S50inet     S85postgresql
K08autofs      K34yppasswdd  S05apmd     S55named    S85sound
K10xntpd       K35ypserv     S10network  S55routed   S91smb
K20bootparamd  K45arpwatch   S11portmap  S60lpd      S99linuxconf
K20rusersd     K50snmpd      S15nfsfs    S60nfs      S99local
K20rwalld      K60atd        S20random   S65dhcpd
K20rwhod       K60mars-new   S30syslog   S75keytable
K25squid       K87ypbind     S32gated    S80sendmail
K28amd         K96pcmcia     S40crond    S85gpm
```

The Apache Web server is dependent upon network services (`S10network`) and DNS services (`S55named`). The Apache server also e-mails error messages to the administrator and is therefore dependent upon mail services (`S80sendmail`). If you plan on providing database support for CGI scripting, then your Web server may also be dependent upon your database services (`S85postgresql`, in the above example, though yours could be a MySQL or an Oracle startup script). To start your Apache server after the supporting services, pick a number greater than the highest of those supporting services. Given the above listing, 86 would be a good number.

The converse is true for your Apache server's shutdown script. You want the services to shut down in reverse order. This way, the dependent service may release its supporting service resources. The Apache Web server must be shut down when entering runlevels 0, 1, and 6. Get a directory listing of the /etc/rc.d/rc0.d/ directory:

```
K00linuxconf    K20rusersd      K35dhcpd     K60crond      K89portmap
K05innd         K20rwalld       K35smb       K60lpd        K90killall
K05keytable     K20rwhod        K35ypserv    K60mars-new   K90network
K08autofs       K25squid        K45named     K70syslog     K92apmd
K15gpm          K28amd          K50inet      K75gated      K96pcmcia
K15sound        K30mcserv       K50snmpd     K80random     K98kerneld
K20bootparamd   K30sendmail     K55routed    K85nfsfs      S00halt
K20nfs          K34yppasswdd    K60atd       K87ypbind
```

For your Apache kill script, pick a number less than the lowest of the services that support the Web server; lower than K90network; lower than K45named; lower than K30sendmail. Given the above listing, 29 would be a good number.

These scripts in the /etc/rc.d/rc?.d/ directories are not the actual scripts, but links to scripts kept in the /etc/rc.d/init.d/ directory. For each of these services, a script that takes both the start and the stop command line arguments is placed in the /etc/rc.d/init.d/ directory; and then links to these scripts are created where needed in the /etc/rc.d/rc?.d/ directories. To setup the Apache server for automatic boot-time startup, first copy the apachectl script to the init.d/directory. Type the following commands at the UNIX shell prompt

```
cp /usr/local/apache/bin/apachectl /etc/rc.d/init.d
```

replacing /usr/local/apache with your Apache installation directory. Next, create the startup script links to the apachectl script. At the UNIX shell prompt, type

```
ln /etc/rc.d/init.d/apachectl /etc/rc.d/rc2.d/S86apachectl
ln /etc/rc.d/init.d/apachectl /etc/rc.d/rc3.d/S86apachectl
ln /etc/rc.d/init.d/apachectl /etc/rc.d/rc4.d/S86apachectl
ln /etc/rc.d/init.d/apachectl /etc/rc.d/rc5.d/S86apachectl
```

replacing 86 with the number you picked for your Apache startup scripts. Finally, create the kill script links to the apachectl script, by typing

```
ln /etc/rc.d/init.d/apachectl /etc/rc.d/rc0.d/K29apachectl
```

```
ln /etc/rc.d/init.d/apachectl /etc/rc.d/rc1.d/K29apachectl
ln /etc/rc.d/init.d/apachectl /etc/rc.d/rc6.d/K29apachectl
```

replacing 29 with the number you picked for your Apache kill scripts.

To test that your Apache server will start automatically at boot time, shut down and reboot the system. Log in and type the following command at the UNIX shell prompt

```
ps ax | grep httpd
```

replacing ax with the ps arguments appropriate for your system. If the ps command output looks like this

```
387  ?  S    0:00 /usr/local/apache/bin/httpd
404  ?  S    0:00 /usr/local/apache/bin/httpd
405  ?  S    0:00 /usr/local/apache/bin/httpd
406  ?  S    0:00 /usr/local/apache/bin/httpd
407  ?  S    0:00 /usr/local/apache/bin/httpd
408  ?  S    0:00 /usr/local/apache/bin/httpd
```

then you have successfully installed the Apache server into the system startup.

Creating the Web Site

Strategy

This chapter configures a single-site model. You should configure this model even if you are more interested in a multiple-site model (e.g. an ISP model). This chapter will configure the main Web site for the server. This scenario builds an infrastructure extensible from the single-site model to the multisite model and sets default configurations for other Web sites that you may add. In this scenario, we also create the Web server daemon account—applicable to all models.

Main Concerns

Both the Web server and the webmaster must have agreeable access to the document directory tree. Let's define the webmaster as the one responsible for authoring this Web site's content—versus you, the system administrator, responsible for keeping the Web server running. The most cooperative configuration is to create a user account for the Apache server daemon and a user account for each webmaster. Give the webmaster access to the document directory tree published by the server. Give the server daemon access to the document directory and to the Apache installation directory. This will keep Web authors out of your server. This will keep system administrators out of your content. Good fences make good neighbors.

The document directory tree must get backed up. System volumes are usually backed up less often than user volumes and data volumes. On such segregated systems, be sure to locate the document directory tree on a filesystem that gets backed up.

The infrastructure must be easy to maintain for your kind of Web site. It must adapt to your requirements and grow according to your needs. The structure must allow the webmaster to create a suitable development environment. The webmaster may require more than just a public html directory. For a site receiving contributions from multiple authors/developers, the structure must allow for cooperation. For the ISP model, the structure must be expandable (and, on occasion, contractible).

Solution

In this scenario, there is one Web server, one Web site, one system administrator, and one webmaster. The structure presented here gives the webmaster responsibility for all Web content. The public directories published by the server are subdirectories of the webmaster's home directory (which gets happily backed up with the user volume). The webmaster in this example will be creating HTML and CGI scripted content. This structure provides the webmaster storage for both private and public files—allowing the webmaster to create the development environment of choice.

This single-site configuration provides a baseline for adding new sites to the server. From this baseline, you can create a template for adding user sites and another template for creating virtually hosted sites (discussed in Chapter 7: "Creating Homepage Web Sites" and in Chapter 8: "Creating Virtual Domain Web Sites").

Table 3.1 summarizes the environment to be created for the example server.

Table 3.1
Example environment.

Environment Property	Value in Example		
server host	www.administeringapache.com at 192.168.1.1 on 192.168.1.0		
server operating system	Linux		
Apache server source directory	/usr/local/src/apache/apache_1.3.9/		
Apache server installation directory	/usr/local/apache/		
	permissions	**owner**	**group**
	directories drwx-rwx---	root	httpd
	files -rw-rw-----	root	httpd
	files in bin/ -rwx-rwx---	root	httpd
Apache server daemon user account	httpd		
Apache server daemon group account	httpd		
webmaster user account	webmastr (linux remains more consistent with 8 character user names)		
webmaster home directory	/home/webmastr /		
	permissions	**owner**	**group**
	directories drwxr-xr-x	webmastr	webmastr
	files -rw-rw----	webmastr	webmastr
public HTML document directory	/home/webmastr/pub/html/		
	permissions	**owner**	**group**
	directories drwxr-s---	webmastr	httpd
	^ notice the s		
	files -rw-rw-----	webmastr	httpd

continued on next page

Table 3.1

continued

	Environment Property	Value in Example		
	CGI script binary directory	/home/webmastr/pub/cgi-bin/		
		permissions	**owner**	**group**
	directories	drwxr-s---	webmastr	httpd
	files	-rwxr-x---	webmastr	httpd

We are about to do serious rearrangements. Before proceeding, shut down the Apache web server (as described in Chapter 2 in the section titled "Starting, Stopping, and Restarting the Server").

Creating the Daemon Account

Adding the User

Most UNIX systems have utilities for adding users and groups. If yours does, use it. There may be hidden security features and shadow files that the utility will deal with. On Linux, use the `useradd` command to create the Apache daemon user named `httpd`, and to assign the Apache installation directory as the daemon's home directory. Type

```
useradd -d /usr/local/apache httpd
```

replacing `/usr/local/apache` with your Apache installation directory. The `useradd` command automatically creates a new group with the same name as the new user. If you lack such a user creation utility, you may edit the authentication files directly. Add the `httpd` user to the `/etc/passwd` file. Add the `httpd` group to the `/etc/group` file and make the `httpd` user a member of the `httpd` group. Consult your system man pages for the syntax of these files on your system.

Setting Permissions

Give the `httpd` group-ownership of all the files and directories in the Apache installation directory tree by typing

```
find /usr/local/apache -exec chown root.httpd {} \;
```

In the above command, the `root.httpd` syntax specifies the user and the group. If your `chown` command does not let you specify the group, then you may have to give user ownership and group ownership separately using these two commands

```
find /usr/local/apache -exec chown httpd {} \;
find /usr/local/apache -exec chgrp httpd {} \;
```

Only the `httpd` group should have rights to read files in the Apache installation directory tree (and additionally have execute permissions on the files in the `bin/` subdirectory). Other users and groups should not have any access. Configure this by typing

```
find /usr/local/apache -type d -exec chmod 750 {} \;
find /usr/local/apache -type f -exec chmod 640 {} \;
chmod u+x,g+x /usr/local/apache/bin/*
```

Configuring Apache

With an ASCII text editor, edit the `httpd.conf` configuration file in the `conf/` subdirectory of the Apache installation directory (i.e. `/usr/local/apache/conf/httpd.conf`). Find the `User` and the `Group` directives.

User and Group

These specify the user ID and the group ID under which the Apache server will run. Apache switches to these IDs on the fly, so you will initially have to launch Apache as `root` for it to have the right to do so. They are initially set to the user `nobody` and the group `nobody`. Change them to read:

```
User httpd
Group httpd
```

Creating the Webmaster Account

Adding the User

Create a user named `webmastr` and a group named `webmastr`. In Linux, use the `useradd` command. At the shell prompt, type

```
useradd -d /home/webmastr webmastr
```

(or add them to /etc/passwd and /etc/group files manually, if you have to). The useradd command creates both a user named webmastr and a group named webmastr. Since the /home/webmastr/ directory does not yet exist on the filesystem, the useradd command also creates the home directory and populates it with the default login scripts and user configuration files. For lack of such a command, you can create the home directory manually by typing

```
mkdir /home/webmastr
```

The webmaster will need to log in to this account, so the password must be set. As the root user at the shell prompt, type

```
passwd webmastr
```

The passwd program will ask to you type in the new password and verify it.

Creating the Content Directories

As described in "Strategy" (above), we need to create a public subdirectory to be shared with the World Wide Web. Underneath that public subdirectory, two more subdirectories are required: one for housing HTML documents and another for housing CGI scripts. At the shell prompt, type

```
mkdir /home/webmastr/pub
mkdir /home/webmastr/pub/html
mkdir /home/webmastr/pub/cgi-bin
```

Next, copy the test CGI scripts and the test HTML documents from the Apache installation directory into the new cgi-bin subdirectory and html subdirectory. Type

```
cp /usr/local/apache/cgi-bin/* /home/webmastr/pub/cgi-bin
cp /usr/local/apache/htdocs/* /home/webmastr/pub/html
```

The cp command will likely gripe the following

```
cp: /usr/local/apache/htdocs/manual: omitting directory
```

which is all right. We don't want to copy the manual/ subdirectory. It would be convenient for the Web server to serve up its own manual. We therefore create a link to the manual/ subdirectory. Type

```
ln -s /usr/local/apache/htdocs/manual /home/webmastr/pub/html/manual
```

In this case, a link is better than copying the directory. On upgrade of the Apache server, the new manual documents will be installed in the `/usr/local/apache/htdocs/manual/` directory. A link to this directory will keep the Web-served manual current.

Setting Permissions

Give the webmastr user and group ownership of all of the files in the webmaster's home directory, by typing

```
find /home/webmastr -exec chown webmastr.webmastr {} \;
```

(use `chown` and `chgrp` separately, if you have to). Only the `webmastr` user and the `webmastr` group should have permissions in the webmaster's home directory. To configure such restrictions, type

```
find /home/webmastr -type d -exec chmod 770 {} \;
find /home/webmastr -type f -exec chmod 660 {} \;
```

At this point, the daemon has access to the Apache installation directory and the webmaster has access to the webmaster's home directory and the Web site content. To serve up the content, we need to give the Apache daemon read-only access to the Web site content. Change the group ownership of the public files to the `httpd` group and remove the group's write permissions. Type

```
find /home/webmastr/pub -exec chgrp httpd {} \;
find /home/webmastr/pub -exec chmod g-w {} \;
```

The webmaster retains access to the content through user ownership. The Apache Web server daemon gains access to the content through group ownership. We need to configure the public directories so that new files created in these directories by the webmaster will have the `httpd` group ownership. To do this, set the group `set-uid` bit on the public directories. Type

```
find /home/webmastr/pub -type d -exec chmod 2750 {} \;
```

Executable permissions must be added to the CGI scripts. Type

```
chmod u+x,g+x /home/webmastr/pub/cgi-bin/*
```

One last touch up on permissions. At this point, the `/home/webmastr/`
directory has these permissions

```
drwxrwx--- webmasr webmastr /home/webmastr
```

Which means that the `httpd` daemon will not be able to search the
`/home/webmastr` directory to find the `/home/webmastr/pub/` subdirectory. There are two ways to grant the `httpd` daemon search permissions
on the webmaster's home directory: 1) give read and execute permissions
to others, or 2) give the `httpd` group group-ownership of the directory
and give read/execute permissions to the group.

For the first method, type

```
chmod o+r,o+x /home/webmastr
ls -ld /home/webmastr
```

The permissions should then be

```
drwxrwxr-x webmastr webmastr /home/webmastr
```

For the second method, type

```
chgrp httpd /home/webmastr
chmod 750 /home/webmastr
ls -ld /home/webmastr
```

The permissions should then be

```
drwxr-x--- webmastr httpd /home/webmastr
```

Configuring Apache

With an ASCII text editor, edit the `httpd.conf` configuration file in the
`conf/` subdirectory of the Apache installation directory (i.e.
`/usr/local/apache/conf/httpd.conf`). Find and modify the following
directives.

ServerAdmin

This specifies the e-mail address of the person who is to receive error
messages from the Web server. This e-mail address may also show up on
the browser in error messages and other server-generated replies. Your
first instinct might be to set this to root user's e-mail address or to an
administrator's e-mail address. Observe that most "breakage" seen by the

browser is a result of bad content (missing or obsolete links, or forgetting to set execute permissions on CGI scripts, etc.), not server errors. Set the `ServerAdmin` directive to the e-mail address of the webmaster. In our example

```
ServerAdmin webmastr@administeringapache.com
```

Let the webmaster deal with the content errors and user questions. Rest assured that the webmaster will come to you when a true server error is reported. The above example sends the e-mail to the `webmastr` user account we created earlier. You may choose to create (with an ASCII editor) a file named `.forward` in the webmaster's home directory (e.g. `/home/webmastr/.forward`). Whoever is webmaster at the time can put the appropriate and current e-mail address in that file. This assumes that the host on which Apache is installed provides e-mail to the user account. If it does not, you may point the `ServerAdmin` directive directly to whatever address the webmaster currently uses.

DocumentRoot

This specifies the top of the directory tree containing this server's content. The browsers connecting to this server will see this as the root directory. This needs to point to the public `html/` subdirectory, in our scenario

```
DocumentRoot "/home/webmastr/pub/html"
```

ScriptAlias

This specifies the directory in which CGI scripts reside. This directive maps a URL path to a filesystem directory. In this scenario, we would set `ScriptAlias` to

```
ScriptAlias /cgi-bin/ "/home/webmastr/pub/cgi-bin/"
```

Given the above setting, when a browser requests a file in the `/cgi-bin/` directory, the Apache server looks for the requested file in the `/home/webmastr/pub/cgi-bin/` directory, executes that file as a program, and pipes that program's output back to the browser.

<Directory>

This block directive specifies permissions and services for a specified directory. Whenever you change the `DocumentRoot` directory, you must make the same change to the appropriate <Directory> block directive. Find the directive reading

```
<Directory "/usr/local/apache/htdocs">
```

and change it to read

```
<Directory "/home/webmastr/pub/html">
```

Whenever you change the ScriptAlias directory, you must make the same change to the appropriate <Directory> block directive. Find the directive reading

```
<Directory "/usr/local/apache/cgi-bin">
```

and change it to read

```
<Directory "/home/webmastr/pub/cgi-bin">
```

AddModule

This specifies that Apache is to activate the specified module. A list of AddModule directives specifies the order in which Apache is to activate the modules. Order is important. This directive is required for a module regardless of whether the module was compiled as a static module or as a dynamically loaded module. Supporting CGI requires that the server include the mod_cgi module. This is a default module, so your server has it, unless you explicitly disabled it (in which case, you would need to recompile the server). Look for the following directive

```
AddModule mod_cgi.c
```

If this directive is not found, then you will need to add it in the correct place in the list. Refer back to the discussion of the AddModule directive in the "Configuring the Installed Server" section of Chapter 2, where there is a list of AddModule directives in their proper order.

LoadModule

This specifies that Apache is to load the specified module in the specified shared object file. A list of LoadModule directives specifies the order to be loaded. This directive is required for all dynamically loaded modules. If you compiled mod_cgi as a DSO, then the following directive is required

```
LoadModule cgi_module          libexec/mod_cgi.so
```

If you had compiled the server with the APACI utility, and specified --enable-shared=max or --enable-shared=mod_cgi, then this LoadModule directive should have been added for you in its proper order. If you have to add this directive manually, refer back to the discussion of the LoadModule directive in the "Configuring the Installed Server" section of Chapter 2, where there is a list of LoadModule directives in their proper order.

Accepting Content

Most content authors prefer to create content remotely with a visual editor and then deliver the content to the Web server using FTP. Configuring FTP is a must. Some developers prefer to log in using telnet and pound code with vi. Allowing telnet logins is a matter of system administration and security policy (see Chapter 1: "Planning Ahead"). If the webmaster is allowed to write CGI scripts in a third-generation language (e.g. C), telnet will be required in order to allow the webmaster to log in and compile the source code. Web sites supporting a large development effort may also require telnet login. The webmaster, acting as librarian for the development team, will need to move files around (from staged, to QA, to production). Developers may need to check files in and out of a version control system. Such development efforts usually use a single-site server dedicated to the team. Trust is high and telnet does not pose a security risk. An ISP, on the other hand, supporting the masses, may wish to disable telnet or, at least, severely restrict it use. If you are an ISP, you will need to provide certain basic CGI services to be shared by all the customer sites. Go ahead and set up telnet services for the webmastr user account, who will be maintaining your main Web site.

The FTP and telnet configurations described herein are Linux oriented. Please refer to your system's MAN pages for the syntax and arguments appropriate for your system. Applicable MAN pages are: inetd, tcpd, hosts_access, host.allow, host.deny, telnetd, ftpd, login, securetty, and syslog.

Telnet and FTP are launched by the inetd internet daemon, which requires that ports be assigned to these services in the file named /etc/services and that the manner of launching these services be described in the file named /etc/inetd.conf file. With an ASCII editor, edit the /etc/services file. Look for the following lines and add them, if you do not find them

```
ftp-data      20/tcp
ftp           21/tcp
telnet        23/tcp
```

Edit the /etc/inetd.conf file. Look for the following lines and add them, if necessary

```
telnet   stream   tcp   nowait   root   /usr/sbin/tcpd   in.telnetd
ftp      stream   tcp   nowait   root   /usr/sbin/tcpd   in.ftpd -l -a
```

If you had to modify either of the above files, you will need to tell the running inetd daemon to reread its configuration. First, obtain the process ID of the inetd daemon. At the shell prompt, type

```
ps ax | grep inetd
```

The above command should respond with

```
324   ?   S     0:00 inetd
```

Send a hangup signal to the inetd process by typing

```
kill -HUP 324
```

replacing 324 with the process ID obtained by the ps command.

The inetd.conf entries described above specify that inetd use the tcpd wrapper to launch the telnet and FTP services. The tcpd daemon adds simple access control mechanisms to several internet services (such as: finger, rsh, rlogin, tftp, etc.). The tcpd daemon grants or denies service to a client based on entries in the file /etc/hosts.allow and the file /etc/hosts.deny. If the client is found in the hosts.allow file, access is granted; otherwise, if the client is found in hosts.deny, access is denied; otherwise, access is granted—in that order. Note that if the client is not found in either file, access is granted. The syntax for these hosts access files is as follows

```
<service>:<client>
```

where <service> is the TCP service requested (specified as the service daemon's command name) and <client> is the host requesting the service (specified by an IP address, a network address, a host name, or by a `user@hostname` pair). To disable all `tcpd`-wrapped services, add this entry to the file `/etc/hosts.deny` (with an ASCII editor)

```
ALL:ALL
```

Make this the only command in the file either by removing any other commands in the file or by commenting them out with a pound sign.

To restrict access to TCP services, first deny all services (as described above), then allow service to specific hosts or networks in the `/etc/hosts.allow` file. To allow all TCP services to all hosts on the local area network, add the following line to the file `/etc/hosts.allow`:

```
ALL:LOCAL
```

and make it the only command in the file. To allow only the FTP and telnet services only to a specific host, edit `/etc/hosts.allow` to read as follows

```
in.ftpd:192.168.1.7
in.telnetd:192.168.1.7
```

replacing `192.168.1.7` with the IP address of the desired host. The host access file syntax supports a variety of patterns for matching the service and the client. The purpose here is to allow FTP and telnet for the `webmastr` user account. The host access files are discussed in detail (with numerous examples) in Chapter 6: "Securing the Server, the Content, and the Connection."

The server is now ready to accept content from the webmaster. The next chapter, "Manipulating Content," explains how to deliver that content to the browser.

Manipulating Content

This chapter is for both the system administrator and the webmaster. The system administrator must configure Apache to deliver different types of content. The webmaster must know how Apache supports different types of content. This requires a few agreements between the system administrator and the webmaster. They must agree on default file names (i.e. what file is delivered when the browser requests a directory). They must agree on what file name extensions are to be given to files of various mime-types. They must agree on what directories will contain files of various types. You, as the system administrator, might let the webmaster read this chapter to know what is available and how to use it. The webmaster can then approach you with what features need to be enabled and configured. If you are an ISP, then the content you are willing to transmit for your customer sites is a matter of policy (e.g. you may or may not allow CGI scripting; or you may provide your customers with a directory of pre-canned scripts).

First, consider the most basic agreement: identifying the default file names.

Displaying Directories

When the browser requests a directory (i.e. enters an URL ending with a /), the Apache server first looks for a default document in the requested directory and, if one is found, transmits that document to the browser. If no such default document is found, the Apache server builds and transmits a listing of the requested directory. You specify the names of default documents and you specify how directories are to be built in the Apache configuration file (e.g. /usr/local/apache/conf/httpd.conf). Open the configuration file in an ASCII text editor and modify the following directives.

DirectoryIndex

This specifies the name of the default document to be transmitted to the browser when a directory is requested. If a file name passed to the DirectoryIndex directive does not begin with a /, then the file is relative to the requested directory. Multiple file names may be specified, separated by white space. The first match found is returned to the browser. For example, the following directive

```
DirectoryIndex index.html index.htm index.cgi
```

tells the Apache server to first look for the file named index.html in the requested directory and, if it is found, return that file to the browser. If index.html is not found, then search next for index.htm in the requested directory and return it if found. It is a good idea to include both index.html and index.htm in the DirectoryIndex directive. Web authors with a UNIX background are likely to use the former while those from a Windows background are likely to use the latter. If neither is found in the requested directory, the above example searches next for a file named index.cgi. If it is found, the index.cgi CGI script is executed and its output is transmitted to the browser. This presumes that the Apache server is configured such that files ending with a .cgi extension are recognized as CGI scripts (see the AddHandler directive discussed in the section "Implementing the Common Gateway Interface (CGI)," below).

The specified file need not be relative to the requested directory. An absolute path (beginning with a /) may be specified. In the example

```
DirectoryIndex index.html index.htm /cgi-bin/ls.cgi
```

if neither index.html nor index.htm is found in the requested directory, then the /cgibin/ls.cgi script is executed and its output is sent to the browser. Apache performs a redirection of the requested URL to the specified script. The Apache server makes the URL of the original request available to the script through the REDIRECT_URL environment variable (environment variables and CGI are discussed the section "Implementing the Common Gateway Interface (CGI)," below).

If none of the files listed in the DirectoryIndex directive is found, then the server would build and return a listing of the requested directory. The Apache server must be given permission to build such a listing for a given directory. This permission is given with the Indexes option.

Indexes

As a parameter to the Options directive, this grants Apache permission to build a directory listing when the user requests a directory and the directory does not contain a default file. Placed within a <Directory> block directive, this allows listings to be built for the specified directory. Find the <Directory> block pertaining to the DocumentRoot directory, in our example:

```
<Directory "/home/webmastr/pub/html">
Options Indexes FollowSymLinks
    AllowOverride Limit
    Order allow,deny
```

```
        Allow from all
</Directory>
```

The `Indexes` option in the example above permits Apache to build a directory listing when the browser requests the `DocumentRoot` directory and that directory does not contain a default file. Subdirectories inherit the parent's `<Directory>` specifications; so, the above example allows the server to build a directory listing for any directory within the document directory tree—provided a given subdirectory does not have its own overriding `<Directory>` block in which the `Options` directive lacks the `Indexes` argument.

Lacking the `Indexes` option, the server would not be allowed to build and transmit a directory listing for the requested directory. If the browser requests a directory for which indexing has not been enabled (and that directory does not contain a default file), the server returns a `403 Forbidden` error to the browser.

If indexing is enabled for a given directory, Apache can build either a standard directory listing or a fancy directory listing. Figures 4.1 and 4.2 compare the browser's view of these listings.

Figure 4.1

Standard directory listing.

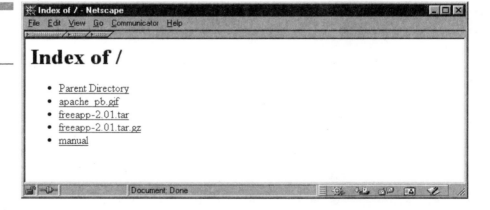

Figure 4.2

Fancy directory listing.

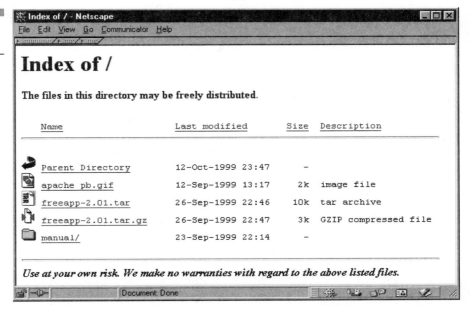

Figure 4.2

Fancy directory listing.

The differences between the two figures result from the following configuration directives.

HeaderName

This specifies the name of the text file whose contents are to be displayed above the listing. Thus, each directory can have its own heading.

```
HeaderName HEADER
```

tells the Apache server to look for a file named HEADER in the requested directory and, if found, display its contents. In our example, the file named HEADER reads: "The files in this directory may be freely distributed."—which appears at the top of the document window in Figure 4.2. How this text came to be bolded took a bit of fix-up. The Apache server sets up the HTML document before outputting the text file. Specifically, the server outputs the <HTML>, <HEAD>, <TITLE>, and <BODY> tags. Unfortunately, the server puts your header text within a <PRE> pre-format block (and char quotes your tag markers, to boot). If you try to make your text bold with a <B></B> block, all you'll get is the <B> and </B> tags displayed in the browser. To make use of HTML formatting, create a complete HTML document—complete with its own <HTML>, <HEAD>, and <BODY> tags. When Apache sees your <HTML> start tag, it will not pre-format your header file. The HTML file used to create the header shown in Figure 4.2 reads as follows:

```
<HTML>
     <HEAD>
          <TITLE>Index of /</TITLE>
     </HEAD>
     <BODY>
          <H1>Index of /</H1>
          <B>
               The files in this directory may be freely
               distributed.
          </B>
     </BODY>
</HTML>
```

ReadmeName

This specifies the name of the text file whose contents are to be displayed after the listing. Thus, each directory can have its own readme-footer. The following directive

```
ReadmeName README
```

tells the Apache server to look for a file named README in the requested directory and, if found, display its contents. In our example, the file named README reads, "Use at your own risk. We make no warranties with regard to the above listed files."—which appears at the bottom of the document window in Figure 4.2. Formatting this text requires the same fix-up described in the HeaderName directive, above. The server outputs your README text within a <PRE> pre-format block. To use HTML format tags in your README file, code your README file as a complete HTML document. When Apache sees your <HTML> start tag, it will not pre-format your README file. Our example HTML file reads

```
<HTML>
     <BODY>
          <B><I>
               Use at your own risk. We make no warranties
               with regard to the above listed files.
          </I></B>
     </BODY>
</HTML>
```

IndexIgnore

This prevents the specified files from appearing in server-generated directory listings. You may wish to hide the files named by the `HeaderName` and `ReadmeName` directives (above). The browser sees the contents of those files above and below the server-generated directory index; but you might not want these files to show up *in* the directory index. The pre-configured `IndexIgnore` directive

```
IndexIgnore .??* *~ *# HEADER* README* RCS CVS *,v *,t
```

already hides these files and shows how the `IndexIgnore` directive accepts wildcards. All files that begin with `HEADER` or begin with `README` are hidden from directory indexes. If you change the `HeaderName` and/or `ReadmeName` directives (and you still want those files hidden), be sure to make the appropriate changes to the `IndexIgnore` directive. The other files hidden by the above `IndexIgnore` directive are:

- `.??*`—all file names beginning with a period and are at least three characters long. This hides user configuration files (all of the dot-files normally hidden by the shell's `ls` command). It also hides directory access files (typically named `.htaccess`, which are discussed in Chapter 6: "Securing the Server, the Content, and the Connection." Yet, the parent directory (named `..`) still appears in the directory index because it is less than three characters long.
- `*~`—all file names ending with a tilde.
- `*#`—all file names ending with a pound sign.
- `RCS CVS`—all files named `RCS` or `CVS`. Source code revision control systems often create subdirectories named `RCS` or named `CVS`. If you submit your HTML content to a revision control system, then the RCS or CVS directories will be hidden from directory listings.
- `*,v *,t`—all file names ending with `,v` or `,t`. Typically, these are revision control system archive files.

IndexOptions

This governs the appearance of directory listings built by the Apache server. The following directive

```
IndexOptions FancyIndexing
```

enables the features seen in the directory listing shown in Figure 4.2—specifically: sortable columns, file type icons, the last-modified and size columns, and file descriptions. If you prefer the standard directory listing, then specify the IndexOptions directive with no arguments or comment the directive out altogether with a pound sign.

The following options may also be added to the IndexOptions directive. All of them (save the last one) tweak the appearance of fancy indexing and are ignored if FancyIndexing is not enabled.

IndexOptions IconHeight

This specifies the height, in pixels, of the file type icons (e.g. IconHeight=25). The AddIcon, AddIconByType, and AddIconBy Encoding directives (discussed below) associates file types (or content types) with icon image files. Without the IconHeight option, each associated image file prescribes the height of that icon image. The IconHeight option enforces the same height on all icon images—causing Apache to output a HEIGHT= attribute in the <IMG> tag placed in the directory listing. Apache will *not* enforce the specified height unless an enforced width is also specified using the IconWidth option (see below). Requires FancyIndexing.

IndexOptions IconWidth

This specifies the width, in pixels, of the file type icons (e.g. IconWidth=20). The AddIcon, AddIconByType, and AddIconBy Encoding directives (discussed below) associates file types (or content types) with icon image files. Without the IconWidth option, each associated image file prescribes the width of that icon image. The IconWidth option enforces the same width on all icon images—causing Apache to output a WIDTH= attribute in the <IMG> tag placed in the directory listing. Apache will *not* enforce the specified width unless an enforced height is also specified using the IconHeight option (discussed above). Requires FancyIndexing.

IndexOptions IconsAreLinks

Each file name in the Name column resides within an HTML link for retrieving the named file. The IconsAreLinks option tells Apache to include the icon within the link anchor so that clicking on the icon will also retrieve the named file. Requires FancyIndexing.

IndexOptions SuppressColumnSorting

By default, the column headings are links for sorting the directory listing by the values in that column. You can turn this behavior off by adding the SuppressColumnSorting option. Requires FancyIndexing.

IndexOptions NameWidth

The width of the file Name column defaults to about 200 pixels. You may specify a different width using with this option (e.g. NameWidth=150). If you specify an asterisk for the width value (e.g. NameWidth=*), the Apache server will make the file Name column as wide as the longest file name. Requires FancyIndexing.

IndexOptions SuppressLastModified

This removes the Last modified date column from the directory listing display. Suppressing the last modified date column frees up 19 more bytes for the width of the Description column (see AddDescription directive, below). Requires FancyIndexing.

IndexOptions SuppressSize

This removes the Size column from the directory listing display. Suppressing the Size column frees up seven more bytes for the width of the Description column (see AddDescription directive, below). Requires FancyIndexing.

IndexOptions SuppressDescription

This removes the Description column from the directory listing display. Requires FancyIndexing.

IndexOptions ScanHTMLTitles

Normally, the verbiage in the Description column derives from a file's type (i.e. file name extension). The AddDescription directive (described below) associates file types with their descriptions. If an HTML file's extension does not have an associated description, this ScanHTMLTitles option directs the Apache server to take the description from the title of the HTML document. Note that there is a performance hit when this option is enabled. Requires FancyIndexing.

IndexOptions SuppressHTMLPreamble

Normally, Apache outputs an HTML preamble (`<HTML>`, `<HEAD>`, `<TITLE>`, and `<BODY>` tags) before outputting the server-generated directory listing. If you specify this `SuppressHTMLPreamble` option, then Apache will not output its HTML preamble—leaving it up to you to code these tags in your header file (see the `HeaderName` directive, above). Apache doe not assume that you will do so. If you don't, Apache will add these tags, even if your have suppressed the preamble (and it will `<PRE>`-format your header file). Also, if the listed directory does not contain a header file, then Apache will output its own HTML preamble, regardless of this setting. Does *not* require `FancyIndexing`.

The `IndexOptions` directive may appear on its own or it may appear within a `<VirtualHost>` block directive or within a `<Directory>` block directive. The `IndexOptions` directive may also appear within an access file (e.g. `.htaccess`). The `IndexOptions` directive declared on its own in the configuration file (outside any block directive) acts as the default options. Options are inherited from the most global scope to the most local scope. In order the most global to most local, these are: default, `<VirtualHost>`, `<Directory>`, and access file. The more local `IndexOptions` directive completely overrides the more global directive. Consider the following:

```
IndexOptions FancyIndexing

<Directory "/home/webmastr/pub/html/plainolddir">
    IndexOptions SuppressHTMLPreamble
</Directory>
```

When a directory listing is generated for `plainolddir/`, the above example not only suppresses the HTML preamble, but also turns off fancy indexing, since the local directive does not contain the `FancyIndexing` option. The local directive completely overrides the global directive.

There is a way to merge local options with the global options. Add an option to the inherited options by prefixing a plus sign to the added option. For example:

```
<Directory "/home/webmastr/pub/html">
    IndexOptions FancyIndexing
</Directory>

<Directory "/home/webmastr/pub/html/hasaheader">
```

```
        IndexOptions +SuppressHTMLPreamble
</Directory>
```

The `hasaheader/` subdirectory adds the `SuppressHTMLPreamble` option to the `FancyIndexing` option already in effect (inherited from the `/home/webmastr/pub/html/` parent directory).

By the same token, you can cancel an inherited option by prefixing a minus sign to the option. In this example

```
IndexOptions FancyIndexing SuppressHTMLPreamble

<VirtualHost 192.168.1.8>
    IndexOptions -SuppressHTMLPreamble
</VirtualHost>
```

the `SuppressHTMLPreamble` option is turned off (though `FancyIndexing` remains in effect) when Apache lists a directory belonging to the specified `VirtualHost`.

IndexOrderDefault

This sets the sort order for a fancy index. Fancy indexes are usually sorted by file name in ascending order. With this directive, you may specify that the directory listing be sorted in either ascending order or descending order by either name, date, size, or description. For example:

```
IndexOrderDefault Descending Date
```

would sort the listing in descending date order—displaying the most recent files first.

AddDescription

This assigns a description to the specified file names. File names may be file name extensions, full file names, or file names with wildcards. For example:

```
AddDescription "GZIP compressed file" .gz
AddDescription "core dump" core
AddDescription "HTML document" *.htm*
```

Your description can be up to 23 characters long. If you suppress the `size` column, you may use an additional seven characters (see the `SuppressSize` option of the `IndexOptions` directive, above). If you suppress the Last modified date column, you may use an additional 19 characters (see the `SuppressLastModified` option of the `IndexOptions` directive, above).

Alias

This maps a requested URL to a local filesystem directory. This directive allows Apache to serve up documents stored in directories outside the directory tree specified by the `DocumentRoot` directive. Apache ships with a set of icons for fancy indexing. These icons are installed in the `icons/` subdirectory under the Apache installation directory (e.g. `/usr/local/apache/icons/`). The default configuration file declares this alias

```
Alias /icons/ "/usr/local/apache/icons/"
```

so that Apache can serve up the icon image files from that directory. If you move these icons to another directory (or if you supply your own icons in another directory), you must modify the `Alias /icons/` directive accordingly. You must also modify the appropriate `<Directory>` block directive (see below). If you plan to supplement Apache's icon images with some of your own (in another directory), then add an `Alias` directive and a `<Directory>` block for your image file directory. Be sure that the user or group under which Apache runs has access to your alternate (or additional) image file directory.

The `Alias /icons/` directive instructs Apache to deliver files from the `/usr/local/apache/icons/` directory whenever a browser requests a file from the `/icons/` virtual directory. Note that both the URL and the file system directory end with a slash. If the browser requests `/icons`, it will not be aliased and Apache will return a `404 Not Found` error.

<Directory>

This block directive specifies permissions and services for a specified directory. Apache pre-configures a `<Directory>` block directive for the `/usr/local/apache/icons/` directory (in which Apache installs the icon image files for fancy indexing). This block reads as follows:

```
<Directory "/usr/local/apache/icons">
    Options Indexes MultiViews
    AllowOverride None
    Order allow,deny
    Allow from all
</Directory>
```

If you move the icon image files to another directory (or if you use your own icon image files in another directory), then modify the icon directory's <Directory> block directive accordingly. Be sure to fix up the Alias /icons/ directive as well (see above).

AddIcon????

This assigns an icon image file (for fancy indexing) to the specified files. Each of the AddIcon???? directives (AddIconByType, AddIconByEncoding, AddIcon) is discussed in detail below. In general, these directives take two or more parameters: a path to an image file, and one or more file specifiers. For example

```
AddIcon /icons/layout.gif .html .htm
```

displays the layout.gif icon image next to all files ending with .html or .htm. Note that the path to the image file, in the above example, uses the /icons/ alias, not the local file system path. The path to the image must be an URL accessible to the browser. In all of the AddIcon???? directives, you can specify alternate text to be displayed in lieu of the icon for graphically-challenged browsers. Add the alternate text in front of the image file name, as is done with HTM in this example

```
AddIcon (HTM,/icons/layout.gif) .html .htm
```

For the second and subsequent parameters, the file specifier used depends on the directive. AddIcon accepts file names, file name extensions, and wildcards; AddIconByType accepts MIME type specifications; and AddIconByEncoding accepts mime encoding schemes.

Apache displays the icon for the first matching AddIcon???? directive. When you add or change an AddIcon???? directive, do put it on a line above all of the other AddIcon???? directives. This way, the icon you want to see won't be preempted by a pre-existing AddIcon???? directive. Given the order of these examples

```
AddIcon /icons/layout.gif .html .shtml .htm .pdf
AddIconByEncoding /icons/pdf.gif application/pdf
```

the layout.gif icon image would appear next to Acrobat files (.pdf)—not the pdf.gif image.

AddIconByType

This assigns an icon image file (for fancy indexing) to the specified MIME content type. The following example

```
AddIconByType /icons/text.gif text/*
```

directs Apache to display the /icons/text.gif image next to the names of files belonging to any of the text/ MIME content types. This includes files of type text/html, text/plain, etc. The MIME content type specified in the AddIconByType directive must be a valid MIME content type. MIME content types and their associated file name extensions are defined in the TypesConfig file (e.g. /usr/local/apache/conf/mime.types) and by the AddType directive (see the section "Configuring MIME," below).

AddIconByEncoding

This assigns an icon image file (for fancy indexing) to files that have been encoded with the specified encoding scheme. The following example

```
AddIconByEncoding /icons/compressed.gif x-compress x-gzip
```

directs Apache to display the /icons/compressed.gif image next to the names of files that have been encoded with either the x-compress encoding scheme or the x-gzip encoding scheme. (See more on encoding schemes in the section "Configuring MIME.")

AddIcon

This assigns an icon image file (for fancy indexing) to files whose names match any of the specified file names. The specified file names may be file name extensions. The following example

```
AddIcon /icons/layout.gif .html .shtml .htm .pdf
```

causes the /icons/layout.gif image to appear next to file names ending with either .html, .shtml, .html, or .pdf.

The specified file name may also be a full file name or a file name with wildcards. The AddIcon directive recognizes the normal UNIX shell wildcards. AddIcon also accepts two special file names: ^^DIRECTORY^^ (matching any file that is a directory) and ^^BLANKICON^^ (that matches when Apache is skipping the icon column, as in the row for the column titles). The following examples show these uses:

```
AddIcon /icons/bomb.gif core
AddIcon /icons/layout.gif *.htm*
AddIcon /icons/folder.gif ^^DIRECTORY^^
AddIcon /icons/blank.gif ^^BLANKICON^^
```

DefaultIcon

This specifies the icon image file (for fancy indexing) to display when a file does not match any other icon. Apache ships with this setting

```
DefaultIcon /icons/unknown.gif
```

As with the AddIcon???? directives (above), the DefaultIcon directive requires that the path to the icon image file be an URL accessible to the browser (not a local file system path).

AddAlt????

This assigns alternate text when fancy indexing the specified files. The alternate text will be displayed in lieu of an icon on graphically challenged browsers. Given the following two directives

```
AddIcon /icons/layout.gif .html .htm
AddAlt "HTM" .html .htm
```

Apache's fancy indexing will display the layout.gif icon image next to hypertext file names on image-enabled browsers and will display the text HTM next to those files on image-incapable browsers.

Apache provides an analogous AddAlt???? directive for each of the AddIcon???? directives (discussed above). AddAlt assigns alternate text to file names, file name extensions, and wildcards; AddAltByType assigns alternate text to mime type specifications; and AddAltByEncoding assigns alternate text to MIME encoding schemes.

Note that the icon and the alternate text can be assigned in one AddIcon directive, taking advantage of the extended syntax:

```
AddIcon (HTM,/icons/layout.gif) .html .htm
```

This is the way all of the icon assignments are done in the default configuration file shipped with Apache.

Configuring MIME

Brief History

In 1982, the format of internet mail messages was standardized on the Simple Mail Transport Protocol (SMTP—RFC821) and the Standard for the Format of ARPA Internet Text Messages (RFC 822). These standards permitted only text messages using the ASCII character set. Mail servers would not accept anything else (e.g. no images, audio, application data, program binaries). In 1990, Internet hypertext messages became standardized on the HyperText Transport Protocol (HTTP/0.9); it, too, allowed only ASCII text messages. The need to send other content types gave rise to encoding schemes (such as uuencode), which would translate an 8-bit binary file into ASCII text to get it through the mail servers. The receiver of such a message would then decode the message back into 8-bit binary (using the complementary decoder, such as uudecode). The sender and the receiver would have to agree, of course, on what encoding scheme was to be used. In 1993, the Multipurpose Internet Mail Extensions protocol (MIME—RFC 1521 and 1522) automated this agreement. The MIME protocol added a few headers to the mail protocol to describe the contents of the mail message's body. These headers described the content type (e.g. image or audio) and the content transfer encoding (e.g. uuencode or Base64). The MIME standard also provides for the transfer of multipart messages containing various content types and encoding. MIME-like headers were added to the hypertext protocol in 1996 (HTTP/1.0—RFC 1945).

Configuring Content Types

MIME headers allow the server to tell the browser what it is getting. When the browser makes a request for a document, the server sends a ContentType: header to tell the browser what the MIME media type is for the file that's it's about to receive. This conversation might look like this (headers only, bodies omitted):

Browser says

```
GET /a.html HTTP/1.1
Host: www.administeringapache.com
```

and Server says

```
HTTP/1.1 200 OK
Date: Fri, 15 Oct 1999 21:47:49 GMT
```

```
Server: Apache/1.3.9 (Unix)
Last-Modified: Fri, 15 Oct 1999 18:08:41 GMT
ETag: "28392-5b9-38076da9"
Accept-Ranges: bytes
Content-Length: 1465
Content-Type: text/html
```

The last header line, `Content-Type: text/html`, tells the browser that it is about to receive a text file that is a hypertext file (the syntax is `type/subtype`). The browser then knows to render the HTML document onto the screen. Other MIME types that a browser might receive include: `text/plain`, `image/bmp`, `image/gif`, `application/pdf`, `video/mpeg`, or `audio/x-realaudio`. The browser displays the content with the viewer appropriate to the content type. The viewer could be an internal routine (such as the browser's document window for text files and image files) or an external program (such as the RealAudio software that plays audio/x-realaudio files). If the browser doesn't know how to display the specified content type, it might ask you to pick the application with which to view the file; or it might ask you if you wish to save the file to your local file system.

In Apache, there are three ways to associate a file with its appropriate content type:

■ By file name extension
■ By the directory in which the file resides
■ By examining the contents of the file

Apache ships with a text file named `mime.types`, installed in the `conf/` subdirectory of the Apache installation directory (e.g. `/usr/local/apache/conf/mime.types`) in which each line associates a content type with one or more file name extensions. This line from `mime.types`, for example

```
text/html html htm
```

associates the `text/html` content type with any file that has either a .html or a .htm file name extension. Note that, in the `mime.types` syntax, the specified file name extensions are not prefixed with a period. Most of the standard MIME content types are already defined in this file. You should not modify the contents of this file. When you upgrade Apache, you'll want the new `mime.types` file, which may contain MIME types newly standardized by the Internet Assigned Numbers Authority (IANA). Apache provides other means (i.e. configuration directives) for you to define MIME content types. If you do wish to maintain your own MIME types file, and obligate yourself to manual updates thereof, be sure to tell the Apache configuration (e.g. /usr/local/apache/conf/httpd.conf) what the name of your MIME types file is with the TypesConfig directive.

TypesConfig

This specifies the name of the MIME content type definition file. The default value for this directive uses the pre-configured MIME types file shipped with Apache

```
TypesConfig /usr/local/apache/conf/mime.types
```

If you used the APACI utility to compile and install Apache, then this directive already points to the pre-configured MIME types file. You may have to correct the path specified in this directive if you manually compiled and installed your Apache server; or if you have created your own MIME types definition file (not recommended).

AddType

This assigns a MIME content type to files having the specified file name extensions. This directive may be used to add MIME types not defined in the TypesConfig file or to override types already defined in the TypesConfig file. Using the AddType directive is preferable to editing the TypesConfig file directly. Here is a good example. When a user installs the RealPlayer software, its installation procedures define several media types in the user's browser. These content types are not defined in Apache's pre-configured mime.types file. If your Web server will be serving up RealPlayer files, then you may wish to add the following directives to the Apache configuration file:

```
AddType video/vnd.rn-realvideo .rv
AddType audio/vnd.rn-realaudio .ra
AddType application/vnd.rn-realmedia .rm
AddType image/vnd.rn-realpix .rp
AddType image/vnd.rn-realflash .rf
AddType text/vnd.rn-realtext .rt
AddType application/vnd.rn-realplayer .prx
```

The first directive, in the above examples, associates the video/vnd.rn-realvideo content type with all files whose names have the .rv file name extension[1]. This syntax is the same as that of the

TypesConfig file, except that the file name extensions may be prefixed with a period.

ForceType

This assigns a MIME content type to all of the files in a specific directory. The ForceType directive takes one parameter: the MIME type to be assigned. To enforce the specified type onto a particular directory, place the ForceType directive inside of that directory's <Directory> block directive—as in

```
<Directory /home/webmastr/pub/qt>
    Options Indexes
    AllowOverride Limit
    Order allow,deny
    Allow from all
    ForceType video/quicktime
</Directory>
```

Given the above <Directory> block, any file served from the /home/webmastr/pub/qt directory will be assigned the video/quicktime MIME content type, even if it does not have the .qt or the .mov file name extension.

MIMEMagicFile

This enables Apache to assign MIME types and encoding schemes to files based on each file's contents. This directive points to a file that associates magic numbers to MIME content types and encoding types. Before delivering a requested file, Apache searches the requested file for any of the magic numbers listed in the magic file. If a match is found, Apache assigns to the requested file the content type and encoding type associated with that magic number. Apache has a preconfigured magic file, named magic, in the conf/ subdirectory of the Apache installation directory (e.g. /usr/local/apache/conf/magic).

To perform this magic, Apache must be compiled with the mod_mime_magic module. This is not a default module. Given this requirement, it is best to enclose the MIMEMagicFile directive within an <IfModule> block directive:

---

1 Realplayer MIME types have changed through the various versions of the Realplayer software. Go to **http://service.real.com** for a current list of MIME types.

```
<IfModule mod_mime_magic.c>
    MIMEMagicFile /usr/local/apache/conf/magic
</IfModule>
```

If the server is running the mod_mime_magic module, then Apache will use the magic file; if not, then the MIMEMagicFile directive will be ignored.

To compile this module with the APACI utility, use the parameter --enable-module=mime_magic. The parameter --enable-module=most will also include the mod_mime_magic module. See Chapter 2: "Creating the Web Server."

LoadModule

This loads the specified dynamically shared module. If you are enabling MIME magic processing, and you compiled the mod_mime_magic module as a DSO, then you will need to load the module (before activating the module) with the following directive:

```
LoadModule mime_magic_module  libexec/mod_mime_magic.so
```

AddModule

This activates the specified module. To enable MIME magic processing, add the directive:

```
AddModule mod_mime_magic.c
```

Magic processing takes a performance hit, but it isn't outrageously expensive. You can reduce computational costs by placing the mod_mime_magic module's AddModule directive above that of the mod_mime module. The order is in increasing importance, so this will give the mod_mime module first shot at discovering a file's content type by file name extension. Failing that, the server will then go searching through the magic file. If you can rely on your webmaster to name files with the appropriate file name extensions, then you may wish to comment out the mod_mime_magic's AddModule directive to disable magic processing altogether.

DefaultType

This assigns the specified MIME content type to any file whose content type cannot be determined. The preconfigured default type is

```
DefaultType text/plain
```

which assumes that files lacking file name extensions are likely to be text files. If such files are likely to be HTML documents, then you may wish to change this to

```
DefaultType text/html
```

If these unrecognized files are likely to be binary files, then you might default to the `application/octetstream` content type.

Configuring Encoding Schemes

Whatever the file's MIME content type might be, the file might also be encoded. For instance, a hypertext document might have been compressed using the gzip utility. When the server sends an encoded file, it adds a `Content-Encoding` header to tell the browser how the file was encoded. For example, the header

```
ContentEncoding: x-gzip
```

tells the browser that the file has been encoded by the gzip compression utility. The browser then decodes the file (with the appropriate decoder) before viewing the file (with the appropriate viewer).

In Apache, there are two ways to associate a file with its appropriate encoding type: by file name extension or by examining the contents of the file.

AddEncoding

This assigns an encoding scheme to files having the specified file name extensions. The default Apache configuration file predefines these encoding schemes

```
AddEncoding x-compress Z
AddEncoding x-gzip gz tgz
```

which assigns the `x-compress` encoding scheme to files having the `.Z` file name extension and the `x-gzip` encoding scheme to files with either the `.gz` or the `.tgz` file name extension. Though you may tell the browser about a file's encoding scheme, the browser may not know how to decode the file before displaying it. Figure 4.3 shows the results of my quick test.

Figure 4.3

Browser support for encoding.

Browser	Compress	GZip
Netscape Navigator 4.5 for Linux	✔	✔
Netscape Navigator 4.61 for Windows 98		✔
Internet Explorer 4.0 for Windows 98		✔

A checkmark (✔) indicates that the browser natively supports decoding the given encoding scheme.

MIMEMagicFile

This enables Apache to assign MIME types and encoding schemes to files based on each file's contents. The `MIMEMagicFile` associates magic numbers with MIME types and encoding schemes. Before transmitting a requested file, Apache will search the file for any magic number listed in the `MIMEMagicFile`. MIME magic processing, its dependencies, and its consequences are discussed in detail in the "Content Types" subsection above.

Configuring Languages

In addition to telling the browser about a file's content type and encoding scheme, the server might also tell the browser what natural (i.e. human) language was used to write the content, using the `Content-Language` header. For example, the header

```
ContentLanguage: fr
```

specifies to the browser that the content is in French.

In Apache, there is only one way to associate a file with its natural language content and that is by file name extension. The following Apache configuration directives apply to languages.

AddLanguage

This associates the specified natural language with files that have the specified file name extension. Apache comes pre-configured with these associations:

```
AddLanguage en .en
AddLanguage fr .fr
AddLanguage de .de
AddLanguage da .da
AddLanguage el .el
```

```
AddLanguage it .it
```

Each `AddLanguage` directive first specifies the language code then the file name extension to be associated with that language. The language code and the file name extension do not necessarily have to be the same (as they are in the preconfigured directives shown above). The language code parameter should be a two-letter code listed by the ISO 639 standard. Many web sites display this list (e.g. **http://sunsite.berkeley.edu/ amher/iso_639.html**). The registration authority for ISO 639 is Infoterm, Osterreiches Normungsinstitut (ON), Postfach 130, A-1021 Vienna, Austria.

DefaultLanguage

This assigns the specified ISO 639 natural language code to any file whose language cannot be determined by the file's filename extension. For example

```
DefaultLanguage de
```

sets the default language to German. The HTTP/1.1 specification (RFC 2616) does not require the server to send a `Content-Language` header to the browser (unlike the `Content-Type` header, which is required). Apache's default configuration file does not pre-configure a `DefaultLanguage` directive.

A `DefaultLanguage` directive outside any block directive sets the default language for all files served. You can use `DefaultLanguage` within a `<Directory>` block directive to set a default language for the files in a given directory.

If you are serving up the same content in files of different languages, you may find the `DefaultLanguage` directive useful for making sure that all files have an assigned language during content negotiation.

Content Negotiation

The browser can use MIME headers to tell the server what the browser prefers. The browser might say, "Send me the document named /a.html. I will accept any textual version of the file, but I prefer a hypertext file. I speak French, but I can read English tolerably well. I can deal with encoded files, too. I prefer that the file be compressed with the UNIX compress utility; but I can accept gzipped files as well." The server (which may have the document stored in files of different flavors) does its best to deliver the most satisfactory document. The server might respond with, "I'm giving you a.html.fr.Z. I selected this file because you have a language preference and an encoding preference. The file you are about to receive is a text file (that is hypertext) and it was encoded with the UNIX compress utility." In their native language, the conversation would sound like this

Browser says

```
GET /a HTTP/1.1
Host: spot.ael.com
Accept: text/*; q=0.2, text/html; q=1.0
Accept-Encoding: compress; q=1.0, gzip; q=0.5
Accept-Language: fr; q=1.0, en; q=0.6
```

and Server says

```
HTTP/1.1 200 OK
Date: Sat, 16 Oct 1999 00:04:49 GMT
Server: Apache/1.3.9 (Unix)
Content-Location: a.html.fr.Z
Vary: negotiate,accept-language,accept-encoding
TCN: choice
Last-Modified: Sat, 16 Oct 1999 00:04:25 GMT
ETag: "28398-2c5-3807c109;3807c109"
Accept-Ranges: bytes
Content-Length: 709
Content-Type: text/html
Content-Encoding: compress
Content-Language: fr
```

The browser's Accept headers declare the browser's preferences. The q= values in these Accept headers give a *quality factor* to a preference. A q= value may range from 0.0 to 1.0, where 0.0 means "not acceptable" and 1.0 means "most preferred." An Accept header value with no q= parameter is assigned a quality factor of 1.0 by the server. The server states the name of the chosen file with the Content-location header and why it chose that file with the Vary header. The Content-type header reports the MIME content type of the file. The Content-encoding header reports the encoding scheme that was applied to the file. The Content-language header specifies the natural language in which the content was written.

The conversation quoted above is an example of "server-driven" negotiation. The server considers the browser's wishes, but the server makes the choice. Apache supports server-driven negotiation as well as the experimental negotiation protocol known as *transparent negotiation* (RFC

2295 and 2296), wherein the browser selects from the available variants. If this is enabled, Apache will perform transparent negotiation if a browser asks for it; otherwise, Apache will perform server-driven negotiation. By default, however, Apache performs no negotiation. You must explicitly enable it.

There are two ways to implement server-driven content negotiation in Apache:

- Manually define and weight the server's choices with type-maps
- Allow Apache to automatically define and weight the choices.

Implementing Type-maps

A type-map is an ASCII text file that assigns a content type, an encoding scheme, and/or a natural language to each "variant" of a "resource." A resource is the conceptual representation of the web content you are publishing. A variant of that resource is one of the physical representations of the resource. You may, for instance, want to publish a Web page describing a pair of boots. The description of the boots is the resource. The Web page describing the boots in English is one variant. The Web page describing the boots in Spanish is another variant. By convention, you would name these files using the ISO 639 language codes: `boots.html.en` and `boots.html.es`, respectively. Place both these files in the same directory; then, in that same directory, create an ASCII text file named `boots.var` that reads as follows

```
URI: boots

URI: boots.html.en
Content-type: text/html
Content-language: en
Content-length: 16382
Description: in English

URI: boots.html.es
Content-type: text/html
Content-language: es
Content-length: 15472
Description: en español
```

Type-map files list variants separated by an empty line. Empty lines are not allowed within a variant. Each variant first declares its file name with the `URI:` tag, then describes that variant's contents with `Content-type:`, `Content-language:`, and/or `Content-encoding:` headers The

`Content-length` header saves Apache the time of having to go to the file system to get the file size. The `Description` header is used in error messages. If the server cannot find a variant that can satisfy the browser, then it transmits a 406 Not Acceptable page that displays the available variants with the text specified by the `Description` header. By convention, the first variant describes the resource as a whole—typically using the same base file name as the variants, but without any file name extensions. Since no content headers follow, this empty variant is ignored. The example above, true to convention, first declares an empty resource variant. The second variant describes the English version of the resource and the third variant describes the Spanish version. These sample Web pages differ by the natural language of their content. Thereby, they differ by what `Content-language` header that the server will send to the browser when transmitting one of the variants. The attribute by which the variants differ is known as a "dimension" of the content negotiation. A dimension might be the content type, the natural language, or the encoding scheme. Variants may differ by more than one dimension. It is not likely that you will provide every possible variant for a resource. When a browser requests the type-map file, the Apache server searches the type-map file for the variant whose dimensions best match the browser's preferences; and then transmits the file named by the selected variant's `URI:` tag. Note that the browser is requesting the type-map file directly (e.g. the browser is requesting **http://administeringapache/boots.var**).

Let's say you've digitized a picture of these boots that you scanned into a GIF image file. Each of the variants needs to display a picture of these boots. In an effort to please as many browsers as you can, you copied/converted the GIF image file to a JPEG image file and both are available on your Web site. Assume that the JPEG converter did a satisfactory job; but you like the GIF image better—it looks cleaner. You want each browser to receive a picture that it can display; but, for browsers that can display both formats, you would prefer they receive the GIF file. You can make this happen with a type-map file.

Each of our example `boots.html.??` variants has an anchor link to a type-map file named `bootpic.var`, which you would create as follows

```
URI: bootpic

URI: bootpic.gif
Content-type: image/gif; qs=1.0

URI: bootpic.jpg
Content-type: image/jpeg; qs=0.5
```

When a browser requests `bootpic.var`, Apache compares the browser's capabilities and preference to that of the server. The server's preferences are defined by `qs=` parameters to the dimension values in the type-map file. A `qs=` parameter assigns a source quality factor to a dimension value. The syntax is the same as the `q=` parameter in the `Accept` headers of a browser's request (which assign quality factors to the browser's preferences—discussed in the "Content Negotiation" subsection above). A `qs=` parameter may have a value ranging from `0.0` to `1.0`, where `0.0` means "I will not serve this" and `1.0` means "I'd most like to serve this." The `bootpic` example, above, assigns a higher source quality factor to the `image/gif` variant than to the `image/jpeg` variant, thus defining the server's preference to serve up the GIF file.

Note that there can be only one value for a given dimension in a type-map file. The browser may be able to say, "I can accept all these kinds of things;" whereas the server must say, "I am giving you *this* one."

When there are type-map files to process, you must tell the Apache server how they are named and how to process them. Enable type-map processing with the `AddHandler` directive.

AddHandler

This assigns the specified handler routine to files whose names contain the specified file name extensions. Apache sends a matching file to the handler and the output from the handler is transmitted to the browser. To enable type-map processing, add the following directive to your Apache configuration:

```
AddHandler type-map var
```

This directive instructs Apache that all files having the `.var` file name extension are to be processed by the `type-map` handler. Note that the file name extension specified in the `AddHandler` directive does not contain the period. The example above uses the `.var` file name extension because that's how we named our type-map files in the boots example, above (`boots.var` and `bootpic.var`).

The `type-map` routine resides in the `mod_negotiation` module, which is a default module. If, when you compiled Apache, you explicitly disabled `mod_negotiation`, then you will need to recompile Apache for the `type-map` handler to be available.

Type-maps enforce file typing and content preferences on a very granular level. Maintaining a type-map file for every resource on a Web site might be more than a webmaster would be inclined to do. If the system administrator and the webmaster can agree on a file naming convention, then Apache can negotiate content automatically. The webmaster will still be able to use type-maps where needed, but the server can do the work in most situations.

Automated Content Negotiation

If you have defined the file name extensions discussed in the sections "Configuring Content Types," "Configuring Encoding Types," and "Configuring Languages" (above), then Apache can determine all of a file's attributes automatically. When content negotiation is automated, the browser requests the resource without a filename extension (e.g., http://administeringapache.com/boots). Then the server decides which variant to transmit (e.g., boots.html.en). You enable automated content negotiation per directory with the MultiViews directory option.

MultiViews

As an argument to the Options directive, MultiViews enables automated content negotiation. This option is usually localized within a <Directory> block directive. In the Apache configuration file, find the <Directory> block pertaining to the directory for which you wish to enable MultiViews (or create the <Directory> block, if necessary). The following, for example

```
<Directory "/home/webmastr/pub/html">
    Options Indexes MultiViews FollowSymLinks
    AllowOverride Limit
    Order allow,deny
    Allow from all
</Directory>
```

allows Apache to perform automated content negotiation in the /home/webmaster/pub/html/ directory (the DocumentRoot directory of our example server). Since <Directory> configurations are inherited, this enables MultiViews for all subdirectories in the document directory tree. Since content negotiation requires some overhead, it would be best to allow MultiViews only for those directories in which you actually provide variants. For all other directories (those for which MultiViews is not enabled), there should only be one variant for each resource; and the browser must request that file by the file's full name—including file name extensions.

Figure 4.4 shows the order in which the `MultiViews` algorithm considers dimensions in deciding which variant to deliver to the browser (from highest to lowest precedence).

Figure 4.4
Automated content negotiation order of precedence.

Dimension	Browser Request Header	Server Response Header
MIME content type	`Accept`	`ContentType`
Natural language	`AcceptLanguage`	`ContentLanguage`
MIME content type version	`level=` parameter to `AcceptLanguage`	`level=` parameter to `AcceptLanguage`
Character set	`AcceptCharset`	`charset=` parameter to `ContentType`
Encoding scheme	`AcceptEncoding`	`ContentEncoding`
Smallest file size		`ContentLength`
First listed in either the type-map file or the directory listing sorted by file name		

The details of the `MultiViews` algorithm are discussed in the *Apache User's Guide*—**manual/content-negotiation.html**. The automated `MultiViews` algorithm does not allow you to assign source quality factors. You can always use a type-map where needed to override the `MultiViews` order of precedence. `MultiViews` does, however, allow you some control over the server-sided preferences for natural language—using the `LanguagePriority` directive.

LanguagePriority

This defines the server's natural language preference when the browser does not specify a language preference. The default setting is

```
LanguagePriority en fr de
```

The two-character ISO 639 language codes specified in the `LanguagePriority` directive are listed in order, from highest preference to lowest. Given the above directive and a choice between `boots.html.en` and `boots.html.fr`, the server would transmit `boots.html.en`—provided the browser does not specify a preference. Most HTTP/1.1 compliant browsers will explicitly negotiate natural language; so the `LanguagePriority` directive will come into play most often in conversing with HTTP/1.0 browsers. Be sure that each language code that you use in the LanguagePriority directive is also declared with an AddLanguage directive (see "Configuring Languages," above).

This last directive related to content negotiation governs the behavior of proxy servers between the browser and the server.

CacheNegotiatedDocs

This instructs proxy servers that they may cache content-negotiated documents. Normally, Apache instructs proxy servers that they cannot cache such documents—by sending the Pragma: no-cache header. If CacheNegotiatedDocs is enabled, Apache does not send the no-cache header. In the default configuration file, this directive is commented out. CacheNegotiatedDocs takes no parameters; so to enable it uncomment the line by removing the pound sign. Enabling the caching of negotiated documents reduces network traffic and reduces download time at the browser. The downside is that a browser might not get its most preferred content. The greatest risk is to pre-HTTP/1.1 browsers. The HTTP/1.1 protocol (RFC 2616) provides the browser with a great deal of control over caching.

The MIME-like headers of HTTP/1.1 are not the only server response headers a content author can send to the browser. When MIME is not enough, the webmaster can send metadata.

Sending Metadata and Other Headers

HTTP's MIME-like headers are understood and agreed upon by the browser and the server. That is, the HTTP/1.1 protocol defines them. The Internet Engineering Task Force also provided extension headers so that you can invent your own. Use these to pass messages between the server and customized user agents (proprietary browsers, plug-ins, search engine spiders, etc.). The content author and the user agent must agree, of course, on what the added header means. Some of the invented headers have come into common usage. Content authors often add keywords to their documents for the search engine spiders to find. They achieve this by adding a tag as follows:

```
<META    HTTP-EQUIV=Keywords
    CONTENT="shoes boots work-boots snakeskin ostrich"
>
```

The tag shown above instructs the browser to create a header named `keywords` whose value is `"shoes boots work-boots snakeskin ostrich."` When the browser sees a `<META>` tag with an `HTTP-EQUIV` attribute, it adds the specified header to those it has already received in the server response header (overwriting the value of any response header having the same name). The problem is that `<META>` tag information travels with the document body, not with the server response headers. Some search engines peruse your site using the `HEAD` method, which doesn't retrieve the document body.

Apache's support of metafiles allows content authors to write their own headers into the server response header. The content author writes the desired headers into an ASCII text file. Apache reads (as is) the metafile into the response header. In this sample metafile

```
Keywords: "shoes boots work-boots snakeskin ostrich"
Expires: Friday, 30-Oct-99 12:00:00 GMT
```

the `Keywords` header has been added for the search engines and the `Expires` header has been added to control browser and proxy caching. One might apply this metafile to the `boots.html` example. The metafile must have the same name as the document but with an added file name suffix (conventionally `.meta`, as in `boots.html.meta`). It is also common practice to place the metafiles in a hidden subdirectory.

The metafiles feature may be enabled on a per-directory basis in the Apache configuration file. The following `<Directory>` block directive would enable metafile processing in our example server's products subdirectory: The `Meta????` directives used therein are discussed thereafter:

```
<Directory "/home/webmastr/pub/html/products">
    Options Indexes FollowSymLinks
    AllowOverride Limit
    Order allow,deny
    Allow from all
    MetaFiles on
    MetaDir .web
    MetaSuffix .meta
</Directory>
```

MetaFiles

Within a `<Directory>` block directive, this enables or disables metafile processing for the specified directory. Use the `on` parameter to enable and the `off` parameter to disable. The `<Directory>` block attributes are inherited; so, metafile processing will be enabled or disabled for subdirectories of the specified <Directory>.

MetaDir

Within a <Directory> block directive, this specifies the subdirectory in which the Apache server will find the metafiles for documents in the specified <Directory>. For example:

```
MetaDir .web
```

instructs Apache to look in the .web subdirectory of the specified <Directory>. Since the .web subdirectory name begins with a period, UNIX hides the directory; but Apache will still list it in a directory listing. Use the IndexIgnore directive (described earlier in this chapter) to prevent Apache from listing the .web subdirectory.

The specified metafiles subdirectory is relative to the <Directory>. Use

```
MetaDir .
```

to instruct Apache to look for a document's metafile in the same directory as the document.

MetaSuffix

Within a <Directory> block directive, this specifies the file name suffix by which Apache will find the metafile associated with a document from that <Directory>. The following:

```
MetaSuffix .meta
```

instructs Apache to obtain the name of a document's metafile by adding the .meta suffix to the document's file name (e.g. index.html's metafile is named index.html.meta). Note that this commonly used example uses a period so that the suffix will look like a file name extension. The period is not required (but then you would name your metafile index.htmlmeta).

The Meta???? directives, above, transmit particular headers with particular files. Maintaining metafiles for every Web document might be overwhelming. The Header directive, below, allows you to specify that particular headers be transmitted with any file from a group of files, or with any file from a particular directory, or with any file requested by a particular URL.

Header

This provides control over server response headers. The Header directive allows you to perform the following actions on a specified header.

- set—Create the specified response header, overwriting any pre-existing response header with the same name.
- append—Create the specified response header. If a response header with the same name already exists, then the value of the specified header is appended to the value of the pre-existing header.
- add—Create the specified response header. If a response header with the same name already exists, then the transmission will contain duplicate headers. Don't use add. Use append, instead.
- unset—Remove the specified response header from the transmission, if the specified header already exists.

The Header directive takes at least two parameters: the action to be taken and the name of the header. When you use any of the actions that create a response header (the first three listed above), the directive requires a third parameter specifying the value of the header. For example, assume a custom application: maybe an add-on Apache module that talks to a browser plug-in. You might use these directives

```
Header set AutoECheck program/3.4
Header append AutoECheck schema/8.3
```

to construct the following header

```
AutoECheck: program/3.4, schema/8.3
```

and add it to every document served by the server. The browser plug-in would check the AutoECheck header to test if it is in sync with the server. The reason the header is added to every document served is because the Header directive in the above example is not within a block directive that would limit its scope—which you can do.

You can manipulate headers for every file served from a particular directory by enclosing the directive within a <Directory> block. For example

```
<Directory /home/tperson/pub/html>
    Options FollowSymLinks
    AllowOverride Limit
    Order allow,deny
```

```
        Allow from all
        Header set Author: "Thomas Person"
</Directory>
```

would force an `Author` header on every file served from Thomas' home directory Web site (see Chapter 7: "Creating Homepage Web Sites"). Notice that the value of the header must be surrounded by double quotes if it contains spaces.

The `Header` directive can also be used within the `<Location>` block directive to manipulate the headers of documents requested by a matching URL. Let's say you are serving up stock quotes, updated every five minutes. You could use the following block to control caching:

```
<Location ~ "/quotes/(NYSE|NASDAQ)/" >
    Header set Cache-Control max-age=300
</Location>
```

The above block puts the `Cache-Control` header in all responses to requests for files from either the `/quotes/NYSE/` directory or the `/quotes/NASDAQ/` directory. The tilde in the `<Location>` tag allows you to use an extended regular expression for the specified URL, like the one above. Note that `<Location>` block is matching the requested URL, not the directory on the file system. The `Header` directive within the above example specifies that the document expires when it becomes 300 seconds old.

The `Header` directive may be used within the `<VirtualHost>` and `<Files>` block directives as well. Since the `Header` actions consider pre-existing headers, order of processing is important. Apache processes `Header` directives in the following contextutal order:

```
no block → <VirtualHost> → <Directory> → <Location> → <Files>
```

`Header` directives are processed by the `mod_headers` module, which is *not* a default module. To compile the `mod_headers` module into Apache using the APACI utility, use the parameter `--enable-module=headers` or the parameter `--enable-module=most`.

One last header directive is shown below.

ServerTokens

This defines the verbosity of the `Server:` response header sent with every document served. `ServerTokens` takes one parameter, which may be one of:

- Minimal—sends the most basic header, which reads

      Server: Apache/1.3.9

- OS—adds the operating system, as in

      Server: Apache/1.3.9 (Unix)

- Full—adds module information, such as

      Server: Apache/1.3.9 (Unix) PHP/3.0

The default setting is Full. The ServerTokens directive is global and cannot be placed inside a block directive.

Sending Files As-Is

The MIME-types, the metafiles, and the header directive enable you to add response headers. What if you want the document itself to have (almost) full control over its own response headers? The mod_asis module (a default module) offers the send-as-is handler, which will transmit files with almost no headers (Apache will always add the headers Date: and Server: so do not include them in the files to be sent as is). Note that the HTTP protocol requires the server response to include a Status: header and a Content-type: header, which should be written into any file sent as-is.

To enable as-is processing, use one configuration directive, AddHandler or SetHandler to tell Apache which files are to be sent as is.

AddHandler

This associates the specified handler with the specified file name extension. A *handler* is a named procedure made available in one of the Apache modules. Toward the end of sending files as is, we use this directive to associate files having the .asis file name extension with the send-as-is handler:

```
AddHandler send-as-is .asis
```

SetHandler

Within a block directive, this instructs Apache to process all matching files with the specified handler. For sending as is, you can specify that matching files be processed with Apache's `send-as-is` handler. For example, the following block

```
<Directory "/home/webmastr/pub/html/asis">
    SetHandler send-as-is
</Directory>
```

instructs Apache to send as-is all files residing in the `asis/` subdirectory.

Implementing the Common Gateway Interface (CGI)

Overview

CGI interfaces the Web content with the operating system. Content authors commonly use CGI to retrieve data from and submit data to a database (and for other data-processing tasks). When a browser requests a document that is a CGI script (or program), the Web server calls upon the operating system to execute the script. The Web server passes the browser's request to the script through environment variables and through the script's standard input. The script performs its processing and the outputs HTML response headers and HTML text to its standard out, which the server then transmits back to the browser.

Enabling CGI

In Chapter 3: "Creating the Web Site," we enabled CGI for the webmaster. Here is a quick review. We created the `webmastr` user account and moved Apache's `cgibin/` directory to a subdirectory of `webmastr`'s home directory, giving the new subdirectory these permissions:

```
drwxr-s---    webmastr httpd  /home/webmastr/pub/cgi-bin/
```

All the files within the webmastr's `cgibin/` directory where given the permissions `-rwxr-x---`. We instructed Apache that all files in the new `cgibin/` file system directory are to be executed as scripts when requested by the `/cgibin/` URL by adding the following configuration directive:

```
ScriptAlias /cgi-bin/ "/home/webmastr/pub/cgi-bin/"
```

We created a `<Directory>` block directive to give browsers access to the new `cgi-bin/` directory.

```
<Directory "/home/webmastr/pub/cgi-bin">
    AllowOverride None
    Options None
    Order allow,deny
    Allow from all
</Directory>
```

We loaded and activated Apache's CGI executor (the mod_cgi module, a default module) as a DSO with these configuration directives:

```
LoadModule cgi_module libexec/mod_cgi.so
AddModule mod_cgi.c
```

The end result of the above configuration is that Apache executes as scripts all files in the directory specified by the ScriptAlias directive. You can configure Apache to recognize CGI scripts outside of the ScriptAlias directory with the following configuration directives.

AddHandler

This associates the specified handler with the specified file name extension. A handler is a named procedure made available in one of the Apache modules. To handle CGI, we use this directive to associate files having a .cgi file name extension with Apache's CGI executor—cgi-script.

```
AddHandler cgi-script .cgi
```

SetHandler

Within a block directive, this instructs Apache to process all matching files with the specified handler. For CGI, you can specify that matching files be processed with Apache's cgi-script handler. For example, the block

```
<Files ~ ".*sql\.ksh">
    SetHandler cgi-script
</Files>
```

would execute as scripts all files whose names end with sql.ksh (such as custsql.ksh or prodsql.ksh). The tilde in the <Files> tag allows extended regular expressions, like the one above.

The directives AddHandler and SetHandler do not give Apache permission to run the scripts. You must grant such permission to the directory in which the script resides. Do this with the ExecCGI option.

ExecCGI

As an argument to the `Options` directive, this grants permission for the execution of CGI scripts. The `Options` directive may be global in scope (outside any block directive) and may be used to grant CGI execute permissions everywhere. The `Options` directive may be localized within a `<VirtualHost>` block, a `<Directory>` block or a directory access file (e.g. `.htaccess`); which is preferable since CGI programs may be malicious or hackable. Most administrators grant CGI execution permission to one directory shared by all the Web sites on the server. The system administrator, as the only one who can create files in that directory, can then test scripts for security flaws and malicious intent before placing them in the CGI directory. Such a one-directory grant is usually achieved with the `ScriptAlias` directive, which both associates the `cgi-script` handler with all files in the specified directory and grants CGI execute permissions on that directory. This `ExecCGI` option, on the other hand, is used for directories other than that specified by the `ScriptAlias` directive. Say you have a directory dedicated to database scripts. You could enable CGI for that directory with this `<Directory>` block:

```
<Directory "/home/webmastr/pub/html/dbscripts">
    Options +ExecCGI
</Directory>
```

In the example above, the `dbscripts` directory inherits its options from the parent directory (which is the `DocumentRoot` of our example server). The execute permissions are added to the inherited options with the plus sign. Note that, without the plus sign, the above `Options` directive would completely override the options inherited from the parent directory (wiping out all but the `ExecCGI` option).

Using Apache's CGI Environment

The Web server passes the browser's request headers (and other information) to the script through the script's shell environment. The Web server passes the browser's request body to the script through standard input. Figure 4.5 displays the environment variables created by Apache for use by the script. It also displays the sources for the values of those environment variables and also shows what Apache configuration directives affect those values.

Apache conforms to NCSA's CGI/1.1 specification and sets up all of the environment variables required thereby (point your browser to

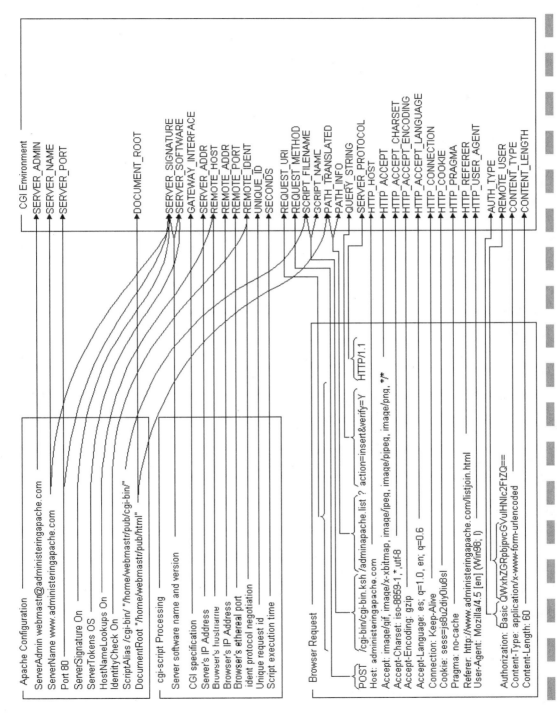

Figure 4.5 *Environment variables that Apache provides for CGI scripts.*

http://hoohoo.ncsa.uiuc.edu/cgi/). Apache provides additional variables not required by the CGI/1.1 standard. All of these environment variables are described below. Those required by the CGI/1.1 standard are marked (CGI). Those added by Apache are marked with (Apache). Note that the (Apache) variables are undocumented and were discovered empirically:

- AUTH_TYPE—(CGI) the algorithm used to authenticate the user requesting the script, for example,

    Basic

    AUTH_TYPE will be set only if the directory in which the script lives requires authentication; in which case, the browser provides this information in the Authorization: request header.
- CONTENT_LENGTH—(CGI) the length, in bytes, of the body of the browser's request, for example,

    60

- CONTENT_TYPE—(CGI) the MIME content type of the body of the browser's request. For example, an HTML form submitted by a POST request might have this content type:

    application/x-www-form-urlencoded

- DOCUMENT_ROOT—(Apache) the file-system directory that is the URL root directory for the web site. That is, the file-system directory accessed when the browser requests the / URL. This variable is set to the value of the DocumentRoot configuration directive. For our example server, this is

    /home/webmastr/pub/html

- GATEWAY_INTERFACE—(CGI) the version number of the CGI specification to which the Web server adheres, for example:

    CGI/1.1

- HTTP_????—(CGI) all left-over request headers sent by the browser. According to the CGI/1.1 specification, the Web server should make a variable out of any request header not accounted for by the specifications. The variable is to be given the same name as the header, but prefixed with HTTP_ and with hyphens replaced with underscores. The most common are described below.

- HTTP_ACCEPT—(CGI) the MIME content types that the browser is willing to accept. This variable is set to the value of the Accept: request header, for example:

```
'image/gif, image/x-xbitmap, image/jpeg, image/pjpeg,
image/png, */*'
```

- HTTP_ACCEPT_CHARSET—(CGI) the MIME character sets that the browser is willing to accept. This variable is set to the value of the Accept-Charset: request header, for example:

```
'iso-8859-1,*,utf-8'
```

- HTTP_ACCEPT_ENCODING—(CGI) the MIME encoding schemes that the browser is willing to accept. This variable is set to the value of the Accept-Encoding: request header, for example:

```
gzip
```

- HTTP_ACCEPT_LANGUAGE—(CGI) the natural languages that the browser is willing to accept. This variable is set to the value of the Accept-Language: request header, for example:

```
'es; q=1.0, en; q=0.6'
```

- HTTP_CONNECTION—(CGI) the connection duration as specified by the browser. This variable is set to the value of the Connection: request header, for example:

```
Keep-Alive
```

- HTTP_COOKIE—(CGI) a semi-colon separated list of cookies sent by the browser with the request. This variable is set to the value of the Cookie: request header. For example, session IDs are often placed in cookies:

```
'sess=js8u2diy0iu8sl'
```

- HTTP_HOST—(CGI) the hostname of the server requested by the browser. This variable is set to the value of the Host: request header, for example:

```
www.administeringapache.com
```

- – HTTP_PRAGMA—(CGI) instructs proxy servers and the originating Web server to deliver the authoritative version of the document, not a cached version. This variable is set to the value of the Pragma: request header. Only one value is allowed by the HTTP/1.1 specification:

  ```
  no-cache
  ```

- – HTTP_REFERER—(CGI) the URL of the document containing the link used to request the script being invoked. This link could be an <A HREF=> anchor tag or the ACTION attribute of a <FORM> tag. This variable is set to the value of the Referer: request header, for example:

  ```
  http://wwwadministeringapache.com/listjoin.html
  ```

- – HTTP_USER_AGENT—(CGI) the name and version of the browser software used to make the request. This variable is set to the value of the User-Agent: request header, for example:

  ```
  'Mozilla/4.5 [en] (Win98; I)'
  ```

- ■ PATH_INFO—(CGI) extra path information in the URL specified by the browser's request. This is the part of the URL between the name of the script and the query string, for example, given this URL

  ```
  /cgi-bin/listmaint.ksh/adminapache.list?action=
  insert&verify=Y
  ```

  the PATH_INFO variable would be set to

  ```
  /adminapache.list
  ```

  In the above example, the PATH_INFO variable is used to tell the listmaint.ksh script which list is to be operated on.

- ■ PATH_TRANSLATED—(CGI) a file-system translation of the extra path information in the URL specified by the browser's request. PATH_TRANSLATED takes the PATH_INFO environment variable and translates it into a file-system path relative to the DocumentRoot directory. For example, given the above PATH_INFO example, our example server would set PATH_TRANSLATED to:

  ```
  /home/webmastr/pub/html/adminapache.list
  ```

- QUERY_STRING—(CGI) in the URL requested by the browser, the query information following the question mark. For example, given the URL

  `/cgi-bin/listmaint.ksh/adminapache.list?action=insert&verify=Y`

  the QUERY_STRING variable would be set to

  `action=insert&verify=Y`

- REDIRECT_STATUS—(Apache) the server response status from the redirection of the originally requested URL into a request for the script being invoked. This variable is set when Apache performs certain configured redirects (such as an AliasMatch directive; but not an Alias directive). A successful example would be:

  `200`

- REDIRECT_UNIQUE_ID—(Apache) a unique identifier for the original request before being redirected into the script being invoked. Apache assigns a unique identifier to every request. This variable is set when Apache performs certain configured redirects (such as an AliasMatch directive; but not an Alias directive). An example ID is

  `OBeAi8CoAQEAACFJCio`

- REDIRECT_URL—(Apache) the original URL requested by the browser, before that URL was redirected into a request for the script being invoked. This variable is set when Apache performs certain configured redirects (such as an AliasMatch directive; but not an Alias directive). If set, REDIRECT_URL contains the path and filename of the script being invoked plus any extra path information in the original URL. For example, given this request

  `/listscripts/listmaint.ksh /adminapache.list?action=insert&verify=Y`

  and given this directive

  `AliasMatch /listscripts/ /home/webmastr/pub/cgi-bin/`

  the REDIRECT_URL variable would be set to this segment of the original URL:

  `/listscripts/listmaint.ksh/adminapache.list/`

The REDIRECT_URL variable is handy if you have put the name of a CGI script in the DirectoryIndex configuration directive (e.g., DirectoryIndex index.cgi). Such a script would then use REDIRECT_URL to obtain the originally requested directory.

■ REMOTE_ADDR—(CGI) the IP address of the browser making the request, for example:

    192.168.1.7

■ REMOTE_HOST—(CGI) the hostname of the browser making the request, for example:

    ppp3452.administeringapache.net

This variable will be set if the HostnameLookups configuration directive is set to On and the Web server successfully performs a reverse DNS lookup on the browser's IP address; otherwise, this variable is empty. Beware that turning HostnameLookups to On may cause a considerable performance hit.

■ REMOTE_IDENT—(CGI) the system dependent identification of the user requesting the script. For example

    Doe.DODCSC.j

might be a MULTICS user name. This variable is set only if the IdentityCheck configuration directive is set to On and the Web server successfully negotiates the value with the browser (using the RFC 931 ident protocol). Since the value of REMOTE_IDENT is system-dependent, it should only be used informationally (e.g. for logging purposes).

■ REMOTE_USER—(CGI) the name of the user requesting the script, for example:

    jdoe

This variable will be set only if authentication is required for the directory in which the script resides; in which case, the browser supplies this information in the Authorization: request header. The browser's Authorization: header (containing the user name and password separated by a colon) is encrypted. Apache decrypts the header before scanning the user name into this REMOTE_USER environment variable.

- REQUEST_METHOD—(CGI) the HTTP request method specified in the browser's request, for example:

  ```
  POST
  ```

- REQUEST_URI—(Apache) the full URL as requested by the browser. This variable is set to the segment of the browser request appearing between the request method and the protocol. This includes the URL path and resource name of the script, any extra path information, and the query string, for example:

  ```
  /cgi-bin/listmaint.ksh/adminapache.list?qvar=qval&q2var=q2val
  ```

- SCRIPT_FILENAME—(Apache) the file-system path and file name of the script being invoked. This variable contains the file-system translation of the URL requesting the script. The path mapping used for this translation could be the value of the ScriptAlias directive or the value of the DocumentRoot directive, depending on the directory in which the script resides, for example:

  ```
  /home/webmastr/pub/cgi-bin/listmaint.ksh
  ```

- SCRIPT_NAME—(CGI) the URL path to the CGI script being evoked (as specified in the browser's request). If any redirections have been applied, then the SCRIPT_NAME variable contains the post-redirect URL, for example:

  ```
  /cgi-bin/listmaint.ksh
  ```

- SECONDS—(Apache) the number of seconds required to execute the requested script. For example

  ```
  1
  ```

  would be slow.

- SERVER_ADDR—(Apache) the IP address of the server handling the request, for example:

  ```
  192.168.1.1
  ```

- SERVER_ADMIN—(Apache) the e-mail address of the person responsible for the server handling the request. This variable is set to the value of the ServerAdmin configuration directive, for example:

  ```
  webmastr@administeringapache.com
  ```

■ SERVER_NAME—(CGI) the hostname of the Web server. This variable takes the value of the ServerName configuration directive if that server name is correctly served by a DNS server; otherwise, this variable is set to the IP address of the Web server, for example:

```
www.administeringapache.com
```

■ SERVER_PORT—(CGI) the port number on which the server received the request, for example:

```
80
```

■ SERVER_PROTOCOL—(CGI) the protocol with which the browser made its request and the version number of that protocol, for example:

```
HTTP/1.1
```

■ SERVER_SIGNATURE—(Apache) HTML formatted information about the server handling the request. This variable is set according to the specifications of the ServerSignature configuration directive. If ServerSignature is Off, then the SERVER_SIGNATURE environment variable is not set. If ServerSignature is On, then SERVER_SIGNATURE contains the SERVER_SOFTWARE information and the SERVER_NAME information. If ServerSignature is EMail, then SERVER_SIGNATURE also contains the e-mail address of the server administrator, for example:

```
'<ADDRESS>Apache/1.3.9 Server at <A HREF=
"mailto:webmastr@administeringapache.com"
>www.administeringapache.com</A>Port 80</ADDRESS>
```

■ SERVER_SOFTWARE—(CGI) the name and version of the server software. This variable may also contain the operating system name and the names of Apache add-on modules—as specified by the ServerTokens configuration directive (described above in the section titled "Sending Metadata and Other Headers"), for example:

```
Apache/1.3.9 (Unix)
```

■ UNIQUE_ID—(Apache) a unique identifier for the request. Apache assigns one identifier to every request, for example:

```
OBUEvsCoAQEAABVwDGA
```

Controlling the CGI Environment

Apache provides three configuration directives for manipulating the environment in which CGI scripts run. All these directives can be global (i.e. outside any block directive) or local to a `<VirtualHost>` block directive. These directives are provided by the `mod_env` module, a default module. Each of these directives is described below.

PassEnv

This passes to CGI scripts the specified variable taken from the Apache server's own environment. You could, for example, pass the server's search path environment variable using this directive:

```
PassEnv PATH
```

SetEnv

This creates the specified variable with the specified value and places that variable in the environment of CGI scripts. You could, for example, specify a database path to your CGI scripts using this directive:

```
SetEnv DbPath /var/lib/pgsql
```

UnsetEnv

This removes the specified variables from those that would normally be passed to CGI scripts, for example:

```
UnsetEnv PATH DbPath
```

CGI Caveats

The CGI script must output the `Content-type:` response header. The `Content-type:` response header is required by the HTTP protocol, but Apache has no clue what kind of content your script will be transmitting.

Apache will start the response header for you, but you will have to finish it. After your script has output all the headers that it cares to, the script must output an empty line to mark the end of the response header. The cgi-script handler expects all output prior to a blank line to conform to response header syntax; otherwise, Apache transmits a `500 Internal Server Error`.

The CGI-script handler will output applicable headers defined by metafiles or by `Header` directives. Apache buffers your output and places these headers in their appropriate places in the response header. Note, however, that Apache does not make environment variables out of these added headers; they are not available to the CGI programmer.

Do not redirect scripts that expect to receive `POST` data. All redirections are retrieved via the `GET` method. When the browser submits data with a `POST` request to a CGI script, and that CGI script is redirected, the redirected request will become a `GET` method—losing both the `POST` method and the submitted data.

Apache provides extensive facilities for logging CGI activity. See Chapter 5: "Using Logs."

Security risks come with the power of programming. The system administrator trusts that the CGI programmer will not create hackable or malicious scripts. This is discussed in Chapter 6: "Securing the Server, the Content, and the Connection" in the section "Security Considerations for CGI—Wrappers."

Implementing Server-Side Includes (SSI)

Overview

When HTML is not enough and CGI is too much, SSI might be just right. As its name suggests, SSI allows the HTML author to write an oft-used construct once and then include it where needed. You can also set variables and output their values; test variables and conditionally branch; output file sizes and modification dates; and call CGI scripts.

Enabling SSI

There are three steps to enabling SSI:

1. Instruct Apache how to recognize which files need to be parsed.
2. Grant permission for SSI parsing (usually within a certain scope, like a directory).
3. Communicate to the browser the content-type of the parsed result.

The server-parsed handler in the `mod_include` module (a default module) performs server-side parsing. Use the configuration directives `AddHandler` or `SetHandler` to inform Apache which files are to be parsed.

AddHandler

This associates the specified handler with the specified file name extension. A handler is a named procedure made available in one of the Apache modules. To handle SSI, we use this directive to associate files having a .shtml file name extension with Apache's SSI parser—server-parsed.

```
AddHandler server-parsed .shtml
```

SetHandler

Within a block directive, this instructs Apache to process all matching files with the specified handler. For SSI, you can specify that matching files be processed with Apache's server-parsed handler. For example, the SetHandler directive within the following block

```
<Directory "/home/webmastr/pub/html/parsed">
    Options +Includes
    SetHandler server-parsed
</Directory>
```

would cause all files residing in the /parsed subdirectory to be parsed by the server-parsed handler. The AddHandler and SetHandler directives teach Apache to recognize parsed files, but do grant Apache permission to parse them. You must grant such permission to the directory in which the parsed files reside. Do this with the Includes option or the IncludesNOEXEC option.

Includes

As an option to the Options directive, this enables SSI parsing. The Options directive may be global in scope (outside of any block directive); so you may make server-side parsing available everywhere, through this is not a good idea. Server-side parsing increases the latency of delivering content to the browser. You don't want the server to parse files that don't need parsing. The Options directive may be localized within a <VirtualHost> block, a <Directory> block or a directory access file (e.g. .htaccess). The following example

```
<Directory "/home/webmastr/pub/html/parsed">
    Options +Includes
</Directory>
```

grants permission for parsing files in the /parsed subdirectory. The plus sign adds the Includes option to the options inherited from the parent directory (our DocumentRoot, in this example). Without the plus sign, the subdirectory's Options would completely override those of the parent directory.

IncludesNOEXEC

As an option to the Options directive, this enables SSI parsing but with CGI script execution disabled. SSI's exec command is disabled and the include command will not execute an included CGI script. Otherwise, the IncludesNOEXEC option behaves exactly the same as the Includes option described above.

The last task to enable SSI is to tell the browser what the MIME content-type is for parsed files. SSI is an extended HTML, so the content-type should be text/html. If your parseable documents have the .shtml file name extension (by use of the AddHandler directive), then you need to tell Apache that .shtml files are text/html with the AddType directive.

AddType

This assigns a MIME content type to files having the specified file name extensions. The following example

```
AddType text/html .shtml
```

instructs Apache to output a Content-Type: text/html header with files having the .shtml file name extension.

Using SSI

SSI commands are embedded within HTML comment tags. For example:

```
<!--#include file="header.inc" -->
```

includes the file named header.inc into the document being parsed at the position of the include command. Observe that the command is prefixed with a pound sign, which comes immediately after the beginning of the HTML comment <!--. Also note that there is white space preceding the HTML end-of-comment tag -->. All SSI commands accept named parameters (name = value). In the above example, file is the parameter name and "header.inc" is the parameter value. Literal string values are double quoted. To include a double quote within a literal string, precede it with a backslash (e.g. `"\"To quote a phrase\""`).

SSI Variables

The SSI parser provides several predefined variables for use within parsed files, including almost all of the predefined CGI variables (see the subsection "Using Apache's CGI Environment" above). CGI's `SECONDS` variable is not provided; and, since the `POST` method is not allowed for HTML files, the request header `CONTENT_TYPE` and `CONTENT_LENGTH` variables are omitted, as well. In addition to the CGI variables, Apache predefines the following variables for SSI.

DATE_LOCAL

This is the local date and time on the server at the time the browser request is served, for example:

```
Sunday, 31-Oct-1999 04:17:16 CST
```

DATE_GMT

This is the Greenwich Mean Time at the time the browser request is served, for example:

```
Sunday, 3-1-Oct-1999 10:17:16 GMT
```

DOCUMENT_URI

This is the URL of the requested document, plus any extra path information, for example:

```
/parsed/listjoin.shtml/adminapache.list
```

DOCUMENT_NAME

This is the file name of the requested document. This variable does not contain any path or extra path information, for example:

```
listjoin.shtml
```

DOCUMENT_PATH_INFO

This gives extra path information in the URL specified by the browser's request. This variable is the same as CGI's `PATH_INFO` environment variable. It is the segment of the requested URL between the name of the script and the query string. For example, given this URL

```
/listjoin.shtml/adminapache.list?action=insert&verify=Y
```

the DOCUMENT_PATH_INFO variable would be set to

```
/adminapache.list
```

LAST_MODIFIED

This is the date the requested file was last modified (according to the file system date-time stamp). For example:

```
Sunday, 31-Oct-1999 03:20:16 CST
```

QUERY_STRING_UNESCAPED

In the URL requested by the browser, the query information following the question mark. This is the same as the QUERY_STRING CGI environment variable, except that HTML special characters are preceded with a backslash. For example, given the URL

```
/listjoin.shtml/adminapache.list?action=insert&verify=Y
```

the QUERY_STRING_UNESCAPED variable would be set to

```
action=insert\&verify=Y
```

USER_NAME

This is the owner of the requested file according to the file system, for example:

```
USER_NAME=webmastr
```

Using SSI Variables

Variables are used within quoted strings as arguments to SSI commands. A variable's name may be replaced by that variable's value by placing a dollar sign in front of the variable name. The example

```
<!--#set
   var="JoinStr"
   value="Send email to $SERVER_ADMIN to join the list."
```

```
-->
<!--#echo var="JoinStr" -->
```

uses the `set` command to create a variable named `JoinStr` and then uses the `echo` command to output the created variable. For our example server, the resulting output would read

```
Send email to webmastr@administeringapache.com to join the list.
```

If you place two variable references next to each other, and you don't get the results you expected, then you may delineate the variables with curly braces. For instance, you may need to distinguish the `HTTP_ACCEPT` predefined variable plus a user-defined variable named `LANGUAGE` versus the predefined variable `HTTP_ACCEPT_LANGUAGE`:

```
<!--#set
    var="LANGUAGE"
    value="English"
-->
<BR><P>
<!--#set
    var="OutStr"
    value="${HTTP_ACCEPT}_${LANGUAGE}"
-->
```

If you wish to include a dollar sign in a literal string, quote it with a backslash, as in

```
<!--#set
    var="OutStr"
    value="The \$HTTP_USER_AGENT is $HTTP_USER_AGENT"
-->
```

SSI Commands

Apache's SSI provides these commands:

config

This sets the value of an SSI configuration variable. There are three variables:

errmsg

Defines the text of an error messages to be transmitted to the browser upon any error encountered during parsing. Apache does not automatical-

Chapter 4

ly generate an error message page for parsed HTML files (as it does for regular HTML files). You must generate your own:

```
<!--#config errmsg="An error has occurred. Please email
webmastr@spot.administeringapache.com" -->
```

The error message within the double quotes can be formatted HTML text and can span multiple lines, as in

```
<!--#config errmsg="
    <P>
        Please inform the
        <I><A HREF=\"mailto:$SERVER_ADMIN\">
            System Administrator
        </A></I>
        that an error was encountered processing the
        document...
    </P>
    <P>
        $DOCUMENT_URI
    </P>
"
-->
```

sizefmt

Specifies whether file sizes are to be displayed in bytes or in an abbreviation of kilobytes or megabytes. Use

```
<!--#config sizefmt="bytes" -->
```

to display file sizes in bytes with no units (to output 3,132). Use

```
<!--#config sizefmt="abbrev" -->
```

to display file sizes in kilobytes or megabytes with the abbreviated units included (to output 3k).

timefmt

Specifies the format in which date/time variables are displayed. The value of the `timefmt` format string consists of a mixture of regular characters plus date-component references, each of which is a single character preceded by a percent sign. When a date/time variable is output, each date-component reference is replaced by the appropriate segment from the date/time value. For example

```
<!--#config timefmt="%m/%d/%Y" -->
```

would display October 31, 1999 as

```
10/31/1999
```

To convert a date/time variable into a printable string, Apache takes the format string you specify for the `timefmt` value and passes it directly to the `strftime()` standard C library function. The date-component references accepted by `strftime()` are:

`%A`—the name of the weekday (e.g. Friday)

`%a`—the abbreviated name of the weekday (e.g. Fri)

`%B`—the name of the month (e.g. October)

`%b`—the abbreviated name of the month (e.g. Oct)

`%c`—the date and time representation as specified for the current locale (e.g. Sunday, 31-Oct-1999 14:18:31 CST)

`%d`—the numeric day of the month (e.g. 31)

`%H`—the numeric hour in 24-hour format (e.g. 14)

`%I`—the numeric hour in 12-hour format (e.g. 2)

`%j`—the Julian day count (e.g. 364)

`%M`—the numeric minute (e.g. 47)

`%m`—the numeric month (e.g. 10)

`%p`—the 12-hour morning/evening specifier (e.g. am)

`%S`—the numeric second (e.g. 47)

`%U`—the numeric week number (e.g. 51). The first Sunday of the year marks the beginning of the first week of the year.

`%W`—the numeric week number (e.g. 51). The first Monday of the year marks the beginning of the first week of the year.

`%w`—the numeric day of the week (e.g. 5). Sunday is day 0.

`%X`—the time representation as specified for the current locale (e.g. 14:18:31 CST)

`%x`—the date representation as specified for the current locale (e.g. Sunday, 31-Oct-1999)

`%y`—the numeric year without the century (e.g. 99)

`%Y`—the numeric year including the century (e.g. 1999)

`%Z`—the time zone (e.g. CST)

`%%`—a percent character (percent quotes a percent)

The following `config` command

```
<!--#config timefmt="%A, %d-%b-%Y %H:%M:%S %Z" -->
```

would produce the following output

```
Sunday, 31-Oct-1999 14:38:29 CST
```

echo

This outputs the value of the specified variable. The following example outputs the value of the DATE_LOCAL variable:

```
<!--#echo var="DATE_LOCAL" -->
```

Notice that the variable is specified by name, not by reference; so do not precede the variable name with a dollar sign. If the variable has not been set, the string (none) is output. This might happen, for instance, if you try to echo the HTTP_REFERER variable when the browser has accessed the document directly.

exec

This executes the specified CGI script or Bourne shell commands. When passed a parameter named cgi, the exec command executes the specified URL as a CGI script. When passed a parameter named cmd, the exec command executes the specified command line in a Bourne shell.

The following example uses the cgi argument to execute the listmaint.ksh CGI script:

```
<!--#exec cgi="/cgi-bin/listmaint.ksh" -->
```

The cgi parameter must be a %-encoded URL accessible to the browser (and subject to aliasing). If it does not specify an absolute path, then the path is taken as relative to the directory in which the parsed file caller resides. Wherever the cgi script lives, that directory must have CGI execute permissions granted with the ScriptAlias directive or with the ExecCGI option to the Options directive. Be sure that the specified cgi parameter is actually a script. Apache will try to execute whatever is specified—regardless of whether or not an AddHandler or SetHandler directive is applicable to the file. Notice that the above example does not include any extra path information nor any query string. The exec command syntax does not allow it. The exec command automatically places the PATH_INFO and QUERY_STRING variables of the parsed file into the environment of the called CGI script. As a matter of fact, the exec command puts all of the parsed file's variables into the called script's environment.

The following example uses the cmd argument to execute Bourne shell commands (echo, cut, and sed) to extract and decode parts from the query string:

```
The query string variable named
<!--#exec cmd="echo \"$QUERY_STRING\" | cut -d \& -f 1 | cut -d =
-f 1" -->
has a value of
<!--#exec cmd="echo \"$QUERY_STRING\" | cut -d \& -f 1 | cut -d =
-f 2 | sed 's/+/ /g'" -->
<P>
```

If the browser requested the parsed file as

```
/parsed/listjoin.shtml?RealName=John+Doe&EMail=jdoe@some.com
```

then the output resulting from the above example would read

```
The query string variable named RealName has a value of John Doe
```

The executables specified in the cmd argument must be file system paths (not URLs). As such, they are not subject to any browser access restrictions, alias mapping, or ExecCGI option. They *are* subject to file system restrictions. That is, the specified shell commands run under a system user account—the same user account under which the Apache Web server runs (as specified by the User configuration directive). The user account must have execute permissions for the specified shell commands. Also, if the shell commands are not in the user's search path, then the specified shell commands must include a directory path. That directory path may be absolute (begin with a slash) or relative to the directory in which the parsed file caller resides. The cut and sed shell commands used in the example above are usually in everyone's search path (on almost all UNIX systems). Note that the echo command within the example cmd strings is the Bourne shell built-in echo command (not the SSI echo command discussed above).

If SSI was enabled using the IncludesNOEXEC option, then the exec command is disabled. An attempt to use the exec command (with either the cgi or cmd arguments) would output an error message to the browser (see the command config errmsg= above). You will also see the following error message:

```
exec used but not allowed in
/home/webmastr/pub/html/parsed/listjoin.shtml
```

in the appropriate error log file (see Chapter 5: Using Logs).

One last caveat for the `exec` command: if the `cgi` script attempts a redirection by outputting a `Location:` header, the parsed file will not automatically redirect. That is, the `exec` command will not pass the `Location:` header on to the browser because it can't. These SSI commands reside within a parsed HTML document. The response headers have already been output and HTML text may have been output before the `exec` command is encountered by the parser. The `exec` command will, instead, output an `<A HREF=>` link.

fsize

This outputs the size of the specified file or URL. The `fsize` command takes either a parameter named `file` or a parameter named `virtual`. The `file` argument specifies a file on the local file system. The `virtual` argument specifies a %-encoded URL, in which case `fsize` first resolves the URL to a file on the local file system (through `DocumentRoot` or through aliasing) before obtaining the file's size. The URL, therefore, must point to a document on the local Web server.

The following example uses the `file` argument to display the size of the file named `header.inc`:

```
<!--#fsize file="inc/header.inc" -->
```

The above example shows that the `file` argument must be relative to the directory in which the parsed file resides. The `file` argument does *not* allow absolute paths or dot notation for the current and parent directories.

This next example uses the `virtual` argument to specify a URL that resolves to a file whose size is then output:

```
<!--#fsize virtual="/cgi-bin/listmaint.ksh" -->
```

The above example shows that the `virtual` argument may be an absolute path. In our example server, the URL specified above would resolve to the file `/home/webmastr/pub/html/cgibin/listmain.ksh` via the `ScriptAlias` directive. Relative paths (those not beginning with a slash) are relative to the directory in which the parsed file resides.

The `config` command's `sizefmt` parameter (described above) governs the appearance of the output from the `fsize` command.

flastmod

This outputs the last-modified date/time of the specified file or URL. The flastmod command takes either a parameter named file or a parameter named virtual. The file argument specifies a file on the file system. The virtual argument specifies a %-encoded URL. These parameters fall under the same restrictions here as they do with the fsize command, above. That is, file must be relative and virtual may be absolute. Take the fsize examples and change the command name and you will have suitable syntax examples for the flastmod command.

The config command's timefmt parameter (described above) governs the appearance of the output from the flastmod command.

include

This inserts the specified file or URL at the point where the include command is encountered. The include command takes either a parameter named file or a parameter named virtual. The file argument specifies a file on the file system. The virtual argument specifies a %-encoded URL. These parameters fall under the same restrictions here as they do with the fsize command, above. That is, file must be relative and virtual may be absolute.

The following example inserts a parsed HTML file from the relative inc/ subdirectory:

```
<!--#include file="inc/header.shtml" -->
```

If Apache recognizes the included file or URL as a server-parsed file, then Apache inserts the included file's parsed output at the position of the include command. That is to say, parsed files may be nested. The included file inherits all the variables of the including file. A query string may be added to the specified file or URL and it will override the query string variables within that included file. You cannot, however, add any extra path information to the file or URL.

If Apache recognizes the specified file or URL as a CGI script, then the script is executed and the script's output is inserted at the position of the include command. The parsed script caller exports all of its variables to the called CGI script's environment. The included CGI script would, therefore, inherit its extra path information and query string from the parsed file caller. Extra path information and a query string may be added to the specified file or URL and will override the appropriate environment variables within the called script. Beware that passing a query string to an included file side-effects the QUERY_STRING variable of the including file.

If you enabled SSI using the IncludesNOEXEC option, a file recognized as a CGI script will not be executed, nor will its contents be included (it might be a binary, after all). Instead, the browser will be sent an error message (see the errmsg parameter to SSI's config command, above) and an error message will also be recorded in the appropriate error log.

printenv

This outputs all of the parsed file's variables as name = value pairs, each terminated with a carriage-return/line-feed. The command accepts no parameters, for example:

```
<!--#printenv -->
```

The listing output by this command is plain text, not HTML. In the browser, all the name = value pairs appear run together. This command is wonderful for debugging, though.

set

This creates the variable with the specified name and value. The following example:

```
<!--#set var="DOC_TITLE" value="Join the Mailing List" -->
```

would create a variable named DOC_TITLE with the value Join the Mailing List.

Any variable created will be passed along to any include or exec files. Imagine a header that you would like to use on several different web pages. You don't want every page to have the same title. Make each page server parsed and have each define its own DOC_TITLE variable. Then, have each page include the common header, which is also a parsable file. The included file could then use the value of the DOC_TITLE variable. The including server-parsed file would read:

```
<!--#set var="DOC_TITLE" value="Join the Mailing List" -->
<!--#include file="inc/header.shtml" -->
```

The included server-parsed file would read:

```
<HEAD>
    <TITLE>
```

```
     <!--#echo var="DOC_TITLE" -->
     </TITLE>
</HEAD>
<BODY>
     <IMG SRC="/images/logo.gif" ALIGN="left">
     <H1><!--#echo var="DOC_TITLE" --></H1>
     <HR>
```

Implementing Server-Sided Image Maps

Overview

An image map links regions of a graphic image to Web pages. When the end-user clicks the mouse on one of the mapped regions of the image, the browser jumps to the associated Web page. Image maps may be client-sided; the browser determines which Web page is associated with the clicked region and requests the associated page. Image maps may be server-sided; the browser tells the server the coordinates at which the mouse was clicked and the server determines which page is associated with the clicked region and redirects the browser to the associated page. Client-sided image maps take the map processing load off of the server, but the server must deliver the map to the browser. The converse is true for server-sided image maps. Image maps defining just a few regions should be client-sided; those defining many regions, server-sided.

The content author implementing a server-sided image map creates an image map file separate from the HTML document that refers to it. The map file describes regions of an image and associates a URL with each mapped region. In the HTML document referencing the mapped image, the content author adds the ISMAP attribute to the image's <IMG> tag. This tells the browser that the image is mapped by a server-sided image map. The image's <IMG> tag is then embedded within a link anchor that refers to the image map file residing on the server. The following example specifies to the browser that the groupphoto.gif image is mapped by the personnel.map server-sided image map.

```
<A HREF="/maps/personnel.map">
     <IMG ISMAP SRC="/images/groupphoto.gif">
</A>
```

When the end-user clicks the mouse anywhere within the displayed groupphoto.gif image, the browser requests the personnel.map file. Because the image has the ISMAP attribute, the browser adds the coordinates of the click with a query string. In our example, the browser might make the request:

```
http://administeringapache.com/maps/personnel.map?116,107
```

Receiving the above request, Apache would then search the `personnel.map` image map file for the first mapped region containing the coordinates x = 116 and y = 107. If a containing region is found, then the server transmits to the browser a redirect notice specifying the location of the URL associated with the clicked region. In our example, the clicked region refers to the document `jdoe.html`. The header of the server's response would then read:

```
HTTP/1.1 302 Found
Date: Wed, 03 Nov 1999 13:20:34 GMT
Server: Apache/1.3.9 (Unix)
Location: http://administeringapache.com/personnel/jdoe.html
Transfer-Encoding: chunked
Content-Type: text/html
```

The browser should then request the document specified by the `Location:` header in the redirect notice.

If the mouse click coordinates do not fall within any mapped region, then the server responds with a `204 No Content` error; in which case, the browser should continue to display the referring page. Alternately, Apache can be instructed to respond with a hypertext menu instead of an error. The generated menu will contain a hypertext link for each URL mapped by the image map file.

Enabling Server-Sided Image Maps

The `imap-file` handler in the `mod_imap` module (a default module) performs image map processing. Use the configuration directives `AddHandler` or `SetHandler` to inform Apache as to which files are to be processed as image maps by the `imap-file` handler.

AddHandler

This associates the specified handler with the specified file name extension. A handler is a named procedure made available in one of the Apache modules. To handle image maps, we use this directive to associate files having a `.map` file name extension with Apache's image map processor—`imap-file`.

```
AddHandler imap-file .map
```

SetHandler

Within a block directive, this instructs Apache to process all matching files with the specified handler. For image maps, you can specify that matching files be processed with Apache's `server-parsed` handler. For example, the block

```
<Directory "/home/webmastr/pub/html/maps">
    SetHandler imap-file
</Directory>
```

would treat every file residing in the `/maps` subdirectory as an image map file. Image map processing does not require any special permissions to the `Options` directive (as do CGI and SSI).

URLs and URL Keywords

Each mapped region of an image refers to a Web page. The URL specifying the associated Web page may be any valid URL, even non-HTTP protocols (e.g. `ftp://administeringapache.com` may be used and `mailto:` may be used). The specified URL may be absolute or it may be relative to a base URL. This base URL is specified by the `ImapBase` configuration directive (see below), which may be overridden by a `base` directive within a map file. The `..` notation may also be used in a URL to represent the parent of the base URL.

Alternately, the specified URL may be one of several keywords recognized by the `imapfile` handler, as follows:

- `map`—Stands for the URL of the map file itself with no image coordinates. When Apache encounters this keyword, it behaves as if the browser requested the map file with an unmapped region. Apache will then respond with either a `204 No Content` error or with a generated menu (see the `ImapMenu` configuration directive described below).
- `menu`—Same as map
- `referer`—Stands for the referring document (i.e. the HTML document containing the `<A HREF=>` link to the server-sided image map file). If the browser requests the image map file directly (that is, if the browser does not send a `Referer:` header), then Apache replaces the referer URL keyword with the `DocumentRoot` directory (e.g. `http://administeringapache/`).

- nocontent—Instructs Apache to generate a 204 No Content error.
- error—Instructs Apache to generate a 500 Server error.

Configuring Server-Sided Image Map Processing

The following Apache configuration directives control the behavior of image map processing.

ImapMenu

Specifies the action to take when the user clicks on an unmapped region of the image. If the region clicked by the user does not have a Web page associated with it, Apache can generate a hypertext menu from the regions that are mapped. For example, the directive

```
ImapMenu formatted
```

instructs Apache to generate such a hypertext menu automatically. The ImapMenu directive accepts any one of the following parameters:

- none—Specifies that no menu is to be generated. The server returns a 204 No Content error and the browser continues to display the referring page.
- formatted—Specifies that Apache is to generate and format a menu automatically. Apache creates the simplest menu. It contains the <HTML>, <HEAD>, <TITLE>, and <BODY> tags; an <H1> header with the map file's name; an <HR> hard rule; and a hypertext link for each region defined in the map file. The hypertext links in the menu are <A HREF=> tags surrounded by <PRE>-formatting tags, and are formatted into a column using spaces.
- semiformatted—Specifies that Apache is to generate a menu with the same hypertext links as is done with the formatted argument; but, the <H1> header and the <HR> hard rule are left out. Instead, any comments you've written into the map file appear as text in the menu (without the pound sign comment character). The generated links are still <PRE>-formatted, but your comment text is not. You may write HTML tags into your comments for formatting. Apache places your comment text and the menu links within its prefabricated <BODY>. You cannot output your own <HTML>, <HEAD>, or <TITLE> tags.
- unformatted—Specifies that Apache is to generate a menu with hypertext links, but with no <PRE>-formatting. This gives you more control over the body of the menu. The comments within the map file

must contain HTML formatting tags, or the text and links will be run together when rendered by the browser. Apache still provides the `<HTML>`, `<HEAD>`, and `<TITLE>` tags, over which you have no control.

The `ImapMenu` directive may be global in scope (outside any block directive) or may be localized within a `<VirtualHost>` block, a `<Directory>` block, or within a directory access file (e.g. `.htaccess`).

ImapDefault

This specifies a default action to be taken when the end-user clicks on an unmapped region of the image. For example

```
ImapDefault nocontent
```

instructs Apache to deliver a `204 No Content` error under such circumstances (in which case, the browser should continue displaying the referring page). Any URL or any of the keywords described in "URLs and URL Keywords" (above) may be used as an argument to the `ImapDefault` directive.

The `ImapDefault` directive may be global in scope (outside any block directive) or may be localized within a `<VirtualHost>` block, a `<Directory>` block, or within a directory access file (e.g. `.htaccess`). The default action specified by the `ImapDefault` directive may be overridden within a map file using the `default` map file directive (see "Writing a Server-Sided Image Map" below).

ImapBase

This specifies the base URL to which non-absolute image map URLs are relative. The example

```
ImapBase http://administeringapache/personnel/
```

sets the base URL to the `personnel/` subdirectory under the `DocumentRoot` directory. The following relative URL in the image map file:

```
jdoe.html
```

would then resolve to

```
http://administeringapache/personnel/jdoe.html
```

The base may be specified by a URL or by either the `map` keyword or the `referer` keyword (see "URLs and URL Keywords" above).

Lacking an `ImapBase` directive, Apache resolves non-absolute image map URLs to the directory in which the image map file resides. If you keep your map files in a different directory from your HTML files, then you need an `ImapBase` directive to correctly resolve relative URLs.

The `ImapBase` directive may be global in scope (outside of any block directive) or may be localized within a `<VirtualHost>` block, a `<Directory>` block, or within a directory access file (e.g. .htaccess). It makes sense to localize the `ImapBase` directive. A Web site organized by topic would not want to impose a site-wide URL base. The URL base specified by the `ImapBase` directive may be overridden within a map file using the `base` map file directive (see "Writing a Server-Sided Image Map" below).

Writing a Server-Sided Image Map

An image map file contains geometric directives that divide the image into shapes (`circle`, `point`, `poly`, or `rect`) and associate an URL with each defined shape. Each geometric directive receives, as its first parameter, the associated URL—which may be specified by an actual URL or by any one of the URL keywords described in the subsection "URLs and URL Keywords" above. After the URL, you define the size and location of the shape with a list of X,Y pixel coordinate pairs (0,0 is at the top left of the image). How may of these pairs you specify depends upon which shape you are defining. After the coordinate pairs, you may opt to add double quoted menu text describing the associated URL. Apache will use this text if allowed to generate a menu when the user clicks on an unmapped region of the image. The allowable shapes are:

circle

This defines a circular region by specifying its center point and one point on the circle's edge. The example

```
circle jdoe.html 49,49 49,19 "John Doe's Bio"
```

defines a circle at the top left of the image. The circle is centered on the coordinates 49,49. The point at 49,19 is on the top edge of the circle, thus giving the circle a radius of 20 pixels. The jdoe.html URL will be selected when the end user clicks anywhere on the circle. You might use a circle around John's face in a group picture.

point

This defines a single point on the image by specifying the coordinates of the point. The point shape is peculiar in that the end-user need only click on it or near to it. When the end-user clicks on an unmapped region of the image, the nearest `point` is selected. If a point is defined anywhere on the image, then all mouse clicks will resolve to a URL. There can be no default action. Note that this effectively disables automatic menu generation (although you can explicitly define a region to generate a menu).

Note also that a point is selected only if no other shape contains the coordinates of the mouse click. Apache tests all non-point shapes for a match before testing the defined points. Thus a point residing on top of another shape will never be selected.

If the regions you wish to define are evenly distributed, then all you need do is define a single point in the middle of each region. If the regions are a little less than evenly distributed, you may define multiple points within each region. The `point` directive will accept a list of points to be associated with the specified URL. The example

```
point mailto:jdoe@administeringapache.com 10,85 40,85 "John Doe's
Email"
```

associates two points with John's e-mail address. You might use this example `point` directive to put a couple of points on a mailbox pictured below John in a group photo.

poly

This defines a polygon by specifying its vertices. Polygons describe irregular shapes. The example

```
poly rbrown.html 129,19 149,35 149,69 99,69 99,35 "Robert (Bobby)
Brown's Bio"
```

defines a pentagon you might use to surround Bobby sitting at his desk.

rect

This defines a rectangle by specifying two of its opposing corners. The example

```
rect map 0,130 199,160 "Personnel Menu"
```

uses the `map` keyword to generate a map file menu when the end-user clicks on the rectangle. You might define such a rectangle across the bottom of an image (where you have overlaid some appropriate text) so that end-users can fetch a map menu, even if a `point` has been defined somewhere in the map file.

The `imapfile` handler recognizes two additional non-geometric map file directives (`base` and `default`) that control map file processing:

- `base`—Sets the root URL to which all non-absolute URLs are relative. This map file directive has the same syntax as the `ImapBase` configuration directive (described above) and will locally override the `ImapBase` directive.
- `default`—Specifies the default action to take when the user clicks on an unmapped region of the image. This map file directive uses the same syntax as the `ImapDefault` configuration directive (described above) and will locally override the `ImapDefault` directive. Note that the default directive will never be selected if the map file contains any `point` directive.

Comments may be added to the map file with a pound sign. If the `ImapMenu` configuration directive specifies `semiformatted` or `unformatted`, then Apache will use your comments when generating a map file menu. You may use HTML tags within your comments for formatting.

The following example map file maps a group photo. The image pictures the personnel of a mythic company. The image map associates each person in the photo with an HTML document containing that person's bio. A mailbox is pictured below each person and each person's mailbox links to that person's e-mail address. A `default` action generates a `map` file menu when the end-user clicks on an unmapped region of the image. For this reason, no `point` directives are used in the map file. For this example, the `ImapMenu` configuration directive has been set to `unformatted` and the comments in the map file define the appearance of the generated menu. The `base` map directive resolves all non-absolute URLs relative to the `personnel/` subdirectory. on the `http://administeringapache.com` server.

```
base http://administeringapache.com/personnel/
#<IMG SRC=/images/logo.gif ALIGN="left">
#<H1> <I>Personnel</I></H1>
#<HR>
#<P>
circle jdoe.html 49,49 49,19 "John Doe's Bio"
#<P>
rect mailto:jdoe@administeringapache.com 0,70 69,99 "John Doe's
Email"
```

```
#<P>
poly rbrown.html 129,19 149,35 149,69 99,69 99,35 "Robert (Bobby)
Brown's Bio"
#<P>
rect mailto:rbrown@administeringapache.com 129,70 149,99 "Robert
(Bobby) Brown's Email"
#<P>
default map "Personnel Menu"
#<P>
```

Map File Caveats

Apache processes map file directives in order. You should, therefore, place your `base` directive early in the map file, above any directives containing relative URLs that rely upon that defined `base`. Order of processing becomes important if you define overlapping shapes—in which case, Apache selects the region first listed in the map file. This is true for all shapes except the `point`. Apache will select a `point` only if the clicked coordinates do not fall within any other shape. If the image is rendered with a border, beware that the browser will offset the mouse click by the width of the border. If you must be that precise (e.g. a "find the secret" image map), then you might want to add the `BORDER=0` attribute to the image's `<IMG>` tag.

CHAPTER **5**

Using Logs

Logging errors and file transfers helps you to:

- Maintain the server
- Debug content
- Improve site ergonomics
- See who is visiting your site
- Improve the effectiveness of your advertising
- Pay other sites on which you advertise,

among other things. You can use Apache's standard log files or create your own. You can log everything or just transfers of interest. Apache's logging facilities are very adaptive, but be careful. The more you log, the more overhead you create for the server.

Logging Errors

Apache's error log helps you maintain your server and your Web site. The error log records both server errors (file open errors, process errors, and the like) and content errors (CGI script errors, file not found errors, and etc.). Thus the error log is useful to both the system administrator and the webmaster.

In each line of the error log text file, Apache records the date, the priority of the error, the IP address of the browser making the request that caused the error, and text describing the error. All fields except the descriptive text are enclosed in square brackets. The following line, taken from an Apache error log, illustrates this format:

```
[Sun Oct 31 05:56:36 1999] [error] [client 192.168.1.7] unable to
include "inc/header.inc" in parsed file
/home/webmastr/pub/html/index.shtml
```

In the Apache configuration file (e.g. /usr/local/apache/conf/httpd.conf), you specify where the error log resides and the verbosity of error logging. Open the configuration file with an ASCII text editor and modify the directives noted below.

LogLevel

This controls the verbosity of Apache's error log file. Each message written to the log file has a priority. With the LogLevel directive, you specify the priority at which logging begins. All messages of greater or equal priority will be logged. The specified priority may be one of the following (from highest to lowest)

- emerg—The error has completely crippled the Apache server. When such an error occurs, it is usually present at server startup, though it sometimes presents itself during the startup of a child server launched to handle requests.
- alert—The main Apache server survives, but a child server died from a condition that requires immediate attention.
- crit—Apache can usually recover from the error (though sometimes not), but an important subsystem has been compromised and particular browser requests are not being satisfied.
- error—An error has occurred in the content or in a request. This level of error is most useful in debugging content, such as invalid links to local URLs or CGI scripts that do not properly generate HTTP response headers.
- warn—Apache has fully recovered from the error and the content was delivered; but you should find some time to remedy the source of the problem (by doing, for instance, a server recompile or a configuration change).
- notice—Apache has encountered a minor problem, such as a configuration directive value that was ignored. Some non-error conditions are logged with this priority. These mark important moments in the life of the server, such as server startup or server shutdown.
- info—These messages mark minor events; such as when a child process is launched or terminated, or when a browser disconnects before receiving all the requested content. It is with a message of the info priority that Apache will tell you that all the child processes are busy and that the server may become overloaded.
- debug—These messages detail of the workings of the server, such as file openings and closings, socket management, and signal passing. You can increase the volume of these messages even further by defining the DEBUG macro while compiling the server. If you use the APACI utility to compile the server, then enter the following at the shell prompt

```
CFLAGS=-DDEBUG
```

before running APACI's configure command. If you are compiling the server manually, you can add -DDEBUG to the EXTRA_CFLAGS= setting in the src/Configure script. (See the section "Downloading and Compiling the Source Code" in Chapter 2: "Creating the Web

Server.") If you are debugging at the source code level, then you will find other macros therein that may be similarly defined for debugging specific subsystems (`DEBUG_CFG_LINES`, `IPHASH_STATISTICS`, and the like).

Lowering the `LogLevel` setting increases the verbosity of the error log. A system administrator should be interested in messages of `crit` or higher. You might set the level down to `error`, if the content author is interested in reading the error log. Allowing the lowest-priority messages may incur a hit on server performance, but may be useful in tracking an elusive problem.

ErrorLog

This specifies where Apache is to record errors. The `ErrorLog` directive accepts one parameter that may be a file system path and file name, or the keyword `syslog`, or a piped command.

Sending Errors to a File

A specified file system path may be absolute (i.e. begins with a slash) or relative (i.e. does not being with a slash). If a relative path is specified, that path is relative to the Apache installation directory (specified by the `ServerRoot` directive—e.g. `/usr/local/apache`). The following example

```
ErrorLog /usr/local/apache/logs/error_log
```

uses an absolute path to instruct Apache to write errors to the text file named `error_log` in the `logs/` subdirectory under Apache's installation directory.

Sending Errors to Syslog

Passing the keyword `syslog` to the `ErrorLog` directive instructs Apache to send error messages to the UNIX `syslogd` daemon which centralizes logging for UNIX applications. The `syslogd` daemon categorizes applications into groups called *facilities*. When an application sends a message to `syslogd`, the application specifies the facility in which the error message should be logged. For example, all mail programs (mail, SMTPD, sendmail) would log errors under the mail facility. An application submitting a log message to `syslogd` specifies the priority of the message—informational messages having the lowest priority and emergency error messages having the highest. The `syslogd` configuration file (e.g. `/etc/syslog.conf`) prescribes where to log messages of a specified priority for a specified facility. The default is for Apache to submit messages to the `local7` facility. You can specify a different facility in the `ErrorLog` directive by adding a colon plus a facility name to the `syslog` keyword parameter. The following Apache configuration directive

```
ErrorLog syslog:local3
```

instructs Apache to log errors to syslog's `local3` facility. Note that, given the above example, the webmaster will see messages from other (non-Apache) applications if other applications submit messages to the `local3` facility.

The system administrator would be interested in server errors; whereas the webmaster would interested in debugging content. You might configure syslog to log all errors to a file in the webmaster's home directory; but log only critical errors to a system log file. Adding the following lines to the syslog configuration file will do just that:

```
*.info;mail.none;authpriv.none;local3.none   /var/log/messageslocal3.crit   /var/log/local3
local3.*   /home/webmastr/site-error_log   #*.*   /dev/tty8
```

The above example uses Linux extensions to the syslog configuration file syntax. Consult your system's man pages for the syntax appropriate for your version of syslog. In the above example, the first line instructs syslog to log all messages with a priority of `info` or greater to the `/var/log/messages` system message file—except for messages submitted to the `mail` facility, the `authentication` facility, and the `local3` facility. The second line causes syslog to log `local3` messages with a priority of `critical` or greater to the file `/var/log/local3` (for the system administrator). The third line logs all `local3` facility messages to the `site-error_log` file in the webmaster's home directory. The last line in the above example sends *all* messages to the `tty8` terminal (console screen F8)—which is handy for debugging your `syslog` configuration. That last line has been commented out with a pound sign. To enable that line, remove the pound sign and restart the syslogd daemon.

When you make a change to the `syslog` configuration file, you must restart the `syslog` daemon for the changes to take effect (just like restarting Apache after modifying Apache's configuration file). To restart the `syslogd` daemon on a Linux system, enter the following at the shell prompt:

```
/etc/rc.d/init.sd/syslog restart
```

Also beware that, if your `syslogd` daemon doesn't flush its buffers or if your file system performs write-back caching, then you may need to produce several errors while testing before you will see your new error messages show up in the log file.

Sending Errors to a Piped Command

Apache can pipe error messages to the standard input of a script or program binary. You might want to send error messages to a program that would store the messages into a database from which you could generate a variety of reports. To do this, follow the `ErrorLog` directive with a pipe character and the desired command. The following example pipes error messages to an example script named `errordb` that I added to the `bin/` subdirectory of the Apache installation directory:

```
ErrorLog "|/usr/local/apache/bin/errordb insert"
```

The `ErrorLog` directive accepts only one parameter. Do not put a space between the pipe character and the command. If you need to pass any command-line parameters to the command, enclose the whole thing in double quotes (as in the above example). Note that the path to the piped command is absolute. My example `errordb` script is a korn shell script that inserts the message into a `postgres` database table named `siteerr`. The script reads

```
#!/bin/ksh

#
# Get the action from the first command line parameter
#
action="$1"

#
# If the action is to insert a new record...
#
if [ "x_$action" = x_insert ]; then

    #
    # read the error message from standard input
```

```
#
read buf

#
# Convert the message into a tab delimited variable
#
buf=`echo "$buf" | sed 's/\] \[/    /g'`
buf=`echo "$buf" | sed 's/^\[//g'`
buf=`echo "$buf" | sed 's/\] /   /g'`

#
# extract fields from the message
#
indate=`echo "$buf" | cut -f 1`
prior=`echo "$buf" | cut -f 2`
client=`echo "$buf" | cut -f 3 | sed 's/client //g'`
msg=`echo "$buf" | cut -f 4`

#
# scan out the date field components
#
mo=`echo "$indate" | cut -d ' ' -f 2`
day=`echo "$indate" | cut -d ' ' -f 3`
tm=`echo "$indate" | cut -d ' ' -f 4`
yr=`echo "$indate" | cut -d ' ' -f 5`

#
# get the timezone with the date command
#
tz=`date '+%Z'`

#
# arrange the date components into a postgres
# datetime field
#
outdate=`echo "$yr-$mo-$day $tm $tz"`

#
# insert a new record into the siteerr table
#
psql -d siteerr -c "insert into siteerr \
    (errtime, priority, client, msg) \
    values \
    ('$outdate', '$prior', '$client', '$msg');"

fi   ###
# end if action is insert
#
```

Both the `ErrorLog` and `LogLevel` directives may be global in scope (outside any block directive) or they may be localized within a `<VirtualHost>` block directive. This way, each virtual host may have its own error log. If these directives appear in a `<VirtualHost>` block directive, then they override those directives in the global scope. If a `<VirtualHost>` block does not contain these directives, then those in the global scope will apply.

`ErrorLog` and `LogLevel` are both core Apache features—not supplied by any module.

Logging Document Transfers

Logging document transfers will tell you the who, what, when, and where of your server's interaction with the planet. (The how might be gotten by the Agent Log and the Referer Log, described later.) The system administrator might be interested in when the server experiences peaks in requests. The webmaster might be interested in what pages are most popular and who is requesting them.

In each line of the transfer log text file, Apache records the requesting host, the requesting user's identification, the requesting user's authenticated name, the time of the request, the first line of the request, the status of the response to the request, and the number of bytes transferred. If information is not available for a given field a hyphen is inserted in place of that field. This format conforms to the Common Log Format convention proposed by CERN (point your browser to **http://www.cern.ch/ WebOffice/Services/WWWlogfiles/Common LogFormat.html**). Several third-party tools are available for reading and reporting on files following CLF specification. The following line from an Apache transfer log illustrates this format:

```
192.168.1.7 - - [17/Nov/1999:10:19:12 -0600] "GET
/manual/mod/mod_log_config.html HTTP/1.0" 200 15924
```

The `TransferLog` Apache configuration directive (discussed below) and the `LogFormat` directive (discussed in the next section) oversee Apache's logging of document transfers:

TransferLog

This specifies where Apache is to log document transfers. The `TransferLog` directive accepts one parameter that may be either a file system path or a piped command.

Logging Transfers to a File

A specified file system path may be an absolute (i.e. begin with a slash) or a relative path (i.e. not being with a slash). If a relative path is specified, that path is relative to the Apache installation directory (specified by the `ServerRoot` directive—e.g. `/usr/local/apache`). The following example

```
TransferLog /usr/local/apache/logs/access_log
```

uses an absolute path to instruct Apache to log document transfers to the text file named `access_log` in the `logs/` subdirectory under Apache's installation directory.

Logging Transfers to a Piped Command

Apache can pipe log messages to the standard input of a script or program binary. You might want to send transfer log messages to special program to collect the log data. To do this, follow the `TransferLog` directive with a pipe character and the desired command. The following example pipes transfer log messages to an mythic script named `accessdb`:

```
TransferLog "|/usr/local/apache/bin/accessdb insert"
```

The `TransferLog` directive accepts only one parameter. Do not put a space between the pipe character and the command. If you need to pass any command-line parameters to the command, enclose the whole thing in double quotes (as in the above example). Note that the path to the command is absolute.

`TransferLog` (unlike `ErrorLog`) will receive a log message for every request. To reduce latency, you might not want to pipe transfer log messages to an external program. If you log transfers to a file instead, a third-party CLF reporting utility can process the file nightly—during non-peak hours.

The `TransferLog` directive may be global in scope (outside any block directive) or it may be localized within a `<VirtualHost>` block directive. This way, each virtual host may have its own transfer log. A `TransferLog` directive within a `<VirtualHost>` block overrides any `TransferLog` defined in the global scope.

The `mod_log_config` module, a default module, provides the `TransferLog` directive.

Creating Custom Logs

If the Common Log Format does not present the information you require, you may change the TransferLog format or create additional logs of your own design. This section describes the tools you need. Subsequent sections use these tools to create various kinds of logs.

You can define the format of a log with the LogFormat configuration directive. You can then apply that format to the TransferLog or to a log you create with the CustomLog directive. The CustomLog directive has the added feature of conditional logging, so that you can log only the information in which you are interested. A conditional CustomLog directive tests environment variables defined by the SetEnvIf directive. The SetEnvIf directive defines an environment variable based on values from the request headers and response headers of the current transfer.

Some of the logs discussed in following sections require the identification of individual browsers. You can't just use the browser's hostname or IP address for this, since these are dynamically assigned (for most people) by their internet service provider. The mod_usertrack module (*not* a default module) provides directives for tagging browsers with cookies: CookieTracking, CookieName, and CookieExpires.

LogFormat

This creates a log format specification. The LogFormat directive accepts one or two parameters. The first parameter specifies what is to be written to a log (i.e. the format of the log). The optional second parameter associates a name with that format. If the second parameter is omitted, then the format will be applied to the next encountered TransferLog directive. If the second parameter is given, then the LogFormat directive will associate the name with the format, but will not apply the format to any log. You can then use the name to specify a format to the CustomLog directive (discussed below).

Format Strings

The first parameter is a double-quoted string containing the text that should be written to a log. This string may contain substitutions (a character preceded by a percent sign) which will be replaced with data from the transfer. To write a literal double-quote character to the log, precede it with a backslash. The following example

```
LogFormat "%a requested \"%r\" from %v"
```

passes only one parameter to the `LogFormat` directive. It therefore defines what is to be written to the file named by the next `TransferLog` directive. Each line in that `TransferLog` will then display the browser's IP address (`%a`), the request line (`%r`), and the server name (`%v`)—which would look like:

```
192.168.1.7 requested "GET / HTTP/1.0" from administeringapache.com
```

The format string may contain any of these replacements :

- `%a`—the IP address of the browser making the request.
- `%A`—the IP address of the server.
- `%b`—the number of bytes sent in the response to the request, excluding HTTP headers.
- `%{environ}e`—the value of the environment variable named by *environ*. For example, `%{PATH}e` would be replaced by the value of the `PATH` environment variable of the server process.
- `%f`—the file system path to the requested document. This is the requested virtual URL translated to the file system through any applicable alias, such as `DocumentRoot` or `ScriptAlias`.
- `%h`—the hostname of the browser making the request. That hostname will be available only if the `HostNameLookups` directive has enabled reverse DNS lookups (for which you will pay a price in performance). If the hostname is not available, the `%h` metacharacter will be replaced by the IP address of the requesting browser.
- `%{reqheader}i`—the value of the request header named by *reqheader*. For instance, `%{Accept}i` would be replaced by the value of the `Accept:` request header.
- `%l`—the system-dependent identification of the user making the request. This value is available only if the `IdentityCheck` directive is set to `On` and Apache successfully negotiates the value with the browser (using the RFC 931 ident protocol).
- `%{modnote}n`—the value of the note named by *modnote*. An Apache module, when it processes a request, may create a named note and attach that note to the request. For example, the `mod_usertrack` module uses a cookie to assign a session ID to the browser, so that it can track the user's activity on the web site. To each request within the session, `mod_usertrack` attaches a note named `cookie` containing the value of the session ID. You may write this session ID to the log using `%{cookie}n`.
- `%p`—the TCP/IP port on which the server received the request.

- %P—the process ID of the child server that serviced the request.
- %r—the first line of request. This includes the method, the URL, any extra path information, the query string, and the protocol.
- %s—the original response status (before any internal redirection has been performed).
- %>s—the response status returned to the browser (after any internal redirection has been performed).
- %t—the date and time that the request was made. The time is formatted according to CERN's Common Log Format and looks like this

  ```
  [18/Nov/1999:13:02:58 -0600]
  ```

  (see **http://www.cern.ch/WebOffice/Services/WWWlogfiles/ CommonLogFormat.html**).
- %{*timefmt*}t—the date and time that the request was made, formatted according to the specified *timefmt* string, which is passed directly to the strftime() standard C library function. The date-component references accepted by strftime() are:

%A the name of the weekday (e.g. Friday)

%a the abbreviated name of the weekday (e.g. Fri)

%B the name of the month (e.g. October)

%b the abbreviated name of the month (e.g. Oct)

%c the date and time representation as specified for the current locale (e.g. Sunday, 31-Oct-1999 14:18:31 CST)

%d the numeric day of the month (e.g. 31)

%H the numeric hour in 24-hour format (e.g. 14)

%I the numeric hour in 12-hour format (e.g. 2)

%j the Julian day count (e.g. 364)

%M the numeric minute (e.g. 47)

%m the numeric month (e.g. 10)

%p the 12-hour morning/evening specifier (e.g. am)

%S the numeric second (e.g. 47)

%U the numeric week number (e.g. 51). The first Sunday of the year marks the beginning of the first week of the year.

%W the numeric week number (e.g. 51). The first Monday of the year marks the beginning of the first week of the year.

%w the numeric day of the week (e.g. 5). Sunday is day 0.

%X time representation as specified for the current locale (e.g. 14:18:31 CST)

%x the date representation as specified for the current locale (e.g. Sunday, 31-Oct-1999)

%y the numeric year without the century (e.g. 99)
%Y the numeric year including the century (e.g. 1999)
%Z the time zone abbreviation (e.g. CST)
%z the time zone number (e.g. -600)
%% a percent character (percent quotes a percent)

Leaving out the {*timefmt*} string (i.e. using just %t) is equivalent to

```
%{[%d/%b/%Y:%H:%M:%S %z]}t
```

which outputs a date that is compliant with the Common Log Format.

- %T—the number of seconds required to service the request.
- %u—the login name of the user making the request. The value is taken from the Authorization: request header. If the response status is 401 Unauthorized, then the login name has not been authenticated.
- %U—The requested URL. This includes the URL path and any extra path information. For example, given the request

```
GET /cgibin/listmaint.ksh/adminapache.list?action=
insert&verity=Y HTTP/1.1
```

the log will display

```
/cgibin/listmaint.ksh/adminapache.list
```

- %v—the name of the server. This is the name specified by the Server-Name directive (see the section "Configuring the Installed Server" in Chapter 2: "Creating the Web Server").
- %V—the name of the server according to the UseCanonicalName directive. If UseCanonicalName is set to Off, then the %V is replaced by the server name requested by the browser's Host: request header. If UseCanonicalName is set to On, then %V will be replaced by the canonical name of the server specified by the ServerName directive.

The Common Log Format (the default TransferLog format) is equivalent to

```
LogFormat "%h %l %u %t \"%r\" %>s %b"
```

Each replacement value can be printed conditionally by placing a list of status codes between the percent sign and the character. If the response status is among those in the condition list, then the value is written to the log; otherwise, a hyphen is written to the log (as if the value were empty).

For example, to log all users that failed authentication, use the following conditional format:

```
LogFormat "%401u"
```

With the above example, the user name is displayed only if the response status is 401 Unauthorized. Any other response status will cause a hyphen to be written to the log.

You can negate the condition list by preceding it with an exclamation mark; in this case, the value will be written to the log only if the response status is *not* in the condition list. For example, you can discover bad links by logging the Referer: request header when the response status does not indicate success:

```
LogFormat "%!200,302,304,307{Referer}i"
```

Format Names

The optional second parameter to the LogFormat directive assigns a name to the format string. That name can then be used in a CustomLog directive (discussed below). When such a format name is specified, all that the LogFormat directive will do is associate the name with the format. It will not assign the format to any log. Apache's configuration file ships with these named log formats:

```
LogFormat "%h %l %u %t \"%r\" %>s %b \"%{Referer}i\"
\"%{Useragent}i\"" combined
LogFormat "%h %l %u %t \"%r\" %>s %b" common
LogFormat "%{Referer}i -> %U" referer
LogFormat "%{User-agent}i" agent
```

Apache's default configuration file does not use the TransferLog directive. Instead, it creates a common log format (the second line in the above listing) and uses it to create an equivalent custom log.

CustomLog

This creates a log file. The CustomLog directive requires two parameters: the log's location and the log's format. The directive accepts an optional third parameter: a condition that must be met to log a transfer. The location can be a file system path (a text file is written) or a piped command (the error message is sent to the command's standard input). The log format may be specified as a double quoted string or by a format name previously defined with a `LogFormat` directive. For example, Apache's default configuration file creates the equivalent of a `TransferLog` log with this `CustomLog` directive:

```
CustomLog /usr/local/apache/logs/access_log common
```

The above example creates the text file name `access_log` in which transfers will be logged using the `common` format.

The first parameter, the location parameter, follows the same rules as the `TransferLog`'s single parameter. That is, if a file system path is specified, that path may be absolute or it may be relative to the Apache installation directory (named by the `ServerRoot` directive). If a piped command is specified, then it must be surrounded by double quotes if it contains any spaces. The following example

```
CustomLog "|/usr/local/apache/bin/refererdb insert" "%{%Y-%b-%d
%H:%M:%S %Z}t|%{Referer}i|%r"
```

could be used to log referring pages into a database. The first `CustomLog` parameter pipes the error message to an example korn shell script named `refererdb`, passing the word `insert` as an argument to the script. Note that the path to the command is absolute. The second parameter to `CustomLog` formats the error message for consumption by the script. The log message consists of three pipe-delimited fields: the time, the URL of the referring page, and the request. Observe how the example log format string outputs the time in a format acceptable to a postgres datetime field.

A `CustomLog` will log *every* transfer. This could affect server performance, especially if the invoked command has a lot of work to do. You can reduce the number of log entries by logging only selected transfers. The `CustomLog` directive accepts an optional third parameter in which you specify an environment variable that, if defined, causes the transfer to be logged. If it is not defined, then the transfer is not logged. The following example creates a log format named `fmtRefer` and then uses it to create the same `CustomLog` as in the previous example,

```
LogFormat "%{%Y-%b-%d %H:%M:%S %Z}t|%{Referer}i|%r" fmtRefer
CustomLog "|/usr/local/apache/bin/refererdb insert" fmtRefer
env=logrefer
```

the difference being that an entry will be sent to the `refererdb` script only if the environment variable named `logrefer` has been defined. You could invert this logic with an exclamation point. This example

```
CustomLog logs/referer.log fmtRefer env=!suppressrefer
```

would log the transfer only if the environment variable named suppessrefer is *not* defined.

By now you're asking, "How do these environment variables get defined?"

SetEnvIf

This defines an environment variable if a specified condition is true. The SetEnvIf directive accepts at least three parameters: an attribute of the current transfer, a regular expression, and an environment variable name. If the attribute matches the regular expression, then the environment variable is defined. If the attribute does not match the regular expression, then the environment variable is left alone. That is, if the attribute does not match and the specified variable was not defined before the SetEnvIf, then it won't be defined after. If there is no match and the specified variable was defined before the SetEnvIf, then the environment variable retains its previous value. This example

```
SetEnvIf Request_URI ".*referred\.html.*" logrefer
```

examines the requested URI (Request_URI) to see if it any part of it contains the string referred.html. If it does, then the logrefer environment variable becomes defined.

The attribute to be examined (SetEnvIf's first parameter) may be any one of the following keywords recognized by the SetEnvIf directive

- Remote_Addr—the IP address of the browser making the request. This is the same value as the %a replacement in the LogFormat directive.
- Remote_Host—the hostname of the browser making the request. If the HostNameLookups directive is Off or if a reverse lookup using the browser's IP address fails, then the Remote_Host value will be empty. This is the same value as the %h replacement in the LogFormat directive.
- Remote_User—the login name of the user making the request. The value is taken from the Authorization: request header. If the response status is 401 Unauthorized, then the Remote_User has not been authenticated. This is the same value as the %u replacement in the LogFormat directive.
- Request_Method—the HTTP method used in the request (e.g. GET).
- Request_Protocol—the name and version of the protocol by which the request was made (e.g. HTTP/1.1).

- `Request_URI`—The requested URL. This includes the URL path and any extra path information (e.g. `/cgibin/listmaint.ksh/adminapache.list`). This is the same value as the %U replacement in the LogFormat directive.

The attribute may also be any request header sent by the browser. In Chapter 4: "Manipulating Content," the subsection "Using Apache's CGI Environment" shows Figure 4.5, which illustrates many of the request headers that may be sent by the browser. For a full list, refer to the HTTP/1.1 protocol defined by RFC 2616 (**ftp://ftp.isi.edu/in-notes/rfc2616.txt**). The following example

```
SetEnvIf Referer ".*//administeringapache\.com/.*" suppressrefer
```

examines the `Referer:` request header. If it contains the string `//administeringapache.com/`, then the `suppressrefer` environment variable becomes defined. A `CustomLog` directive could then test for `!suppressrefer` before logging the current transfer—to filter out local links. Note that the request header name does not terminate with a colon in the `SetEnvIf` directive.

The regular expression (`SetEnvIf`'s second parameter) is a search pattern applied to the attribute (`SetEnvIf`'s first parameter). The section "Regular Expressions" in the Appendix explains in detail how to build regular expressions. You might also read the `man 7 regex` page on your UNIX system. To explain the regular expressions used in the two `SetEnvIf` examples (above): a period, in a regular expression, means "any character." To refer to a literal period, you must quote the period with a backslash. An asterisk means "zero or more." Thus ".*referred\.html.*" means "any character any number of times followed by the literal string `referred.html` followed by any character any number of times." To paraphrase, this regular expression matches if the string `referred.html` appears anywhere within the attribute.

The specified environment variable (`SetEnvIf`'s third parameter) is defined and given a value of 1, if the attribute matches the regular expression. You may set the environment variable to some other value by following the variable with an equal sign and your desired value. Also, `SetEnvIf` can define more than one environment variable. Just add them as the fourth and subsequent parameters. The following example illustrates both of these features:

```
SetEnvIf Request_URI ".*jpg$" isimage doctype=jpeg
```

The above example sets the environment variable named isimage to 1 and sets the environment variable named doctype to jpeg, if the requested URL ends with jpg (a dollar sign means "end of line" in regular expressions).

Note that the environment variables defined by the SetEnvIf directive become available to CGI scripts and to server-side parsed documents. They are *not*, however, made available to piped log commands.

The SetEnvIf directive may be global in scope (i.e. outside any block directive); in which case the attribute is tested on every request. The SetEnvIf directive may be localized within a <VirtualHost> block directive; in which case the attribute is tested only on requests for documents belonging to the specified virtual host.

The mod_log_config module, a default module, provides the LogFormat and the CustomLog directives. The mod_setenvif module, also a default module, provides the SetEnvIf directive.

CookieTracking

This enables the tagging of browsers with cookies by the mod_usertrack module. This directive accepts one parameter that may be either on or off. Since mod_usertrack is not a default module, it is a good idea to embed the CookieTracking directive within an <IfModule> block directive so that the CookieTracking directive will be ignored if mod_usertrack has not been compiled into the server. For example:

```
<IfModule mod_usertrack.c>
    CookieTracking on
</IfModule>
```

CookieName

This specifies the name of the cookie used to tag browsers by the mod_usertrack module. By default, mod_usertrack's cookie is named Apache. You might be surprised at the number of Apache cookies in your browser's cookie file. The following example instructs Apache to use a different name, browsertag, instead:

```
<IfModule mod_usertrack.c>
    CookieName browsertag
</IfModule>
```

CookieExpires

This sets the time to live for the cookies used to tag browsers by the mod_usertrack module. By default mod_usertrack cookies expire at the end of the browser session (when the user closes the browser). The CookieExpires directive allows you to set the number of seconds between the time the cookie set and the time that the cookie expires. The following example

```
<IfModule mod_usertrack.c>
    CookieExpires 600
</IfModule>
```

instructs mod_usertrack to issue cookies that expire in ten minutes. To track a browser's activity for longer periods, CookieExpires accepts an alternate syntax in which you specify the unit of time for the expiry period. To track each browser's activity over the course of a month, you could use this setting:

```
CookieExpires "1 month"
```

CookieExpires accepts only one parameter, so you must surround the alternate syntax with double quotes (as in the above example). Acceptable units are: years, months, weeks, hours, minutes, and seconds. These units may be combined, as in

```
CookieExpires "3 weeks 2 days 4 hours 22 seconds"
```

All the Cookie??? directives may be global in scope (outside any block directive); in which case browser requests for the entire Web site are tracked. All these directives may be localized within a <VirtualHost> block directive to configure user tracking for each virtual host. The CookieTracking and the CookieName directives can be further localized with a <Directory> block directive and within directory access files (e.g. .htaccess), so that user tracking can be enabled per directory; and so that different directories can use different cookie names. Before these directives can appear within a directory access file, though, the Apache configuration must grant permission to do so. Such permission is granted by adding this directive

```
AllowOverride FileInfo
```

to the appropriate <Directory> block.

AllowOverride

This grants permission to directory access files (e.g. .htaccess) to override particular <Directory> block settings. AllowOverride accepts one parameter that may be one of:

- All—allows directory access files to override all of the following settings
- AuthConfig—allows directory access files to override authorization directives (such as AuthType, AuthName, AuthUserFile, etc.)
- FileInfo—allows directory access files to override document type settings (such as AddEncoding, AddLanguage, AddType, CookieTracking, CookieName, etc.)
- Indexes—allows directory access files to override directory indexing settings (such as FancyIndexing, DirectoryIndex, IndexOptions, etc.)
- Limit—allows directory access files to override access restrictions (such as allow, deny, order, require, etc.)
- None—forbids directory access files from overriding any <Directory> setting
- Options—allows directory access files to override directory options (such as Options and XbitHack).

AllowOverride appears only within the scope of a <Directory> block directive. Since subdirectories inherit <Directory> settings, such permission is granted to all subdirectories of the specified <Directory> (unless a subdirectory's <Directory> block revokes that permission with its own AllowOverride directive).

Although CookieTracking and CookieName may be localized within a <Directory> block or directory access file, CookieExpires cannot. CookieExpires is restricted to the global scope and the virtual host scope. This means that the webmaster can enable cookie tracking and set cookie names through directory access files; but changing the expiry period requires intervention by the system administrator (i.e. a modification to the Apache configuration file).

The mod_usertrack module sends a Set-Cookie: header to the browser when the browser makes its first request to a tracked site or directory. For example, this configuration

```
<IfModule mod_usertrack.c>
    CookieExpires "1 month"
</IfModule>
DocumentRoot "/home/webmastr/pub/html"
<Directory "/home/webmastr/pub/html">
<IfModule mod_usertrack.c>
    CookieTracking on
    CookieName browsertag
</IfModule>
</Directory>
```

would cause `mod_usertrack` to transmit the following HTTP response header

```
Set-Cookie: browsertag=192.168.1.7.9803943937750592; path=/;
expires=Thu, 30-Dec-99 04:55:46 GMT
```

The browser will return the cookie to the server on all subsequent requests within the cookie's scope (`path=/`) up until the expiration time (`expires=Thu, 30-Dec-99 04:55:46 GMT`), with this HTTP request header:

```
Cookie: browsertag=192.168.1.7.9803943937750592
```

When `mod_usertrack` creates or receives one of its cookies, it adds an annotation to the transfer. This annotation is named `cookie` and is available to the `LogFormat` directive through the `%{cookie}n` replacement variable (see `LogFormat`, above).

The `mod_usertrack` module is *not* a default module. If you need your logs to track individual browsers you will need to compile the Apache server with the `mod_usertrack` module. The APACI utility's `configure` command will compile this module when `--enable-module=usertrack` is given as a command line argument. A command line argument of `--enable-module=most` will also include `mod_usertrack` in the compile. Be sure that the module is loaded and enabled with the appropriate `LoadModule` and `EnableModule` directives (see Chapter 2: "Creating the Web Server").

The following sections of this chapter use the `SetEnvIf`, `LogFormat`, `CustomLog`, and `Cookie???` directives to implement several useful logs.

Tracking User Habits—The Clickstream Log

The clickstream log allows you to observe the habits of your visitors: what they download and in what order and how they navigate your site. You can use this information to improve your site's content and ergonomics. The example log described herein tracks, on a per-browser basis, every transfer from the `DocumentRoot` directory tree (e.g. `/home/webmastr/pub/html/`). This requires the ability to identify individual browsers. The `Cookie???` directives (described above) are used to tag each browser with a cookie. Then the `LogFormat` and `CustomLog` directives eat the cookies. A korn shell script is then provided to sort the clickstream log and generate a report in HTML format.

Make sure that your Apache server has been compiled with these modules:

- `mod_log_config` (a default module)
- `mod_setenvif` (a default module)
- `mod_usertrack` (not a default module)

Refer to Chapter 2: "Creating the Web Server" for instructions on selecting and compiling modules and on loading and activating modules in the Apache configuration file.

Meet with the webmaster, the person most interested in a clickstream study. The system administrator will need to provide the accommodating Apache configuration. The webmaster will want to specify the time period over which each browser's activity is to be observed. This affects the `CookieExpires` directive. The webmaster will want to specify what data are logged. This affects the `LogFormat` directive.

To create the accommodating Apache configuration, first add the following in the global scope or within the scope of a `<VirtualHost>` block

```
<IfModule mod_usertrack.c>
    CookieExpires "1 month"
</IfModule>
```

replacing `"1 month"` with the desired expiry period. Next, give the webmaster permission to configure user tracking via directory access files (e.g. `.htaccess`). Permission is granted by adding the `FileInfo` parameter to the `AllowOverride` directive. This example grants such permission to the directory access files in the document root directory tree:

```
DocumentRoot "/home/webmastr/pub/html"
<Directory "/home/webmastr/pub/html">
    AllowOverride Limit FileInfo
    .
    . (The rest of your DocumentRoot's <Directory> block goes here)
    .
</Directory>
```

Next, create the clickstream log. Add the following directives in the global scope or within the appropriate `<VirtualHost>` block:

```
LogFormat "%{Cookie}n %{%Y%m%d%H%M%S}t %f %t %U" fmtClickstream
CustomLog logs/click.log fmtClickstream
SetEnv ClickLog /usr/local/apache/logs/click.log
```

The first three fields in the above LogFormat directive are required by the example viewing script provided at the end of this section. The first field, %{Cookie}n, outputs the cookie that identifies the requesting browser. This will be the primary sorting and grouping key for the viewing script. The second field, %{%Y%m%d%H%M%S}t, outputs the time of the request in an easily sortable format. This is the secondary key for the viewing script. The third field, %f, is the file system path of the requested file, which is the tertiary key for the viewing script. The remaining fields, %t %U, may be changed to suit the requirements of the study and are displayed verbatim in the report. See the LogFormat description in "Creating Custom Logs," above, for a full list of available fields. In the above example, the CustomLog directive creates the clickstream log as a text file in the logs/ subdirectory of the Apache installation directory (/usr/local/ apache, in our example server). The SetEnv directive creates an environment variable named ClickLog, which is used to pass the absolute path of the clickstream log file to the viewing script. If you rotate logs, you might want to point this ClickLog variable to yesterday's log file.

The webmaster can now configure user tracking on a per-directory basis by creating directory access files in the desired directories. Tell the webmaster the value of the AccessFileName directive so that he/she will know what to name the directory access files. By convention and by default, these files are named .htaccess. The webmaster can enable user tracking and specify the user-tracking cookie name by adding these directives to the directory access file:

```
<IfModule mod_usertrack.c>
    CookieTracking on
    CookieName browsertag
</IfModule>
```

The webmaster can disable user tracking for a specific directory by placing these directives in a directory access file:

```
<IfModule mod_usertrack.c>
    CookieTracking off
</IfModule>
```

Note that turning CookieTracking off for a given subdirectory doesn't prevent requests for that directory from being logged. It just prevents the cookie processing for that directory. The CustomLog directive will still log every transfer—placing a hyphen in the log instead of the value of the cookie.

The webmaster will want to view the results. This means you'll have to either *a*) give the webmaster access to the log file or a copy thereof; or *b*) provide a CGI script to sort, group, and report on the log; or *c*) allow the webmaster to write the necessary script. The following korn shell script can be used as a CGI script to report the clickstream log in HTML format:

```ksh
#!/bin/ksh

#
# clicklog.cgi
#
# Description:
#
#   Script to generate an HTML-formatted report on a click
# stream log. This script outputs a Content-type:
# response header and (therefore) can be used as a CGI
# script.
#
# Parameters:
#
#   This script does not accept any command line parameters;
# but it does expect an environment variable named ClickLog
# to contain the absolute path to the clickstream log text
# file on which the report is to be generated.
#
# Input:
#
# The clickstream log is expected to contain the following
# space-separated fields:
#
# 1) the requesting browser's usertrack cookie
#
# 2) the date/time of the request in the following
#     format: YYYYmmddHHMMSS -- which makes sorting
#     easier
#
# 3) the file system path to the requested file
#
# 4) the text to be displayed for this log entry
#
# The first three fields make up the sort key for the report.
# The forth and subsequent fields are displayed verbatim.
#
# The following example Apache configuration directives
# would create such a file:
#
# LogFormat "%{Cookie}n %{%Y%m%d%H%M%S}t %f %t %U" fmtClickstream
# CustomLog logs/click.log fmtClickstream
```

```
# SetEnv ClickLog /usr/local/apache/logs/click.log
#
# The LogFormat directive, above, maintains the appropriate
# keys in the first three fields and then displays the
# date/time of the request (in a more readable format) and
# the virtual path of the requested URL.
#

#
# Get the log file name from the environment
#
LogFile="$ClickLog"

#
# Output HTTP response headers
#
echo Content-type: text/html
echo

#
# Output the start of the HTML document
#
echo "<HTML>"
echo "    <HEAD>"
echo "        <TITLE>"
echo "            Clickstream Log"
echo "        </TITLE>"
echo "    </HEAD>"
echo "    <BODY"
echo "        TOPMARGIN=\"4\""
echo "        LEFTMARGIN=\"4\""
echo "        MARGINWIDTH=\"8\""
echo "        MARGINHEIGHT=\"4\""
echo "        BGCOLOR=\"#ffffff\""
echo "        TEXT=\"#000000\""
echo "        LINK=\"#770022\""
echo "        VLINK=\"#770022\""
echo "        ALINK=\"#770022\""
echo "    >"
echo "        <H1>Clickstream Log</H1>"

#
# The clickPrevTag variable lets us know when we have arrived
# at the next browser tag group; at which time we end the
# HTML table for the previous browser tag group and start a
# new HTML table for the next browser tag group.
#
clickPrevTag=
```

```
##
# Filter out the log entries containing untagged browsers, then
#
# Sort the log file by..
# browser tag, then by
#    date-time, then by
#       file name
#
# then read each line in the log file -- extracting the fields
# within each line
#
grep --revert-match "^-" $LogFile \
    | sort +0 -3 \
    |(
        while read \
            clickTag \
            clickTimeKey \
            clickFile \
            clickDisplay
        do
            ##
            # Group by browser tag:
            #
            # If the current clickTag differs from the clickPrevTag,
            # then we've arrived at the next browser tag group...
            #
            if [ "x_$clickPrevTag" != "x_$clickTag" ]; then
                ##
                # If clickPrevTag is not empty, then this is not the
                # first browser tag group.
                #
                # End the HTML table for the previous browser tag
                # group
                #
                if [ -z $clickPrevTag ]; then
                    :
                else
                    echo "    </TABLE>"
                fi

                #
                # Set previous to current for the next loop iteration
                #
                clickPrevTag="$clickTag"

                #
                # Start the HTML table for the current browser tag
                # group
                #
```

```
           echo "    <BR>"
           echo "    <HR>"
           echo "    <TABLE"
           echo "       BORDER=\"1\""
           echo "       CELLSPACING=\"1\""
           echo "       CELLPADDING=\"3\""
           echo "    >"
           echo "       <TR>"
           echo "          <TH COLSPAN=\"2\">"
           echo "             <B>Browser Tag:</B> $clickTag<BR>"
           echo "          </TH>"
           echo "       </TR>"

     fi ###
        # end if we have arrived at the next browser tag group
        #

     #
     # Output the current log entry
     #
     echo "    <TR>"
     echo "       <TD>"
     echo "          $clickDisplay"
     echo "       </TD>"
     echo "    </TR>"

  done ###
        # end of while loop reading the clickstream log
        #

) ###
     # end of the sorting of the log file
     #

#
# Output the HTML ending tags for the table, body, and document
#
echo "          </TABLE>"
echo "       </BODY>"
echo "    /HTML>"
```

The visitors to your sight probably want to remain anonymous. A clickstream log combined with an ISP's DHCP log could reveal a user's identity. You should secure the clickstream log so that it is not available to the general public. One way to do this would be to require authentication for access to the viewer script. Adding the following directives will do just that:

```
<Location /cgi-bin/clicklog.cgi>
    AuthType Basic
    AuthName adminapache
    AuthUserFile /home/webmastr/pub/auth/authuser
    AuthGroupFile /home/webmastr/pub/auth/authgroup
    require group clicklog
</Location>
```

The above `<Location>` block requires the user to login to the adminapache domain (using HTTP's `Basic` authentication method) before satisfying a request for the `/cgibin/clicklog.cgi` script. The user must successfully authenticate and be a member of the group named `clicklog`. The `AuthUserFile` and the `AuthGroupFile` behave much as the UNIX `/etc/passwd` and `/etc/group` files do. Use Apache's `htpasswd` utility (in the `bin/` subdirectory of the Apache installation directory) to create the `AuthUserFile` and to add users to it. The `AuthGroupFile` is created and maintained manually with an ASCII text editor. To implement the above example, you will need to add and populate the `clicklog` group in the `AuthGroupFile`. See Chapter 6: "Securing the Server, the Content, and the Connection" for a full explanation of the various authentication methods.

Logging Referring Sites

One way to generate traffic to your Web site is to get other sites to link to yours. If your site is advertised on other sites, you might want to log the hits you get from each of these referring sites. With a referer log, you can determine the effectiveness of your advertising.

The Apache configuration file ships with a log format for a referer log:

```
LogFormat "%{Referer}i -> %U" referer
```

The above directive creates a log format named `referer`. The `%{Refer}i` logs the value of the `Referer:` request header sent by the browser. The `%U` logs the requested URL. To create a referer log using the above format, all you have to do is find the following line in the global scope of the configuration file

```
#CustomLog /usr/local/apache/logs/referer_log referer
```

and uncomment it by removing the pound sign. Once this is done, the `CustomLog` directive will log every transfer to the text file named `referer_log`—replacing the `%{Referer}i` field with a hyphen when the `Referer:` request header is missing or empty. You can filter out these uninteresting transfers by replacing the `CustomLog` directive with these three directives:

```
SetEnvIf Referer "^$" suppressreferer
SetEnvIf Referer ".*//administeringapache\.com/.*" suppressreferer
CustomLog logs/referer_log referer env=!suppressreferer
```

The `CustomLog` directive in the above listing logs the current transfer only if the `suppressrefer` environment variable is *not* defined. The first of the `SetEnvIf` directives defines the `suppressreferer` environment variable if the `Referer:` request header is missing or empty. The second `SetEnvIf` directive defines the `suppressrefer` environment variable when our example Web site refers to itself. Such filtering not only makes a cleaner, smaller log; it also enhances server performance—by not having to log every transfer.

You can configure the referer log for a specific virtual host by placing the `SetEnvIf` and `CustomLog` directives within the appropriate `<VirtualHost>` block.

Paying Referring Sites—The Paid Referer Log

If you are running pay-per-hit banner ads on other sites, the paid referer log will tell you how much you need to pay each referring site. Let's say that you've agreed to pay five cents for every "new" visitor—"new" defined as not having visited your site within the last year. Each visitor needs to be counted, then marked so as not to be counted again.

First, make sure that your Apache server has been compiled with these modules:

- `mod_log_config` (a default module)
- `mod_setenvif` (a default module)
- `mod_usertrack` (not a default module).

Refer to Chapter 2: "Creating the Web Server" for instructions on selecting and compiling modules and on loading and activating modules in the Apache configuration file.

The example log described herein uses the `Cookie???` directives to tag each browser as having been counted. Add the following directives to the

Apache configuration file, either in the global scope or within an appropriate <VirtualHost> block:

```
<IfModule mod_usertrack.c>
    CookieExpires "1 year"
    CookieTracking on
    CookieName counted
</IfModule>
```

In the above listing, the <IfModule> block prevents the Cookie??? directives from being processed if Apache has not been compiled with the mod_usertrack module. The Cookie??? directives give a cookie named counted to every browser. This cookie expires after one year. If you are already using the Cookie??? directives for some other log, then you will need to merge the two logs. You will need to specify a CookieExpires with the longer of the two expiry periods. You will have to format the log to contain all of the fields from both logs. And you will need to modify the reporting scripts to read the new format and to sort and filter the log entries. If this paid referer log is the only log relying on the Cookie??? directives, then proceed with the implementation of this example.

Add the following directives just after the <IfModule mod_usertrack.c> block:

```
SetEnvIf Cookie ".*counted.*" suppressreferer
SetEnvIf Referer "^$" suppressreferer
SetEnvIf Referer ".*//adminsteringapache\.com/.*" suppressreferer
LogFormat "%{Referer}i %{%Y%m%d%H%M%S}t" fmtReferer
CustomLog logs/paidref.log fmtReferer env=!suppressreferer
SetEnv PaidRefLog /usr/local/apache/logs/paidref.log
```

The first of the SetEnvIf directives checks to see if the browser has transmitted a Cookie: request header containing a cookie named counted. If so, then the browser has been previously tagged and should not be counted; in which case, the SetEnvIf directive defines the suppressreferer environment variable. The second SetEnvIf directive suppresses the logging of this transfer if the Referer: request header is missing or empty. The third SetEnvIf directive suppresses the logging of this transfer if the referral is from our own server. The LogFormat directive defines a log format (named fmtReferer) that outputs log entries in a format compatible with the reporting script provided below. Each log entry will contain the URL of the referring document and the date/time of the request. The CustomLog directive creates the log as a text file named `paidref.log` is in `logs/` subdirectory (relative to the Apache installation directory). The `CustomLog` directive then outputs each log entry according the `fmtReferer` log format. Before logging the transfer, the `CustomLog` directive checks to see if the environment variable named `suppressreferer` is not defined. In the last line of the above listing, the `SetEnv` directive creates an environment variable named `PaidRefLog`, which contains the full path to the log file. The reporting script expects this environment variable.

The following korn shell script can be used as a CGI script to sort and count referrals. The report displays each referring document and the number of referrals received from that document. The report can be filtered to display the referrals received within a given year, month, or day. Refer to the `Parameters:` section of the script's comments for a description of the query string arguments.

```ksh
#!/bin/ksh

#
# paidref.cgi
#
#
# Description:
#
#    Script to generate an HTML-formatted report on a referer
# log -- displaying the number of referrals for each referring
# document. This script outputs a Content-type: response header
# and (therefore) can be used as a CGI script.
#
#
# Parameters:
#
# This script expects an environment variable named PaidRefLog
# to contain the absolute path to the referer log text file
# on which the report is to be generated. The following Apache
# configuration directive would set such a variable:
#
# SetEnv PaidRefLog /usr/local/apache/logs/paidref.log
#
# This script scans the value of the QUERY_STRING environment
# variable to extract the following parameters:
#
#    1) year -- the 4-digit year for which referrals are to
#            be counted
#
#    2) month -- the numeric month for which referrals are to
#            be counted
```

```
#
#    3) day -- the numeric day of the month for which referrals
#          are to be counted
#
# These three parameters are optional. A parameter not specified
# means "all".  The following example URL counts referrals
# received in the month of December, 1999:
#
# http://administeringapache.com/cgibin/paidref.cgi
# ?year=1999&month=12
#
#
# Input:
#
#    The referer log is expected to contain the following
# space-separated fields:
#
#    1) the URL of the referring document
#
#    2) the date/time of the request in the following
#       format: YYYYmmddHHMMSS -- which makes filtering
#       easier
#
# These fields make up the sort key for the report.
# The following example Apache configuration directive
# would output such a format:
#
# LogFormat "%{Referer}i %{%Y%m%d%H%M%S}t" fmtReferer
#


#
# Get the log file name from the environment
#
LogFile="$PaidRefLog"


#
# Get the year, month, and day from the QUERY_STRING
#
refYear=`expr $QUERY_STRING : '.*year=\(.*\)$' | sed 's/&.*//'`
if [ -z $refYear ]; then
    refYear='[0-9]\{4,4\}'
fi

refMonth=`expr $QUERY_STRING : '.*month=\(.*\)$' | sed 's/&.*//'`
if [ -z $refMonth ]; then
    refMonth='[0-9]\{2,2\}'
fi

refDay=`expr $QUERY_STRING : '.*day=\(.*\)$' | sed 's/&.*//'`
```

```
if [ -z $refDay ]; then
  refDay='[0-9]\{2,2\}'
fi

#
# Output HTTP response headers
#
echo Content-type: text/html
echo

#
# Output the start of the HTML document
#
echo "<HTML>"
echo "   <HEAD>"
echo "      <TITLE>"
echo "         Referral Summary"
echo "      </TITLE>"
echo "   </HEAD>"
echo "   <BODY"
echo "      TOPMARGIN=\"4\""
echo "      LEFTMARGIN=\"4\""
echo "      MARGINWIDTH=\"8\""
echo "      MARGINHEIGHT=\"4\""
echo "      BGCOLOR=\"#ffffff\""
echo "      TEXT=\"#000000\""
echo "      LINK=\"#770022\""
echo "      VLINK=\"#770022\""
echo "      ALINK=\"#770022\""
echo "   >"
echo "      <H1>Referral Summary</H1>"

#
# Start the HTML table in which the counts will
# be displayed
#
echo "   <BR>"
echo "   <TABLE"
echo "      BORDER=\"1\""
echo "      CELLSPACING=\"1\""
echo "      CELLPADDING=\"3\""
echo "   >"
echo "      <TR>"
echo "         <TH>"
echo "            Referring Document"
echo "         </TH>"
echo "         <TH>"
echo "            No. of Referrals"
echo "         </TH>"
```

```
echo "        </TR>"

#
# The refPrevReferer variable lets us know when we have arrived at
# the next referring document; at which time we will need to
# output a table row for the previous referring document.
#
refPrevReferer=

#
# refCount counts the number of referrals for each referring
# document
refCount=0

#
# Extract log entries matching the specified year, month,
# and day. Sort the filtered entries by referring document
# and date/time.
#
grep "[^ ] $refYear$refMonth$refDay" $LogFile \
    | sort +0 -2 \
    | (
        while read \
            refReferer \
            refDate
        do
            #
            # If the current refReferer differs from the
            # refPrevReferer, then...
            #
            # This groups the report by referring document
            #
            if [ "x_$refPrevReferer" != "x_$refReferer" ]; then

                #
                # If refPrevReferer is not empty, then
                # this is not the first referring document.
                #
                # Output an HTML table row for the previous
                # referring document
                #
                if [ -z $refPrevReferer ]; then
                    :
                else
                    echo "        <TR>"
                    echo "          <TD>"
                    echo "            $refPrevReferer"
                    echo "          </TD>"
                    echo "          <TD>"
```

```
                        echo "              $refCount"
                        echo "          </TD>"
                        echo "        </TR>"
                    fi

                    #
                    # Set previous to current for the next loop
                    # iteration
                    #
                    refPrevReferer="$refReferer"

                    #
                    # Clear the counter for the next referring document
                    #
                    refCount=0

            fi ###
                    # end if we have arrived at the next referring
                    # document

            #
            # Increment the referral counter for the current
            # referring document
            #
            refCount=`expr $refCount + 1`

        done ###
                # end of while loop reading the referral log

        #
        # Output the referral count for the last of
        # the referring documents
        #
        if [ -z $refPrevReferer ]; then
            :
        else
            echo "        <TR>"
            echo "          <TD>"
            echo "              $refPrevReferer"
            echo "          </TD>"
            echo "          <TD>"
            echo "              $refCount"
            echo "          </TD>"
            echo "        </TR>"
        fi

) ###
    # end of the filtering and sorting of the log file
```

```
#
# end HTML table, body, and document
#
echo "       </TABLE>"
echo "   </BODY>"
echo "</HTML>"
```

Logging User Agents

Knowing what kinds of browsers visit your site may help you make decisions on which browsers to cater to. Standardization has become a casualty of the browser wars—each browser adding its own extensions to the HTTP protocol. You can also check the agent log to see if you've been indexed by a search engine spider.

The Apache configuration file ships with a log format for an agent log

```
LogFormat "%{User-agent}i" agent
```

which logs the User-agent: request header. To create an agent log using the above format, all you have to do is find the following line in the global scope of the configuration file

```
#CustomLog /usr/local/apache/logs/agent_log agent
```

and uncomment it by removing the pound sign. Once this done, the CustomLog directive will log every transfer to the text file named agent_log.

You can configure the agent log for a specific virtual host by moving this CustomLog directive to the appropriate <VirtualHost> block.

The following korn shell script can be used as a CGI script to sort and count user-agents. The report displays each user agent, the number of hits received from that user agent, and the percentage of total hits for that user agent.

```
#!/bin/ksh

#
# useragent.cgi
#
# Description:
#
#   Script to generate an HTML-formatted report on an agent
# log -- displaying the number of hits for each agent.
```

```
# This script outputs a Content-type: response header
# and (therefore) can be used as a CGI script.
#
# Parameters:
#
# This script expects an environment variable named AgentLog
# to contain the absolute path to the agent log text file
# on which the report is to be generated. The following Apache
# configuration directive would set such a variable:
#
# SetEnv AgentLog /usr/local/apache/logs/agent_log
#
#
# Input:
#
#   The referer log is expected to contain one field --
# the value of the User-agent: request header.
#
# The following example Apache configuration directive
# would output such a format:
#
# LogFormat "%{User-agent}i" agent
#

#
# Get the log file name from the environment
#
LogFile="$AgentLog"

#
# Count the number of lines in the log file, so we
# can display the hit counts as percentages of
# total hits.
#
agentTotal=`cat $LogFile | wc -l`

#
# Output HTTP response headers
#
echo Content-type: text/html
echo

#
# Output the start of the HTML document
#
echo "<HTML>"
echo "   <HEAD>"
echo "      <TITLE>"
echo "         User-Agent Summary"
```

```
echo "        </TITLE>"
echo "    </HEAD>"
echo "    <BODY"
echo "        TOPMARGIN=\"4\""
echo "        LEFTMARGIN=\"4\""
echo "        MARGINWIDTH=\"8\""
echo "        MARGINHEIGHT=\"4\""
echo "        BGCOLOR=\"#ffffff\""
echo "        TEXT=\"#000000\""
echo "        LINK=\"#770022\""
echo "        VLINK=\"#770022\""
echo "        ALINK=\"#770022\""
echo "    >"
echo "        <H1>User-Agent Summary</H1>"

#
# Start the HTML table in which the counts will
# be displayed
#
echo "    <BR>"
echo "    <TABLE"
echo "        BORDER=\"1\""
echo "        CELLSPACING=\"1\""
echo "        CELLPADDING=\"3\""
echo "    >"
echo "        <TR>"
echo "            <TH>"
echo "                User-Agent"
echo "            </TH>"
echo "            <TH>"
echo "                No. of Hits"
echo "            </TH>"
echo "            <TH>"
echo "                Percentage"
echo "            </TH>"
echo "        </TR>"

#
# The agentPrevUserAgent variable lets us know when we have
# arrived at the next user-agent; at which time we will need
# to output a table row for the previous user-agent.
#

agentPrevUserAgent=

#
# agentCount counts the number of hits for user-agent
#
agentCount=0
```

```
#
# Sort the user-agent log
#
cat $LogFile \
    | sort \
    |(
      while read \
          agentUserAgent
      do
          #
          # If the current agentUserAgent differs from the
          # agentPrevUserAgent, then...
          #
          # This groups the report by User-Agent
          #
          if [ "x_$agentPrevUserAgent" != "x_$agentUserAgent" ]
          then

              #
              # If agentPrevUserAgent is not empty, then
              # this is not the first User-Agent
              #
              # Output an HTML table row for the previous
              # User-Agent
              #
              if [ -z $agentPrevUserAgent ]; then
                  :
              else
                  echo "    <TR>"
                  echo "        <TD>"
                  echo "            $agentPrevUserAgent"
                  echo "        </TD>"
                  echo "        <TD>"
                  echo "            $agentCount"
                  echo "        </TD>"
                  echo "        <TD>"
                  agentPercent='expr $agentCount \* 100 / $agentTotal'
                  echo "            $agentPercent%"
                  echo "        </TD>"
                  echo "    </TR>"
              fi

              #
              # Set previous to current for the next loop iteration
              #
              agentPrevUserAgent="$agentUserAgent"

              #
```

```
            # Clear the counter for the next User-Agent
            #
            agentCount=0

      fi ###
            # end if we have arrived at the next User-Agent

      #
      # Increment the referral for the current
      # User-Agent
      #
      agentCount=`expr $agentCount + 1`

   done ###
      # end of while loop reading the agent log

   #
   # Output the referral count for the last of
   # the user agents
   #
   if [ -z $agentPrevUserAgent ]; then
      :
   else
      echo "       <TR>"
      echo "          <TD>"
      echo "             $agentPrevUserAgent"
      echo "          </TD>"
      echo "          <TD>"
      echo "             $agentCount"
      echo "          </TD>"
      echo "          <TD>"
      agentPercent=`expr $agentCount \* 100 / $agentTotal`
      echo "             $agentPercent%"
      echo "          </TD>"
      echo "       </TR>"
   fi
) ###
   # end of the filtering and sorting of the log file

#
# end HTML table, body, and document
#
echo "      </TABLE>"
echo "   </BODY>"
echo "</HTML>"
```

Rotating Log Files

Log files can get big in a hurry and should be periodically purged to prevent them from filling up your file system. You could manually shutdown the server, back the log files to tape, remove the log files, and then restart the server. Your server, however, will be down for a while and you won't have recent log information readily available (it's off on tape). Log rotation solves these problems. The process of rotation involves moving the current log file to a backup file (first removing any previous backup file) and then restarting the server so that it will create a new (empty) log file. You can then analyze, back to tape, and remove the backup file at your leisure. You could perform this procedure manually. To rotate the error log, for example, type the following at the shell prompt:

```
cd /usr/local/apache/logs
rm error_log.1
mv error_log error_log.1 ../bin/apachectl restart
```

Many UNIX systems provide a logrotate command to automate this process. Apache offers the rotatelogs command. I remember which is which by asking, "Does Apache rotatelogs? Yes." The UNIX command, logrotate, is a very verbose and adaptive system that handles log rotation for many of the UNIX subsystems. The UNIX command can automatically compress backup files and remove older backup files. It also allows you to add pre- and post-rotate scripts for custom processing. Most post-rotate scripts restart some server daemon after rotation. The Apache command, rotatelogs, is a very specific program used as a filter in the Apache logging process. It moves the current log file to a backup file, but that is all it does. The advantage of Apache's rotatelogs is that it performs the rotation on the fly. You don't have to restart the server after the rotation.

logrotate (UNIX)

The logrotate command is usually launched on a daily basis by cron, the scheduled-command daemon. The logrotate configuration file (e.g. /etc/logrotate.conf) defines what needs to be backed up and how often. In this configuration file, you specify a log file and a block of configuration directives to be applied to that log file. Configuration directives outside a file block are global in scope and define default actions—which may be overridden by directives within a file block. The following (abbreviated) example

```
weekly
rotate 4
errors root
create
```

```
/var/log/xferlog {
}

/var/log/messages {
    postrotate
    /usr/bin/killall -HUP syslogd
    endscript
}
```

rotates logs once per week (`weekly`), keeping four backup files (`rotate 4`) in the same directory as the log file. Given a log file named `messages`, for example, these files would be named messages.1, messages.2, messages.3, and messages.4. When it's time to rotate, `logrotate` deletes the fourth backup file, moves the third file to the fourth file, moves the second to the third, and the first to the second, and then moves the current log file to the first backup file. Any errors encountered during the rotation are e-mailed to the root user (`errors root`). Then `logrotate` creates a new, empty log file (`create`). These default actions are performed on the log files named `/var/log/xferlog` and `/var/log/messages`. After `/var/log/messages` has been rotated, `logrotate` restarts the `syslogd` daemon by sending it a HUP signal.

If you add one of Apache's logs to the `logrotate` configuration file, you need to have `logrotate` restart the Apache server after the rotation. You may also wish to override some of the default settings, as this example does:

```
/usr/local/apache/logs/click.log {
    daily
    nocreate
    postrotate
    /usr/local/apache/bin/apachectl graceful
    endscript
}
```

The above example rotates the clickstream log. Since the clickstream log records every transfer, it grows fast. Consequently, the rotation period has been reduced to `daily`; which overrides the `weekly` global setting and keeps four days' worth of log entries instead of four weeks' worth. The `postrotate` script restarts Apache `gracefully`—allowing current connections to finish up before the server is shut down and restarted. Since Apache will recreate missing log files when it starts up, the `nocreate` directive overrides the `create` directive in the global scope—allowing

Apache to create the new log file instead of this being done by
logrotate.

You could add your log files to the logrotate.conf configuration file,
but there may be a more appropriate place. A logrotate configuration
file may include other configuration files with the include directive. The
include directive can specify a file name (in which case the file is included inline at the occurrence of the include directive); or it can specify a
directory (in which case all regular files in that directory are included).
The logrotate configuration on my Linux system includes this directory:

```
include /etc/logrotate.d
```

Packages installed with the RedHat Linux RPM system place their own
logrotate configuration files in this directory. If your Apache server was
installed from the RedHat installation CD, then you already have the file
/etc/logrotate.d/apache, which looks like this:

```
/var/log/httpd/access_log {
    postrotate
    /usr/bin/killall -HUP httpd
    endscript
}

/var/log/httpd/agent_log {
    postrotate
    /usr/bin/killall -HUP httpd
    endscript
}

/var/log/httpd/error_log {
    postrotate
    /usr/bin/killall -HUP httpd
    endscript
}

/var/log/httpd/referer_log {
    postrotate
    /usr/bin/killall -HUP httpd
    endscript
}
```

If you have been seeing system error messages saying, "Error rotating
logs," they may be due to this file's being out of sync with your current
Apache configuration.

There are 24 configuration directives recognized by `logrotate`. Handy ones include: the `size` directive, which specifies that it is time to rotate when the log file has exceeded the specified number of bytes; and the `compress` directive, which instructs `logrotate` to compress the backup files with the gzip utility. Consult your system's MAN pages for a complete list of options.

rotatelogs (Apache)

The `rotatelogs` command is a filter program that you can include in your `ErrorLog`, `TransferLog`, and `CustomLog` Apache configuration directives as a piped command. Logging to a piped command is discussed in detail in the first section of this chapter, "Logging Errors," in the subsection "Sending errors to a piped command." The `rotatelogs` program accepts two command line parameters: the absolute path to the log file and the rotation period in seconds. The following example:

```
ErrorLog "|rotatelogs /usr/local/apache/logs/error_log 86400"
```

rotates the error log daily (every 86400 seconds). The `rotatelogs` filter captures the log entry, rotates the log if it is time to do so, then writes the log entry. This is done on the fly, on every log entry. The server does not have to be restarted after a rotation. This does require some overhead. You might not want to do this to a verbose log, such as a clickstream log.

Apache's `rotatelogs` command names the backup files a little differently from the way the UNIX `logrotate` command does. Instead of adding a simple counter as a filename extension, `rotatelogs` adds the date of the rotation in UTC format (the number of seconds elapsed since midnight, January 1, 1970). The log file with the most recent UTC stamp is the log file currently in use by the server. Given the above `ErrorLog` example, these files would be named

```
error_log.0944006400    12/01/99 00:00 GMT
error_log.0944092800    12/02/99 00:00 GMT
error_log.0944179200    12/03/99 00:00 GMT <-- most recent
```

The last file, `error_log.0944179200`, created at midnight last night, is the error log file currently being written to by the server. Note that `rotatelogs` does not delete older backup files; it just keeps creating new ones. You could remove them manually or you could set up a `cron` job to do it automatically.

Securing the Server, the Content, and the Connection

The more locks we invent, the more picks they invent. You can watch this little war on the Bugtraq discussion list—**http://hysteria.sk/lists/bugtraq/index.html**, hosted by Elias Levy of Security Focus (**http://www.securityfocus.com/**). A searchable archive of the BugTraq database is available at **http://geek-girl.com/bugtraq/search/ghindex.html**. The database lists the vulnerabilities of a variety of systems and the measures you can take to harden those systems against attacks.

In this chapter, we discuss the basic means of hardening your system and hardening your Apache server. We also discuss how you can use the public internet to publish private data only to authorized individuals; and how you can safely exchange sensitive data (like credit-card information) with your e-commerce customers.

Securing the Server

Configuring a Firewall

I thought web servers were public. Why do I need a firewall?

- Intranet web servers are private to the company and need protection.
- If you've got personnel out in the field, a firewall will allow them access to the intranet server without letting everyone else in.
- If a web server talks to a database server, it's a good idea to protect the database server.
- Apache proxy services can be made transparent, if the proxy server is running on a firewall computer that can redirect HTTP requests.
- A firewall running on the web server's machine can block out ports not being listened to. It's one thing not to listen. It's another to cover your ears.

A firewall restricts traffic between networks. It can be as simple as a router that performs packet filtering. It can be as complex as a software package running on a multi-homed computer—performing packet filtering, IP masquerading, statistics, logging, user authentication, and Virtual Private Network encryption. A variety of firewall software packages are available for various systems (see the section "Where in the Web" in the Appendix).

Later in this section, we show examples of Apache's relations to firewalls. The examples will configure a packet-filtering router and an IP masquerading firewall. This requires a basic understanding of TCP/IP networking, briefly described herein.

TCP/IP Basics

Networking allows a program running on one computer on one network to send messages to a program running on another computer on another network. Very much like a letter sent through the postal service, network messages have a destination address and a return address. The postal service delivers a letter to the correct house in the correct city (most of the time) and then it's up to the occupants of the house to get the letter into the hands of the person named on the envelope. On the Internet, the IP address gets the message to the right computer on the right network, then the port number gets the message to the right program on that computer. A letter may be mailed in a legal-size manila envelope or in a letter-size envelope. Internet messages may be packaged in a TCP packet (which includes error checking) or a UDP packet (which does not). A letter may change carriers several times on route, from truck to plane to truck. An Internet packet may be carried by an ethernet network to a token ring network to an ethernet network. A letter must be unloaded from the truck and loaded on the plane. A router between two networks takes the packet off the ethernet network, repackages it, and puts it on the token ring network. The postal service has bomb-sniffing dogs to remove explosives from the system. Routers have packet filters that drop unwanted packets.

IP addresses have two components: a host number portion and a network portion (compare to a letter's number/street line and city/state line). For example, the IP address 192.168.1.56 reads as host number 56 on network 192.168.1. This is an example of a class C address license, the first three bytes being the network portion and the last byte being the host number. The one-byte host number can accommodate up to 256 hosts on the network. Those 3 high-order bytes that make up the network number are 24 bits long. Thus the network is said to have a 24-bit network mask. The network address would commonly be written as 192.168.1.0/24. Larger networks use less of the address for the network portion and more of the address for the host-number portion. A class B license uses two bytes for the network and two bytes for the host number, accommodating up to 65,536 host numbers. For example, 172.16.1.56 would read as host number 1.56 on network 172.16.0.0/16. A class A license uses only one byte for the network. For example, 10.43.145.32 reads as machine number 43.145.32 on network 10.0.0.0/8. Let's say that a host whose address is 192.168.1.56 sends a message to the host at 10.43.145.32. This message from network 192.168.1.0/24 must pass through a router to get to network 10.0.0.0/8. When the source host throws a packet onto the wire, the router must determine if that packet should stay on the source host's network or be passed on to the other network. The router extracts the network portion of the destination address. If the destination network number equals the network number of the other network to which the router is connected, the router passes the packet on to the other network. To extract the network number from the destination address, the router performs a binary *AND* operation on the destination address and the network mask of the other network. This operation removes the host number from the destination address, leaving the network number of the destination address. Mathematically speaking:

Does this destination address	reside on ?	this other network
10.43.145.32	=	10.0.0.0/8
---	|	
10.43.145.32	|	10.0.0.0
AND 8-bit mask	|	
---	|	
00001010.00101011.10010001.00100000	|	
AND 11111111.00000000.00000000.00000000	|	
---	|	
00001010.00000000.00000000.00000000	|	
---	|	
10.0.0.0	=	10.0.0.0 ✔

Firewall Basics

A firewall is often placed between a local area network and the Internet to allow LAN hosts to request services from the Internet; but not allow Internet hosts to request services from the LAN hosts. A firewall in this context would be configured to disallow everything, except outgoing requests for selected services and their incoming responses. Figure 6.1 shows a browser connecting to a web server through such a firewall.

The simplest firewall is a router that performs packet filtering. A packet filter passes or refuses packets depending on each packet's protocol, source IP address, source port, destination IP address, and destination port. The network administrator configures the router with filter rules to tell the router which combinations are acceptable and which are not. The example firewall in Figure 6.1 connects network 192.168.1.0/24 to network 192.168.2.0/24. One of its filter rules says, "accept tcp from 192.168.1.0/24 1024:65535 to 0.0.0.0/0 80". This rule allows TCP requests from any ethereal port (1024:65535) from any host on network 192.168.1.0/24 destined for the HTTP port (80) of any host on any network (0.0.0.0/0). Ports below 1024 are service ports—ports on which a server listens for requests. By convention, port 80 is HTTP; port 25 is SMTP (email); port 23 is telnet. You'll find a long list of these ports in the text file /etc/services. Ports numbered 1024 and above are ethereal ports—ports on which a client listens for server responses. These four numbers combined—the source address and port and the destination address and port—uniquely identify a connection between two computers on the Internet. Another of the router's filter rules says, "accept tcp from 0.0.0.0/80 to 192.168.1.0/24 1024:65535". This allows TCP responses from the HTTP port of any host on any network destined for an ethereal port of any host on the 192.168.1.0/24 network.

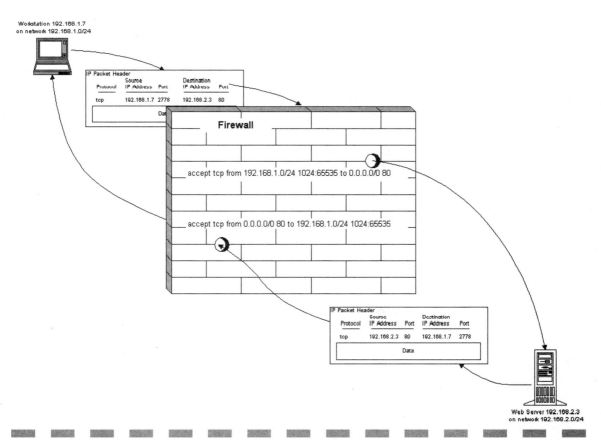

Figure 6.1 *Browser connecting to a Web server through a firewall.*

The following sections configure two example firewalls. The first, in "Configuring a Corporate Firewall," is a router that performs packet-filtering. The second, in Configuring a Small Business Firewall, is a computer configured to be a router that performs packet filtering and IP masquerading (masquerading is explained in that section).

Configuring a Corporate Firewall

Figure 6.2 illustrates a typical corporate local area network (extracted from Figure 1.1 in Chapter 1: "Planning Ahead").

Figure 6.2
Corporate LAN configuration.

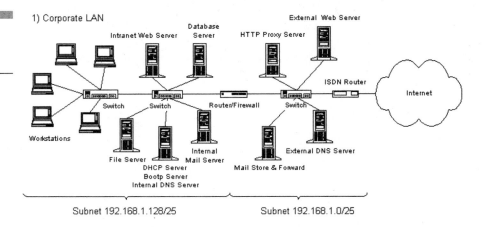

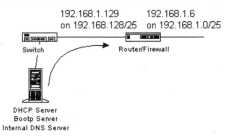

1) Corporate LAN

The corporation illustrated in Figure 6.2 divides its network into two subnets: an internal/private subnet and an external/public subnet. A router/firewall connecting these subnets restricts traffic between them. The firewall protects the private workstations and servers, yet allows these Internal hosts to connect to selected services on the Internet. Most of the requests for Internet services have to pass through some sort of forwarding server or proxy server on the public subnet—rather than allowing direct connections between private hosts and Internet hosts. Some direct connections, however, must be allowed. Hosts on the public subnet, in contrast, are not protected. These servers publish data to the web, sacrificed to the web; so back up their hard drives daily.

The corporation owns a class C license, namely 192.168.1.0/24. (This is an example. The numbering of private internets is discussed in the next section.) The corporation divides this license into two subnets by adding one bit to the subnet mask. The public network number is thus 192.168.1.0/25. The private network number is thus 192.168.1.128/25. It is actually easier to think of it in binary terms (as the router does):

```
192.168.1.0      =     11000000.10101000.00000001.00000000
192.168.1.128    =     11000000.10101000.00000001.10000000
25-bit netmask   =     11111111.11111111.11111111.10000000
```

2) Bootp server gives the router its configuration

How you configure a router depends on the brand of router. Some routers are configured by attaching a terminal to the router and entering filter rules. Others are configured by logging into the router with telnet and entering the rules. Some routers support the SNMP protocol and are managed by an administrative software client. The router in this example supports the Remote Bootstrap Protocol (bootp), wherein you create a configuration text file on a bootp server that delivers the configuration to the router every time the router is turned on. When the router is turned on, it broadcasts a request for a bootp server. The bootp server receives the request and searches its bootp configuration text file (usually /etc/bootptab) for an entry matching the router's hardware address. The matching bootptab entry might look like this:

```
gateway:\
   ht=ether:\
   ha=00E0292F4597:\
   ip=192.168.1.129:\
   sm=255.255.255.128:\
   bf=filtercfg.2:\
   hd=/tftpboot:\
   sa=192.168.1.2
```

This entry says, "When a bootpd request is received from a machine whose hardware type is ethernet and whose hardware address is

00E0292F4597, tell that machine that its TCP/IP hostname is gateway. Tell the machine that its IP address is 192.168.1.129 on a network whose subnet mask is 255.255.255.128 (a 25-bit mask). Tell the machine to fetch its boot file from the home directory named /tftpboot on the TFTP server running on 192.168.1.2." This boot file from the \tftpboot directory is the router's configuration file. It prescribes the router's internal and external interfaces and its packet filter rules. The syntax of a router's configuration file is very specific to the brand of router. The rest of this section generically describes what the router must do.

The router's external interface is given a host number of 6 on the network 192.168.1.0/24—which works out to 192.168.1.6. The router's internal interface is given a host number of 1 on network 192.168.1.128/25—which works out to 192.168.1.129. The binary addresses are:

```
      host number:          1
on    network:             192.168.1.128/25
-------------------------------------------------------------
      host number:               .         .        . 0000001
on    network (25-bit):    11000000.10101000.00000001.1
-------------------------------------------------------------
yields IP address          11000000.10101000.00000001.10000001
-------------------------------------------------------------
                           192.168.1.129
```

The router's configuration file also instructs the router that it is the default gateway for the 192.168.128/25 subnet. Next, the router's configuration file gives the router its packet-filter rules, as shown in Figure 6.3.

3) Deny all. Then allow the LAN to request specific services from the Internet

The first filter rule given to the router instructs the router to deny all packets that are not specifically allowed. All subsequent filter rules instruct the router what packets are to be allowed. This first group of "accept" rules prescribes what connections can be made directly between internal hosts and external hosts. The corporate LAN model does its best to put some kind of forwarding server or proxy server between the internal network and the Internet; but there some direct connections that you must allow: ICMP and DNS.

The very first connections that should be allowed through the firewall are ICMP connections. ICMP is a low-level protocol required by other protocols. Echo requests and echo replies (ping and pong) are transmitted through

Figure 6.3
Corporate LAN packet filter rules.

3) Deny all. Then allow the LAN to request specific services from the Internet.

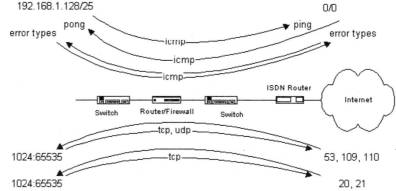

192.168.1.128/25

0/0

pong
error types

ping
error types

icmp

icmp

icmp

ISDN Router

Internet

Switch   Router/Firewall   Switch

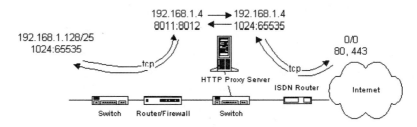

tcp, udp

1024:65535   tcp   53, 109, 110

1024:65535   20, 21

4) Allow internal hosts to browse the web via the HTTP proxy server.

192.168.1.4 ⟶ 192.168.1.4
8011:8012 ⟵ 1024:65535

192.168.1.128/25
1024:65535

0/0
80, 443

tcp

tcp

HTTP Proxy Server

ISDN Router   Internet

Switch   Router/Firewall   Switch

5) Allow connections between specific internal servers and specific external servers.

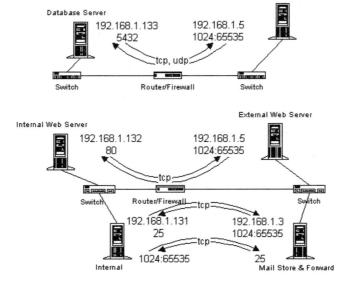

External Web Server

Database Server

192.168.1.133
5432

192.168.1.5
1024:65535

tcp, udp

Switch   Router/Firewall   Switch

External Web Server

Internal Web Server

192.168.1.132
80

192.168.1.5
1024:65535

tcp

Switch   Router/Firewall   tcp   Switch

192.168.1.131
25

192.168.1.3
1024:65535

tcp

1024:65535   25

Internal   Mail Store & Forward

ICMP. Connection and routing errors are reported through ICMP. You should not accept all ICMP packet types. The *flood-ping attack* comes through ICMP. A flood-ping attack occurs when a hacker tries to break a machine by sending ping requests faster than the TCP/IP stack can handle them. The *ping-of-death attack* also comes through ICMP: a hacker sends an ICMP packet that is too large—attempting to break the machine by overflowing the TCP/IP stack's packet buffer. The firewall should restrict ICMP traffic to those ICMP message types that are absolutely necessary. The firewall should pass ICMP error messages (destination-unreachable, source-quench, time-exceeded, and parameter-problem) in both directions. The firewall should allow hosts on the internal network to ping hosts on the Internet; but should disallow external hosts from pinging internal hosts. That is, the firewall should accept outgoing ICMP echo-request packets and incoming ICMP echo-reply packets; but not the inverse. You could further reduce your exposure to flood-ping attacks if your router can impose a rate cap on ICMP packets. You could further reduce your exposure to ping-of-death attacks if your router can disallow ICMP fragments (packets that are so large that they have to be broken up into smaller packets). An ICMP packet should not be so large as to be fragmented; if your firewall allows control of fragments, then you might explicitly reject ICMP fragments. (You might want to accept TCP and UDP fragments, or some connections might not work. This section of the router configuration file, early on, would be a good place to do that. Fragments have a protocol and they have source and destination addresses, but they do not have port numbers. The rest of the filter rules herein accept packets based on the service port number.) These measures can reduce your exposure, but do not guarantee immunity. Risk reduction is about all you can do with a packet filter.

The second kind of connection that should be allowed through the firewall is DNS connections. Many other services use DNS while setting up their own connections. The corporate LAN model has both internal and external DNS servers. The internal one serves up the addresses of the internal server farm to the internal hosts. The external one serves up the addresses of the public servers to anyone who asks. You could configure the firewall to allow DNS connections only between the internal DNS server and the external DNS server. Then the internal DNS server could serve up Internet addresses to the internal hosts (requesting lookups from the external server as needed). The problem with this is that an internal host might (at some point) require an authoritative answer, which must be gotten from some authoritative DNS server on the web. Your firewall should, then, allow DNS requests from any internal host and allow DNS responses from any external host. Specifically, accept both TCP and UDP packets from any ethereal port on any internal host destined for the DNS port of any external host. This connection is bidirectional; so also accept both TCP and UDP packets from the DNS port of any external host destined for any ethereal port on any internal host.

If workstation users demand it, you might need to open up direct connections to other Internet services for which you are not providing a proxy server (e.g. POP-2, POP-3, FTP, or telnet). Beware that the more direct connections that you allow, the less secure your internal subnet will become. There are some direct connections that may be inappropriate for a corporate LAN. News services (NNTP) might be a real help to developers who need to ask questions of the technical community. But opening up all news services to everyone might allow inappropriate content (i.e. porn) into the corporate LAN. If your users demand NNTP, it would be better to supply them with a news server that publishes only selected news groups. RealPlayer connections to RealServers (audio and visual) will eat up a lot of bandwidth. In addition, RealServers turn around and send connection requests back to the RealPlayer to establish a data channel; they turn the LAN host from a client into a server (which is exactly what we're trying to avoid with the packet-filtering router). ICQ chat connections also turn the client into a server and require the firewall open up a huge number of ports. Internet Relay Chat (IRC) may be well-behaved (that is, a client remains a client), but you may not want users chatting on company time.

4) Allow internal hosts to browse the web via the HTTP proxy server

An HTTP proxy server makes HTTP requests (port 80) and HTTPS requests (port 443) on behalf of the workstations. This allows you to hide the IP addresses of your internal browsers. The only IP address seen by the Internet web servers is that of the proxy server. An HTTP proxy server also allows you to log every web request (useful information for the thought police) and reduces latency by caching HTTP server responses (how many times per day do your users hit the Microsoft site). The HTTP proxy server (with an attached database and a bit of work) could also be used to censor LAN requests. To configure the proxy server, refer to Chapter 9: "Proxying with Apache." Here, we configure the firewall to allow connections to the HTTP proxy server. Our example proxy server listens for HTTP requests on port 8011 and listens for secure HTTP requests on port 8012 (both of which are configurable). The firewall must accept TCP requests from the ethereal port of any internal host destined for port 8011 or port 8012 on the proxy server. The firewall must also accept the bidirectional responses.

Each workstation browser must be configured to make requests via port 8011 and 8012 on the proxy server. For Netscape, select Edit, then Preferences, then Advanced, then Proxies, then Manual Proxy Configuration, then View. In the row labeled HTTP:, enter the IP address of the proxy server and 8011 for the port. In the row labeled Security:, enter the IP address of the proxy server and 8012 for the port. For MS Explorer, select View, then Internet Options, then Connection. Check the box labeled "Access the Internet using a proxy server", then click the Advanced button. In the row labeled HTTP:, enter the IP address of the proxy server and port number 8011. In the row labeled Secure:, enter the IP address and port 8012. You could avoid this hassle if your router were a dual-homed computer performing both router services and proxy services. Then you could have the router software redirect all port 80 and port 443 requests to port 8011 and 8012 on the routing computer—regardless of the destination address of the request. The proxy service would then be transparent to the browsers. The section "Configuring a Small Business Firewall," below, depicts just such a machine.

5) Allow connections between specific internal servers and specific external servers

This group of filter rules allows servers on the public subnet to make requests to selected servers on the private subnet—without providing those private services to the rest of the world.

The external web server needs to publish to the web selected data stored on the internal database server. It also needs to save data collected from site visitors back to the internal database server. Make doubly sure that the external web server cannot overwrite any of its CGI scripts (see the section "Security Considerations for CGI—Wrappers" later in this chapter). Otherwise, a hacker might modify a database script and gain access to private data (or, worse yet, destroy the database). The internal database server listens for TCP and UDP connections on port 5432 (which is a configurable postgres example). The firewall must accept TCP and UDP requests from any ethereal port on the external web server destined for port 5432 on the internal database server. It must also accept the bidirectional responses.

The internal web server serves up private documents to the private subnet. The external web server publishes documents to the world. There are some documents on the internal web server that the company would like published to the web. The *reverse proxy* service on the external web server publishes those selected documents (see more on reverse proxy in Chapter 9). The firewall must accept TCP requests from any ethereal port on the external web server destined for the HTTP port of the internal web server. It must also accept the bidirectional responses.

The external mail server forwards internet email to the internal mail server (from whence the internal hosts retrieve their mail). The firewall must accept TCP requests from any ethereal port on the external mail server destined for the SMTP port on the internal mail server. The firewall must also accept the bi-directional responses. The internal email server also forwards outgoing mail to the external email server. The firewall must accept TCP requests from any ethereal port on the internal mail server destined for the SMTP port on the external mail server. It must also accept the bidirectional responses.

Configuring a Small-Business Firewall

Figure 6.4 illustrates a typical small-business LAN (extracted from Figure 1.1 in Chapter 1: "Planning Ahead").

Figure 6.4

A typical small-business LAN.

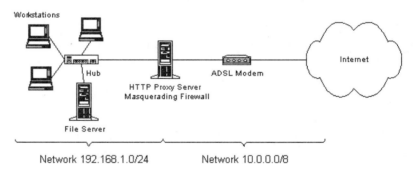

1) Small Business LAN

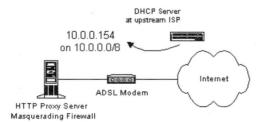

2) The firewall receives its external IP configuration from the upstream ISP's DHCP server.

1) Small Business LAN

The small business reduces costs and the number of machines by combining the router/firewall with the HTTP proxy server. The limited amount of traffic across the firewall permits this combination without creating a bottleneck. The small business further reduces costs by being able to connect to the Internet without purchasing an IP address license from the Internet Assigned Numbers Authority. This can be done because the firewall performs *IP masquerading*. The firewall masquerades as the LAN host on all Internet connections. It keeps track of all connections between LAN hosts and Internet hosts. On all outbound traffic, the firewall replaces the source IP address with its own and the source port with a port allocated on the firewall. The firewall then maintains the connection with the external host and relays the incoming traffic back to the appropriate LAN host. The only IP address the Internet can see is that of the firewall. The addresses of the internal LAN hosts are hidden—adding a layer of security of the internal LAN hosts. Only one public IP address is used (taken from the upstream ISPs pool)—which conserves our shrinking supply of public IPv4 addresses.

In this example, the firewall is a UNIX computer with two network interface cards—one connected to the internal network and one connected to the Internet. Configuring this firewall is a matter of editing configuration files and restarting the network subsystem.

2) The firewall receives its external IP configuration from the upstream ISP's DHCP server

First, configure the firewall's interfaces. The firewall in this example receives its external IP address from the upstream ISP via the DHCP protocol. The Dynamic Host Configuration Protocol is similar to bootp, except that the configurations it delivers are dynamically generated. The upstream ISP configures its DHCP server with a block of IP addresses, known as a *pool* of available addresses. When a new host is connected to the network, the DHCP server removes an IP address from the pool and gives it to the new host. The new host can use that IP address for a given period of time, known as a *lease*. When the lease expires, the given address is returned to the pool and the host must request a new address from the DHCP server. All of this negotiation occurs automatically within the DHCP protocol. On our example firewall, the external interface device is named eth0. The firewall is a Linux box, so some of the configuration examples may differ from your system. The concepts are all applicable. To configure the external interface to receive its configuration from the

DHCP server, edit the file /etc/sysconfig/network-scripts/ifcfg-eth0 to read like this:

```
DEVICE=eth0
ONBOOT=yes
BOOTPROTO=dhcp
BROADCAST=
NETWORK=
NETMASK=
IPADDR=
DEFROUTE=yes
```

In the above listing, ONBOOT instructs the Linux network subsystem to bring this interface up when the operating system boots up. BOOTPROTO=dhcp specifies that this interface is to use DHCP to receive its configuration. The BROADCAST, NETWORK, NETMASK, and IPADDR parameters are left blank, since they will be set by the DHCP server. The DEFROUTE=yes directive instructs Linux that this interface is the default route (i.e. this interface is the network's gateway).

For the router's internal interface (and for the LAN workstations), you can use any numbering scheme you like; but there is a convention. RFC 1918, "Address Allocation for Private Internets," reserves three blocks of addresses for use by private networks. These blocks are described in Table 6.1.

Table 6.1
Private IP address blocks

IP Address Blocks Reserved for Private Networks				Network Addresses in Block					No. of Networks	No. Hosts Per Network
From: 10.	0.	0.	0		10.	0.	0. 0	/8	1	16,777,216
To: 10.	255.	255.	255							
From: 172.	16.	0.	0	From: 172.	16.	0. 0	/16		16	65,536
To: 172.	31.	255.	255	To: 172.	31.	0. 0	/16			
From: 198.	168.	0.	0	From: 192.	168.	0. 0	/24		255	255
To: 198.	168.	255.	255	To: 192.	168.	255. 0	/24			

The size of your network determines which addressing scheme you use. The first block in Table 6.1 acts like one big class A license; the second block as 16 class B licenses; the third as 255 class C licenses. Use as many of these network addresses as you like. The IP addresses in these blocks are not directly reachable from the Internet (which is why the examples in this book use IP addresses from these blocks). In our example firewall, the network interface card connected to the internal network is a device named eth1, which we configure as host number 1 on network 192.168.1.0/24. Edit the file /etc/sysconfig/network-scripts/ ifcfg-eth1 to read like this:

```
DEVICE=eth1
ONBOOT=yes
BOOTPROTO=none
BROADCAST=192.168.1.255
NETWORK=192.168.1.0
NETMASK=255.255.255.0
IPADDR=192.168.1.1
```

In the above listing, the device's IP configuration (BROADCAST, NETWORK, NETMASK, and IPADDR) is hard coded. The BOOTPROTO parameter is set none since the interface doesn't have to go anywhere else to get its configuration.

The Linux network subsystem must be instructed to forward packets between the two interfaces. Edit the file /etc/sysconfig/network to read like this:

```
NETWORKING=yes
FORWARD_IPV4=yes
DEFRAG_IPV4=yes
HOSTNAME=gw.administeringapache.com
GATEWAYDEV=eth0
```

In the above listing, NETWORKING=yes enables the network subsystem. FORWARD_IPV4=yes enables the kernel to perform packet forwarding (a must for any firewall). The DEFRAG_IPV4=yes instructs the kernel that it should reassemble fragmented packets before filtering them or routing them. This will reduce the number of filtering rules required. Without defragmentation, you'll have to deal with fragments separately. They match differently. Defragmentation occurs just behind the interface. Use this option only if this machine is the *only* route to the external network (otherwise, fragments might sneak in through other routes). The HOSTNAME parameter prescribes this computer's host-domain name. GATEWAYDEV=eth0 tells Linux that the device named eth0 is the external interface (i.e. the network's gateway).

Next, configure the firewall to perform the masquerading and proxy services as shown in Figure 6.5.

Figure 6.5

Configure the firewall to perform masquerading and proxy services.

3)The workstations browse the web via the HTTP proxy server.

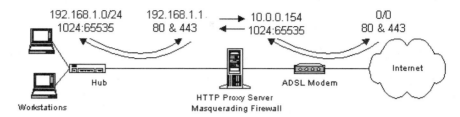

4) The firewall masquerades as the workstations for all other connections

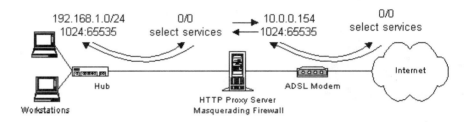

5) A remote administrator telnets in to maintain the firewall.

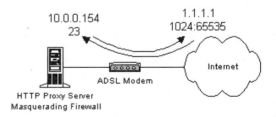

3) The workstations browse the web via the HTTP proxy server

The HTTP proxy server provides the small-business LAN with the same advantages that it provides the corporate LAN: logging of transfers and caching (and, possibly, censoring). The HTTP proxy server illustrated here has an advantage over the one in the corporate model because this proxy server straddles the firewall. This allows the firewall to divert all HTTP requests to the proxy server—regardless of the actual destination address. Forget the hassle of configuring every browser to use the proxy server. The browsers address their requests to the usual port 80 and port 443. This makes the proxy transparent. The browsers don't even know they're using a proxy.

4) The firewall masquerades as the workstations for all other connections

For all non-HTTP/non-HTTPS connections, the firewall masquerades as the workstations making the requests. This is similar to a proxy service in that, in both cases, the firewall replaces the source address with its own. The difference is that masquerading operates in the transport layer and proxy services operate in the application layer. The operating system's kernel performs packet filtering and masquerading, which is fast. Server software performs the proxy, where additional processing may be performed (logging, caching, etc).

The firewall must be configured to accept and masquerade connections for particular services. As with the corporate LAN, selected DNS and ICMP connections should be allowed between the LAN and the Internet. Unlike the corporate LAN, the small business does not provide a farm of servers and services. All services that LAN users rely on are provided by remote servers out on the Internet. Our example small business gets its email from the upstream ISP's mail server. Furthermore, many of the workstation users have personal email accounts (which they also use for work) at various ISPs around the web. The company's web site is hosted on a web server at the upstream ISP and the company updates its web site with FTP. The firewall must allow the LAN workstations to request connections to the POP-2, POP-3, SMTP, and FTP ports of servers on the internet. Internet hosts, on the other hand, must not be allowed to request those connections to LAN hosts or to the firewall. Even though direct connections are being made between LAN hosts and the Internet, the LAN hosts are still safe. Since the firewall performs masquerading, hosts on the Internet cannot request connections from LAN hosts. We still need to protect the firewall itself from inbound connection requests.

5) A remote administrator telnets in to maintain the firewall

The ISP that provides the Internet connection also provides the firewall. A system administrator working for the ISP periodically logs into the firewall to perform maintenance. The firewall specifically allows the system administrator's machine (and no other machine) to request a telnet connection to the firewall. Note that the firewall does not allow just any machine residing on the same network as the administrator. For the ISP to provide this service in mutual trust, the remote administrator's machine cannot receive its IP address dynamically (e.g. via DHCP). This is a potential security risk. A hacker might spoof the firewall by sending packets with the source address set to that of the remote administrator's machine. Weigh this risk against requiring the administrator to come on site to maintain the firewall.

Now we configure the firewall. Linux provides the *ipchains system* for packet filtering and IP masquerading (for kernel versions 2.1.102 and above). Ipchains provides three filters—input, forward, and output—each with its own list of filter rules. The input filter processes all packets coming into the firewall. This includes packets addressed to the firewall itself and packets that the firewall must forward from one network to another. If the input filter approves of the packet, then it sends the packet to a routing process that converys the packet to either a local process (if it is addressed to the firewall) or to the forward filter (if it is addressed to a remote host). If the forward filter approves of the packet, the packet is sent to the output filter. All packets leaving the firewall pass through the output filter. This includes packets from the forward filter and packets originating from a local process.

Masquerading takes place between the forward filter and the output filter. If a rule in the forward filter accepts the packet, the packet is sent directly to the output filter. If a rule in the forward filter specifies that this packet should be masqueraded, the packet is sent to the masquerade process. The masquerade process stores a copy of the packet's header information; replaces the packet's IP address with that of the firewall; allocates a temporary port on the firewall; replaces the packet's source port with the temporary port; and then sends the packet to the output filter. Observe that the packet goes into the output filter with the firewall's address as the source address. Write your output filter rules accordingly.

When remote server responds on the masqueraded connection, the response packet will have the firewall's address as the destination address. Write your input filter rules accordingly. Demasquerading takes place just after a packet passes through the input filter. After the input filter has accepted a packet, the kernel checks to see if this packet is addressed to a temporary port allocated for a masqueraded connection. If so, the packet is sent directly to the output filter—skipping the forward filter.

The whole thing looks like Figure 6.6.

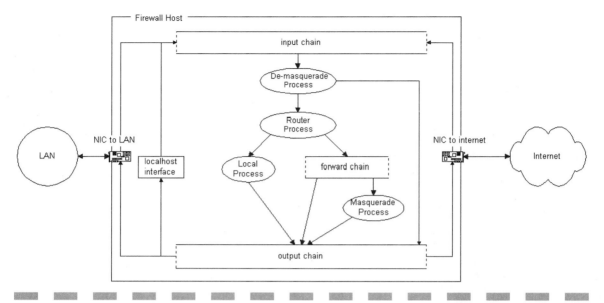

Figure 6.6 *Ipchains firewall.*

You can create your own chains and jump to them from the built-in chains. The called chain can return to the previous chain, somewhat like a function call. You can build chains that ease administration by building chains that modularly perform specific filtering tasks. Alternatively, you can build chains for performance by creating chains that branch like a decision tree. For this example, we will not be creating any user-defined chains. That would require far too much explanation. Paul Russell has written a most eloquent treatise on the subject for the Linux HOWTO docs. You will find it in the text file /usr/doc/HOWTO/IPCHAINS-HOWTO. We'll give you the rules you need to implement the small business firewall. Then, with the help of the HOWTO and the man pages, you can optimize\it or modularize it at your discretion.

Use the program named ipchains to add and remove rules and chains in the kernel networking subsystem. When the network system starts up, the ipchains system is completely open. This presents an important timing issue. You want the ipchains system secured before the network interfaces come up (so that you don't forward possibly malicious packets during network startup). However, the DHCP ports need to be opened for the gateway interface to receive its configuration from the upstream ISP. To get around this, we write two shell scripts. The first locks down the ipchains system, yet allows DHCP. We call this first script just before the network interfaces are initialized (I'll show you where later). The second script configures ipchains for the running firewall. We call this second script just after the network interfaces are initialized. As root at the UNIX shell prompt, create the directory /etc/ipchains. Put the following script in that directory:

```bash
#!/bin/bash

##################################################################
# ipchDhcpOnly
#
# Description:
#    Script to lock down the kernel packet filtering
# system before the initialization of the network
# interfaces.
#
# Command line parameters:
#    None
##################################################################

#
# Set ipchDhcpDev to the name of the network interface
# device that needs to get its IP from a DHCP server.
# Change this setting for your system.
#
ipchDhcpDev="eth0"

#
# Set the default policy of the built-in chains to DENY
# packets not matched by a filter rule.
#
ipchains -P input DENY
ipchains -P forward DENY
ipchains -P output DENY

#
# Flush all filter rules from all chains.
#
ipchains -F

#
# Delete all chains. This will delete all of the
# user-defined chains. The built-in chains cannot be
# deleted.
#
ipchains -X

#
```

```
# Add rules to the output filter to allow outgoing DHCP
# requests.
# DHCP uses the same ports as bootp. Accept TCP and UDP
# packets going out of the interface to the internet and
# destined for a bootp server port.
#
ipchains -A output -i $ipchDhcpDev -p tcp --dport bootps \
    -j ACCEPT
ipchains -A output -i $ipchDhcpDev -p udp --dport bootps \
    -j ACCEPT


#
# Add rules to the input filter to allow incoming DHCP
# responses.
# Accept TCP and UDP packets coming in from the interface
# to the internet and destined for the bootp client port
#
ipchains -A input -i $ipchDhcpDev -p tcp --dport bootpc \
    -j ACCEPT
ipchains -A input -i $ipchDhcpDev -p udp --dport bootpc \
    -j ACCEPT
```

And put this script in the /etc/ipchains directory, too.

```
#!/bin/bash

###############################################################
# ipchFirewall
#
# Description:
#    Script to configure the ipchains packet filtering
# system for the running firewall. This script implements
# the firewall policy and should be called after the network
# interfaces have initialized.
#
# Command line parameters:
#    None
###############################################################

###############################################################
# Configuration
#
# Set the following variables for your system.
#    ipchGateDev    the device name of the interface to
#                   the internet.
#
#    ipchLanDev     the device name of the interface to
#                   the internal network.
```

```
#
#     ipchLoDev        the device name of the loop-back
#                      interface.
#
#     ipchHttpProxyPort  the port number on which the
#                      HTTP proxy server listens for HTTP
#                      connections. Set to nothing if the
#                      firewall is not providing this proxy
#                      service.
#
#     ipchHttpsProxyPort the port number on which the
#                      HTTP proxy server listens for secure
#                      HTTP connections. Set to nothing if
#                      the firewall is not providing this
#                      proxy service.
#
#     ipchRemoteAdmin    the IP address of the remote
#                      machine from which the remote
#                      administrator is allowed to telnet
#                      into the firewall to perform
#                      maintenance. Set to nothing if all
#                      maintenance is done on-site.
#
ipchGateDev="eth0"
ipchLanDev="eth1"
ipchLoDev="lo"
ipchHttpProxyPort=
ipchHttpsProxyPort=
ipchRemoteAdmin=

###################################################################
# Globals
#
# These variables are set through calls to ifconfig.
#
# ipchGateIp   the IP address of the firewall's network
#              interface to the internet
#
# ipchGateNet  the network address of the upstream ISP
#              (the network to which the firewall's
#              gateway interface is connected)
#
# ipchLanIp    the IP address of the firewall's network
#              interface to the LAN
#
# ipchLanNet   the network address of the LAN
#
# ipchLoIp     the IP address of the firewall's loop-back
```

```
#               interface (almost always 127.0.0.1)
#
# ipchLoNet    the network address of the loop-back
#              interface (almost always 127.0.0.0/8)
#
ipchGateIp=
ipchGateNet=
ipchLanIp=
ipchLanNet=
ipchLoIp=
ipchLoNet=



################################################################
#
# These functions obtain the IP configuration of the
# specified interface. We don't hard code these IP
# configurations because they may be dynamic (e.g.
# obtained through DHCP).
#
################################################################
# ipchIpFromDev
#
# Description:
#   Obtains the IP address of the specified network
# interface (via ifconfig).
#
# Parameters:
#       1) a string naming the interface (e.g. eth0).
#
# Returns:
#   Echoes, to stdout, the IP address as a 4-octet string
#(e.g. 192.168.1.1)
#
################################################################
function ipchIpFromDev
    {
    ifconfig "$1" \
        | grep "inet addr:" \
        | sed 's/.*inet addr://' \
        | cut -d ' ' -f 1
    }



################################################################
# ipchMaskFromDev
#
# Description:
```

```
#    Obtains the subnet mask of the specified interface
#    (via ifconfig)
#
#
# Parameters:
#        1) a string naming the interface (e.g. eth0)
#
# Returns:
#        Echoes, to stdout, the subnet mask as a 4-octet
# string (e.g. 255.255.255.0).
#
################################################################
function ipchMaskFromDev
    {
    ifconfig "$1" \
        | grep "Mask:" \
        | sed 's/.*Mask://' \
        | cut -d ' ' -f 1
    }



################################################################
# ipchNetFromIpAndMask
#
# Description:
#   Calculates the network address from the specified IP
# address and subnet mask.
#
# Parameters:
#        1) an IP address as a 4-octet string
#           (e.g. 192.168.1.1).
#
#        2) a subnet mask as a 4-octet string
#           (e.g. 255.255.255.0).
#
# Returns:
#        Echoes, to stdout, the calculated network
# address as a 4-octect string plus a slash plus a
# number indicating the number of bits in the network's
# subnet mask (e.g. 192.168.1.0/24).
#
#####
# Notes:
#        This function relies on bash shell bit-wise
# arithmetic.
#
################################################################
function ipchNetFromIpAndMask
```

```
{
IPAddr="$1"
NetMask="$2"

#
# test params
#
[ -z $IPAddr ] && return
[ -z $NetMask ] && return

#
# Calculate network address
#
# For every octet in the address and in the subnet
# mask...
#
NetAddr=
IPByteNdx=1
NetLen=0
while [ $IPByteNdx -le 4 ]; do
    #
    # ...perform a bit-wise AND on the two octets
    # and append the result to the network address
    #
    IPByte=`echo "$IPAddr" \
        | cut -d '.' -f $IPByteNdx`
    MaskByte=`echo "$NetMask" \
        | cut -d '.' -f $IPByteNdx`
    [ -z $NetAddr ] || NetAddr="$NetAddr."
    NetAddr="$NetAddr$(($IPByte & $MaskByte))"

    #
    # Keep a running count of the number of contiguous,
    # high-order set bits. That is, keep a running
    # count of the length of the subnet mask.
    #
    while [ "$MaskByte" -gt 0 ]; do
       NetLen=`expr "$NetLen" + 1`
       MaskByte=$((($MaskByte << 1) & 0xFE))
    done

    IPByteNdx=`expr "$IPByteNdx" + 1`

done


#
# echo the results
#
```

```
                echo "$NetAddr/$NetLen"

        }


        ##############################################################
        # ipchNetFromDev
        #
        # Description:
        #    Obtains the network address of the specified network
        # interface.
        #
        # Parameters:
        #        1) a string naming the interface (e.g. eth0)
        #
        # Returns:
        #        Echoes, to stdout, the calculated network address
        # as a 4-octect string plus a slash plus a number
        # indicating the number of bits in the network's subnet
        # mask (e.g. 192.168.1.0/24).
        #
        ##############################################################
        function ipchNetFromDev
            {
            IPAddr=`ipchIpFromDev "$1"`
            NetMask=`ipchMaskFromDev "$1"`
            ipchNetFromIpAndMask "$IPAddr" "$NetMask"
            }



        ##############################################################
        # Main
        # Script execution begins here
        ##############################################################
        #
        # Discover the IP configurations of all of the
        # interfaces.
        #

        #
        # Discover the gateway interface
        #
        ipchGateIp=`ipchIpFromDev "$ipchGateDev"`
        ipchGateNet=`ipchNetFromDev "$ipchGateDev"`

        #
        # Discover the LAN interface
        #
        ipchLanIp=`ipchIpFromDev "$ipchLanDev"`
```

```
    ipchLanNet=`ipchNetFromDev "$ipchLanDev"`

    #
    # Discover the loopback interface
    #
    ipchLoIp=`ipchIpFromDev "$ipchLoDev"`
    ipchLoNet=`ipchNetFromDev "$ipchLoDev"`

    #
    # Flush all filter rules from all chains and delete all
    # user-defined chains.
    #
    ipchains -F
    ipchains -X

    #
    # Set the default policy of the built-in chains.
    # The input and forward chains are locked down. Specific
    # services will allowed through them by rules added later
    # by this script. The output chain is left open. (You
    # can't shoot yourself if the gun is pointed away from
    # you.)
    #
    ipchains -P input DENY
    ipchains -P forward DENY
    ipchains -P output ACCEPT


    ###############
    # input chain
    #     Built-in chain through which all incoming
    # packets must pass.
    #

    ###########
    # input chain
    #     Anti-spoof
    #
    #     Prevent spoof attacks by checking that the source
    # address really belongs to the network of the interface
    # that the packet came in on.
    #
    ipchains -A input -i $ipchLoDev -s ! $ipchLoNet \
        -j DENY
    ipchains -A input -i $ipchLanDev -s ! $ipchLanNet \
        -j DENY

    #
    # Packets coming in on the gateway interface could
```

```
# have any source address. We detect spoofing on these
# packets by making sure that they don't have a source
# address belonging to the LAN or the loop-back.
#
ipchains -A input -i $ipchGateDev -s $ipchLoNet \
    -j DENY
ipchains -A input -i $ipchGateDev -s $ipchLanNet \
    -j DENY


#
###########
# input chain
#    from localhost
#
# Accept all. After spoof-detection, the loop-back is a
# trusted network.
#
ipchains -A input -i $ipchLoDev -j ACCEPT


#
###########
# input chain
#    from LAN
#


#
#####
# input chain
#    from LAN
#        to firewall
#
# Accept all. After spoof-detection, the LAN is a trusted
# network.
#
# Firewall serves LAN
#
#    If the firewall provides services to the LAN,
# requests for those services are accepted here.
#
# Firewall as client to the LAN
#
#    If the firewall uses any services provided by a
# server on the LAN, responses to requests for those
# services will be accepted here.
#
ipchains -A input -i $ipchLanDev -d $ipchLanIp -j ACCEPT


#
#####
```

```
# input chain
#     from LAN
#          to internet
#


#
# If HTTP/HTTPS requests are being proxied, redirect
# them to the proxy ports on this firewall.
#
if [ "x_$ipchHttpProxyPort" != "x_" ]; then
    ipchains -A input -i $ipchLanDev -p tcp \
        --dport http -j REDIRECT $ipchHttpProxyPort
fi

if [ "x_$ipchHttpsProxyPort" != "x_" ]; then
    ipchains -A input -i $ipchLanDev -p tcp \
        --dport https -j REDIRECT $ipchHttpsProxyPort
fi

#
# Accept all other LAN-to-internet packets. They will be
# filtered and masqueraded by the forward chain.
#
ipchains -A input -i $ipchLanDev -j ACCEPT

#
###########
# input chain
#     from internet
#

#####
# input chain
#     from internet
#          Safe ICMP
#
# We reduce our exposure to flood-ping and ping-of-death
# attacks by limiting the types of ICMP messages that
# are accepted.
#
# This ICMP check should only be performed on packets
# coming in from the internet (unless you have some
# malicious users on your LAN).
#

#
# Drop ICMP fragments
#
ipchains -A input -i $ipchGateDev -p icmp -f -j DENY
```

```
#
# Allow only ICMP packets that carry error messages.
#
ipchains -A input -i $ipchGateDev -p icmp \
    --icmp-type destination-unreachable -j ACCEPT
ipchains -A input -i $ipchGateDev -p icmp \
    --icmp-type source-quench -j ACCEPT
ipchains -A input -i $ipchGateDev -p icmp \
    --icmp-type time-exceeded -j ACCEPT
ipchains -A input -i $ipchGateDev -p icmp \
    --icmp-type parameter-problem -j ACCEPT


#
# Allow internet hosts to respond to pings from
# the LAN, but not visa versa (i.e. let pong
# in, but not ping).
ipchains -A input -i $ipchGateDev -p icmp \
    --icmp-type pong -j ACCEPT


#
# Deny all other icmp message types
#
ipchains -A input -I $ipchGateDev -p icmp \
    -j DENY

#####
# input chain
#    from internet
#        to firewall
#


#
# Masquerade responses: These rules accept
# responses to masqueraded connections.
#
# Accept packets for allowed services based on the
# source port. Note that the destination IP address
# of these packet's will be that of the firewall,
# not the IP address of the original LAN host.
#

# DNS
ipchains -A input -i $ipchGateDev -p tcp \
    -d $ipchGateIp --sport domain -j ACCEPT
ipchains -A input -i $ipchGateDev -p udp \
    -d $ipchGateIp --sport domain -j ACCEPT

#
```

```
# If HTTP/S are being masqueraded (not proxied),
# accept responses to those masqueraded connections
# here.
#
if [ "x_$ipchHttpProxyPort" = "x_" ]; then
    ipchains -A input -i $ipchGateDev -p tcp \
        -d $ipchGateIp --sport http -j ACCEPT
fi

if [ "x_$ipchHttpsProxyPort" = "x_" ]; then
    ipchains -A input -i $ipchGateDev -p tcp \
        -d $ipchGateIp --sport https -j ACCEPT
fi

# email
ipchains -A input -i $ipchGateDev -p tcp \
    -d $ipchGateIp --sport pop-2 -j ACCEPT
ipchains -A input -i $ipchGateDev -p tcp \
    -d $ipchGateIp --sport pop-3 -j ACCEPT
ipchains -A input -i $ipchGateDev -p tcp \
    -d $ipchGateIp --sport smtp -j ACCEPT

# FTP
ipchains -A input -i $ipchGateDev -p tcp \
    -d $ipchGateIp --sport ftp -j ACCEPT
ipchains -A input -i $ipchGateDev -p tcp \
    -d $ipchGateIp --sport ftp-data -j ACCEPT

#telnet
# If you decide to allow it…
#ipchains -A input -i $ipchGateDev -p tcp \
#     -d $ipchGateIp --sport telnet -j ACCEPT

#
# Firewall as internet client
#
# If the firewall is allowed to use services on the
# internet, allow the incoming responses to those
# connections here. Accept packets based on the source
# port. If a given source port is already being accepted
# as part of the masquerade services, that port does not
# need to be duplicated here.
#

#
# If HTTP/S are being proxied (not masqueraded),
# accept responses to the proxy connections here.
#
if [ "x_$ipchHttpProxyPort" != "x_" ]; then
```

```
        ipchains -A input -i $ipchGateDev -p tcp \
            -d $ipchGateIp --sport http -j ACCEPT
fi

if [ "x_$ipchHttpsProxyPort" != "x_" ]; then
    ipchains -A input -i $ipchGateDev -p tcp \
        -d $ipchGateIp --sport https -j ACCEPT
fi


#
# Firewall serves the internet
#
# If this firewall provides services to the internet,
# accept incoming requests for those services here.
# Accept packets based on the destination port
#
# Currently, the firewall provides no services to the
# internet; but here's a commented-out example.
#
#ipchains -A input -i $ipchGateDev -p tcp \
#    -d $ipchGateIp --dport http -j ACCEPT


#
# Remote administration
#
# Allow the remote administrator to login to the firewall
# with telnet. Specifically, check the source address of
# the packet.
#
if [ "x_$ipchRemoteAdmin" != "x_" ]; then
    ipchains -A input -i $ipchGateDev -p tcp \
        -d $ipchGateIp --dport telnet \
        -s $ipchRemoteAdmin -j ACCEPT
fi


###############
# forward chain
#    Built-in chain through which must pass all packets
# to be forwarded from one network to another.
#

#
# Bad boys.
#
# If you need to keep your LAN users off of particularly
# nasty web servers, specifically DENY those connections
```

```
# here (before they get ACCEPTed by one of the
# "LAN as client" rules, below.
#
# If you specify hosts by name (instead of IP), then
# be sure the firewall has access to DNS before
# issuing the ipchains command.
#
# ipchains -A forward -d www.inappropriatecontent.com \
#    -j DENY
# ipchains -A forward -s www.inappropriatecontent.com \
#    -j DENY


##########
# forward chain
#    from LAN to internet
#

# LAN as client
#
# All connection requests from the LAN to the internet
# are masqueraded. A MASQ rule must be added here for
# every ACCEPT rule placed in the section
# input chain - from internet - to firewall -
# Masquerade responses (above).
#
# In the forward chain, the -i option specifies the
# interface through which the packet will be sent out
# (not the interface that the packet came in on).
#
# Allowed services are accepted based on the
# destination port.
#

# icmp
# Let the LAN ping out
ipchains -A forward -I $ipchGateDev -p icmp \
    --icmp-type ping -j MASQ
# DNS
ipchains -A forward -i $ipchGateDev -p tcp \
    -s $ipchLanNet --dport domain -j MASQ
ipchains -A forward -i $ipchGateDev -p udp \
    -s $ipchLanNet --dport domain -j MASQ

#
# If HTTP/S are being masqueraded (not proxied),
# then masquerade them here.
#
if [ "x_$ipchHttpProxyPort" = "x_" ]; then
    ipchains -A forward -i $ipchGateDev -p tcp \
```

```
                   -s $ipchLanNet --dport http -j MASQ
fi

if [ "x_$ipchHttpsProxyPort" = "x_" ]; then
    ipchains -A forward -i $ipchGateDev -p tcp \
        -s $ipchLanNet --dport https -j MASQ
fi

# email
ipchains -A forward -i $ipchGateDev -p tcp \
    -s $ipchLanNet --dport pop-2 -j MASQ
ipchains -A forward -i $ipchGateDev -p tcp \
    -s $ipchLanNet --dport pop-3 -j MASQ
ipchains -A forward -i $ipchGateDev -p tcp \
    -s $ipchLanNet --dport smtp -j MASQ

# FTP
ipchains -A forward -i $ipchGateDev -p tcp \
    -s $ipchLanNet --dport ftp -j MASQ
ipchains -A forward -i $ipchGateDev -p tcp \
    -s $ipchLanNet --dport ftp-data -j MASQ

# telnet
# If you decide to allow it...
#ipchains -A forward -I $ipchGateDev -p tcp \
#     -s $ipchLanNet --dport telnet -j MASQ

#
# LAN serves internet
#
# Accept responses from a server on the LAN to a client
# on the internet. Only specific servers on the LAN
# should provide such services, so check the source IP
# address. Allowable services are accepted based on the
# source port.
#
# This is pretty much impossible with masquerading; but
# here is a commented out example, in case you get
# an IP license and turn masquerading off.
#
# ipchains -A forward -i $ipchGateDev -s 192.168.1.4 \
#     -p tcp --sport http -j ACCEPT


##########
# forward chain
#     from internet to LAN
#
```

```
#
# LAN as client
#
# Accept responses from an internet server to a LAN
# client. Allowable services are accepted based on the
# source port.
#
# This is pretty much impossible with masquerading
# (all responses to masqueraded connections skip the
# forward chain); but here is a commented out example,
# in case you turn masquerading off. If you do, change
# all of the MASQ rules to ACCEPT rules. Then move
# all of the ACCEPT rules in the section
# input chain - from internet - to firewall -
# Masquerade responses (above)
# to here. For each such moved rule, set the destination
# address to the LAN's network addresss and remove the
# -i interface specification.
#
# DNS
# ipchains -A input -p tcp -d $ipchLanNet \
#    --sport domain -j ACCEPT
# ipchains -A input -p udp -d $ipchLanNet \
#    --sport domain -j ACCEPT


#
# LAN serves internet
#
# Accept requests from internet clients to LAN servers.
# Only specific servers on the LAN should provide such
# services, so check the source IP address. Allowable
# services are accepted based on the destination port.
#
# This is pretty much impossible with masquerading; but
# here is a commented out example, in case you get
# an IP license and turn masquerading off.
#
# ipchains -A forward -d 192.168.1.4 -p tcp --dport http \
#    -j ACCEPT


###############
# output chain
#
#    Built-in chain through which must pass all packets
# leaving the firewall.
#
```

```
# The output chain is completely open.
#
```

Finally, modify the network startup script to call the two scripts at the appropriate points. Edit the file /etc/rc.d/init.d/network and find the section that reads like this:

```
for i in $interfaces_boot; do
    action "Bringing up interface $i" ./ifup $i boot
done
```

and change it to read like this:

```
#
# Lock out all but dhcp
#
/etc/ipchains/ipchDhcpOnly

#
# Bring up the interfaces
#
for i in $interfaces_boot; do
    action "Bringing up interface $i" ./ifup $i boot
done

#
# Bring up the firewall
#
/etc/ipchains/ipchFirewall
```

Locking Down Internet Services

There are a number of quick and easy things you can do to close up large holes in security. Edit the /etc/inetd.conf file and comment out (by inserting a pound sign at the beginning of the line) all services that the server is not actually serving. The rsh, rlogin, and rexec services (ports 514/tcp, 513/tcp, and 512/tcp) are especially dangerous because they allow automatic login.

Don't allow the root user to log in on any terminal other than the console. The file /etc/securetty lists those terminals that root is allowed to login on. It should look like this:

```
tty1
tty2
tty3
```

```
tty4
tty5
tty6
tty7
tty8
```

This prevents root from logging over the network using a pseudo terminal. If you need to telnet in as root, telnet in as a normal user and then su to root. This way, the actions that the root user performs can be traced back to a real user.

Don't let power users and daemon users log in to FTP. The file /etc/ftpusers lists those usernames that are not allowed to log in to FTP. It should read like this:

```
root
bin
daemon
adm
lp
sync
shutdown
halt
mail
news
uucp
operator
games
nobody
httpd
```

How your web server accepts content from the webmaster is a matter of policy. Most ISPs provide FTP for their web-hosting customers to deliver content; though there are market pressures for allowing webmasters to telnet in and edit the content directly on the server. This is especially true if the webmasters are writing CGI scripts in a compiled language; which, as an ISP, you may or may not support. An intranet web server, on the other hand, lives in a more trusted environment. Login access by the webmaster doesn't pose such an anonymous threat. You can configure FTP and telnet services to allow access based on where the login is coming from. You might want to allow access to these services only to connections made from within the LAN. Or your might allow FTP from anywhere, but telnet from only within the LAN. You might also allow telnet over the Internet to selected users working from home.

To implement FTP access policies, edit the file /etc/ftpaccess. This describes who is authorized to use FTP services and from where. In this file, you define authorized classes of users with the `class` directive. With this directive, you define a class name and then describe what kind of users from what IP addresses belong to that class. The `class` directive accepts several parameters. The first is the class name. The second parameter is a comma-separated list of user types: which may be one of the following keywords: `real` (any user defined in `/etc/passwd`), `guest` (any user listed in the `guestgroup` or `guestuser` directives), or `anonymous` (anyone logging in as the anonymous user). Next, the `class` directive accepts a space separated list of IP address specifications. For a user to belong to the defined class, the user must be one of the specified user types and must be connecting from one of the specified addresses. This example:

```
class all real,guest,anonymous *
```

defines the class named `all`. A user is a member of this class if the user is either a `real` user, a `guest` user, or an `anonymous` user logging in from anywhere. This would be a standard configuration for a public FTP server. For a more restrictive policy, you could define this class instead

```
class lanusers real 192.168.1.0/24
```

which allows FTP login for any valid user logging in from the local area network. You could additionally allow FTP login from selected hosts on the Internet by adding this class

```
class rmtusers real 1.1.1.1 2.2.2.2
```

which allows FTP login for any valid user connecting from the specified IP addresses. You can also explicitly deny FTP login for users connecting from particular IP addresses. The `deny` directive takes two parameters: an IP address and the name of a text file containing a message to be displayed when someone attempts to log in from the specified address. For example:

```
deny !192.168.1.0/24 /etc/ftpreject.txt
```

The exclamation point negates the address match. The above directive would deny FTP login to anyone *not* connecting from the LAN; in which case, FTP displays to the rejected user the `ftpreject.txt` file.

Your telnet daemon may provide options for using different login methods and for calling custom login programs. Consult `man 8 telnetd` for available options.

FTP, telnet, and any other services launched by the inetd daemon can be secured with the tcpd wrapper. Normally, the inetd daemon listens to all services ports and passes connections to the appropriate service daemons (e.g. telnet connections are passed to telnetd, etc.). With the tcpd wrapper installed, inetd is tricked into passing each connection to the tcpd wrapper (by renaming the service daemon program in inetd's configuration file /etc/inetd.conf—see man 8 tcpd). Tcpd performs various security checks on each connection before passing the connection on to the appropriate service daemon. Tcpd logs all connections to the syslogd daemon. For rsh and rlogin connections (which you really shouldn't be using), tcpd does a reverse DNS lookup to verify that the requesting host really is who it says it is. Tcpd fights spoofing in general by turning off source-routing on all connections. Most importantly, tcpd performs configurable access control through the two hosts-access files named /etc/hosts.allow and /etc/hosts.deny. When a service request is received, tcpd looks for a match on the requested service and the requesting client in the hosts-access files. These files are searched in this order:

- If the service:client pair appears in hosts.allow, the connection is accepted.
- If the service:client pair appears in hosts.deny, the connection is refused.
- The connection is accepted.

Chances are that you already have the tcpd wrapper installed and all you have to do is edit the hosts-access files. The syntax for these files is

```
<daemon list>:<client list>[:<shell command>]
```

where <daemon list> is a comma-separated list of service daemons (as named in the /etc/inetd.conf file—e.g. to add telnet, add the name in.telnetd). <client list> is a comma-separated list of client hostnames or IP addresses. The <shell command>, which is optional, is executed if this line is the first match for the requested service and requesting client. Certain keywords are available as wildcards. ALL, for example, matches anything. The original installation of tcpd will be quite open, with ALL:ALL in the hosts.allow file and nothing in the hosts.deny file. To completely disable telnet, put in.telnetd:ALL in the hosts.deny file and make sure that in.telnetd is not present in the hosts.allow file. To allow FTP from everywhere and allow telnet only from the LAN, put ALL:ALL in the hosts.deny file, then put these two entries in the hosts.allow file:

```
in.ftpd:ALL
in.telnetd:192.168.1.0/24
```

Consult `man 5 hosts_access` for a complete list of pattern matching options.

Secure sockets layers is available for FTP and telnet, which you can configure to require the client to present a certificate for authentication. The application of SSL to the Apache web server is discussed in great detail later in this chapter. To apply SSL to FTP or telnet, obtain the SSLeay toolkit and SSL aware applications from **http://www2.psy.uq. edu.au/ ~ ftp/Crypto/**.

Configuring Apache's Self-Defenses

Apache can defend itself from some types of hacker attacks, with the following configuration directives:

LimitRequestBody

`LimitRequestbody` limits the maximum size of the HTTP request body. If a request exceeds this limit, the request will be rejected with an error response. This reduces exposure to a denial-of-service attack, in which a hacker ties up the server with an infinitely long request. `LimitRequest-Body` accepts a single numeric parameter that may be from 0 to 2147483647, where 0 means "no limit." The default is 0. Request bodies are usually received with `POST` and `PUT` requests. If you impose a `LimitRequestBody`, you will need to set this limit high enough to allow for the largest file that you expect the server will receive via a `PUT` request and high enough to allow for the largest form-data submission that you expect to receive via a `POST` request. The `LimitRequestBody` directive may appear in the configuration file's global context, or within `<VirtualHost>` or `<Directory>` block, or within an `.htaccess` file.

LimitRequestFields

`LimitRequestFields` limits the allowable number of request header fields in any one request. If a request exceeds this limit, the request will be rejected with an error response. This reduces exposure to a denial-of-service attack, where a hacker ties up the server with an infinitely long list of request headers. `LimitRequestFields` accepts a single numeric parameter that may be from 0 to 32767, where 0 means "no limit." The default is 100. This limit should be set high enough to allow for normal requests that may have a large number headers (e.g. session id cookies, cache control headers, proxy headers, MIME headers, and the like). The `LimitRequestFields` directive may appear only in the configuration file's global context.

LimitRequestFieldSize

`LimitRequestFieldSize` limits the size of each request header. If a request exceeds this limit, the request will be rejected with an error response. This reduces exposure to a buffer-overflow attack, where a hacker might try to overflow Apache's request header buffer and thus corrupt memory. `LimitRequestFieldSize` accepts one numeric parameter that may be from 0 to 8190, where 8190 is the currently compiled size of Apache's request header buffer. The default is 8190. The default value prevents buffer-overflow attacks. You could reduce this limit if you are under a denial-of-service attack in which the hacker repeatedly sends a long list of large request headers. The `LimitRequestFieldSize` directive may appear only in the configuration file's global context.

LimitRequestLine

`LimitRequestLine` limits the length of each request line. If a request exceeds this limit, the request will be rejected with an error response. This reduces exposure to a buffer-overflow attack, in which a hacker might try to overflow Apache's request line buffer and thus corrupt memory. `LimitRequestLine` accepts one numeric parameter that may be from 0 to 8190, where 8190 is the currently compiled size of Apache's request line buffer. The default is 8190. The default value prevents buffer-overflow attacks. You could reduce this limit if you are under a denial-of-service attack in which the hacker repeatedly sends long request lines. The `LimitRequestLine` directive may appear only in the configuration file's global context.

RLimitCPU

`RLimitCPRU` limits the number of seconds that a process can occupy the CPU. This limit is imposed on the forked children of Apache child daemons, such as CGI scripts and SSI `exec` calls. This directive accepts one or two numeric parameters, the first being a soft limit and the second a maximum limit. The default value is set to that of the operating system. If a child process exceeds this limit, the child is killed and an error response is returned and logged. This directive normally prevents runaway CGI scripts, but could be useful in defending against attacks on poorly written CGI scripts. If a CGI script is accepting `POST` data, and runs those data through various shell commands (like `sed`, `cut`, etc.), a hacker could embed a semicolon into the data to break out of the shell command and run destructive commands. For example, if a CGI script blindly accepts these data

```
;; while true ; do; : done
```

and runs them through sed, the semicolons will cause the shell to stop the sed command and run the above infinite loop. If you detect such an attack, reduce the `RLimitCPU` value and consult the webmaster about pre-processing semicolons in `POST` data. The `RLimitCPU` directive may appear within the configuration file's global context, or within a `<VirtualHost>` block.

RLimitMem

`RLimitMem` limits the number of bytes of memory that a process can allocate. This limit is imposed on the forked children of Apache child daemons, such as CGI scripts and SSI exec calls. This directive accepts one or two numeric parameters, the first being a soft limit and the second a maximum limit. The default value is set to that of the operating system. If a child process exceeds this limit, the child is killed and an error response is returned and logged. This directive is normally used to shut down leaky CGI binaries, but could be useful in defending against attacks on poorly written CGI. If a CGI script allocates memory based on the amount of `POST` data or `PUT` data being received, a hacker could submit unreasonably long data in an attempt to cause out-of-memory errors. If you detect such an attack, reduce the `RLimitMem` value and contact the webmaster about buffer management. You might also reduce the `LimitRequestBody` value. The `RLimitMEM` directive may appear within the configuration file's global context, or within a `<VirtualHost>` block.

RLimitNProc

`RLimitNProc` limits the number of processes that can be forked by any one process. This directive accepts one or two numeric parameters, the first being a soft limit and the second a maximum limit. The default value is set to that of the operating system. If a child process exceeds this limit, the child and forked children are killed and an error response is returned and logged. This directive normally stops fork-happy CGI scripts, but could be useful in defending against attacks on poorly written CGI scripts. If a CGI script is accepting POST data, and runs those data through various shell commands (like sed, cut, etc.), a hacker could embed a semicolon into the data to break out of the shell command and run destructive commands. For example, if a CGI script blindly accepts these data

```
;; while true ; do; find / -exec ls -l {} \; &; done
```

and runs them through sed, the semicolons will cause the shell to stop the sed command and run the above infinite loop—which forks a long running process with each iteration. If you detect such an attack, reduce the RLimitNProc value and contact the webmaster about preprocessing semicolons in POST data. The RLimitNProc directive may appear within the configuration file's global context, or within a <VirtualHost> block.

KeepAlive

KeepAlive enables persistent connections. This increases performance because the client can make several requests without establishing a separate connection for each request. The KeepAlive directive accepts one parameter, which may be either on or off. Disabling KeepAlive is a defense against denial-of-service attacks in which the hacker makes a connection and then just sits on it. Set KeepAlive to off if you detect that you are under such an attack; otherwise, set it to on for the sake of performance. The KeepAlive directive can appear only within the configuration file's global context.

KeepAliveTimeout

KeepAliveTimeout limits the number of seconds that Apache will wait for additional requests on the same connection. The default is 15 seconds. This directive could be used to defend against a denial-of-service attack in which the hacker repeatedly makes persistent connections that are never closed. The KeepAliveTimeout directive can appear only within the configuration file's global context.

MaxKeepAliveRequests

MaxKeepAliveRequests limits the number of requests that can be made over one connection. The default is 100. Lowering this defends against a denial-of-service attack in which the hacker makes a persistent connection and launches an infinite loop of requests through that connection. The MaxKeepAliveRequests directive may appear only within the configuration file's global context.

ContentDigest

ContentDigest enables the generation of the Content-MD5 response header. This directive accepts one parameter, which may be either on or off. The default is off. If it is enabled, Apache calculates an MD5 message digest on the content body of the response and places the result in the Content-MD5 response header. The client can then recalculate the digest on the received content body and compare the recalculated digest to that transmitted in the Content-MD5 response header. If the digests do not match, then the browser knows that the message has been altered en route. This provides some protection against a *man-in-the-middle attack*. You may want to enable this directive only if you suspect you are under such an attack. The digest is calculated on every response and is never cached, which affects performance. This directive doesn't provide complete protection. A good hacker would modify the content body and then recalculate the digest—transmitting to the client a digest that the client would believe to be correct. The ContentDigest directive may appear in the configuration file's global context, or within a <VirtualHost> or <Directory> block, or within an .htaccess file.

The Apache core provides all the directives discussed in the above section.

Securing the Content

Allowing/Blocking Content Access

The most obvious defense against publishing private data is the appropriate use of the User and Group directives.

User

User specifies the user ID under which the Apache child daemons run. The User directive accepts one parameter that may be either a valid username from /etc/passwd or a number (preceded by a pound sign) specifying a numeric user ID from /etc/passwd.

Group

Group specifies the group ID under which the Apache child daemons run. The Group directive accepts one parameter that may be either a valid group name from /etc/group or a number (preceded by a pound sign) specifying a numeric group ID from /etc/group.

The User and Group directives may appear within the configuration file's global context, or within a <VirtualHost> block. The Apache core provides the User and Group directives.

The APACI utility will default these directives to nobody during installation. You should change this. You should create a user and group specifically for the web server child daemons. The new user and group should have absolutely no permissions other than the ability to read the DocumentRoot and ScriptAlias directory trees. The user and group should especially not have write permissions anywhere within the ServerRoot or ScriptAlias directory trees. Otherwise, a hacker might be able to trick the Apache child daemons into modifying server binaries and CGI scripts and binaries. See the section titled "Creating the Daemon Account" in Chapter 3: "Creating the Web Site."

Apache provides directives for selectively allowing access to various parts of your file system and public data. These access directives (Order, deny, and allow) may appear within a <Directory>, <Files>, or <Location> block or within an .htaccess file to grant or deny access to the resource specified by the block directive. Consider the following:

```
<Directory "/">
    order allow,deny
    deny from all
</Directory>

DocumentRoot "/home/webmastr/pub/html"

<Directory "/home/webmastr/pub/html">
    order deny,allow
    allow from all
</Directory>
```

The above directives first deny access to the root directory. Since <Directory> configurations are inherited by subdirectories, this denies access to the entire file system. After defining the public data area with the DocumentRoot directive, the above example explicitly grants access to the DocumentRoot directory tree.

deny

Denies specified clients access to the resource defined by an enclosing block directive. The deny directive expects at least two parameters. The first must be the keyword from, which is then followed by a space-separated list of IP address specifications. If the IP address of the client requesting the specified resource matches any of the IP specifications in the list, then access is denied to that client, in which case the server responds with 403 Forbidden error.

allow

Allows specified clients access to the resource defined by an enclosing block directive. The allow directive expects at least two parameters. The first must be the keyword from, which is then followed by space-separated list of IP address specifications. If the IP address of the client requesting the specified resource matches any of the IP specifications in the list, then access is granted and the server transmits the requested resource.

An IP address specification accepted by the deny and allow directives may be any of the following:

- The keyword all matches any client. For example:

  ```
  allow from all
  ```

- A domain name matches any client whose hostname ends with the specified domain name or partial domain name. For example:

  ```
  allow from ourcompany.com
  ```

- An IP address matches any client having the specified IP address; or, if a partial address is specified, matches any client whose IP address begins with the specified IP address. For example:

  ```
  allow from 1.1.1.1
  ```

  or

  ```
  allow from 192.168.1.
  ```

- A network address with netmask matches any client whose IP address contains a network portion (extracted using the netmask) that matches the specified network address. For example:

```
allow from 192.168.1.0/255.255.255.0
```

■ A network address with CIDR matches any client whose IP address contains a network portion (extracted using the CIDR—which species the number of bits in the netmask) that matches the specified network address. For example:

```
allow from 192.168.1.0/24
```

order

Order governs the process of access decision making. The order directive accepts one parameter, which may be one of:

■ `deny,allow`—Processes the `deny` directives first. The initial state of the request is set to OK. Then the `deny` directives are processed. If the host matches any IP specification in the `deny` list, then the request state is set to FORBIDDEN. Next, the `allow` list is processed. If the client matches any IP specification in the allow list, then the state of the request is set to OK. The final state of the request decides access. Requests from clients that don't match either list are thus accepted. Requests from clients that match both lists are thus accepted. The result is that a request is accepted, unless it appears in the `deny` list and only in the `deny` list.

■ `allow,deny`—Processes the `allow` directives first. The initial state of the request is set to FORBIDDEN. Then the `allow` list is processed. If there is a match in the allow list, the state of the request is set to OK. Next, the `deny` list is processed. If there is a match in the deny list, the state of the request is set to FORBIDDEN. The final state of the request decides access. Requests from clients that don't match either list are thus rejected. Requests from clients that match both lists are thus rejected. The sum result is that a request is rejected unless it appears in the `allow` list and only in the `allow` list.

■ `mutual-failure`—Grants access only to clients who appear in the `allow` list and not in the `deny` list.

Note that both the `allow` list and the `deny` list are always processed. There is not logical short-circuiting.

Consider these examples:

The following example allows access to the web site only if the requesting client is connecting from within the local area network.

```
<Directory "/home/webmastr/pub/html">
    order deny,allow
    deny from all
    allow from 192.168.1.0/24
</Directory>
```

The following example allows access to the web site to everyone, except for the internal/ subdirectory, for which access is granted only to connections from the local area network.

```
<Directory "/home/webmastr/pub/html">
    order deny,allow
    allow from all
</Directory>

<Directory "/home/webmastr/pub/html/internal">
    order deny,allow
    deny from all
    allow from 192.168.1.0/24
</Directory>
```

The following example grants access to the admin/ subdirectory only to the administrator's workstation on the LAN and from the administrator's PC at home.

```
<Directory "/home/webmastr/pub/html/admin">
    order deny,allow
    deny from all
    allow from 192.168.1.7 2.2.2.2
</Directory>
```

Note that for any of the access directives to appear within an .htaccess file, a Limit option to the AllowOverride directive must be in effect for the given resource.

The mod_access module, a default module, provides the allow, deny, and order directives.

Watch out for collisions between <Directory>, <Files>, and <Location> blocks and .htaccess directives that may contain conflicting policies. A given request may match more than one block. The access policies specified by the most local context will prevail, which may not yield the results that you expect.

Requiring Authentication to Access Content

You may have private resources you would like to make available only to selected individuals. This requires authentication (verifying who the user is) and authorization (determining if the user has permissions for the resource). Apache provides the `Auth????` directives for authentication and the `require` directive for authorization. These directives are placed inside a `<Directory>`, `<Files>`, or `<Location>` block to control access to the resource specified by that block. These directives can appear within an `.htaccess` file to control access to the directory in which the .htaccess file resides. To appear within an `.htaccess` file, an `AuthConfig` option to an `AllowOverride` directive must be in effect for the given resource. Consider the following:

```
<Location /cgi-bin/clicklog.cgi>
    AuthType Basic
    AuthName adminapache
    AuthUserFile /home/webmastr/auth/authuser
    AuthGroupFile /home/webmastr/auth/authgroup
    require group clicklog
</Location>
```

The above example is taken from the end of the section titled "Tracking User Habits—the Clickstream Log" in Chapter 5: "Using Logs," where we created a click-stream log that is viewable online only to members of the clicklog user group.

AuthType

`AuthType` specifies the authentication protocol to be used between the server and the client. The `AuthType` directive accepts one parameter, which may be either Basic or Digest. The HTTP/1.1 specification provides for two type of authentication summarized as follows:[1]

BASIC ACCESS AUTHENTICATION:
- The client transmits a request.
- The server rejects the request with a 401 Unauthorized error and transmits a WWW-Authenticate response header. The value of the WWW-Authenticate header instructs the browser to use the Basic Access Authentication scheme. The WWW-Authenticate header also tells the browser the name of the realm in which the user needs to authenticate. The realm is just a string to remind the user which password to use.

---

[1] The HTTP/1.1 protocol defined in RFC 2616 adopts the authentication methods described in RFC 2069. RFC 2069 was subsequently made obsolete by RFC 2617. My summary of the Basic and Digest algorithms is my interpretation of RFC 2617.

- The browser displays the name of the realm in a login dialog box in which the user enters the appropriate username and password. The browser then retransmits the request with an added Authorization request header. The Authorization request header contains a Base64 encoding of the username:password.
- The server decodes the username:password from the Authorization request header, locally looks up the password for the username, and compares the password from the Authorization header to the password looked up locally. If they match, the user is considered authenticated.

Basic authentication has a basic problem. The user's password is transmitted in the clear across the Internet. True, it's Base64 encoded; but Base64 doesn't use a key. Anyone can decode it. This problem gave rise to another form of authentication.

DIGEST ACCESS AUTHENTICATION:
- The client transmits a request.
- The server rejects the request with a 401 Unauthorized error and transmits a WWW-Authenticate response header. This header instructs the user to use the Digest authentication scheme. This header also contains the realm in which the user needs to login and a *nonce value* (a server-generated string unique to this connection).
- The browser displays the name of the realm in a login dialog box in which the user enters the appropriate username and password. The browser then combines the username, the user's password, the realm, various information about the request, and the server's nonce value and calculates a digest on the combination. The browser then retransmits the request with an added Authorization request header. The Authorization request header contains, among other things, the username and the calculated digest.
- The server obtains the username from the Authorization request header and locally looks up the username's password. The server calculates the same digest that the browser calculated, using the locally looked up password. The server compares its digest with the digest transmitted in the Authorization request header. If they are the same, then the user must know the username's password and the user is considered authenticated.

The calculated digest is a one-way hash and cannot be reversed to extract the user's password. Thus the user's password is not transmitted in the clear over the Web.

The Digest authentication scheme also has a basic problem. None of the browsers supports it. You're stuck with Basic authentication. Under current conditions, the only way to authenticate without giving away the user's password is to encrypt the whole thing with SSL (discussed later in this chapter).

The Apache core provides the `AuthType` directive.

AuthName

`AuthName` specifies the name of the realm in which the user must authenticate. For Basic authentication, this merely provides a prompt for the user. For Digest authentication, this directive specifies the realm included in the digest calculation.

The Apache core provides the `AuthName` directive.

AuthUserFile

`AuthUserFile` specifies, for Basic authentication, the path and filename to a text file containing the usernames and passwords of user accounts recognized by the server. The following sample line illustrates the format of this file:

```
jdoe:CDcpxLaWpiuRg
```

Each line contains two colon-separated fields. The first field is the username. The second is the encrypted password for the given username. Use the `htpasswd` program to create and maintain such files. The `mod_auth` module, a default module, provides the `AuthUserFile` directive.

htpasswd

`htpasswd` creates and maintains user account text files for Basic authentication. You will find this binary in the `bin/` subdirectory of the Apache installation directory (e.g. `/usr/local/apache/bin/htpasswd`). The `htpasswd` program expects two parameters: 1) the path and filename to the text file to be manipulated, and 2) the username whose record therein is to be created or altered. The program will prompt the terminal for entry of the password for the username specified on the command line. Then the program will prompt for reentry of the password for verification. Then the program searches the specified text file for the specified username. If found, the username's password is updated. If not found, the username and password are added to the file. The two required parameters may be preceded by the following options:

- ▪ −c—Creates a new password file. This option informs htpasswd that you are aware that the file does not exist. Without this option, htpasswd exits with a "No such file or directory" error.
- ▪ −d—Instructs htpasswd to use the crypt() function from the C standard library (a DES cipher) to encrypt the password, which is the default encryption method on all systems except Windows.
- ▪ −m—Instructs htpasswd to use the MD5 cipher to encrypt the password, which is the default encryption method on Windows systems.
- ▪ −p—Instructions htpasswd not to encrypt the password at all, but to save it as plain text instead. This option should only be used on Windows systems. UNIX systems will not authenticate unencrypted passwords.
- ▪ −s—Instructs htpasswd to use the SHA cipher to encrypt the password.
- ▪ −b—Instructs htpasswd to obtain the password from the command line (instead of the terminal); in which case, a third parameter specifying the password is required. The password thus given on the command line must be pre-encrypted. This option is useful for CGI scripts that accept POST data from forms in which the user creates his/her own account.

The following example would create the Basic password file used in the clicklog example that begins this section:

```
/usr/local/apache/bin/htpasswd -c \
    /home/webmastr/auth/authuser \
    jdoe
```

AuthGroupFile

AuthGroupFile specifies, for both Basic and Digest authentication, the path and filename of the text file containing group names and member lists. The following sample line illustrates the format of this file:

```
clicklog:jdoe tsmith
```

Each line contains two colon-separated fields. The first is the group name. The second is a space-separated list of the usernames who are members of the given group. Create and edit this file manually with a text editor.

The mod_auth module, a default module, provides the AuthGroupFile directive.

require

`require` authorizes the specified users for access to a resource. The `require` directive expects at least one parameter; which may be one of:

- `user`—Followed by a space-separated list of usernames, specifies which users are authorized to access the resource
- `group`—Followed by a space-separated list of group names, specifies the groups whose members are authorized to access the resource.
- `valid-user`—By itself, specifies that any authenticated user is authorized to access the resource.

The Apache core provides the `require` directive.

This concludes the list of directives used in the clicklog example that begins this section. The remaining authentication directives are discussed below.

If you are guaranteed that all the browsers hitting your site are Digest-aware (e.g. you are running an intranet web server and control the browser configurations), then you can use the more secure Digest Access Authentication scheme (as described in `AuthType`, above). Digest authentication requires a different username/password text file, which you specify with the `AuthDigestFile` directive, instead of the `AuthUserFile` directive. The `AuthGroupFile` directive would remain the same. The clicklog example's `<Location>` block would then be configured like this:

```
<Location /cgi-bin/clicklog.cgi>
    AuthType Digest
    AuthName adminapache
    AuthDigestFile /home/webmastr/auth/authuser
    AuthGroupFile /home/webmastr/auth/authgroup
    require group clicklog
</Location>
```

AuthDigestFile

`AuthDigestFile` specifies, for Digest authentication, the path and filename to a text file containing the usernames, realms, and passwords of user accounts recognized by the server. The following sample line illustrates the format of this file:

```
jdoe:clicklog:233c3e34b82b019cd9b3ce98e4275fdb
```

Each line contains three colon-separated fields. The first is the username. The second is the authentication realm for the username. The third is the MD5-encrypted password for the given username. Use the `htdigest` program to create and maintain such files.

The `mod_digest` module, which is *not* a default module, provides the `AuthDigestFile` directive. To compile this module into your Apache server use the `--enable-module=digest` parameter to the APACI utility's `configure` command. Or use the `--enable-module=most` parameter.

htdigest

`htdigest` creates and maintains user account text files for Digest authentication. You will find this binary in the `bin/` subdirectory of the Apache installation directory (e.g. `/usr/local/apache/bin/htdigest`). The `htdigest` program expects three parameters: 1) the text file, 2) the realm and 3) the username. The program will prompt the terminal for entry of the password for the username specified on the command line. Then the program will prompt for reentry of the password for verification. It then searches the specified text file for the specified username and realm. If found, the password is updated. If the password is not found, the username, realm, and password are added to the file. The three required parameters may be preceded by the following option:

- –c creates a new password file. This option informs `htdigest` that you are aware that the file does not exist. Without this option, `htdigest` exits with a " Could not open passwd file" error.

The following command line could be used to create the password file for the `clicklog` example:

```
/usr/local/apache/bin/htdigest -c \
    /home/webmastr/auth/authuser \
    clicklog \
    jdoe
```

Searching large text files is a slow process. You can enhance performance by storing the users and groups in a database file. Apache provides directives and utilities for storing users and groups in DBM-style and Berkeley DB 2-style databases. Of the two, Apache prefers the latter. Both will be discussed herein. In the DB 2 style, the `clicklog` example's `<Location>` block would be coded like this:

```
<Location /cgi-bin/clicklog.cgi>
    AuthType Basic
    AuthName adminapache
```

```
         AuthDBUserFile /home/webmastr/auth/authuser
         AuthDBGroupFile /home/webmastr/auth/authgroup
         require group clicklog
</Location>
```

AuthDBUserFile

AuthDBUserFile specifies the path and filename to a Berkeley DB 2-style database containing the usernames and passwords of user accounts recognized by the server. The key for the database is the username. The data is the crypt()-encrypted password. Use the dbmmanage program to create and maintain such files.

AuthDBGroupFile

AuthDBGroupFile specifies the path and filename to a Berkeley DB 2-style database containing the group names and member lists. The key for the database is the username. The data for the database are in a comma-separated list naming the groups of which the given username is a member. Use the dbmmanage program to create and maintain such files.

The mod_auth_db module, which is *not* a default module, provides the AuthDBUserFile and the AuthDBGroupFile directives. To compile this module into your Apache server, use the --enable-module=auth_db parameter to the APACI utility's configure command. Or use the --enable-module=most parameter.

dbmmanage

dbmmanage creates and maintains Berkeley DB 2-style database files for storing user account information. You will find this perl script in the bin/ subdirectory of the Apache installation directory (e.g. /usr/local/apache/bin/dbmmanage). The first line in the script is a shebang line pointing to the perl interpreter:

```
#!/usr/local/bin/perl
```

You may need to correct this line before running the script. On my Linux box, I had to change it to:

```
#!/usr/bin/perl
```

The dbmmanage script expects at least two parameters. The first parameter specifies the path and filename of the database to be manipulated. The second parameters specifies the action to take; which may be one of:

- ■ add—Adds a user account record to the database. Two additional parameters are expected: the username and the crypt()-encrypted password to be assigned to the username.
- ■ adduser—Adds a user account record to the database. One additional parameter is expected: the username. The program prompts the terminal for entry of the password for the username, and then prompts for reentry for verification.
- ■ check—Checks if the specified user exists in the database and has the specified password. One additional parameter is expected: the username. The program prompts the terminal for entry of the password. If the specified user exists and has the entered password, then the program echoes "password ok" to stdout and exits with an exit code of 0. If the user exists in the database, but has a password different from the one entered, then the program echoes "password mismatch" to stdout and exits with an exit code of 0. If the specified username does not exist in the database, then the program echoes "Sorry, user 'zzz' doesn't exist!" and exits with an exit code of 255. If the specified database file does not exist, the program echoes " Sorry, user 'zzz' doesn't exist!" and exists with an exit code of 2.
- ■ delete—Deletes the user account record of the specified username. One additional parameter is required: the username.
- ■ import—Imports user account records into the database. No additional parameters are expected. The user account data are taken from stdin. The data are expected to be in one of two forms: either <username>:<encrypted password> or <username>:<encrypted password>:<group list>, where group list is a comma-separated list of group names of which the username is a member.
- ■ update—Updates the password for the specified username. One additional parameter is expected: the username. The program prompts the terminal for entry of the username's new password, and prompts for reentry for verification.
- ■ view—Views the database. One additional parameter is optional. If no additional parameter is given on the command line, the program displays the entire database. If an additional parameter is given, it specifies the username whose record is to be displayed.

The clicklog example's user and group files would be created with these two commands:

```
/usr/local/apache/bin/dbmmanage \
    /home/webmastr/auth/authuser \
```

```
    adduser \
    jdoe

/usr/local/apache/bin/dbmmanage \
    /home/webmastr/auth/authgroup \
    add \
    jdoe \
    admin,clicklog,users
```

The first command creates the user file and adds jdoe as its first user. The program prompts for jdoe's password, prompts for verification of the password, then encrypts the password into jdoe's record. The second command creates the group file and adds jdoe's group list as its first record—granting jdoe membership to the admin, clicklog, and users groups. The add action is specified to the dbmmanage command because we don't want the group list encrypted.

When using database files, you can combine the user and the group files into one file. The key for the file is the username. The data for each record consist of the user's encrypted password, a colon, and then a comma-separated list of groups of which the user is a member. The following command would create a single file for our clicklog example:

```
/usr/local/apache/bin/dbmmanage \
    /home/webmastr/auth/authuser \
    add \
    jdoe \
    MVyH9enn12DB.:users,clicklog,admin
```

The above command creates the database and adds jdoe as its first record. The last parameter to the dbmmanage command contains the data to be stored under the jdoe key (which includes the encrypted password and the group list). A CGI script that accepts POST data from user's creating the own accounts might issue the above command. This CGI script or binary must have access to the crypt() function in the C standard library in order to encrypt the password. You would then set the AuthDBUserFile and the AuthDBGroupFile to point to the same file— /home/webmastr/auth/authuser.

Another way to set up the single-file database would be first to use the htpasswd program to create and populate a flat file (which will prompt for passwords and then encrypt them). Then edit the flat file to append each user's group memberships. Each line in the flat file would then have this format:

```
jdoe:MVyH9enn12DB.:users,clicklog,admin
```

Finally, import the flat file into the database with this command:

```
cat /home/webmastr/auth/flatfile \
    |   /usr/local/apache/bin/dbmmanage \
    /home/webmastr/auth/authuser \
    import
```

The `dbmmanage` script can create DB 2 style and DBM style databases. The script searches your system for DB and DBM libraries. You system probably has more than one. The script picks the one it likes best from those available on your system. The script's preferences are defined by the following two lines in the script:

```
#                                 -ldb    -lndbm    -lgdbm
BEGIN { @AnyDBM_File::ISA = qw(DB_File NDBM_File GDBM_File) }
```

`DB_File` refers to the Berkeley DB 2 library. `NDBM_File` refers the New Database Manager library. `GDBM_File` refers to the GNU Database Manager library. You may reorder these to match your own preferences. Be sure similarly to reorder the libraries shown in the comment line above.

If the `dbmmanage` script chooses the NDBM or the GDBM libraries, then your Apache configuration file will need to use the `AuthDBMUserFile` and the `AuthDBMGroupFile` directives, instead of the `AuthDBUserFile` and `AuthDBGroupFile` directives. The `AuthDBM???` directives behave the same as their `AuthDB???` counterparts.

AuthDBMUserFile

`AuthDBMUserFile` specifies the path and filename to the NDBM or GDBM style database containing usernames and their passwords.

AuthDBMGroupFile

`AuthDBMGroupFile` specifies the path and filename to the NDBM or GDBM style database containing usernames and their groups lists.

Like the DB style databases, the `AuthDBMUserFile` and the `AuthDBMGroupFile` database may be combined into one database.

The `mod_auth_dbm` module, which is *not* a default module, provides the `AuthDBMUserFile` and the `AuthDBMGroupFile` directives. To compile this module into your Apache server, use the `--enable-module=auth_dbm` parameter to the APACI utility's `configure` command. Or use the `--enable-module=most` parameter.

The `Auth???` directives described above authenticate users who have user accounts on the server. You can also configure a resource to allow anonymous access, like the anonymous login on a public FTP site. Apache provides the `Anonymous???` directives to govern anonymous login. Consider the following:

```
<Directory /home/webmastr/pub/html/downloads">
    Anonymous guest anonymous guestuser
    Anonymous_MustGiveEmail on
    Anonymous_LogEmail on
    Anonymous_VerifyEmail on
    Anonymous_NoUserId off
    require valid-user
</Directory>
```

Anonymous

`Anonymous` specifies the usernames allowed to login without a password (or with just an email address as the password). The `Anonymous` directive accepts as parameters a space-separated list of magic usernames. You should always include the `anonymous` username in this list.

Anonymous_MustGiveEmail

`Anonymous_MustGiveEmail` requires the user to enter an email address for the password. This directive accepts one parameter; which may be `on` or `off`. The default is `on`. If you require the user to enter the email address as the password, you can log it. In proper netiquette, you would publish a policy statement on your site, describing what you will and will not do with the collected addresses.

Anonymous_LogEmail

`Anonymous_LogEmail` enables the logging of the email addresses entered as passwords for anonymous logins. This directive accepts one parameter; which may be either `on` or `off`. The default is `on`. When the parameter is `on`, the email addresses are logged to the error log (as prescribed by the `ErrorLog` directive). These log entries are submitted with an error level of info; so you will have to set `LogLevel` to `info` or `debug` for these addresses to make it into log.

Anonymous_VerifyEmail

`Anonymous_VerifyEmail` requires that an email address entered as the password be valid. This directive accepts one parameter; which may be `on` or off. The default is off. When the parameter is on, the user must enter a string containing at least one @ sign and at least one period.

Anonymous_NoUserId

Anonymous_NoUserId enables the user to log in without entering any username. This directive accepts one parameter; which may be on or off. The default is off.

The mod_auth_anon module, which is *not* a default module, provides the Anonymous??? directives. To compile Apache with this module, use the --enable-module=auth_anon parameter to the APACI utility's configure command. Or, use the --enable-module=most parameter.

You probably don't want registered users to have to log in as themselves for the private parts of the web site and then log in again as anonymous to get to the downloads area. You can include both sets of authentication requirements in the same <Directory> block. Consider the following:

```
<Directory "/home/webmastr/pub/html/downloads">
   AuthType Basic
   AuthName "Downloads (Anonymous allowed. Use email as password)"
   AuthDBUserFile /home/webmastr/auth/authuser
   AuthDBGroupFile /home/webmastr/auth/authuser
   require valid-user
   AuthDBAuthoritative off
   Anonymous anonymous guest nobody
   Anonymous_LogEmail on
</Directory>
```

When the user logs in (that is, when the browser sends an Authorization header), the server first tries to authenticate the user against the DB database of user accounts. An authentication that fails is deferred to the anonymous authentication scheme. AuthDBAuthoritative allows this fall-through processing.

AuthDBAuthoritative

AuthDBAuthoritative specifies whether or not the DB database authentication scheme is the authoritative login scheme for the resource specified by the enclosing block. This directive accepts one parameter; which may be on or off. The default is on. When the parameter is on, the DB database(s) are considered to be the authoritative login scheme and failure to authenticate therein will cause the request to be rejected. When the parameter is off, the DB database(s) are not considered to be the authoritative login scheme and failure to authenticate therein will allow authentication to fall through to the next lower-level authentication scheme. The modules that provide all these authentication schemes are listed in the file `/usr/local/src/apache/apache_1.3.9/src/Configuration`. Those that appear earlier in this file are lower-level authentication schemes. Those that appear later are higher-level authentication schemes. The modules appear in that file in this order:

```
mod_auth
mod_auth_anon
mod_auth_dbm
mod_auth_db
```

This means that DB authentication can defer to anonymous authentication, but not vice versa. Each of the authentication schemes has an `???Authoritative` directive for allowing that scheme to fall through to the next lower-level scheme.

AuthDBMAuthoritative

`AuthDBMAuthoritative` specifies whether or not the DBM database authentication scheme is the authoritative login scheme for the resource specified by the enclosing block. When it is `on`, failed DBM logins are rejected. When it is `off`, failed authentication falls through to the next lower-level scheme.

Anonymous_Authoritative

`Anonymous_Authoritative` specifies whether or not the anonymous login scheme is the authoritative login scheme for the resource specified by the enclosing block. When it is `on`, failed anonymous logins (now there's a concept) are rejected. When it is `off`, failed authentication falls through to the next lower level scheme.

AuthAuthoritative

`AuthAuthoritative` specifies whether or not the flat-file authentication scheme is the authoritative login scheme for the resource specified by the enclosing block. When it is `on`, failed flat-file logins are rejected. When it is `off`, failed authentication falls through to the next lower-level scheme.

These `???Authoritative` directives also arbitrate collisions between `.htaccess` files and the Apache configuration file. Let's say, for example, that the configuration file uses flat-file authentication to require membership in the admin user group before granting access to a particular directory. Let's also say that the directory contains an .htaccess file that uses DB authentication to require a valid-user. The .htaccess file could contain AuthDBAuthoritative off setting to allow failed user authentication to fall through to the admin authentication prescribed by in the configuration file.

A given resource may have both access requirements (Order, deny, allow directives) and authentication requirements (Auth??? directives). Both sets of requirements must be satisfied before access is granted to the resource. For example:

```
<Directory "/home/webmastr/pub/html/internal">
    order deny,allow
    deny from all
    allow from 192.168.1.0/24
    AuthType Basic
    AuthName "Internal Private Area"
    AuthDBUserFile /home/webmastr/auth/authuser
    AuthDBGroupFile /home/webmastr/auth/authuser
    require valid-user
</Directory>
```

The <Directory> block above instructs Apache to grant access to the internal/ subdirectory only if the request originates from the local area network and the user successfully authenticates as a valid user account. You could change this so that only one or the other is required with the Satisfy directive.

Satisfy

Satisfy specifies whether or not access and authentication policies must both be satisfied before granting access to the resource specified by the enclosing block. This directive accepts one parameter, which may be either any or all. When it is all (or when the Satisfy directive is omitted), both access and authentication requirements must be satisfied. When it is any, access to the resource is granted if either requirement is satisfied. For example:

```
<Directory "/home/webmastr/pub/html/internal">
    order deny,allow
    deny from all
    allow from 192.168.1.0/24
    AuthType Basic
    AuthName "Internal Private Area"
```

```
          AuthDBUserFile /home/webmastr/auth/authuser
          AuthDBGroupFile /home/webmastr/auth/authuser
          require valid-user
          Satisfy any
</Directory>
```

Given the `<Directory>` block above, a user connecting from the local area network can access the `internal/` subdirectory without having to login. Users connecting from outside the LAN must log in and authenticate as valid users before accessing the directory.

Authenticating PUT Requests

Content authors usually edit content on their local systems and then upload the content to the web server. Many of the web-authoring tools automate the process of updating the server by performing FTP transfers in the background. Some web-authoring tools allow the choice of updating the server via FTP or via HTTP with the `PUT` request method. Apache can accept `PUT` requests, but you must write your own CGI script to handle the request. You would want to require the user sending a `PUT` request to log in and be authenticated as a webmaster with authorization to deposit files into the web site. You would not want to require normal site visitors to have to log in. Here is how to do it:

```
<Directory "/home/webmastr/pub/html">
     Script PUT /cgi-bin/rcvput.cgi
     AuthName "Upload to web site"
     AuthType Basic
     AuthUserFile /home/webmastr/auth/authuser
     AuthGroupFile /home/webmastr/auth/authuser
     <Limit PUT>
          require group webauthors
     </Limit>
</Directory>
```

The `Script` directive in the above `<Directory>` block associates the `PUT` request method with the `/cgi-bin/rcvput.cgi` script (which you have to write yourself). Apache will reject any request using a request method other than `GET` or `POST`, unless a `Script` directive defines a script for that request method. Next, the `Auth???` directives set up the authentication scheme to be used. Then, the `require` directive prescribes that only members of the web authors user group are authorized to access the content. This `require` directive is enclosed within a `<Limit>` block, which limits the authorization requirement to requests that use the `PUT` request method. GET and POST requests can access the content without having to log in. PUT requests must log in.

Script

Script associates the specified CGI script with the specified request method. This directive accepts two parameters. The first specifies the request method and may be one of GET, POST, PUT, or DELETE. The second parameter specifies the path and filename of the CGI script (or binary) that will handle requests of the given method. Apache will not accept PUT or DELETE requests unless they have been associated with a CGI script by a Script directive.

The Script directive may appear within the configuration file's global context, or within a <VirtualHost> or <Directory> block. The mod_actions module, which is a default module, provides the Script directive.

<Limit>

<Limit> limits the evaluation of the enclosed directives to requests using the specified request method(s). The <Limit> directive accepts as parameters a space-separated list of request methods, each of which may be one of: CONNECT, COPY, DELETE, GET, OPTIONS, LOCK, MKCOL, MOVE, PATCH, POST, PROPFIND, PROPPATCH, PUT, TRACE, or UNLOCK. HEAD requests are treated as GET requests.

LimitExcept

LimitExcept limits the evaluation of the enclosed directives to requests not using the specified request method(s). This is the reverse logic of the <Limit> directive. The following example.

```
<LimitExcept GET POST>
    require valid-user
</LimitExcept>
```

would require the user to login except when doing a normal site-visitor thing like GET or POST.

The <Limit> and <LimitExcept> directives may appear within any configuration file context or block directive and within .htaccess files. The Apache core provides these directives.

Here is a simple PUT-handling script to use for testing an authentication scheme:

```
#!/bin/bash

read buf
if [ "x_$buf" != "x_" ]; then
    ( echo "$buf" > $PATH_TRANSLATED ) || exit $?
fi
while read buf; do
    ( echo "$buf" >> $PATH_TRANSLATED ) || exit $?
done

echo "Content-type: text/plain"
echo
echo "<HTML>"
echo "    <BODY>"
echo "        File accepted."
echo "        <BR>"
echo "        Saved to $PATH_TRANSLATED"
echo "    </BODY>"
echo "</HTML>
```

When Apache routes the PUT request to the CGI script, it sets the PATH_INFO environment variable to the path and filename specified in the PUT request. The PATH_TRANSLATED environment variable is a file system translation of the PATH_INFO value (translated via DocumentRoot or any applicable Alias directives). Thus the PUT-receiving CGI script saves the content body of the request (which is the contents of the file being uploaded) to the file named by the PATH_TRANSLATED environment variable. Note that the user ID under which the Apache child daemons run (as specified by the User directive) must have write permissions to the directory in which the uploaded file is being stored. This, in itself, is a security risk. Note that all our test script does is write the request's content body to the specified file. It does not perform the normal things that a PUT-receiving script should do, like:

- Error checking
- File system permissions checking
- Testing that the target file resides within the DocumentRoot directory tree
- Buffer length management—watch out for unbelievably long lines and large files
- Use of the Content-length request header to determine how many bytes are to be read.

Preventing/Allowing Search Engine Site Inspection

Robots are automated clients used to traverse web sites. Researchers use them to find specific data. Webmasters use them to search for broken links throughout the site. Search engines use them to gather data for indexing. Getting indexed by a search engines brings traffic to your site, which is a good thing. Getting your private (or unfinished) pages indexed is, at best, embarrassing. You should, of course, secure very sensitive data with permanent access restrictions or authentication/authorization requirements. The webmaster could secure unfinished pages or directories with temporary access restrictions placed in an .htaccess file, if permitted to do so by a Limit option to the AllowOverride directive.

There are other reasons to keep robots out of part or all of your web site. Some misbehaving robots generate requests pages at such a rapid-fire rate that they strain the server and shoulder out regular site visitors. Also, you would not want search engines to index dynamic data, especially time-dependant data like stock quotes; so you will want to keep the robots out of your CGI scripts.

Most robots will voluntarily adhere to your robot policies, as prescribed in a file named robots.txt placed in your DocumentRoot directory. The syntax for this file is described in an Internet draft called "A Method for Web Robots Control" proposed by M. Koster of WebCrawler (**http://info.webcrawler.com/mak/projects/robots/norobots-rfc.html**). In that file, you specify which robots may access which areas of your site, and which areas of your site are off limits. You define a policy regarding a specific robot with a User-agent: directive followed by Allow: and Disallow: directives prescribing where that robot can and cannot go. An asterisk in the User-agent: directive means "all robots." For example:

```
User-agent: WebCrawler
User-agent: excite
Disallow: /cgi-bin
Disallow: /private
Allow: /

User-agent: *
Disallow: /
```

The above /robots.txt allows the WebCrawler and the Excite robots to retrieve any documents except those in the cgi-bin/ and private/ subdirectories. All other robots are denied access to everything. The WebCrawler web site publishes a list of robots at **http://info.webcrawler.com/mak/projects/robots/active.html**.

A webmaster who does not have permission to modify /robots.txt can prescribe robot policy regarding a specific document by placing this meta tag in that document:

```
<META NAME="ROBOTS" CONTENT="NOINDEX, NOFOLLOW">
```

The NOINDEX value instructs the robot not to index this document in the search services for whom the robot is gathering data. The NOFOLLOW value instructs the robot not to follow the links in this document.

A robot's compliance with the /robots.txt file and the ROBOTS meta tag is voluntary. Some robots completely ignore /robots.txt. Some can be quite rude: hogging connections, revisiting too often, reindexing pages unmodified since the previous visit. If you're being pestered by bad robot, set up a transfer log or a user-agent log (see Chapter 5: "Using Logs") and get the bad robot's User-agent name. Then you can exclude that User-Agent with these directives:

```
BrowserMatchNoCase ^BadBotName badbot
BrowserMatchNoCase ^OtherBadBot badbot
<Location ~ .*>
    deny from env=badbot
</Location>
```

BrowserMatchNoCase

BrowserMatchNoCase sets the specified environment variable when a request is received from the specified user-agent. This directive accepts two parameters: a regular expression used to match the user-agent; and the name of the environment variable to be set when the user-agent matches the regular expression. Pattern matching on the regular expression is not case sensitive (The BrowserMatch directive is case sensitive). This directive can appear only in the configuration file's global context. The mod_setenvif module, a default module, provides this directive.

Location

Location causes its enclosed directives to be evaluated only on requests for the specified URL. In the above example, we use the tilde to indicate that the specified URL is a regular expression (.* meaning "match any character any number of times").

deny from env=

`deny from env=` denies access to the resource specified by the enclosing block if the specified environment variable is set. This directive may appear in a resource block (`<Directory>`, `<Files>`, `<Location>`, `.htaccess`). The `mod_access` module, a default module, provides this directive.

If you are running a robot or writing a robot, you'll find guidelines for polite behavior at **http://info.webcrawler.com/mak/projects/robots/guidelines.html**.

Securing the Server-Browser Connection with Secure Sockets Layer (SSL)

Understanding SSL

Secure sockets layer enables private connections across a public medium. As a process, SSL performs encryption in a layer between the TCP transport layer and the application layer. It encrypts all data flowing from an application and decrypts all data flowing into the application. The code that performs the SSL processing can be added to any TCP application (telnet, FTP, HTTP) to make the application "SSL aware." For HTTP, this secures documents (e.g. proprietary data), posted forms (e.g. credit card info), request headers (e.g. the Authentication: header containing the user's password), response headers (e.g. session ID cookies), and *everything* above the TCP layer transmitted between the server and the client. The TCP/IP headers (needed for routing) are not encrypted. SSL is also a protocol that defines how two machines agree on an encryption scheme. The server listens to port 443 (by convention) for a request for a secure connection. The browser makes this request by specifying the `https://` protocol (instead of the `http://` protocol) in the requested URL. Be aware that since SSL adds both a layer of processing and a layer of negotiation, your web server will take a very noticeable performance hit. If you need security, you have to have it.

SSL achieves:

- **Message Integrity**—Assurance that a message hasn't been tampered with.
- **Privacy**—An eavesdropper cannot understand the messages sent through the connection.
- **Authentication**—The parties of a connection are each who they say they are.

It accomplishes these with the following cryptographic techniques:

Message Digest

The sender performs a calculation, called a *one-way hash*, on the contents of the message. This calculation yields a number, called a message authentication code, which the sender transmits with the message. The recipient performs the same one-way hash on the received message. If this yields a number different from the message authentication code transmitted with the message, then the message has been altered in transit.

Encryption

The sender transforms the message into garbage using a mathematical equation called a *cipher*. The cipher performs its calculations based on an arbitrary number called a *key*. The recipient can then decrypt the message only if he/she has the key. If the same key is used to encrypt the message as to decrypt the message, the encryption is called *symmetric encryption*. If one key is used to encrypt the message and a different key is used to decrypt the message, the encryption is called *asymmetric encryption*. SSL uses symmetric encryption for the bulk of its data transfers. The problem with symmetric encryption is that the sender and the recipient have to agree, ahead of time, on what key to use—without anyone else's overhearing their agreement. At the beginning of a connection, SSL uses a form of asymmetric encryption, called *public-key encryption*, to privately negotiate the key that will be used later for symmetric encryption. In public-key encryption, one of the asymmetric keys is published and the other is kept secret. Only the private key can decrypt messages encrypted by the public key. Other people with the public key cannot decrypt the message. You use someone's public key to whisper into their ear the symmetric key that you have chosen to continue the conversation.

Digital Signatures

The sender computes a message digest, encrypts it with a private key, and sends this signature with the message. If the recipient knows the sender's public key and can decrypt the message digest using it, then he/she also knows that the message came from that sender (and that the message was not altered in transit).

Certificates

A certificate certifies that a public key belongs to a particular live person, company, or server. The certificate contains information about the real entity (name, address, hostname, etc) plus that entity's public key. The certificate is then signed with the digital signature of a certificate authority, a company that (usually for a fee) verifies who you are before putting their digital signature on your public key. Clients and servers keep a list of the public keys of the certificate authorities they trust. Upon receiving someone's certificate, the recipient checks to see if the authority who signed the certificate is one they trust. If it is, the recipient uses the known public key of the certificate authority to decrypt the certificate authority's signature on the certificate. This verifies that the signature on the certificate really is that of the trusted authority. The recipient then calculates a message digest of the certificate. If the calculated digest equals the digest extracted from the signature, then the data in the certificate (including the sender's public key) are valid.

On the web, certificates are most often used to authenticate the server to the client; to prove to the browser user that the server belongs to the company that the user thinks it does. The user can then, with confidence, give the to server the user's credit card number (or other such sensitive data). On intranets, certificates are most often used to authenticate the client to the server. The server can then, in trust, serve up proprietary data to the client.

The SSL protocol defines how, and in what order, the above methods are used to ensure an authentic and private connection.[2] Netscape invented the protocol and put it in the public domain. You'll find its latest draft (version 3) at: **http://home.netscape.com/eng/ssl3/draft302.txt**. Netscape submitted the protocol to the Internet Engineering Task Force, who put the specification on the standards track under the new title Transport Layer Security protocol (TLS version 1—RFC 2246), which may be viewed at: **ftp://ftp.isi.edu/in-notes/rfc2246.txt**. The RFC describes how various cipher algorithms can be used to perform the key exchange, authentication, encoding, and digest procedures. The protocol itself may be in the public domain, but the ciphers mentioned therein are patented. If you use the DSA or RC5 ciphers, you might need to negotiate a license with RSA Data Security, Inc. (**http://www.rsasecurity.com/**) The patent on the RSA ciphers expires September 29, 2000. (**http://www.rsasecurity.com/rsalabs/faq/6-3-1.html**) To use the IDEA ciphers, you will need to license them from Ascom. (**httpl://www.ascom.ch/infosec/idea/online_order_form.html**) The

---

2 Netscape publishes a lot of good documentation on SSL. You'll find an introduction to SSL at: **http://developer.netscape.com/docs/manuals/security/sslin/contents.htm**; an explanation of how it works at: **http://developer.netscape.com/tech/security/ssl/howitworks.html**; and an explanation of public-key cryptography at: **http://developer.netscape.com/docs/manuals/security/pkin/index.htm**.

Diffie-Hellman patent expired April 29, 1997.[3] To complicate things further, it is illegal to export from the United States products built using ciphers stronger than 40 bits—168-bit Triple DES, 128-bit RC4, 56-bit DES.[4] They are so secure that the U.S. government can't break them and spy on you. All this has a bearing on what ciphers you choose and on how you build and configure SSL in Apache. If you are running an intranet web server and are guaranteed that all connecting browsers support strong encryption, then you may want your server to restrict connections to the stronger ciphers. If you are running an Internet web server, you will probably want to support the strong ciphers (if you can) and you will want to support the 40-bit ciphers, too (so you don't block out the weaker browsers). Browsers that support the stronger ciphers can usually step down to a weaker cipher, if the server requires it. The SSL protocol allows the server and the client to negotiate what ciphers they can mutually use.

Building SSL into Apache

Apache does not ship with SSL. You have to gather the parts: the encryption ciphers, the network-layer software, and the patches for the Apache source code. Some vendors have gathered the parts for you, and licensed the ciphers for you, too—the Secure Web Server included in the Redhat Linux 6.1 Professional package (**https://www.redhat.com/commerce/more_rhl_prof.html**), the Raven SSL Module for Apache by Covalent Technologies (**http://www.covalent. net/raven/ssl/**), and Stronghold by C2Net (**http://stronghold.c2.net/**). If you want it free, you'll have to build it. Building it is not a "walk in the park." There are two ways to do it. You can add an SSL module with a package called mod_ssl. Or you can patch the Apache core with a package called Apache-SSL (Apache earns its name again). Personally, I find the mod_ssl package easier to compile and install. It produces a true Apache module. It can be compiled as a sharable object. At server startup, mod_ssl can be activated or not. Also, I appreciate its integration of its documentation into the Apache User's Guide. On the other hand, Apache-SSL patches the Apache core, presumably to gain slightly better performance. Also, Apache-SSL uses the

---

3 The Diffie-Hellmman patent title Cryptographic Apparatus and Method can be viewed at the U.S. Patent Office web site. Go to the **http://164.195.100.11/netahtml/srchnum.htm** and search for patent number 4200770.

4 Netscape has a good summary at **http://developer.netscape.com/docs/manuals/enterprise/admnunix/encrypt.htm**. To get it from the horse's mouth, wade through the Bureau of Export Administration site at **http://www.bxa.doc.gov/homepage.htm**.

SSLeay toolkit, which can be used to compile SSL-awareness into other TCP service daemons. It's a matter of choice. We'll show you both.

Building an SSL Module with mod_ssl

Building `mod_ssl` creates an Apache module to perform the SSL negotiation and encryption. This `mod_ssl` module can be treated like any other Apache module. You can choose whether or not to load the module in the Apache configuration file. You could load the module dynamically, as well.

The `mod_ssl` package requires the OpenSSL package. If you want to use the RSA ciphers, then OpenSSL will require the RSAref package. These packages have to be built from the ground up.

Building RSAref

RSAref provides the 128-bit RSA ciphers. If you are going to use them in a commercial application, you will need to work out a license agreement with RSA Security, Inc (**http://www.rsasecurity.com/**). If you don't need the RSA ciphers, then you can skip this section and go to the section "Building OpenSSL." OpenSSL comes with other ciphers you can use, but they are the less-secure variety.

The source code for RSAref is available from Spinnaker Systems at **http://www.spinnaker.com**. From their home page, click on the link titled "Cryptography and PGP archives," then click on the `rsaref/` directory. On your UNIX box, create the directory `/usr/local/src/rsaref/rsaref-2.0/` and download the file named `rsaref.tar.Z` into that directory. Alternately, you can download the file via FTP from **ftp.spinnaker.com** using an anonymous login (using your email address as your password). You will find the file in the `/pub/crypt/rsaref/` directory.

After downloading, uncompress and untar the `rsaref.tar.Z` tar-ball. If you need procedures for uncompressing and untarring a tar-ball, refer to Chapter 2: "Creating the Web Server." This tar-ball does not extract itself to a subdirectory named after its version, like many do, so untar the file from within the `/usr/local/src/rsaref/rsaref-2.0/` directory.

Before compiling the RSAref library, you must decide if you need to apply a security patch to the RSAref-2.0 source code. Alberto Solíño and Gerardo Richarte at Core SDI S.A. discovered that the RSAref library was vulnerable to a particular buffer-overflow attack. The OpenSSL library shields the RSAref library from such attacks; the `mod_ssl` package is not vulnerable. If you will be using the RSAref-2.0 library for building SSH (the secure shell) or other packages, then you may want to apply the patch available from Core SDI S.A. at **http://www.core-sdi.com/advisories/ buffer % 20overflow % 20ing.htm**.

To compile RSAref-2.0, create a subdirectory named `local/` under the `/usr/local/src/rsaref/rsaref-2.0/` directory and copy the UNIX makefile into it:

```
cp -a install/unix local
```

Change directory into the `local/` subdirectory and build the `rsaref` library there:

```
cd local
make
```

This will produce the library named `rsaref.a`. For the benefit of your linker, copy this file to a file named `librsaref.a`:

```
cp rsaref.a librasref.a
```

Building OpenSSL

OpenSSL performs the negotiation and cryptographic processing. SSL is available from the OpenSSL Project. From their home page at **http://www.openssl.org/**, click on the link titled "available" in the phrase "OpenSSL 0.9.3 is now available". On your UNIX box, create the directory `/usr/local/src/openssl/` and download the file named `openssl-0.9.4.tar.gz` into that directory. Alternately, you can download the file via FTP from `ftp.openssl.org` using an anonymous login. You will find the file in the `source/` directory.

After downloading, uncompress and untar the `openssl-0.9.4.tar.gz` tar ball. This tar-ball extracts itself to a subdirectory named after its version, `openssl-0.9.4/`. Go into the `openssl-0.9.4/` directory and read the file named `INSTALL` for installation instructions and options regarding your platform. If you are using the RSA ciphers, you'll have to point OpenSSL back to your RSAref build. From the shell prompt in the openssl-0.9.4 `directory/`, enter these commands:

```
./config -L/usr/local/src/rsaref/rsaref-2.0/local rsaref
make
make test
```

If you will not be using the RSA ciphers, then enter these three commands instead:

```
./config
make
make test
```

Either compile (with or without RSAref) will create the libraries named `libRSAglue.a`, `libcrypto.a`, and `libssl.a` in the `/usr/local/src/openssl/openssl-0.9.4/` directory.

Given a successful compile and test, you can now install the OpenSSL command line utility. OpenSSL comes with a utility for creating certificates, revoking certificates, and the like. To install this utility, enter:

```
make install
```

This will install the OpenSSL utility package into the `/usr/src/ssl/` directory. This installation directory is hard-coded in the Makefile. Do not change this. The utility binary relies on it.

Building mod_ssl

The `mod_ssl` package creates an Apache module wrapper around the OpenSSL code. You will need to download the source code for `mod_ssl` from **http://www.modssl.org/**. Click on the link titled "mod_ssl 2.4.10" in the phrase "Current Version: mod_ssl 2.4.10 (08-Jan-2000) for Apache 1.3.9." This will download the file named `mod_ssl-2_4_10-1_3_9_tar.gz`. On your UNIX box, create the directory named `/usr/local/src/mod_ssl/` and save the file in that directory. Alternately you can download the file via FTP at **ftp.modssl.org**. Log in as anonymous and you'll find the file in the `/source/` directory.

Uncompress and untar the tar-ball in the `/usr/local/src/mod_ssl/` directory. The tar-ball will extract itself into the subdirectory named `mod_ssl-2.4.10-1.3.9/`. Go into that subdirectory and read the file named `INSTALL` for installation instructions. The `INSTALL` file will tell what other parts are required, what parts are optional, what parts are legal in the U.S. and in Europe, and how to build them all. For this example, we build it this way:

```
./configure --with-apache=/usr/local/src/apache/apache_1.3.9
```

The above `configure` command adds the `mod_ssl` source code to the Apache source code tree specified by the `--with-apache=` parameter.

Then you must go to your Apache source code directory and rebuild Apache to compile and link to the new mod_ssl module.

Building Apache with mod_ssl

First, prepare the Apache source code tree for the build. At the UNIX shell prompt, in the /usr/local/src/apache/apache_1.3.9/ directory, enter:

```
SSL_BASE=/usr/local/src/openssl/openssl-0.9.4 \
RSA_BASE=/usr/local/src/rsaref/rsaref-2.0 \
./configure \
    --prefix=/usr/local/apache \
    --enable-module=most \
    --enable-shared=max \
    --enable-shared=ssl
```

The above command creates the Makefiles that will be used to build the Apache server. The configure command in the above command string is Apache's APACI utility (see Chapter 2: "Creating the Web Server," "Downloading and Compiling the Source Code"). I prefer to load modules dynamically, including the new ssl modules. Before making the call to the configure command, two variables are set to point to the libraries we just previously built—the SSL layer library and the RSA cipher library. Note that these two variables must be set in the same line as the configure command (hence the backslashes). If you did not build the RSAref-2.0 library, then leave out the RSA_BASE line.

If configure has no gripes, then we can build the Apache server binary. At the UNIX shell prompt, type: make. This will compile and link the Apache server binary. A successful make will display the screen

```
+---------------------------------------------------------------+
| Before you install the package you now should prepare the SSL
|
| certificate system by running the 'make certificate' command.
|
| For different situations the following variants are provided:
|
|
|
| % make certificate TYPE=dummy   (dummy self-signed Snake Oil cert)
|
| % make certificate TYPE=test    (test cert signed by Snake Oil CA)
|
| % make certificate TYPE=custom   (custom cert signed by own CA)
```

```
|
| % make certificate TYPE=existing (existing cert)
|
|        CRT=/path/to/your.crt [KEY=/path/to/your.key]
|
|
|
| Use TYPE=dummy  when you're a  vendor package maintainer,
|
| the TYPE=test   when you're an admin but want to do tests only,
|
| the TYPE=custom when you're an admin willing to run a real server
|
| and TYPE=existing when you're an admin who upgrades a server.
|
| (The default is TYPE=test)
|
|
|
| Additionally add ALGO=RSA (default) or ALGO=DSA to select
|
| the signature algorithm used for the generated certificate.
|
|
|
| Use 'make certificate VIEW=1' to display the generated data.
|
|
|
| Thanks for using Apache & mod_ssl.        Ralf S. Engelschall
|
|                                           rse@engelschall.com
|
|                                           www.engelschall.com
|
+-------------------------------------------------------------------+
make[1]: Leaving directory '/usr/local/src/apache/apache_1.3.9'
<=== src
```

The above instructions say to use the make certificate command to create your server's certificate (or to point Apache to your real certificate). I prefer to use the OpenSSL command line utility (which we installed previously) to create the server certificate—which we will do after installing the compiled Apache server.

Apache with mod_ssl installs like any other Apache build—using the make install command. At the UNIX shell prompt, in the directory /usr/local/apache/apache_1.3.9, enter:

```
make install
```

If this is successful, make install will tell you that:

```
+--------------------------------------------------------------+
| You now have successfully built and installed the            |
| Apache 1.3 HTTP server. To verify that Apache actually        |
| works correctly you now should first check the                |
| (initially created or preserved) configuration files         |
|                                                              |
|   /usr/local/apache/conf/httpd.conf                          |
|                                                              |
| and then you should be able to immediately fire up           |
| Apache the first time by running:                            |
|                                                              |
|   /usr/local/apache/bin/apachectl start                      |
|                                                              |
| Or when you want to run it with SSL enabled use:             |
|                                                              |
|   /usr/local/apache/bin/apachectl startssl                   |
|                                                              |
| Thanks for using Apache.        The Apache Group             |
|                                  http://www.apache.org/      |
+--------------------------------------------------------------+
```

The make install command installed the Apache server binary, and all of its support files into the Apache installation directory (e.g. /usr/local/apache/ in this example). The make install command also merged the new mod_ssl documentation in with the Apache User's Guide in /usr/local/apache/htdocs/manual/.

Creating the Server Certificate with OpenSSL

On a normal Apache compile, our next step would be to edit the Apache configuration file. Before we do that, we need to create a test certificate for the server. If you already have a real server certificate from a certificate authority, then you can skip the creation of this test certificate. We will use OpenSSL's command line utility to create the test certificate and private key. At the UNIX shell prompt, go to the /usr/local/ssl/bin/ directory and enter:

```
./openssl req -new -x509 \
    -keyout /usr/local/ssl/private/serverkey.pem \
    -out /usr/local/ssl/certs/servercert.pem \
    -days 365
```

The above command will create the server's private key in the file named `serverkey.pem` in the directory `/usr/local/ssl/private/`. It will also create the server's certificate (with the server's public key) in X.509 format in the file `servercert.pem` in the directory `/usr/local/ssl/certs/`. The test certificate will expire in 365 days. The `openssl` program will ask you to:

```
Enter PEM pass phrase:
```

Make up a password and enter it here. This password will be used to encrypt the private key file. Don't forget this password; you'll need it to start up the Apache server. After entering the PEM pass phrase, you will be asked to retype the pass phrase for verification; and then you will be asked a series of questions. The answers to these questions are used to create your server certificate's Distinguished Name—the name by which browsers will authenticate the server. For this test certificate, answer the questions any way you like—except when asked:

```
Common Name (eg, YOUR name) []:
```

To the above question, you must reply with the domain-dot-hostname of your Apache server (e.g. **www.administeringapache.com**) as served by your DNS server. When the certificate and key have been created, you might want to doubly lock down the private key with this UNIX shell command:

```
chmod 700 /usr/local/ssl/private
```

This will give the root user (and no one else) read, write, and execute permissions on the `private/` directory.

With the server certificate and private key created, we can now edit the Apache configuration file to make use of them.

Configuring Apache with mod_ssl

The `mod_ssl` documentation regarding the new SSL directives is available at **http://www.modssl.org/docs/2.5/ssl_reference.html**. You will be able to view this documentation on your own Apache server, once we get it running. To configure Apache with `mod_ssl`, edit the Apache configuration file in the `conf/` subdirectory of the Apache installation directory (e.g. `/usr/local/apache/conf/httpd.conf`). If this is a brand-new installation of Apache, the `make install` command will already have configured most of the SSL directives for you. You will still have to set your non-SSL directives (see the section "Configuring the Installed Server" in Chapter 2: "Creating the Web Server") and you still have to point the configuration to your new server certificate and key. If you are adding mod_ssl to an existing Apache installation, your pre-existing configuration file will have been preserved; in which case, the SSL directives will not have been set for you. Verify, modify, or add (as need be) the following...

If you compiled mod_ssl as a shareable module, then you will need to add the following block to the end of the list of LoadModule directives:

```
<IfDefine SSL>
    LoadModule ssl_module libexec/libssl.so
</IfDefine>
```

LoadModule specifies that Apache is to load the specified module in the specified shared object file. The above LoadModule directive is enclosed within the <IfDefine> block because of the way Apache with mod_ssl is started up. The <IfDefine> block makes the evaluation of its enclosed directives conditional upon a command line parameter passed to the parent HTTPD server daemon. The apachectl startup script passes the -DSSL command line parameter to HTTPD if Apache is being started up with SSL support; in which case, SSL is defined and the directives within the <IfDefine> block will be evaluated.

Add the following at the end of the list of AddModule directives in the configuration file:

```
<IfDefine SSL>
    AddModule mod_ssl.c
</IfDefine>
```

The AddModule directive instructs Apache to activate the specified module. It is required whether or not mod_ssl was compiled as a sharable object. Here, again, we evaluate the directive only if the HTTPD daemon is being started with the -DSSL parameter.

We need to instruct Apache to listen to both the HTTP port and the HTTPS port. Add the following block to the configuration file's global context:

```
<IfDefine SSL>
    Listen 80
    Listen 443
</IfDefine>
```

Listen directs Apache to listen to the specified TCP port. The Listen directive may be specified multiple times in order to get Apache to listen to more than one port.

Add the following to the configuration file's global context:

```
<IfDefine SSL>
    AddType application/x-x509-ca-cert  .crt
    AddType application/x-pkcs7-crl     .crl
</IfDefine>
```

AddType assigns a MIME content type to files having the specified file name extensions. The above MIME types aid in downloading certificates and certificate revocation lists:

Add the following section to the configuration files global context, just after your <VirtualHost> declarations:

```
<IfModule mod_ssl.c>
  SSLPassPhraseDialog  builtin
  SSLSessionCache dbm:/usr/local/apache/logs/ssl_scache
  SSLSessionCacheTimeout  300
  SSLMutex  file:/usr/local/apache/logs/ssl_mutex
  SSLRandomSeed startup /dev/urandom
  SSLRandomSeed connect builtin
  SetEnvIf User-Agent ".*MSIE.*" nokeepalive ssl-unclean-shutdown
</IfModule>
```

The <IfModule> block causes its enclosed directives to be evaluated only if mod_ssl has been activated by a prior AddModule directive. These directives are described individually as follows:

SSLPassPhraseDialog

SSLPassPhraseDialog specifies how mod_ssl is to obtain the pass phrase key used to unlock the server certificate and private key. This directive accepts one parameter, which may be one of:

- builtin—Instructs Apache to prompt the terminal on startup for entry of the pass phrase. If you have more than one <VirtualHost>, each with its own server certificate, Apache will try to reuse all of the previously entered pass phrases before prompting you to enter another one.
- exec:<path>—Instructs Apache to obtain the pass phrase by calling the program specified by <path>. The program is called for every required pass phrase. Apache passes the program two command line parameters: 1) the server name and port number of the <VirtualHost> for whom a pass

phrase is being requested, and 2) the keyword RSA or the keyword DSA indicating which cipher used to encrypt the server certificate and private key. You can write whatever security checks you please into the program.

SSLPassPhraseDialog may appear only within the configuration file's global context.

SSLSessionCache

SSLSessionCache specifies how the Apache child daemons are to store and share session information. A browser usually makes multiple requests to the server for the various elements displayed on a given web page. The various requests may end up getting handled by connections to different Apache child daemons. Using a session cache allows the child daemons to share session information for clients who have already established an SSL connection to the server. This way, the client and server don't have to renegotiate the authentication and encryption key for each of the multiple requests. The SSLSessionCache accepts one parameter; which may be one of:

- none—Instructs Apache not to use SSL session cache.
- dbm:<path>—Instructs Apache to store and share session information in the DBM style database specified by <path>. Apache will create the specified database file on startup.
- shm:<path>—Instructs Apache to store and share the session information in a shared-memory hash table. The specified <path> points to a device file that Apache will create on startup. Use of the shm: option requires that Apache be compiled with the MM shared-memory manager available from **http://www.engelschall.com/sw/mm**. The <path> specification may optionally be followed by a number specifying the size (in bytes) of the hash table.

The <path> specified by either the dbm: or shm: parameter should name a file outside of the DocumentRoot directory tree. The parent Apache daemon, running as the root user, needs read and write permissions on the directory specified within the <path>. The Apache child daemons require read permission for that directory. Commonly, the logs/ subdirectory of the Apache installation directory is used. The parent daemon, running as the root user, creates the database and sets its owner as the user ID under which the child daemons will run (as specified by the User directive).

`SSLSessionCache` may appear only within the configuration file's global context.

SSLSessionCacheTimeout

`SSLSessionCacheTimeout` specifies the number of seconds that the session data can live in the cache. This directive may appear within the configuration file's global context or within a `<VirtualHost>` block.

SSLMutex

`SSLMutex` specifies how the Apache child daemons are to handle locks for mutually exclusive operations. This directive accepts one parameter; which may be:

- `none`—Don't use this option.
- `file:<path>`—Instructs Apache to use a physical file specified by `<path>`. Like Apache's `PidFile`, this lock file must be located on a local filesystem (not on an NFS mounted partition). This option cannot be used in Windows. The `<path>` should point to a file outside of the `DocumentRoot` directory tree. The Apache parent daemon requires read and write permissions on the directory specified in `<path>`. The Apache child daemons require read permissions to that directory. The parent daemon will create the lock file and set its owner to the user ID under which the child processes will run (as specified by the `User` directive).
- `sem`—Instructs Apache to use a System V IPC semaphore for mutually exclusive lock management. This option must be used for Windows.

`SSLMutex` may appear only within the configuration file's global context.

SSLRandomSeed

`SSLRandomSeed` specifies how Apache is to seed the random number generator used to generate session-unique keys. The random number generator is seeded on startup and again just before each connection. Use the `SSLRandomSeed` twice within the configuration file to specify a seed method for each of these contexts. Seed methods producing the most random seed data usually take more processing time. You use the most random method on startup and the quickest method on connections. The `SSLRandomSeed` directive accepts two parameters. The first parameter specifies the context; which may be either `startup` or `connect`. The second parameter specifies the seed method; which may be one of:

- `builtin`—Uses random data from the Apache scoreboard file. It is fast, but not the most random. Use this method for connect, but not for startup—especially given that the Apache scoreboard file doesn't have much data in it at startup.
- `file:<path>`—Uses the entire contents of the file specified by `<path>` as seed data. On our example Linux box, we use the `/dev/urandom` device—which was made for just such an occasion. This method usually produces good seed data, but is slower than the `builtin` method. Use this method for startup, but not for connect.

`SSLRandomSeed` accepts an optional third parameter specifying how many bytes of seed data are to be obtained by the given method. Make sure that the specified number of bytes is available within the specified method; otherwise, Apache will block until the specified number of bytes becomes available within the specified method.

`SSLRandomSeed` may appear only within the configuration file's global context.

SetEnvIf

`SetEnvIf` sets the specified environment variable(s) if the specified conditions prove true. We use this directive in the SSL configuration block to set the `ssl-unclean-shutdown` environment variable for misbehaving SSL clients. This directive

```
SetEnvIf User-Agent ".*MSIE.*" nokeepalive ssl-unclean-shutdown
```

tests the User-Agent request header against a regular expression that matches the Microsoft Internet Explorer browsers. If the browser is an MSIE browser, the `nokeepalive` and the `ssl-unclean-shutdown` environment variables are set. Otherwise, they are not set and remain undefined. These are special environment variables recognized by the Apache server. The `nokeepalive` variable instructs Apache not to allow this connection to become persistent. The `ssl-unclean-shutdown` variable is recognized by `mod_ssl`. It causes `mod_ssl`, when closing down a connection, not to wait for the client to send a close notify alert message. Some browsers forget to do this.

The following directives govern SSL negotiations and processing on a per-server or per-virtual host basis. Add the following block to the configuration file's global context or to the `<VirtualHost>` blocks for those web-host customers requiring SSL:

```
<IfDefine SSL>
    SSLEngine on
    SSLCertificateFile /usr/local/ssl/certs/servercert.pem
    SSLCertificateKeyFile /usr/local/ssl/private/serverkey.pem
</IfDefine>
```

SSLEngine

SSLEngine enables or disables SSL negotiation and processing. This directive accepts one parameter, which may be either on or off. SSL negotiation and processing may be enabled or disabled for the entire server. It may be enabled and disabled for specific virtual hosts. When it is enabled, the server listens on port 443 for HTTPS connections. When it is disabled, the server listens to port 80 for HTTP connections. Basically what you get is an SSL server or a normal server. You cannot disable SSL in general and then turn it on for a given resource or directory. The closest you can get to this would be to define, for each web-host customer, two different <VirtualHost> blocks—one listening to port 80 and the other to port 443, placing the appropriate SSL directives in the port 443 host. For example, given a host named ahost.com, create the block <VirtualHost ahost.com:80> and the block <VirtualHost ahost. com:443>. The DocumentRoot for the port 80 host will be public and insecure. The DocumentRoot for the port 443 host will be secure.

SSLCertificateFile

SSLCertificateFile specifies the path and filename to the server's certificate file. We set this value to point to the certificate we created in the subsection titled "Creating the Server Certificate with OpenSSL" above.

SSLCertificateKeyFile

SSLCertificateKeyFile specifies the path and filename to the server's private key. We set this value to point to the private key we created in the subsection titled "Creating the Server Certificate with OpenSSL" above. A certificate file can be created to contain both the certificate and the private key. If your certificate contains the private key, then you do not need to configure a SSLCertificateKeyFile directive.

The following SSL directives configure SSL negotiation and processing on a per-resource basis. These directives may appear within a <Directory>, <Files>, or <Location> block or within an .htaccess file.

SSLRequireSSL

`SSLRequireSSL` denies all non-HTTPS requests to the resource specified by the enclosing block. This directive accepts no parameters. This directive does not enable or disable SSL. It is a safety net for protecting sacred resources should SSL become disabled by the configuration.

The following per-resource directives are useful for private intranet web servers, but not really useful for public Internet web servers:

SSLCipherSuite

`SSLCipherSuite` prescribes the ciphers to be used in SSL negotiation and processing for requests made for the resource specified by the enclosing block. This directive accepts as parameters a space-separated list of keywords referring to particular ciphers. Consult the `mod_ssl` documentation for a complete list of these keywords. This directive can be used to require the client to use only the strongest ciphers, which you might want to do if you are running an intranet server and you have control over the browser configurations. You would not want to use this on a public web server, because you would end up rejecting browsers that have only the less-secure ciphers (such as those exported by the United States).

SSLVerifyClient

`SSLVerifyClient` requires the client to authenticate itself to the server when requesting the resource specified by the enclosing block. The SSL protocol requires that the server authenticate to the client; but not vice versa. With this directive, you can instruct the server to require client authentication. This will require, of course, that each client have its own personal certificate.

SSLCACertificatePath

`SSLCACertificatePath` specifies the directory in which you keep the certificates of the certificate authorities that your server trusts. These certificates are consulted when you are authenticating a client. If the client presents a certificate signed by one of these trusted authorities, then access for the resource is granted to the client. Otherwise, the server may go up the certificate authority chain, looking for a trusted authority, depending on the value of the `SSLVerifyDepth` directive.

SSLVerifyDepth

SSLVerifyDepth specifies the maximum number of certificate authorities that the server will consult while authenticating a client. If the client presents a certificate signed by an unknown certificate authority (i.e. an authority for whom there is no CA certificate in the SSLCACertificatePath directory), then the server may contact the unknown CA and ask for its issuing CA. If that CA is unknown, then the server can ask that CA for the certificate of its CA, and so on up the chain until either a trusted CA is found or the root CA is reached. The SSLVerifyDepth directives specifies the number of times the server will traverse up the CA chain before giving up and denying access to the client. Normally, this directive is set to 1—requiring the client to present a certificate signed by a trusted authority listed in the SSLCACertificatePath directory.

The directives described above do not exhaust the list of those available. Consult the mod_ssl documentation. This example server is configured sufficiently to run that documentation.

Starting and Stopping Apache with mod_ssl

At the UNIX shell prompt, go to the bin/ subdirectory of the Apache installation directory (/usr/local/apache/bin in our example). In this directory you will find the familiar apachectl script.

apachectl is an Apache server control script used to stop and start the server daemon. The mod_ssl patch has modified this script to accept the following parameters:

- start—Starts the server with SSL disabled. The -DSSL command line parameter is *not* passed to the parent httpd daemon. <IfDefine SSL> configuration blocks are skipped.
- startssl—Starts the server with SSL enabled. The -DSSL command-line parameter is passed to the parent httpd daemon. <IfDefine SSL> configuration blocks are evaluated.
- stop—Stops the running server.
- restart—Restarts the server by sending a HUP signal to the parent httpd server daemon.
- graceful—Restarts the server by sending a USR1 signal to the parent httpd server daemon. The server attempts to complete the current connections before shutting down and restarting.
- fullstatus—Displays a status screen characterizing the running server. The use of the parameter requires that the Apache server be compiled with the optional mod_status module.

- status—Displays an abbreviated status screen characterizing the running server. The use of the parameter requires that the Apache server be compiled with the optional mod_status module.
- configtest—Tests the syntax of the configuration file.

At the UNIX shell prompt, in the bin/ subdirectory of the Apache installation directory, enter the following command line to test the syntax of your modifications to the configuration file:

```
./apachectl configtest
```

If there are no gripes, then start the server in non-SSl mode with this command:

```
./apachectl start
```

This will start the server running in normal mode—without SSL enabled. Test that the normal server is running. Hit the server with a browser. If you installed the server over an existing Apache installation, you should see your site's normal home page. If this is a new installation, you should see the page shown in Figure 6.7.

Figure 6.7
mod_ssl installation successful.

Hey, it worked !
The SSL/TLS-aware Apache webserver was successfully installed on this website.

If you can see this page, then the people who own this website have just installed the Apache Web server software and the Apache Interface to OpenSSL (mod_ssl) successfully. They now have to add content to this directory and replace this placeholder page, or else point the server at their real content.

ATTENTION!
If you are seeing this page instead of the site you expected, please **contact the administrator of the site involved.** (Try sending mail to <webmaster@domain>.) Although this site is running the Apache software it almost certainly has no other connection to the Apache Group, so please do not send mail about this site or its contents to the Apache authors. If you do, your message will be **ignored**.

The Apache online documentation has been included with this distribution. Especially also read the mod_ssl User Manual carefully.

Your are allowed to use the images below on your SSL-aware Apache Web server. Thanks for using Apache, mod_ssl and OpenSSL!

Thankfully, the mod_ssl patch added its documentation to the Apache server docs. From the "Hey, it worked!" page, you can take a mod_ssl tutorial by clicking on the link titled "mod_ssl User Manual." (Directly, this is **http://your.server.name/manual/mod/mod_ssl/**) Or you can read about the new SSL directives in the Apache User's Guide by clicking on the link titled "documentation," then click on the link titled "Run-time configuration directives," and scroll down. (Directly, this is **http://your.server.com/manual/mod/directives.html**.)

To stop the running server, at the UNIX shell prompt, and in the directory /usr/local/apache/bin/, enter:

```
./apachectl stop
```

To start the Apache server with mod_ssl enabled, enter:

```
./apachectl startssl
```

Apache will display the server's hostname, the SSL port number, and the encryption in use

```
Server administeringapache.com:443 (RSA)
```

and, if you encrypted your server certificate, it will ask you to…

```
Enter pass phrase:
```

Enter here the password key you created in the subsection titled "Creating the Server Certificate with OpenSSL." To test the running server, hit the server with a browser, but this time use the https protocol (note the spelling), as in **https://your.server.com/**. You browser should tell you that you've requested a secure document. If your browser doesn't tell you this, then you didn't use the https protocol. Continuing through the "secure document" dialog, the browser will tell you about your server's certificate and the fact that it can't authenticate that certificate. Your browser will give you the option to continue. Doing so should bring you again to the page shown in Figure 6.7.

Patching Apache with Apache-SSL

The Apache-SSL package does build a module named mod_apache_ssl.c; but it also patches the Apache core such that you cannot treat the apache_ssl module like a normal Apache module. Loading the apache_ssl is not optional. You *cannot* comment out the

`AddModule apache_ssl.c` in the Apache configuration file and then embed the SSL directives within an `<IfModule>` block. The `AddModule apache_ssl.c` line and the SSL directives must appear in the Apache configuration file. Also, you cannot load the `apache_ssl` module dynamically. Basically, Apache-SSL builds a completely different server. It will only accept https requests (e.g. **https://administeringapache.com/**). It will *not* accept http requests. The server binary even has a different name: httpsd instead of httpd.

Before getting started, you may wish to read the Apache-SSL documentation at **http://www.apache-ssl.org/**. If you click on the link titled "What do I get?," you will learn that you'll need either the OpenSSL package or the SSLeay toolkit; plus the Apache-SSL patch. I have not gotten Apache-SSL to compile without the both OpenSSL and SSLeay. If you performed the compilations in the previous section titled "Building an SSL Module with mod_ssl," then you might be able to reuse that compile of the OpenSSL package—provided that you didn't link in the RSAref library. SSLeay provides its own RSAref implementation and doesn't use the same "glue." You will have to recompile OpenSSL without the RSAref package.

Building OpenSSL

OpenSSL performs the negotiation and cryptographic processing. SSL is available from the OpenSSL Project. From their home page at **http://www.openssl.org/**, click on the link titled "available" in the phrase "09-Aug-1999: OpenSSL 0.9.4 is now available, a major release." On your UNIX box, create the directory `/usr/local/src/openssl/` and download the file named `openssl-0.9.4.tar.gz` into that directory. Alternately, you can download the file via FTP from **ftp.openssl.org** using an anonymous login. You will find the file in the `source/` directory.

After downloading, uncompress and untar the `openssl-0.9.4.tar.gz` tar-ball. This tar-ball extracts itself to a subdirectory named after its version, `openssl-0.9.4/`. Go into the `openssl-0.9.4/` directory and read the file named `INSTALL` for installation instructions and options regarding your platform. If you wish to use the RSA ciphers, do nothing. They will be added by the SSLeay package discussed below. If you previously performed the OpenSSL compile with the RSAref package (i.e. for `mod_ssl`), then remove the results of that compile by entering this command in the `openssl-0.9.4` directory:

```
make clean
```

To build the OpenSSL package, enter these commands:

```
./config
make
make test
```

This compile will create the libraries named libcrypto.a, and libssl.a in the /usr/local/src/openssl/openssl-0.9.4/ directory.

Do *not*, at this point, perform a make install. We will reserve the /usr/local/ssl application directory for the SSLeay package discussed below. If you previously installed OpenSSL applications (i.e. for mod_ssl), remove the /usr/local/ssl directory tree.

Building SSLeay

SSLeay is an application programmer interface to the OpenSSL library. It also provides a suite of applications for creating server certificates, for creating certificate authority certificates, for revoking certificates, etc. The SSLeay home page is hosted by the school of Psychology at the University of Queensland. You can read about the SSLeay applications (and about SSLeay in general) at **http://www2.psy.uq.edu.au/ ~ ftp/Crypto/**. The anchor titled "Is this legal?" is especially interesting. You can download the SSLeay source code via anonymous FTP from **ftp.psy.uq.oz.au**. Go to the directory /pub/Crypto/SSL, where you will find the file SSLeay-0.9.0b.tar.gz. On your UNIX box, create the directory /usr/local/src/SSLeay and download the file into that directory. If that FTP site is too slow, you can download the source from one of the mirror sites listed on the SSLeay home page. I got mine from **ftp.funet.fi**, where I found the tar-ball file in the directory /pub/crypt/mirrors/ ftp.psy.uq.oz.au/SSL/. Uncompress and untar the tar-ball in the /usr/local/src/SSLeay directory. The tar-ball will extract its files into the subdirectory SSLeay-0.9.0b/. Go into that subdirectory. Read the INSTALL file for installation instructions and tips for compiling the package on your system. Next, prepare the SSLeay code for compilation by running the Configure command, which sets configuration variables in the Makefile. The script assumes you have a perl script interpreter in the /usr/local/bin/ directory. If your perl interpreter is in a different place, you will need to correct the first line in the Configure script. On my Linux box, I had change this line from #!/usr/local/bin/perl to #!/usr/bin/perl. If you do not have a perl interpreter, then read the INSTALL file on how to edit the Makefile manually. The Configure command requires at least one command-line parameter to specify the operating system and compiler you are using. If you enter the `Configure` command without any command-line parameters, you will see this list:

```
BC-16              BC-32              FreeBSD            NetBSD-m86
NetBSD-sparc       NetBSD-x86         SINIX-N            VC-MSDOS
VC-NT              VC-W31-16          VC-W31-32          VC-WIN16
VC-WIN32           aix-cc             aix-gcc            alpha-cc
alpha-gcc          alpha400-cc        cc                 cray-t90-cc
debug              debug-irix-cc      debug-linux-elf    dgux-R3-gcc
dgux-R4-gcc        dgux-R4-x86-gcc    dist               gcc
hpux-cc            hpux-gcc           hpux-kr-cc         irix-cc
irix-gcc           linux-aout         linux-elf          ncr-scde
nextstep           purify             sco5-cc            solaris-sparc-cc
solaris-sparc-gcc  solaris-sparc-sc4  solaris-usparc-sc4 solaris-x86-gcc
sunos-cc           sunos-gcc          unixware-2.0       unixware-2.0-pentium
```

The `Configure` command accepts other command-line parameter options to specify the inclusion or exclusion of particular cipher algorithms. These options are listed in the comments at the top of the `Configure` script. The most notable are:

- `-DRSAref`—Build to use RSAref
- `-DNO_IDEA`—Build with no IDEA algorithm
- `-DNO_RC4`—Build with no RC4 algorithm
- `-DNO_RC2`—Build with no RC2 algorithm
- `-DNO_BF`—Build with no Blowfish algorithm
- `-DNO_DES`—Build with no DES/3DES algorithm
- `-DNO_MD2`—Build with no MD2 algorithm

Since our example uses the DSA ciphers, we run the `Configure` script with these parameters:

```
./Configure -DRSAREF linux-elf
```

Notice, that -DRSAREF is in all caps, which differs from the comments in the script. This does make a difference. Next, we compile the SSLeay libraries by entering

```
make
```

which will create the libraries `libcrypto.a` and `libssl.a` in the current directory (e.g. `/usr/local/src/SSLeay/SSLeay-0.9.0b`) and it will create application binaries is various subdirectories. The SSLeay package comes with demo certificates in the `certs/` subdirectory. The next thing to do is recalculate the hash code files for these demo certificates. At the shell prompt, enter:

```
make rehash
```

The above command will create/recreate the numbered hash files in the `certs/` subdirectory. Next, we need to test that everything compiled and the cipher algorithms work properly. At the shell prompt, enter:

```
make test
```

If `make test` has no gripes, we can install the SSLeay applications. Enter the following:

```
make install
```

The compiled libraries will be installed in the directory `/usr/local/ssl/lib/`; the header files will be installed in the directory `/usr/local/ssl/include`; and the application binaries will be installed in the directory `/usr/lib/ssl/bin/`. This base installation directory, `/usr/local/ssl`, is hard coded. The Apache-SSL patch relies on finding it there, so don't change the SSLeay installation directory.

Building Apache with Apache-SSL

You can download Apache-SSL via anonymous FTP from Oxford University at **ftp.ox.ac.uk**. In the directory `/pub/crypto/SSL/Apache-SSL/` you will find several files with names like `apache_1.3.9+ssl_1.37.tar.gz`. On your UNIX box, create the directory `/usr/local/apache-ssl/` and download into that directory the file named for your version of Apache. The Apache-SSL package will make changes to the Apache source code, so it is important that you get the Apache-SSL package appropriate to your version of Apache. Do not untar the downloaded tar-ball into the `/usr/local/apache-ssl/` directory. The files in this tar-ball need to be extracted into your Apache server source code directory. (If you have not installed the Apache source code, refer to Chapter 2: "Creating the Web Server".) At the shell prompt, in the Apache source code directory (e.g. `/usr/local/src/apache/apache_1.3.9`), enter this command:

```
gzip -d -c \
/usr/local/src/apache-ssl/apache_1.3.9+ssl_1.37.tar.gz \
| tar xvf -
```

The above command will simultaneously decompress and extract the files from the tar-ball in the remote directory into the current directory (and leave the original tar-ball compressed). After untarring the tar-ball, read the file README.SLL for installation instructions regarding this patch. Two methods of applying the patch are described. One calls the patch diff patch utility directly. The other method calls a script named FixPatch, which does some extra fix-up and then calls the patch utility. Of the two methods described in the README.SSL file, we will use the one that calls the FixPatch script. To apply the patch, enter the following at the shell prompt:

```
./FixPatch
```

FixPatch is a script that goes out and looks for your OpenSSL source code directory and for your SSLeay installation directory. If it finds them, it will test whether your version of OpenSSL, SSLeay, Apache-SSL, and Apache all agree with one another. If they do, the script continues by asking

```
Do you want me to apply the fixed-up Apache-SSL patch for you?
[n]
```

Upon entering the letter Y, the script continues by fixing up a copy of the SSLpatch file and applying the patches therein. This patch adds an SSL module and modifies several source files in the Apache core and in other Apache modules. It modifies the Makefiles to link the Apache objects into the binary file named httpsd, instead of httpd. It also adds an AddModule apache_ssl.c directive to the default Apache configuration file.

With the patch applied, we now prepare the Apache source code tree for compilation. We'll use the APACI utility's configure script to do so:

```
./configure --prefix=/usr/local/apache \
    --enable-module=most \
    --enable-shared=max
```

Notice that the above call to configure does not mention the new apache_ssl module. The apache_ssl has joined the default modules included in the --enable-module=most parameter. If you do use that parameter (that is, if you are explicitly enabling selected modules), then you could enable the apache_ssl module with the --enable-module=apache_ssl parameter. If you don't want to enable the apache_ssl module, then too bad. This patched server requires it. Passing the `--disable-module=apache_ssl` will break the server. Don't try it. In the command above, the `--enable-shared=max` parameter instructs APACI to compile as many modules as it can as shared modules. You cannot load the `apache_ssl` module as shared; so do not specify the parameter `--enable-shared=apache_ssl`. In the above command, `--prefix=/usr/local/apache` specifies the Apache installation directory.

With the Apache source code tree configured, we now compile Apache with this command:

```
make
```

After a successful compile, we install the patched Apache server with the command:

```
make install
```

This copies the compiled server binary (`httpsd`) and all of its support files to the Apache installation directory (e.g. `/usr/local/apache/`).

Creating the Server Certificate with SSLeay

On a normal Apache compile, our next step would be to edit the Apache configuration file. Before we do that, we need to create a test certificate for the server. If you already have a server certificate from a certificate authority, then you can skip the creation of this test certificate. The `README.SSL` file in the Apache source code directory will tell you to create your test certificate with the command `cd src; make certificate`. If you go that route, you'll create the file `/usr/local/src/apache/apache_1.3.9/SSLconf/conf/httpsd.pem`, which will contain both the server certificate and the server private key. I prefer to use the SSLeay toolkit to create the test certificate.

At the UNIX shell prompt, go the SSLeay application directory: `/usr/local/ssl/bin`. In that directory, enter this command:

```
./ssleay req -new -x509 \
    -keyout /usr/local/ssl/private/serverkey.pem \
    -out /usr/local/ssl/certs/servercert.pem \
    -days 365
```

The above command will create the server's private key in the file named `serverkey.pem` in the directory `/usr/local/ssl/private/`. It will also create the server's certificate (with the server's public key) in X.509 format in the file `servercert.pem` in the directory

`/usr/local/ssl/certs/`. The test certificate will expire in 365 days. The SSLeay program will ask you to

```
Enter PEM pass phrase:
```

Make up a password and enter it here. This password will be used to encrypt the private key file. Don't forget this password; you'll need it to start up the Apache server. After entering the PEM pass phrase, you will be asked to retype the pass phrase for verification; and then you will be asked a series of questions. The answers to these questions are used to create your server certificate's Distinguished Name—the name by which browser's will authenticate the server. For this test certificate, answer the questions any way you like—except when asked

```
Common Name (eg, YOUR name) []:
```

To the above question, you must reply with the domain-dot-hostname of your Apache server (e.g. `www.administeringapache.com`) as served by your DNS server. When the certificate and key have been created, you might want to doubly lock down the private key with this UNIX shell command:

```
chmod 700 /usr/local/ssl/private
```

This will give the root user (and no one else) read, write, and execute permissions on the `private/` directory.

If you are using Apache as an intranet web server, you may want to set yourself up as your own certificate authority and issue to each of your company's browsers its own certificate. Then you would configure the Apache server to require any browser to present its certificate before granting access to the company's proprietary data. The `ssleay` command can be used to create your own CA certificate and to issue (and revoke) the browser certificates. See the SSLeay documentation at **http://www2.psy.uq.edu.au/ ~ ftp/Crypto/**.

With the server certificate and key created, we can now edit the Apache configuration file to make use of them.

Configuring Apache with Apache-SSL

Apache-SSL's documentation regarding the added SSL configuration directives are available at **http://www.apache-ssl.org/docs.html**. You might want to save that document into a subdirectory of the `htdocs/manual/` directory (under the Apache installation directory). So you will have it with your local Apache online manual. To configure Apache with Apache-SSL, go to the Apache installation's `conf/` subdirectory (e.g. `/usr/local/apache/conf`) and edit the Apache configuration file with a text editor. Note that the configuration file has a new name: `httpsd.conf`, not `httpd.conf`. In the configuration file, modify or add (as need be) the following directives:

Listen

`Listen` directs Apache to listen to the specified TCP port. The `Listen` directive may be specified multiple times in order to get Apache to listen to more than one port. The `Listen` directive accepts one parameter specifying the port number that you wish to add. The parameter can include an IP address and port number combination (as in `Listen 192.168.1.1:8011`) to instruct Apache to listen to the added port, but only on the specified interface. Toward the end of configuring SSL, we need to instruct Apache to listen to both the HTTP port and the HTTPS port. Find the commented out `Listen` directives already in the configuration file and add these two lines below them:

```
Listen 80
Listen 443
```

The `Listen` directive can only be specified in the configuration file's global context.

User and Group

`User` and `Group` specify the user ID and the group ID under which the Apache server will run. Apache switches to these IDs on fly, so you will have to initially launch Apache as root for it to have the permissions to do so. These directives are initially set to the user `nobody` and the group `nobody`. Change them to read:

```
User httpd
Group httpd
```

This assumes that you have created the UNIX user named `httpd`. Refer to the section titled "Creating the Daemon Account" in Chapter 3: "Creating the Web Site." Along with the `User` and `Group` directives, you might want to modify any other site-specific directives mentioned in that chapter.

Next, add the SSL directives that belong in the configuration file's global context. Insert the following lines just after the virtual host declarations in the configuration file:

```
### Global SSL Directives
#
#
SSLCertificateFile /usr/local/ssl/certs/servercert.pem
SSLCertificateKeyFile /usr/local/ssl/private/serverkey.pem
SSLCacheServerPath bin/gcache
SSLCacheServerPort logs/gcache_port
SSLSessionCacheTimeout 3600
SSLEnable
```

SSlCertificateFile

SSLCertificateFile specifies the path and file name of the server's certificate file. The contents of this file are transmitted to the browser when the browser requests a secure connection. The browser will use the server's public key (extracted from this certificate) to encrypt messages sent to the server during negotiation. We generated this certificate file with the ssleay program, above, into the file /usr/local/ssl/certs/servercert.pem. This directive can be used in the configuration file's global context or within a <VirtualHost> block. If you recreate or change the file pointed to by this directive, then you will need to restart Apache for it to read the new certificate.

A certificate file can be created to contain both the server's certificate and the server's private key. For this example, we created them as separate files; so we must also add the SSLCertificateKeyFile directive.

SSlCertificateKeyFile

SSLCertificateKeyFile specifies the path and file name of the server's private key file. This file contains the key used to decrypt browser messages that have been encrypted using the server's public key (which the browser extracted from the server's certificate). If your server's certificate file contains both the certificate and the private key, then you do not need to specify this SSLCertificateKeyFile directive. Since we created the private key as a separate file, for this example, we give this SSLCertificateKeyFile directive the value of /usr/local/ssl/private/serverkey.pem. If you recreate or change the file pointed to by this directive, then you will need to restart Apache for it to read the new certificate.

This directive can be used in the configuration file's global context or within a `<VirtualHost>` block.

SSLCacheServerPath

`SSLCacheServerPath` specifies the path to the gcache program. The gcache program caches SSL sessions so that the server and client don't have to continually renegotiate their SSL authentication and encryption keys. The Apache-SSL patch should have installed this program in the `bin/` subdirectory of the Apache installation directory; thus our example sets `SSLCacheServerPath` to `bin/gcache`. The specified path may be absolute or relative. If a relative path is specified, it is relative to the Apache installation directory (e.g. `/usr/local/apache/`). This directive is required and can be placed only in the configuration file's global context.

SSLCacheServerPort

`SSLCacheServerPort` specifies the port number or socket file that the Apache server uses to converse with the gcache program (specified by the `SSLCacheServerPath`, above). `SSLCacheServerPort` accepts one parameter. If a number is specified, it is taken to be the TCP port number through which Apache will connect to `gcache`. If a path and file name is specified, then Apache will (on startup) create a local UNIX socket between Apache and `gcache`. If you create a TCP port for `gcache`, secure that port with a firewall or packet filter. If you create a local socket, secure that socket file with appropriate file permissions. The root user needs read and write permissions on the socket. The `httpd` user (or whatever you specified for the `User` directive), requires read permissions on the socket. For this example, we put the cache socket in the `logs/` subdirectory of the Apache installation directory. We secure the `logs/` subdirectory with these UNIX shell commands:

```
chown root.httpd /usr/local/apache/logs
chmod 750 /usr/local/apache/logs
```

The above `chown` command gives the root user ownership of the file and set's the file's group to `httpd`. The above `chmod` command gives the root user full permissions on the `logs/` subdirectory and gives the httpd group (of which the `httpd` user is a member) read and search permissions on the subdirectory. Make doubly sure that the `logs/` subdirectory never becomes part of the server's public document tree (e.g. via a `<Directory>` block).

The `SSLCachServerPort` directive is required and can only be added to the configuration file's global context.

SSLSessionCacheTimeout

`SSLSessionCacheTimeout` specifies the maximum length of time, in seconds, that the server and client can maintain a secure connection without renegotiating the SSL authentication and encryption keys. A high value increases performance, but gives an attacker more time to crack the session's encryption key. A low value makes the session's encryption key a moving target, but slows performance. For testing we set ours to one hour by specifying 3600 seconds.

The `SSLSessionCacheTimeout` directive is required and can only be added to the configuration file's global context.

SSLEnable

`SSLEnable` enables SSL negotiation. It takes no parameters. This directive causes the Apache server to listen for HTTPS connections and not HTTP connections. The browser should specify the `https://` scheme in the URLs transmitted to this server.

SSLDisable

`SSLDisable` disables SSL negotiation. It takes no parameters. This directive causes the Apache server to listen to HTTP connections and not HTTPS connections. The browser should specify the `http://` scheme in the URLs transmitted to this server.

Note that the server will not listen to HTTP connections when `SSLEnable` is specified. The server will not listen to HTTPS connections when `SSLDisable` is specified.

The `SSLEnable` and `SSLDisable` directives can be added to the configuration file's global context or within a `<VirtualHost>` block.

The SSL directives described above are enough to get the SSL server running. Apache-SSL provides several more directives that can be applied to the global context and within `<Directory>` blocks and `.htaccess` files. We discuss the most notable ones below (though we don't use them in this example). For a complete list of SSL directives consult the Apache-SSL documentation at **http://www.apache-ssl.org/docs.html**.

SSLRequiredCiphers

SSLRequiredCiphers limits the ciphers that the server and client can mutually use. You can use this directive to require the use of the more-secure (128-bit) ciphers. This is useful for an intranet, where you want good security and you are assured that all of the browsers hitting your site will have the 128-bit ciphers. You could require the RSA ciphers with the following example:

```
SSLRequiredCiphers SSL3_TXT_RSA_RC4_128_SHA
```

For a public web server, you probably don't want to use this directive because you'll end up denying service to browsers that have only the 40-bit ciphers (U.S. exported browsers). The Apache-SSL documentation provides a complete list of allowable parameters in the section titled "Cipher Suites." The SSLRequiredCiphers may be added to the configuration file's global context or may be added to a <VirtualHost> block.

SSLRequireSSL

SSLRequireSSL requires that all requests in the given context use the HTTPS protocol. This directive takes no parameters and may appear in the configuration file's global context or within a <VirtualHost> block or <Directory> block or within an .htaccess file. HTTP connections to the given context are refused ("port reset by peer" error) if SSL has not been enabled by the EnableSSL directive. Note that this directive does not enable or disable SSL. With Apache-SSL, you cannot have some directories accessed with HTTP and others with HTTPS. This SSLRequireSSL directive is merely a safety net for the Apache configuration. You can specify SSLRequireSSL within a <Directory> block for a directory that contains sensitive information. If the server is accidentally configured to DisableSSL, the given directory will still be protected (though no-one will be able to get to it).

SSLVerifyClient

SSLVerifyClient requires the requesting browser to present its own (personal) certificate for authentication by the server. The SSL protocol requires the server to authenticate itself to the browser; but does not require the browser to authenticate itself to the server. The SSLVerify-Client directive is useful for adding privacy to an intranet web server. You can set yourself up as your own certificate authority and issue each of your browsers its own private certificate; or, you can contract with a certificate authority to issue your browsers their certificates. The SSLVerifyClient directive accepts one parameter, which may be one of:

- 0—The client is not required to present a certificate
- 1—The client may present a certificate; in this case the browser is authenticated by the server. That is, the certificate authority that signed the browser's certificate must on the server's list of trusted certificate authorities (see SSLCACertificatePath, below).
- 2—The client must present a certificate (which the server authenticates, see SSLCACertificatePath, below).
- 3—The client may present a certificate, but the certificate does not have to be signed by one of the certificate authorities that the server trusts. That is, the client can present a certificate, but it won't be authenticated.

Of the above parameters, only 0 and 2 are useful. The SSLVerifyClient directive may appear in the configuration file's global context or within a <VirtualHost> block.

SSLCACertificatePath

SSLCACertificatePath specifies the directory in which your server keeps the certificate files of the certificate authorities that the server trusts. For intranet purposes, you can require that a browser hitting your site present its own certificate, signed by one of the server's trusted certificate authorities. This example:

```
SSLCACertificatePath /usr/local/ssl/ca
```

specifies that the certificates of the server's trusted authorities reside in the /usr/local/ssl/ca/ directory (which you will have to create and populate).

The SSLCACertificatePath directive may appear in the configuration file's global context or within a <VirtualHost> block.

SSLVerifyDepth

SSLVerifyDepth specifies the number of levels of certificate authorities that the server is willing to traverse in order to authenticate a client. Certificates are authenticated in chains. A root authority will issue a CA certificate to another company, granting that company the right to distribute certificates on behalf of the root authority. This secondary authority might then issue CA certificates to tertiary authorities. When the browser presents a certificate not signed by an authority listed in the server's SSLCACertificatePath, the server connects to the authority that did sign the browser's certificate and asks that CA for its parent CA. If the parent CA is not listed in the server's list of trusted authorities, the server keeps going up the chain until a trusted CA is found or the root CA is reached. The SSLVerifyDepth directive specifies how many CAs up the chain the server is willing to go in order to authenticate the browser. The SSLVerifyDepth directive accepts one numeric parameter specifying the number of traversals the server is willing to make. A value of 0 will cause the server to traverse all the way to the root CA. A value of 1 causes the server to authenticate a client only if the signer of the client's certificate is among the server's trusted CAs. That is, a value of 1 requires the client to present a certificate signed by a CA for whom the server has a certificate in the SSLCACertificatePath directory. A value greater than 1 specifies how many remote connections up the chain the server will go.

The SSLVerifyDepth directive may appear in the configuration file's global context or within a <VirtualHost> block.

The Apache server is configured, and we can now start up the Apache server daemon.

Starting and Stopping Apache with Apache-SSL

In the bin/ subdirectory of the Apache installation directory (e.g. /usr/local/apache/bin/) there resides a script named httpsdctl.

httpsdctl

httpsdctl is Apache server control script used to stop and start the server daemon. It operates much the same way as the apachectl script used to. The httpsdctl script accepts the following parameters:

- start—Starts the httpsd parent deamon (which then launches its child daemons)
- stop—Shuts down all of the running httpsd daemons.
- restart—Sends a SIGHUP signal to the parent httpsd deamon; which then shuts down all of its children daemons, rereads the Apache configuration file, then restarts its child daemons.
- graceful—Sends a SIGUSR1 signal to the parent httpsd daemon; which then waits for its children daemons to finish up the requests that they are currently processing, and then perform a restart.

- `configtest`—Validates the syntax of the Apache configuration file. If you modify the Apache configuration file while the server is running (and save your changes), the `configtest` command will test your last saved version of the configuration file—not the configuration of the running server.
- `fullstatus`—Provides a detailed display of the current status of the running server. This parameter requires that the server be compiled with the `mod_status` module.
- `status`—Provides an abbreviated display of the current status of the running server. This parameter requires that the server be compiled with the `mod_status` module.
- `help`—Lists the parameters acceptable to the `httpsdctl` script.

At the UNIX shell prompt, in the `bin/` subdirectory of the Apache installation directory, enter the following command line to test the syntax of your modifications to the configuration file:

```
./httpsdctl configtest
```

If there are no gripes, then start the server with this command:

```
./httpsdctl start
```

As Apache starts up, it asks you to:

```
Enter PEM pass phrase:
```

If you created a test certificate (in the subsection titled "Creating the Server Certificate with SSLeay," above), enter the password key that you entered in the `ssleay` program when you created the certificate. If your server has a certificate issued by a certificate authority, then enter the password key used to encrypt that file. If the daemon starts up successfully, it will display this:

```
Launching... /usr/local/apache/bin/gcache
pid=27975
/usr/local/apache/bin/httpsdctl start: httpd started
```

just before disconnecting from the terminal. If the daemon cannot start up or if there are any problems, the daemon will write an error message to the file named `httpsd_error_log` in the `logs/` subdirectory of the Apache installation directory (e.g. `/usr/local/apache/logs/httpsd_error_log`). The most common problem is the misspelling of the path to the server's certificate file or private key file; so check that first.

Barring any problems, you should be able to hit your secure web site using the HTTPS protocol (e.g. **https://www.administeringapache.com**/). If your server is running on a test certificate, the browser will pop up warning dialogs asking if you wish to continue the connection with the unauthenticated server. Clicking through these dialogs should bring you to the homepage displayed in Figure 6.8.

If this page doesn't come up, then recheck the URL that you typed into the browser's location bar. Be sure you used the `https://` protocol and not the `http://` protocol. If you still don't get the page, then make sure that the `SSLEnable` directive is specified in the Apache configuration file.

Figure 6.8
*Apache_SSL
installation successful.*

It Worked! The Apache Web Server is Installed on this Web Site!

If you can see this page, then the people who own this domain have just installed the Apache Web server software successfully. They now have to add content to this directory and replace this placeholder page, or else point the server at their real content.

If you are seeing this page instead of the site you expected, please **contact the administrator of the site involved.** (Try sending mail to <Webmaster@domain>.) Although this site is running the Apache software it almost certainly has no other connection to the Apache Group, so please do not send mail about this site or its contents to the Apache authors. If you do, your message will be **ignored.**

The Apache documentation has been included with this distribution.

The Webmaster of this site is free to use the image below on an Apache-powered Web server. Thanks for using Apache!

Security Considerations for CGI

CGI provides all of the power of the operating system—for good or ill.

Setting Policy

Whom you allow to write CGI scripts and programs is one of your most important policy considerations. On an intranet web server, scripts are developed by an employee (or contractor) in an environment of accountability and trust, especially if the webmaster's user account is set up properly and doesn't have inordinate permissions outside of the web site directories. On an ISP web server, providing hosting services to thousands of customers, accountability is a bit harder to come by. It used to be that, if an ISP allowed CGI at all, it was in a strictly controlled environment. The scripts are maintained in a shared /cgi-bin/ directory to which only ISP administrators have write permissions. All scripts placed in that directory are written by the ISP and are *thoroughly* tested for destructive side-effects and security holes. Due to market pressures, many ISPs are beginning to allow their web-hosting customers to write their own scripts. Special provisions must be made to ensure that these scripts are neither malicious nor vulnerable to attack (see "Wrappers," below). You might also enact a published policy of consequences for customers who intentionally write malicious scripts.

Good Programming Habits

The power of CGI scripts has made them attractive targets for hackers. Your scripts should defend themselves against particular attacks. Hackers will try to trick scripts into overwriting or modifying particular system files. The user ID under which the script runs (the Apache child daemon user set by the User directive), should not have write permissions anywhere (especially not in system areas or system source code areas). If the script must write temporary files, these files should be written only to a very restricted directory. This directory should not contain any links to other directories. This should not be the /cgi-bin/ directory or the directory in which the script resides. Your script should perform a great deal of error checking. Most scripts process data from the browser and through these data hackers will enter your system. Your scripts should be positively anal about verifying user data, especially if the data are to be passed through a shell command such as sed or cut. A hacker could put a semicolon or other shell character into the data to terminate your shell command and then run his/her shell command, as in:

```
;; cat /etc/passwd
```

Strip or quote all special shell characters in the user data—&%${}()|<>*@.

Non-Script Aliased vs. Script Aliased

There are two ways to enable the calling of CGI scripts: the `ScriptAlias` directive and the `AddHandler` directive.

ScriptAlias

`ScriptAlias` specifies the directory in which CGI scripts reside. This directive accepts two parameters: the virtual location of the scripts directory (i.e. the URL), and the physical location of the scripts directory. For example:

```
ScriptAlias /cgi-bin/ "/home/webmastr/pub/cgi-bin/"
```

The `ScriptAlias` directive installs an alias that maps requests to the specified URL to the specified file system directory. The directive also automatically performs an `Options +ExecCGI` on the specified directory in order to enable script execution in that directory.

Addhandler

`AddHandler` instructs Apache to call the specified handler when a requested file ends with the specified filename prefix. This example

```
AddHandler cgi-script .cgi
```

calls the `cgi-script` handler whenever a document ending in `.cgi` is requested.

The `AddHandler` method of enabling CGI script execution is the non-script aliased way of doing it. It enables CGI scripts to appear anywhere within the `DocumentRoot` directory tree. This allows the webmaster to put scripts where he/she would like. The drawback is that the system administrator loses all control over scripting. In a trusted environment (e.g. intranet), this non-script aliased CGI would be handy for the webmaster. On an ISP web-hosting server, this would be a disaster (especially without a CGI wrapper).

Using CGI Wrappers

CGI wrappers run each CGI script under the user ID of the owner of the script. Wrappers are really only useful for ISPs who allow their web-hosting customers to write their own scripts. Wrappers keep the web-hosting customers from trashing the system and each other's sites and directories. If you do not have web-hosting customers writing their own scripts, then all you really need to do is set the User directive to a user that has no privileges. If you do implement CGI wrappers, be warned that performance will be much slower. The wrapper performs 20 security checks before running each script.

To install the CGI wrapper, you must reconfigure and recompile the Apache server. Go to the Apache source code directory and enter the following arguments to the APACI utility's configure command (replacing the --prefix, --enable-module, and --enable-shared values as appropriate for your system):

```
./configure \
--prefix=/usr/local/apache \
--enable-module=most \
--enable-shared=max \
--enable-suexec \
--suexec-caller=httpd \
--suexec-docroot=/home/webmastr/pub/html \
--suexec-logfile=/usr/local/apache/logs/suexec_log \
--suexec-userdir=pub_html \
--suexec-uidmin=500 \
--suexec-gidmin=500 \
--suexec-safepath=/usr/local/bin:/usr/bin:/bin
```

In the above configure command, the --enable-suexec instructs the Makefiles to build the suexec binary, which is the CGI wrapper program. Next, do a make to compile the server and a make install to install the new server and suexec binary. Once installed, the Apache child daemons will call suexec. Suexec performs security checks and, if everything checks out, suexec calls the CGI script. The --suexec-??? parameters to the APACI utility are described below:

■ --suexec-caller—Specifes the user ID under which the Apache child daemons run. This should be the same value as the User directive in the Apache configuration file. The user named by this parameter will be the only user allowed to run the suexec program.

- `--suexec-docroot`—Specifies the directory that will be the current directory when a CGI script is run—usually the same as the `DocumentRoot` directory in the Apache configuration file.
- `--suexec-logfile`—Specifies the text file to which the `suexec` binary writes its error messages. When `suexec` refuses to run a script, you will see a "Premature end of script headers" in Apache's error log and then more details in the `suexec` log.
- `--suexec-userdir`—Specifies the subdirectory under each user's home directory from which CGI scripts may be run. This should be set the same as the `UserDir` directive in the Apache configuration file.
- `--suexec-uidmin`—Specifies the minimum value of the user ID under which `suexec` will run the script. Usually, power users are assigned IDs below 500 and normal users are assigned IDs from 500 on up. Setting this parameter prevents scripts from being run as power users.
- `--suexec-gidmin`—Specifies the minimum value of the group ID under which `suexec` will run the script. Usually, power groups are assigned IDs below 500 and normal groups are assigned IDs from 500 on up. Setting this parameter prevents scripts from being run as members of a power group.
- `--suexec-safepath`—Specifies the executable search path to be set for the script. This parameter should point to directories containing normal user programs (e.g. `/bin:/usr/bin:/usr/local/bin`, *never* `/sbin`).

Beware that the `suexec` binary is installed with the user getuid bit set:

```
-rws--x--x 1 root root 10152 Jan 26 05:03 suexec
```

this causes the shell to set the user ID to root before running `suexec`. Suexec must run as root in order to have permission to `setuid()` to the user ID under which the script will run. A root setuid bit is in itself a security problem. The `--suexec-caller` parameter is supposed to prevent this from being abused. But beware. If you don't really understand all this `setuid()` business, you might not want to enable `suexec`. Read carefully the Apache User's Guide section on `suexec`: **manual/suexec.html**.

If you are getting a lot of "Premature end of script headers" errors in your `error_log`, then your `--suexec-???` parameters to the APACI utility may be incorrect. Suexec will refuse to run a script if anything is suspect—especially if the `suexec` configuration is suspect.

The `suexec` utility requires that the script to be run is owned and grouped by the user id and default group id of the webmaster. The directory in which the script resides must also be owned and grouped by the webmaster's user id and default group id. You will have to grant others read and execute permissions on the directory so that the Apache server daemon can search for the requested script. For example:

```
drwxr-xr-x webmastr users /home/webmastr/pub/cgi-bin
```

See Chapter 7: "Creating Homepage Web Sites" for instructions on setting up multiple user homepages with `suexec`.

Security Considerations for Front Page Extensions

Microsoft offers a web-authoring toolkit called FrontPage. This toolkit is an overall web-site maintenance system. Microsoft also offers a server-sided extension package that the FrontPage authoring software can make use of. The extensions allow the FrontPage web-authoring toolkit to perform maintenance on the web site (such as correcting links when files move around). These extensions also help technically unsophisticated web authors install and use CGI scripts that perform common CGI-sorts-of things (like site-search and discussion groups). You can read about FrontPage and the FrontPage Server Extensions at: **http://officeupdate. microsoft.com/frontpage/wpp/serk98/default.htm**. The UNIX version of the FrontPage Server Extensions is available from Ready-to-Run software at: **http://www.rtr.com/fpsupport/**.

Be aware that installing and maintaining the server extensions requires a fair amount of time from the system administrator. Here is a most eloquent quote from a entry in the discussion group hosted by Ready-to-Run software (**http://www.rtr.com/fp2000disc/_disc1/00000303.htm**):

```
Let's face it--they will never work

From: GAS
Date: 15 Jan 2000
Time: 02:48:40
Remote Name: 204.1.34.130

Comments

I'm through wasting my time trying to install a program that does
not and will not work. We do not receive any help from M$ or from
RTR. We fight insane unnecessary problems for such little gain.
```

```
If I lose customers because of this decision then so be it, I
don't care.

Frontpage sucks.
```

```
Last changed: January 19, 2000
```

Also beware that the FrontPage server extensions are vulnerable to particular kinds of hack attacks. The package keeps its cryptographic key in an environment variable—which is not so hard to discover. You'll find a complete description on how to exploit the Server Extensions to become the bin power user on the server system at: **http://www.worldgate. com/ ~ marcs/fp/**. That page also describes how you can protect yourself from such attacks; but none of the solutions is easily configured.

If you wish to support Front Page server extensions, you would be better off installing it on the Microsoft Web server (and not on your Apache server).

Creating Homepage Web Sites

Strategy

Considerations

Homepages (also called *user sites*) are Web sites that do not have their own registered domain names. They are usually used to publish the Web sites of individuals—who rent the server space through the homepage hosting services of an ISP (which provides the registered domain name). But homepages might also be used on a corporate intranet Web server. User sites may be provided to employees for internal publication of their resumes, bios, pictures, office numbers, phone numbers, etc. User sites may be provided for departments to publish proposed projects, status reports for current projects, financials, target sales figures, etc. A Web development team creating a corporate intranet server might make use of homepages. Each developer could have a user site on which to incrementally test the portions being worked on.

User sites on an intranet Web server need to be feature-rich yet easy to use and administer. Homepages on an ISP server must be secure. On a large ISP server, they must not degrade server performance. These goals must be balanced by user requirements. Will homepage authors be allowed to write their own CGI scripts? Will they be allowed to create CGI scripts as compiled binaries? Will they be allowed to telnet into the server to do online development? Will they be allowed to store more than just Web content on the server? How much disk space will each homepage get? What kind of content will they publish? Will the authors use server-generated directory indexes, image maps, SSI? Will the authors be allowed to set access restrictions on all or part of their site? Will they be allowed to define authentication restrictions on all or part of their site? Authentication restrictions require the storage of a username/password file outside of the published user site directory. The homepage author would also require a telnet log in order to create and maintain the username/password file. In general, the more services you provide to the homepage authors, the more measures you will need to take to ensure that security, performance, ease of use, and administration are not compromised.

All of this affects how you implement user sites. This chapter presents three sample implementations—each solving the above problems in different ways.

Strategy for the Intranet Web Server

The homepage author in this scenario is just a regular system user with a homepage. These user sites are the easiest to configure, but the least secure. This is a trusted environment. Users can deliver remotely developed content via FTP. They can also telnet in and develop content online. They can take full advantage of CGI scripting, or even compiling CGI binaries. The `suexec` wrapper is not used to secure the execution of CGI scripts in this environment. Homepage authors can define access and authentication restrictions on all or part of their site. They can also store private files in their home directories.

Strategy for the Large ISP

Security and performance are the key considerations. Homepage authors get a Web site and that's it; no private storage and no CGI. They must use FTP to deliver content to the server and cannot log in via telnet. Homepage authors can define neither access restrictions nor authentication restrictions. Homepage authors cannot store private files in their home directories. The user site directory *is* their home directory.

Strategy for the Small ISP

You're trying to compete with the big guys and your prices are as low as they can go. Your differentiator—service. In this scenario, homepage authors are allowed to write their own CGI scripts. The `suexec` wrapper is used to secure the execution of these scripts. Homepage authors use FTP to deliver content, but cannot log in via telnet. They can define access restrictions, but not authentication restrictions. They cannot store private files in their home directories.

I have heard of a small ISP that became a large ISP through offering such services. When they got big, they stopped allowing homepage authors to write their own CGI scripts. It wasn't for any technical reason. It was because of the growth of their user support phone calls. This growing ISP conformed to the typical large-model ISP. That is, if the homepage authors want CGI, they have to pay a commercial price for a commercial site. Maybe what one could do is offer a level of hosting service between homepage and commercial. It would allow CGI and maybe database services, but would not offer SSL, credit card verification, and the like. In order to advance to the intermediate level, a homepage author must pass a test covering your directory structure, your rules and policies regarding

CGI development and deployment, and tips for safe-hex. One could offer the test and a preparatory course online. One might even provide a two-hour class (for a fee) with the test at the end. An extended four- to eight-hour class—covering scripting how-to in various languages—might also be justifiable.

The tasks for configuring the server are the same for all of the scenarios: The directory structure must be created. Apache's user directory translation must be enabled. Apache content-services must be configured for the user site. CGI must be configured (where allowed). FTP must be configured to accept homepage site content. This chapter prescribes these tasks and, within each task, describes the differences in implementation between the three scenarios.

Creating User Accounts and Site Directories

Designing the Structure

For each homepage, a system user account must be created. The user account authenticates the homepage author on login to FTP or telnet. You will also need to create a user account home directory and a user site document directory. The user account home directory defines the root directory when the homepage author logs in via FTP. It also defines the current directory when the author logs in via telnet. The user site directory, of course, stores the homepage Web site. The site directory may be created as a subdirectory of the home directory. Or the site directory and the home directory can be the same directory. If they are the same directory, then the Web server will publish all of the files in that home directory. The homepage author will not be able to store private files. There are occasions when the author will need to store private files. If authors are allowed to define authentication restrictions, they will need to store username/password files outside the public Web site. In a most trusted environment (e.g. intranet Web server), where authors might be allowed to compile CGI programs as binaries, authors will need private space for the source code. (They will also need telnet to log in and compile). You, as the system administrator, may want to store private files in the user's home directory: customer profile information or support files. These would all be reasons for creating the Web site directory as a subdirectory of the home directory. If none of these features is required, then a single directory scheme might be best.

One neat trick is first to create the site directory on one hard disk partition, then create the home directory on another partition—as a soft link to the site directory. This offers two advantages: 1) If a homepage-hosting customer doesn't pay, you just remove the soft link. This disables the publishing of the user site without removing the user site directory. When the customer pays up, you just add the soft link back. 2) You can back up the home partition and the site partition separately (keeping backups of system account home directories separate from backups of Web sites). The backups can be performed on different schedules. Be sure to set the backup to not follow symbolic links.

If you allow homepage authors to develop their own CGI scripts, then you may want to provide each user account with an additional subdirectory for scripts (script aliased CGI). The alternative is to allow CGI scripts to reside anywhere within any of the user site directories (non-script aliased CGI). See Chapter 6: "Securing the Server, the Content, and the Connection," the section titled "Security Considerations for CGI," the subsection "Non-Script Aliased versus Script Aliased." In this context, script aliased CGI doesn't offer any security advantages, since the system administrator has given up all control over the deployment of scripts. It does offer organizational advantages. The homepage author knows that anything within the script aliased directory will be executed as a program and anything outside of that directory will not be. Also, the homepage author will not have to follow any file naming convention, as is required by non-script aliased CGI.

A large ISP may have extra file system considerations. Apache performs a large number of directory searches and file status polls. Performance of these operations degrades on directories containing a large number of files and subdirectories—which you will experience if you put thousands of user site directories in one big parent directory. If you can group user site directories into various subdirectories, then you can reduce the number of directory entries in the parent directory. One scheme might be to group the home directories and the user site directories according to the first and second letters of the username. For example, the jdoe user account would have the following home directory created as a link to the following site directory:

```
/home/j/d/jdoe/  ➜  /mnt/webpub/homepages/j/d/jdoe/
```

You could configure such a system to go one, two, or three subdirectories deep—depending on the number of user sites that you host.

Once the user site directory has been created, you might pre-populate the new site with some help pages. Then, you and the new homepage author will be able to use these pages to test that the new site is up and running. And the homepage author can get some help without calling you on the phone. You might put some useful little menu with links to your main Web site—links like "Upload Instructions," "Online Support," "HTML Resources." The easiest thing to do is to keep a template Web site in a directory somewhere and just copy the template directory into each new homepage site. If you provide the authors with separate scripts directories, put test scripts into a separate scripts template directory.

Once the new site is populated, you must set permissions on the directories and files therein. The homepage author must be able to create and overwrite files throughout the home directory. The Web server needs to be able to search for and read files in the homepage site directory. The easiest thing to do would be to give the user account user ownership of the directories and full read/write/execute permissions. Then grant to "others" read/execute permissions on the site directory. This is not very secure; and not all files in a public directory are public (e.g. .htaccess files that point to authentication files). Apache provides the IndexIgnore and Deny directives to hide particular files and exclude them from publication. Giving "others" search privileges on the site directory circumvents these restrictions imposed by Apache. The better way would be to give the user account ownership of the directories; then, give the Web server daemon group ownership of the site directory (i.e. set the directory's group to the group ID under which the server runs, as defined by the Group directive). The directory's owner (thus the user account) is given full permissions; the directory's group (thus the Web server) is given read/execute permissions; and the others are given no permissions. In addition, the group set-gid bit can be set on the site directory so that files created in that directory are automatically assigned the same group as that of the directory (the server daemon group). The files in the site directory should also be owned by the user account and grouped by the server daemon's group. Give the owner (thus the author) read/write permissions on these files; and give the group (thus the Web server) read permissions on these files. For files that are CGI scripts, execute permissions should be given to both owner and group.

This scheme of assigning the server daemon's group to the site directory won't work if you use the suexec wrapper. See Chapter 6: "Securing the Server, the Content, and the Connection," the section "Security Considerations for CGI," the subsection "Using CGI Wrappers." The suexec wrapper requires that the directory in which the script resides be owned by the user account and be grouped by the user's default group (as defined by the user's entry in /etc/passwd). Yet the Web server still needs permissions to search the site directory for the requested script. The only option is to give others read and execute permissions to the site directory. This is a security tradeoff. Script execution is made more secure, but the directory permissions are less secure. The directory permissions are almost a non-issue if a) authors cannot telnet into the server, b) telnet is restricted to the administrators workstation, c) FTP is properly configured to chroot() to the user account's home directory (thus authors cannot get into each other's directories through FTP). If you want to use suexec and still minimize exposure, you could create one directory for static content and a separate directory for scripts. Then, on the static document directory, you can set the group to that of the server daemon and grant no permissions to others. On the scripts directory, you would set the group to the user account's default group and open up the read/execute permissions to others. Note that when suexec is used, the server daemon will not need read permissions on the scripts themselves. The server daemon just needs to be able to search the directory. Thus you can, for the script files, give read/write/execute permissions to the owner and no permissions to the group or to others.

Disk space is always a consideration. You need to provide the homepage users with as much as they need—balancing their needs against the cost of the growth of your server farm. For the large ISP, with thousands of homepages, a small rise in disk space for each user equals an exponential rise in disk space for the system. Large ISPs generally limit each homepage to about 5 megabytes The service-oriented small ISP, with fewer homepage customers, might be able to realize a greater space-to-user ratio—depending on the cash at hand. A small ISP might offer 10 or 15 megabytes per homepage to draw customers away from the large ISP. The intranet Web server that hosts user sites may or may not impose limits on disk space—depending on the size of the company, the number of system users, the individual user requirements (inside and outside the site directory). If you have a small number of home pages (such as a set of developer test sites) you might impose no limit. Or you might limit them to about 20 megabytes per developer for medium sized applications (up to 100 Mb for large ones).

With these considerations in mind, it's time to move on to implementation. First, enable and configure the UNIX quota system.

Configuring the Disk Quota System

The quota system is fairly standard on UNIX systems; though, as always, watch for variations in command parameters. The example here is, again, Linux. The first thing to do is enable quota checking on the filesystem that stores the homepage Web sites—/mnt/webpub, in this example. The first thing to do is tell UNIX which filesystem(s) are to be monitored. Edit the file /etc/fstab. Each line describes how to mount a filesystem. Look for the entry that describes the filesystem that will contain the user sites. The fourth field in that line specifies the mount options. Add the word usrquota to these options. For example, find the line that reads like this:

```
/dev/hda8 /mnt/webpub    ext2    defaults      1      2
```

and make it look like this:

```
/dev/hda8 /mnt/webpub    ext2    defaults,usrquota   1      2
```

Make a note of the hard disk device name (/dev/hda8, in the above example). You will need it later. Next, create the empty quota databases on the root of the filesystem on which quotas are to be imposed. and set the permissions on these files. For our example system, these files would be created by the following shell commands:

```
touch /mnt/webpub/quota.user
touch /mnt/webpub/quota.group
chmod 600 /mnt/webpub/quota.user
chmod 600 /mnt/webpub/quota.group
```

Next, create a template user whose quotas will be copied to new users. On a Linux system, you can create the template user account with this shell command:

```
useradd -d /home/templhp templhp
```

Other UNIX systems will have a comparable command. The above command creates the user account for our example template user, templhp, and a home directory for this user. If this user account will be used solely for assigning disk quotas to future new users (e.g. the large and small ISP models), you might create the user account without creating a home directory—using this shell command:

```
useradd -M templhp
```

Next, assign disk quotas to the template user. At the shell, type:

```
edquota -u templhp
```

This command creates a temporary text file and launches the default editor (usually vi). When you land in the editor, the following text should be presented to you for editing:

```
Quotas for user templhp:
/dev/hda8: blocks in use: 0, limits (soft = 0, hard = 0)
     inodes in use: 0, limits (soft = 0, hard = 0)
```

If all you get is the first line, then the quota.user and quota.group files must not be set up correctly (they may be misnamed or have the wrong permissions). The second line of the text starts the partition quotas, one for each filesystem on which quotas are implemented (i.e. those filesystems that contain quota.user and quota.group files). We want to edit the quotas for the filesystem on which the homepage web sites will be stored—/dev/hda8, in our example. For each hard disk device, two quotas are assigned. The first limits the number of blocks that the user's files may occupy. At 1024 bytes per block, this block limit is expressed in kilobytes. The second limit restricts the number of inodes that the user can consume. This inode limit restricts the number of files that the user can create (well almost, small files take up one inode; large files take up more than one). For both the block limit and the inode limit, a soft limit and a hard limit are set. The soft limit prescribes the point at which warnings are issued to the user. The hard limit prescribes the point at which the kernel cuts off the user (that is, disallows the user from consuming any more blocks or inodes—no more creating files or adding to existing files). Be aware that, on some systems, exceeding the hard limit my disable the user account if the login process creates temporary files on that partition. The soft limit is typically set to about 80% of the hard limit. If users are allowed a large quota, you might set the soft limit to about 90% of the hard limit.

Assigning Quotas for the Intranet Server

Use the edquota command to set the template user's quotas as follows:

```
Quotas for user templhp:
/dev/hda8: blocks in use: 0, limits (soft = 18000, hard = 20000)
     inodes in use: 0, limits (soft = 9000, hard = 10000)
```

Assigning Quotas for the Large ISP

Use the edquota command to set the template user's quotas as follows:

```
Quotas for user templhp:
/dev/hda8: blocks in use: 0, limits (soft = 4000, hard = 5000)
       inodes in use: 0, limits (soft = 1600, hard = 2000)
```

Assigning Quotas for the Small ISP

Use the edquota command to set the template user's quotas as follows:

```
Quotas for user templhp:
/dev/hda8: blocks in use: 0, limits (soft = 12000, hard = 15000)
       inodes in use: 0, limits (soft = 3200, hard = 4000)
```

Once you save the temporary file presented by the edquota command (and exit the editor), edquota will store the template user's new limits into the /mnt/webpub/quota.user database.

Since we've just created new quota databases (quota.user and quota.group), the file system has to be remounted for the quota monitoring to take effect. If these quotas are being applied to the root file system, you will have to reboot the system. Our example file system (/mnt/webpub), is a mounted file system; so we can remount it without rebooting by entering the following shell commands:

```
umount /mnt/webpub
mount /mnt/webpub
```

Finally, turn quota monitoring on. At the shell prompt, enter

```
quotaon -avug
```

The quota command reports the quotas currently in effect. To see if our template user's quotas are in effect, enter the following at the shell prompt:

```
quota -uv templhp
```

You should see the following output:

```
Disk quotas for user templhp (uid 508):
     Filesystem blocks   quota  limit  grace  files  quota  limit   grace
       /dev/hda8     0    4000   5000            0    1600   2000
```

From this point forward, quota monitoring will be turned on for the given filesystem. For Linux, this extends across reboots. On other systems, you may need to create an init script to startup quota monitoring. The init script might look something like this:

```
#!/bin/sh

case "$1" in
    start)
        #
        # This may be /usr/sbin/quotaon on your system
        #
        /sbin/quotaon -avug
        ;;

    stop)
        #
        # This may be /usr/sbin/quotaoff on your system
        #
        /sbin/quotaoff -avug
        ;;
esac
```

As new user accounts are created for the homepage authors, the quotas for our template user will be copied to the new user. To do this, the edquota command is used again, but with different parameters. After adding a new user named jdoe, for example, issue the following shell command:

```
edquota -p templhp jdoe
```

The above command will copy templhp's quotas to jdoe. This form of the edquota command will just do the copy. It will not present you with an temporary file and any editor (as it did when we set the quotas on the template user). That makes this second form of edquota really handy for shell scripts.

With the quota system enabled, we can now explore the directory structure of each unique scenario.

Creating a Homepage User on an Intranet Web Server

The homepage author is a normal system user, with a homepage. All you have to do is add an html/ and a cgi-bin/ subdirectory to the user's home directory. On the html/ directory, the user is given read/write/execute permissions on the directory and read/write permissions on the files therein. The Web server is given read/execute permissions on the directory and read permissions on the files therein. On the cgi-bin directory, the user is given read/write/execute permissions on the directory and on the files therein. The Web server is given read/execute permissions on the directory and on the files therein. No permissions are granted to others on either directory. The set-gid bit is set on both the html/ and cgi-bin/ directories so that files created therein are automatically assigned the group of the directory—which is the group ID under which the Web server runs. Read/execute permissions for others are added to the home directory so that the server can descend into the html/ and cgi-bin/ subdirectories.

The following bash script creates the user account and directories for this scenario. This script populates the new user home directory from a template user's home directory (the same template user created for copying quotas, above). You will need to add an html/ and a cgi-bin/ subdirectory to the template user's home directory. You might also populate these subdirectories with example files. This script was written for Linux. You may need to replace the useradd command with the comparable command on your system. Review the parameters to the cp, ln, chown, and chmod commands for their appropriateness for your system. Before using this script, set the configuration variables near the top of the script.

```
#!/bin/bash

####################################################################
# hpnew.sysuser
#
# Description:
#    Creates a home page user account and associated directories
# for a new homepage site on an intranet server. This script
# creates a normal system log in and then adds directories for
# for the homepage site to the user's home directory. This script
# also imposes disk quotas on the user.
#
# Parameters:
#    The name of the user whose account and site are to be
# created.
#
# Exit Codes:
#    0                    success
#    22                   invalid parameter
#    other-non-zero       error code
#
# Notes:
#    User home directories and web site directories are created
```

```
# as follows. Given the username jdoe...
#
#    /home/jdoe
#    /home/jdoe/html
#    /home/jdoe/cgi-bin
#
# A description of each:
#
#    /home/jdoe...the user's home directory.
#
#    /home/jdoe/html...contains the static portion of the
#    the user's homepage.
#
#    /home/jdoe/cgi-bin...contains the dynamic portion of the
#    the user's homepage.
#
################################################################

################################################################
# Configuration:
#
# Set these configuration variables before using this script.
#
# HP_HOMEROOT...The parent directory under which homepage
#    user account home directories are to be
#    created.
#
# HP_TEMPLATEUSER...Names the user account whose home directory
#    files are to be copied into the new user's home
#    directory and whose disk quotas are to copied to the
#    new user.
##
# HP_SERVERGROUP...The name of the user group under which the
#    web server daemon runs. This should be set the
#    same as the Group Apache configuration directive.
#
################################################################
HP_HOMEROOT=/home
HP_TEMPLATEUSER=templhp
HP_SERVERGROUP=httpd


#
# Get the username from the first command-line parameter.
#
HpUserName=$1


#
# HpUserName cannot be empty
#
```

```
if [ "x_$HpUserName" = "x_" ]; then
     echo
     echo "$0: Username not be specfied"
     exit 22
fi

echo
echo "$0: Creating user account and homepage site for $HpUserName"

################################################
# Create the user account
################################################
#
# The useradd command creates the account AND
# populates the new home directory with the files
# in the template user's directory.
#
echo "$0: Creating the user account: $HpUserName"
useradd -d $HP_HOMEROOT/$HpUserName \
     -m -k $HP_HOMEROOT/$HP_TEMPLATEUSER \
     $HpUserName

#
# Prompt the terminal for the new user account's
# password
#
echo "Please set the new user's password..."
echo
passwd $HpUserName
echo

#
# Set the user's disk quota.
#
# Copy the quotas from the template user.
#
edquota -p $HP_TEMPLATEUSER $HpUserName

################################################
# Set permissions
################################################
echo "$0: Setting permissions on the home and user site directories"

#
# drwxr-s---    jdoe httpd        /home/jdoe/html
# -rw-r-----    jdoe httpd        /home/jdoe/html/*
#
find $HP_HOMEROOT/$HpUserName/html \
     -exec chown $HpUserName.$HP_SERVERGROUP {} \;
```

```
find $HP_HOMEROOT/$HpUserName/html \
    -type d \
    -exec chmod 2750 {} \;

find $HP_HOMEROOT/$HpUserName/html \
    -type f \
    -exec chmod 640 {} \;

#
# drwxr-s---   jdoe httpd        /home/jdoe/cgi-bin
# -rwxr-x---   jdoe httpd        /home/jdoe/cgi-bin/*
#
find $HP_HOMEROOT/$HpUserName/cgi-bin \
    -exec chown $HpUserName.$HP_SERVERGROUP {} \;

find $HP_HOMEROOT/$HpUserName/cgi-bin \
    -type d \
    -exec chmod 2750 {} \;

find $HP_HOMEROOT/$HpUserName/cgi-bin \
    -type f \
    -exec chmod 750 {} \;

#
# To the user's home directory, add read/execute permissions
# for others so that the web server can descend into the
# the html/ and cgi-bin/ subdirectories.
#
chmod o+r,o+x $HP_HOMEROOT/$HpUserName
```

Creating a Homepage User at a Large ISP

For the sake of file system performance, site directories are created in sub-directories according to the first two letters of the username. The home directory is then created as a link to the site directory—which facilitates the disabling of the user site. The user site directories and files are read/write accessible to the homepage author; read accessible to the Web server; and not accessible to others.

The following bash script creates the user account and directories for this scenario. Before using this script, set the configuration variables near the top of the script. This script populates the new homepage site from a template directory that you will need to create. Also, this script was written for Linux. You may need to replace the useradd command with the comparable command on your system. Review the parameters to the cp, ln, chown, and chmod commands for their appropriateness for your system.

```
#!/bin/bash

###############################################################################
# hpnew.secure
#
# Description:
#    Creates a home page user account and associated directories
# for a new homepage site on a large ISP. This configuration
# maximizes security and performance; but restricts the features
# available to the homepage author.
#
# Parameters:
#    The name of the user whose account and site are to be
# created.
#
# Exit Codes:
#    0                   success
#    22                  invalid parameter
#    other-non-zero      error code
#
###############################################################################

###############################################################################
# Configuration:
#
# Set these configuration variables before using this script.
#
# HP_SITEROOT...The parent directory under which homepage
#    web site directories are to be created.
#
# HP_HOMEROOT...The parent directory under which homepage
#    user account home directories are to be
#    created (as links to the site directory).
#
# HP_QUOTATEMPLATE...Names the user account whose disk quotas are
#    to be copied to the new user.
#
# HP_DEPTH...Set the subdirectory depth for creating directory
#    trees. Example values for creating jdoe's site
#    directory:
#
#    HP_DEPTH site and home directories created
#
#    0    /$HP_SITEROOT/jdoe
#         /$HP_HOMEROOT/jdoe
#
#    1    /$HP_SITEROOT/j/jdoe
#         /$HP_HOMEROOT/j/jdoe
#
```

```
#    2    /$HP_SITEROOT/j/d/jdoe
#         /$HP_HOMEROOT/j/d/jdoe
#
#
# HP_SITETEMPLATE...The template website directory. Files herein
#    are copied to each new homepage site.
#
# HP_SERVERGROUP...The name of the user group under which the
#    web server daemon runs. This should be set the
#    same as the Group Apache configuration directive.
#
################################################################
HP_SITEROOT=/mnt/webpub/homepages
HP_HOMEROOT=/home
HP_QUOTATEMPLATE=templhp
HP_DEPTH=2
HP_SITETEMPLATE=/mnt/webpub/homepages/templhp
HP_SERVERGROUP=httpd

#
#
# Get the username from the first command-line parameter.
#
HpUserName=$1

#
# HpUserName cannot be empty
#
if [ "x_$HpUserName" = "x_" ]; then
    echo
    echo "$0: Username not be specfied"
    exit 22
fi

echo
echo "$0: Creating site for $HpUserName"

#
# Create HP_DEPTH subdirectories
# under HP_SITEROOT and HP_HOMEROOT.
#
# e.g. Given a username of jdoe, create
#
#    /mnt/webpub/homepages/j/d
#    /home/j/d
#
HpSubDir=
HpCharNdx=1
HpLastChar=
```

```
HpNextChar=
while [ $HpCharNdx -le $HP_DEPTH ]; do
    #
    # Get the next character from $HpUserName. If
    # we've run out of $HpUserName, then we reuse
    # the last character.
    #
    HpNextChar='echo "$HpUserName" | cut -c $HpCharNdx-$HpCharNdx'
    if [ "x_$HpNextChar" = "x_" ]; then
        HpNextChar="$HpLastChar"
    fi


    #
    # Add a subdirectory, named after the HpNextChar, to
    # the HpSubDir.
    #
    if [ "x_$HpSubDir" != "x_" ]; then
        HpSubDir="$HpSubDir/"
    fi
    HpSubDir="$HpSubDir$HpNextChar"


    #
    # Create the subdirectories under HP_SITEROOT and
    # HP_HOMEROOT, if they don't already exist.
    #
    if [ ! -d $HP_SITEROOT/$HpSubDir ]; then
        echo "$0: Creating $HP_SITEROOT/$HpSubDir"
        mkdir $HP_SITEROOT/$HpSubDir
    fi
    if [ ! -d $HP_HOMEROOT/$HpSubDir ]; then
        echo "$0: Creating $HP_HOMEROOT/$HpSubDir"
        mkdir $HP_HOMEROOT/$HpSubDir
    fi


    #
    # Prep for next iternation
    #
    HpCharNdx='expr "$HpCharNdx" + 1'
    HpLastChar="$HpNextChar"

done

#
# Add the username to the subdirectory.
# Create the site directory under $HP_SITEROOT
# and create the home directory under $HP_HOMEROOT
#--as a link to the site directory.
#
```

```
# e.g. Given a username of jdoe, create
#
#      /mnt/webpub/homepages/j/d/jdoe
#
# and link this directory to
#
#      /home/j/d/jdoe
#
HpSubDir="$HpSubDir/$HpUserName"
if [ ! -d $HP_SITEROOT/$HpSubDir ]; then
    echo "$0: Creating $HP_SITEROOT/$HpSubDir"
    mkdir $HP_SITEROOT/$HpSubDir
fi
if [ ! -L $HP_SITEROOT/$HpSubDir ]; then
    echo "$0: Creating $HP_HOMEROOT/$HpSubDir"
    ln -s $HP_SITEROOT/$HpSubDir $HP_HOMEROOT/$HpSubDir
fi


#
# Populate the site directory from the template
# directory.
#
echo "$0: Populating the new site directory"
cp -a $HP_SITETEMPLATE/* $HP_SITEROOT/$HpSubDir/


#
# Create the user account.
#
echo "$0: Creating the user account: $HpUserName"
useradd -d $HP_HOMEROOT/$HpSubDir -M $HpUserName

#
# Prompt the terminal for the new user account's
# password
#
echo "Please set the new user's password..."
echo
passwd $HpUserName
echo

#
# Set the user's disk quota.
#
# Copy the quotas from the template user.
#
edquota -p $HP_QUOTATEMPLATE $HpUserName
```

```
#
# Make the user account the owner of the files
# and directories in the homepage site. Assign
# the server daemon's group to the group on
# these files and directories.
#
echo "$0: Setting site ownership"
find $HP_SITEROOT/$HpSubDir \
    -exec chown $HpUserName.$HP_SERVERGROUP {} \;


#
# On site directories, give the user account rwx
# perms and give the server daemon r-x perms. --- perms
# to others. Set the group set-gid bit on directories so
# that files created in these directories inherit the
# server daemon's group.
#
echo "$0: Setting directory permissions"
find $HP_SITEROOT/$HpSubDir -type d -exec chmod 2750 {} \;


#
# On regular files in the site, give the user account
# rw- perms and the server daemon r-- perms. --- perms
# to others.
#
echo "$0: Setting file permissions"
find $HP_SITEROOT/$HpSubDir -type f -exec chmod 640 {} \;
```

Creating a Homepage User on a Small ISP

In this scenario, a site directory is created with two subdirectories: an html/ directory in which to store static content and a cgi-bin/ subdirectory in which to store scripts. Permissions are set on the site directory such that the user cannot create files therein—otherwise, they could store private files on the server. The html/ directory and files are read/write accessible to the homepage author; read accessible to the web server; and not accessible to others. The suexec wrapper is used to secure the execution of the scripts—which affects the permissions applied to the cgi-bin directory. The user has read/write/execute permissions on the cgi-bin directory and the files therein. The Web server can search the cgi-bin directory, but cannot read the files therein. The cgi-bin/ directory is not accessible to others. Once the site directory is created, the home directory is created as a link to the site directory—which facilitates the disabling of the user site. Unlike the large ISP model, the small ISP model does not have enough homepages to warrant distributing them under directories named after letters of the username.

The directories created for a user named jdoe, for example, would be as follows:

```
/home/jdoe  ➜  /mnt/webpub/homepages/jdoe
               /mnt/webpub/homepages/jdoe/cgi-bin
               /mnt/webpub/homepages/jdoe/html
```

A bash script to create the user account and directories for this scenario is presented below. This script populates the new site directory from a template directory, which you will need to create before running the script. This template directory should contain an html/ subdirectory (with an example document) and a cgi-bin/ subdirectory (with an example script). Also, this script was written for Linux. You may need to replace the useradd command with the comparable command(s) on your system. Also, review the parameters to the grep, cut, cp, ln, chown, and chmod commands for their appropriateness for your system. The default group for the user being added is taken from the fourth field of the user's entry in the /etc/passwd file. Make sure that this is correct for your system. Before using this script, set the configuration variables near the top of the script.

```bash
#!/bin/bash

################################################################
# hpnew.cgi
#
# Description:
#    Creates a home page user account and associated directories
# for a new homepage site on a small ISP. The homepage author
# can write CGI scripts.
#
# Parameters:
#    The name of the user whose account and site are to be
# created.
#
# Exit Codes:
#    0              success
#    22             invalid parameter
#    other-non-zero  error code
#
# Notes:
#    User home directories and web site directories are created
# as follows. Given the username jdoe...
#
# /home/jdoe -->   /mnt/webpub/homepages/jdoe
#                  /mnt/webpub/homepages/jdoe/cgi-bin
```

```
#                       /mnt/webpub/homepages/jdoe/html
#
# A description of each:
#
#    /home/jdoe...This is a link to the user-site directory tree.
#
#    /mnt/webpub/homepages/jdoe...This is the root of the
#         user-site directory. Stored hereunder
#         are all files and directories to which
#         the web server requires access.
#
#    /mnt/webpub/homepages/cgi-bin...This subdirectory stores
#         CGI scripts developed by the homepage
#         author. A ScriptAliasMatch Apache
#         configuration directive points to
#         this directory to allow the execution
#         of scripts therein. This directory
#         must be searchable by the web server.
#         Since the suexec wrapper is used to
#         secure the execution of scripts,
#         this subdirectory must be owned and
#         grouped by the user account (not
#         grouped by the web server daemon's
#         group). Yet the subdirectory must
#         be searchable by the web server daemon.
#         The scripts are run under the user id
#         of the user account (not the user id
#         of the web server daemon). The web
#         server, thus, does not require any
#         permissions on these scripts.
#
#    /mnt/webpub/homepages/html...This subdirectory stores the
#         web site's static content.  An UserDir
#         Apache configuration directive makes
#         this directory the "document root" of
#         the homepage.
#
################################################################################

################################################################################
# Configuration:
#
# Set these configuration variables before using this script.
#
# HP_SITEROOT...The parent directory under which homepage
#    web site directories are to be created.
#
# HP_HOMEROOT...The parent directory under which homepage
#    user account home directories are to be
```

```
#      created.
#
# HP_QUOTATEMPLATE...Names the user account whose disk quotas are
#      to be copied to the new user.
#
# HP_SITETEMPLATE...The template website directory. Files herein
#      are copied to each new homepage site.
#
# HP_SERVERGROUP...The name of the user group under which the
#      web server daemon runs. This should be set the
#      same as the Group Apache configuration directive.
#
################################################################
HP_SITEROOT=/mnt/webpub/homepages
HP_HOMEROOT=/home
HP_QUOTATEMPLATE=templhp
HP_SITETEMPLATE=/mnt/webpub/homepages/templhp
HP_SERVERGROUP=httpd


#
# Get the username from the first command-line parameter.
#
HpUserName=$1

#
# HpUserName cannot be empty
#
if [ "x_$HpUserName" = "x_" ]; then
    echo
    echo "$0: Username not be specfied"
    exit 22
fi

echo
echo "$0: Creating user account and homepage site for $HpUserName"

#############################
# Create the site directory
#############################
echo "$0: Creating the site directory in $HP_SITEROOT/$HpUserName"

#
# Create the site directory under $HP_SITEROOT
#
# e.g. Given a username of jdoe, create...
#
#    /mnt/webpub/homepages/jdoe
#
if [ ! -d $HP_SITEROOT/$HpUserName ]; then
```

```
        echo "$0: Creating $HP_SITEROOT/$HpUserName"
        mkdir $HP_SITEROOT/$HpUserName
fi

#
# Populate the site directory from the template
# directory.
#
echo "$0: Populating the new site directory"
cp -a $HP_SITETEMPLATE/* $HP_SITEROOT/$HpUserName/

#####################################################
# Link the site directory into the home directory
#####################################################
echo "$0: Creating the home directory in $HP_HOMEROOT/$HpUserName"
#
# Soft link the web site directory into the home directory.
#
ln -s $HP_SITEROOT/$HpUserName $HP_HOMEROOT/$HpUserName

###################################################
# Create the user account
###################################################
echo "$0: Creating the user account: $HpUserName"
#
# The useradd command is instructed to NOT create the
# user's home directory.
#
useradd -d $HP_HOMEROOT/$HpUserName -M $HpUserName

#
# Prompt the terminal for the new user account's
# password
#
echo "Please set the new user's password..."
echo
passwd $HpUserName
echo

#
# Set the user's disk quota.
#
# Copy the quotas from the template user.
#
edquota -p $HP_QUOTATEMPLATE $HpUserName

#
# Get this user's default group from the 4th field of
# this user's entry in /etc/passwd
#
```

```
HpUserGroup='grep "^$HpUserName" /etc/passwd | cut -d : -f 4'

echo "$0: Setting directory permissions"

#
# r-xr-x---    jdoe httpd      /mnt/webpub/homepages/jdoe
# r--------    jdoe httpd      /mnt/webpub/homepages/jdoe/*
#
echo -n "$0: $HP_SITEROOT/$HpUserName "
chown $HpUserName.$HP_SERVERGROUP $HP_SITEROOT/$HpUserName
chmod 550 $HP_SITEROOT/$HpUserName
chown $HpUserName.$HpUserGroup $HP_SITEROOT/$HpUserName/*
chmod 400 $HP_SITEROOT/$HpUserName/*
echo " done"


#
# rwxr-sr-x    jdoe users     /mnt/webpub/homepages/jdoe/cgi-bin
# rwxr-x---    jdoe users     /mnt/webpub/homepages/jdoe/cgi-bin/*
#
echo -n "$0: $HP_SITEROOT/$HpUserName/cgi-bin "
find $HP_SITEROOT/$HpUserName/cgi-bin \
    -exec chown $HpUserName.$HpUserGroup {} \;
find $HP_SITEROOT/$HpUserName/cgi-bin -type d \
    -exec chmod 2755 {} \;
find $HP_SITEROOT/$HpUserName/cgi-bin -type f \
    -exec chmod 750 {} \;
echo " done"

#
# rwxr-s---    jdoe httpd      /mnt/webpub/homepages/jdoe/html
# rwxr-----    jdoe httpd      /mnt/webpub/homepages/jdoe/html/*
#
echo -n "$0: $HP_SITEROOT/$HpUserName/html "
find $HP_SITEROOT/$HpUserName/html \
    -exec chown $HpUserName.$HP_SERVERGROUP {} \;
find $HP_SITEROOT/$HpUserName/html -type d \
    -exec chmod 2750 {} \;
find $HP_SITEROOT/$HpUserName/html -type f \
    -exec chmod 640 {} \;
echo " done"
```

Configuring the Web Server For User Sites

Configuring User Directory Translation

The browser accesses a homepage Web site with a URL like this:

```
http://www.administeringapache.com/~jdoe
```

The above URL requests the homepage for the ~jdoe user account on the www host in the administeringapache.com domain. The ~jdoe expression works just like the UNIX tilde expansion of home directories. It resolves ~jdoe to jdoe's home directory as prescribed by jdoe's entry in the /etc/passwd file. The Apache Web server then looks for a subdirectory under jdoe's home directory for the "document root" of jdoe's user site. This subdirectory is specified by the UserDir Apache configuration directive:

UserDir

UserDir specifies the subdirectory, under the user's home directory, which contains the user's Web site. In addition to defining the "document root" for the user sites, the UserDir directive automatically grants browsers permission to access the files in that directory (sort of an implicit Allow from all). For example, the following directive:

```
UserDir public_html
```

would translate this reques

```
/~jdoe/
```

to

```
/home/jdoe/public_html/
```

A second form of the UserDir directive is used to enable and disable user directory translation. When passed a single parameter of disabled, as in

```
UserDir disabled
```

all user directory translation is disabled. When passed a parameter of disabled followed by a space-separated list of usernames, user directory translation is disabled for those users. You should disable directory translation for power users by adding these directives

```
UserDir disabled root bin daemon adm lp sync shutdown halt
UserDir disabled mail news uucp operator games nobody httpd
```

The above example illustrates that this second form of the UserDir directive can be specified multiple times. You should disable power users *especially* if you set UserDir to the current directory (UserDir ., as is done in the large ISP model). If you don't, a URL requesting

```
http://www.administeringapache.com/~root
```

would attempt to access the system root directory or the /root directory (depending on root's home directory assignment in /etc/passwd). Such a request would be denied, of course, if you had this group of directive in your configuration file (which you should):

```
Options None
<Directory />
    Order allow,deny
    deny from all
    Options FollowSymLinks
    AllowOverride None
</Directory>
```

but why give them the chance (see Chapter 6: "Securing the Server, the Content, and the Connection" in the section titled "Securing the Content" in the subsection titled "Allowing/Blocking Content Access").

If you don't host a lot of homepages (e.g. homepages on an intranet Web server), then you might run a tighter ship by disabling all homepages and then explicitly enabling the homepage of each user. This would be implemented with these directives:

```
UserDir disabled
UserDir enabled jdoe bbrown
```

Every time you add a new user homepage, you will have to add the new user's name to the enabled list.

The UserDir directive may appear within the configuration file's global context or within a < VirtualHost > block. The UserDir directive is provided by the mod_userdir module—a default module.

Configuring Content Directives for the User Sites

The user sites inherit any features (such as directory index generation, content-negotiation, metafile processing, image map processing, etc.) that are defined in the Apache configuration file's global context. You may wish to add to the user sites features that are not already defined in the global context. To add features to the main Web site, you would add directives to the <Directory> block for the main site's DocumentRoot directory. To add features to the user sites, you add directives to a <Directory-Match> block for the UserDir.

<DirectoryMatch>

< DirectoryMatch > is analogous to the <Directory> block directive, except that the it may refer to more than one directory. The <Directory-Match> directive applies its enclosed directives to any filesystem directory that matches a regular expression. This regular expression is the directive's one and only parameter. The comparison of the regular expression to the requested directory occurs after the virtual URL has been translated to a physical file system path. That is, the directory is matched after the UserDir directive has translated the request to the user site directory. The following block, for example

```
<DirectoryMatch ^/home/[A-Za-z0-9]+/public_html/.*>
    Options Indexes
    AllowOverride None
</DirectoryMatch>
```

would apply its enclosed directives to any directory whose name begins with /home/, followed by one or more alphanumeric characters (the username), followed by /public_html/, followed by any number of characters of any type (the requested file). This would match a directory like

```
/home/jdoe/public_html/index.html
```

The directives within the above < DirectoryMatch > example allow the server to generate directory indexes (Options Indexes) and disallow the homepage author from overriding any Apache configuration directives with a .htaccess file (AllowOverride None). See Chapter 4: "Manipulating Content" for a list of content-directives that can appear within a <DirectoryMatch> block. Any directive that can appear within a <Directory> block can also appear in a <DirectoryMatch> block.

The <DirectoryMatch> directive may appear within the configuration file's global context or within a <VirtualHost> block. The Apache core provides the <DirectoryMatch> block directive.

Configuring CGI Execution

The intranet scenario and the small ISP scenario both use script aliased CGI (see Chapter 6: Securing the Server, the Content, and the Connection, the section "Security Considerations for CGI", the subsection "Non-Script Aliased vs. Script Aliased"). The ScriptAlias directive specifies the scripts directory for the main server. To specify the scripts directories for the user sites, we use the ScriptAliasMatch directive.

ScriptAliasMatch

ScriptAliasMatch is analogous to the ScriptAlias directive, except that it can refer to more than one directory. The ScriptAliasMatch directive accepts two parameters: 1) a regular expression and 2) a file system directory. The Apache server compares the requested URL to the regular expression. If the URL matches the expression, Apache translates the request to the specified file system directory and enables script execution for that directory (sort of an implicit Options +ExecCGI) and also grants the browser permission to request the scripts in that directory (sort of an implicit Allow from all). Substrings from the expression (the first parameter) may be repeated in the directory string (the second parameter). You surround the parts of the expression to be remembered with parentheses. In the directory string, you recall a remembered substring with a numbered variable: $1 means the first substring that was marked with the parentheses; $2 will be replaced by the second remembered substring; and so on. For example:

```
ScriptAliasMatch ^/~([A-Za-z0-9]+)/cgi-bin/(.*) /home/$1/cgi-bin/$2
```

The regular expression, in the above example, matches any request that begins with /~ (a request for a user site), that is followed by one or more alphanumeric characters (the username), followed by /cgibin/, followed by any number of characters of any type (the requested script). This will match a request like this:

```
/~jdoe/cgi-bin/cgitest
```

The example regular expression uses parentheses to store back the username and the script name for use in the directory string. The example directory string translates the request to the file system directory named by /home/, plus the username (the $1), plus /cgi-bin/, plus the script name (the $2). This would translate the above example request into the following file system directory:

```
/home/jdoe/cgi-bin/cgitest
```

The `ScriptAliasMatch` directive may appear within the configuration file's global context or within a `<VirtualHost>` block. The `mod_alias` module, a default module, provides the `ScriptAliasMatch` directive.

Hiding Dot-Files

There are certain files that may be in the user site document directory tree that should not be delivered to the browser. This includes files whose names being with a period. A homepage author might have a `.htaccess` file that points to an authentication file, whose location you should not divulge to the browser. Login shell dot-files (`.profile`, `.bashrc`, and the like) might also appear in the user site directory if the site directory is the same as the home directory. These files should be protected. Place the following directives in the global context of the Apache configuration file:

```
IndexIgnore .??* *~ *# HEADER* RCS CVS *,v *,t
<Files ~ "^\.[A-Za-z0-9].*">
    Order allow,deny
    Deny from all
</Files>
```

The `IndexIgnore` directive prevents matching filenames from appearing in any directory listing generated by Apache. The `.??*` parameter matches files whose names begin with a period and are at least two characters long (so the `..` parent directory will still show up in the directory listing). The `<Files>` block directive, in the above listing, matches files whose names begin with a period. When a matching file is requested, the enclosed directives deny access to the file and return a 403 Forbidden error to the browser. The tilde in the `<Files>` directive tells Apache that the next parameter is a regular expression. The regular expression then matches any file that begins with a period, followed by an alphanumeric character, followed by zero or more characters of any type. This expression will match the normal dot-files; but will not match the `..` parent directory name. Thus the `..` parent directory can then show up in directory listings without causing errors.

Configuring Apache for User Sites on an Intranet Server

The following directives, added to the Apache configuration file, will implement the policies defined for our intranet user site scenario:

```
UserDir html
UserDir disabled root bin daemon adm lp sync shutdown halt
UserDir disabled mail news uucp operator games nobody httpd
<DirectoryMatch ^/home/[A-Za-z0-9]+/html/.*>
    Options Indexes FancyIndexing MultiViews FollowSymLinks
    AllowOverride All
    MetaSuffix .meta
    MetaDir .web
    MetaFiles on
</DirectoryMatch>
IndexIgnore .??* *~ *# HEADER* RCS CVS *,v *,t
<Files ~ "^\.[A-Za-z0-9].*">
    Order allow,deny
    Deny from all
</Files>
ScriptAliasMatch ^/~([A-Za-z0-9]+)/cgi-bin/(.*) /home/$1/cgibin/$2
```

In the above configuration, UserDir instructs Apache that a user's homepage site can be found in the html/ subdirectory of the user's home directory—which is appropriate to the way the directory structures were created for the intranet example in the previous section ("Creating User Accounts and Site Directories"). The UserDir disabled... directives disable user directory translation for the power users.

The <DirectoryMatch> block enables certain Apache features for use by the homepage authors within the html/ subdirectory—namely server-generated indexes (Options Indexes) that have fancy icons (FancyIndexing); and content negotiation (MultiViews). The Web server is given permission to follow symbolic links from within the user site (FollowSymLinks). The AllowOverride All directive grants permission to the homepage author to create .htaccess files that can override any setting in the Apache configuration file (within the context of the html/ subdirectory). This includes document type directives (such as AddEncoding, AddLanguage, AddType, etc.); indexing directives (such as AddDescription, FancyIndexing, HeaderName, etc.); access directives (Order, Allow, and Deny); authentication directives (such as AuthType, AuthName, AuthUserFile, AuthGroupFile, etc.); and directory option directives (Options and XBitHack). Since the homepage author is allowed to define authentication restrictions, the authors will need to use the htpasswd or dbmmanage commands to create the username/password file. (See Chapter 6: "Securing the Server, the Content, and the Connection," the section "Securing the Content," the subsection "Requiring Authentication to Access Content;" and make sure that the content authors who will be using those commands read those sections too.) Users are not normally given permissions to run programs out of the Apache installation directory (e.g. `/usr/local/apache/bin/htpasswd`). You may want to copy or link the `htpasswd` and `dbmmanage` programs into the `/usr/bin/` directory or some other directory in the user's search path. If you find these program are already in the `/usr/bin/` directory, then you may want to refresh them with the latest version from the Apache installation directory.

The `Meta???` directives allow the homepage author to create metafiles to define extra response headers.

The `IndexIgnore` directive and the `<Files>` block are used to hide dot-files—both `.htaccess` files and shell-dot files (should any find their way into the `html/` or `cgibin/` subdirectory).

The `ScriptAliasMatch` directive translates requests that look like this:

```
/~jdoe/cgi-bin/cgitest
```

into this

```
/home/jdoe/cgi-bin/cgitest
```

which is appropriate for the way the directory structures were created for this scenario.

Configuring Apache for User Sites at the Large ISP

The following directives, added to the Apache configuration file, will implement the policies defined for our large ISP user site scenario:

```
UserDir .
UserDir disabled root bin daemon adm lp sync shutdown halt
UserDir disabled mail news uucp operator games nobody httpd
<DirectoryMatch ^/home/[A-Za-z0-9]/[A-Za-z0-9]/[A-Za-z0-9]+/.*>
    Options Indexes FollowSymLinks
    AllowOverride None
</DirectoryMatch>
```

In the above configuration, `UserDir` instructs Apache that a user's homepage site is the same as the user's home directory—which is appropriate to the way the directory structures were created for the large ISP example in the previous section ("Creating User Accounts and Site Directories"). The `UserDir disabled...` directives disable user directory translation for the power users.

The regular expression in the `<DirectoryMatch>` block matches directories like this

```
/home/j/d/jdoe
```

which considers our distribution of the home directories into subdirectories named after letters in the username. The directives within the `<DirectoryMatch>` block enable and disable certain Apache features within the user's site directory. The server may generate indexes (`Options Indexes`). The server is allowed to follow symbolic links within the user site (`FollowSymLinks`). This is not done for the homepage author's sake but for performance. It allows Apache to descend into the user site without polling the file system for each directory to see whether or not it is a link (See Chapter 10: "Troubleshooting," the section "Tuning Apache for Performance"). The `AllowOverride None` directive disallows the homepage author from overriding settings in the Apache configuration file with a `.htaccess` file.

There is no `IndexIgnore` directive or `<Files>` block to hide dot-files (as was done in the intranet scenario). In this scenario, the user was created without a normal system user account directory. There shouldn't be any login shell dot-files in the user's home directory. Homepage authors are not allowed to use `.htaccess` files. If they try to, the `.htaccess` file will be displayed to the browser like an ordinary text file.

There is no `ScriptAlias` directive, because the homepage author is not allowed to write CGI scripts.

Configuring Apache for User Sites at the Small ISP

The following directives, added to the Apache configuration file, will implement the policies defined for our small ISP user site scenario:

```
UserDir html
UserDir disabled root bin daemon adm lp sync shutdown halt
UserDir disabled mail news uucp operator games nobody httpd
<DirectoryMatch ^/home/[A-Za-z0-9]+/html/.*>
    Options Indexes FancyIndexing MultiViews FollowSymLinks
    AllowOverride FileInfo Indexes Limit
    MetaSuffix .meta
    MetaDir .web
    MetaFiles on
</DirectoryMatch>
IndexIgnore .??* *~ *# HEADER* RCS CVS *,v *,t
<Files ~ "^\.[A-Za-z0-9].*">
```

```
    Order allow,deny
    Deny from all
</Files>
ScriptAliasMatch ^/~([A-Za-z0-9]+)/cgi-bin/(.*) /home/$1/cgi-bin/$2
```

In the above configuration, `UserDir` instructs Apache that a user's homepage site can be found in the `html/` subdirectory of the user's home directory—which is appropriate to the way the directory structures were created for the small ISP example in the previous section ("Creating User Accounts and Site Directories"). The `UserDir disabled...` directives disable user directory translation for the power users.

The `<DirectoryMatch>` block enables certain Apache features for use by the homepage authors within the `html/` subdirectory—namely server-generated indexes (`Options Indexes`) that have fancy icons (`FancyIndexing`); and content negotiation (`MultiViews`). The Web server is given permission to follow symbolic links from within the user site (`FollowSymLinks`). The `AllowOverride` directive grants permission to the homepage author to create `.htaccess` files that can override certain settings in the Apache configuration file (within the context of the `html/` subdirectory). The homepage author may override document type directives (such as `AddEncoding`, `AddLanguage`, `AddType`, etc.); indexing directives (such as `AddDescription`, `FancyIndexing`, `HeaderName`, etc.); and access directives (`Order`, `Allow`, and `Deny`). The homepage author *cannot* override authentication directives (such as `AuthType`, `AuthName`, `AuthUserFile`, `AuthGroupFile`, etc.); nor directory option directives (`Options` and `XBitHack`). The `Meta???` directives allow the homepage author to create metafiles to define extra response headers.

The `IndexIgnore` directive and the `<Files>` block are used to hide dot-files. This is mainly for the `.htaccess` files. In this scenario, the user was created without a normal system user account directory. There should be no login shell dot-files in the user's home directory. Also, the "document root" of the user site is a subdirectory of the home directory (not the home directory itself, wherein the login shell dot-files normally reside).

The `ScriptAliasMatch` directive translates requests that look like this:

```
/~jdoe/cgi-bin/cgitest
```

into this:

```
/home/jdoe/cgi-bin/cgitest
```

which is appropriate to the way the directory structures were created for the small ISP example.

Note that the small ISP model secures script execution with the `suexec` wrapper. The `suexec` wrapper and the Apache server have to be recompiled in order to set the directory configurations. This hard codes the `suexec` configurations into the Web server and suexec binaries, which prevents hackers from being able to change these configurations. Instructions for configuring and compiling Apache with the `suexec` wrapper may be found in Chapter 6: "Securing the Server, the Content, and the Connection," in the section "Security Considerations for CGI", in the subsection "Using CGI Wrappers." For compiling the server for this scenario, the following parameters should be among those passed to the APACI utility (the `configure` command used to configure the source code before compiling it):

```
--suexec-userdir=cgi-bin
```

The above APACI parameter tells the `suexec` program that the `cgi-bin/` subdirectory (under the user's home directory) is the directory in which CGI execution is permitted.

Configuring FTP for User Sites

For both the ISP scenarios (large and small), you will want to configure FTP so that the homepage authors cannot see any part of the filesystem besides their own home directory. Edit the file `/etc/ftpaccess` and add these two lines:

```
guestuser *
realuser sysop
```

The `guestuser *` instructs FTP that *all* users are guest users. When a guest user logs in, FTP performs a `chroot()` so that the user cannot see above their own home directory. The second line in the above tells FTP that the user named `sysop` is a real user—and *not* a guest user. This overrides the `guestuser` directive when the `sysop` user logs in. If you have system administrators or if you have fully privileged system account users who need to upload files to the server (possibly into non-home directories), then you will want to tell FTP that each of these users is a `realuser`.

If you do not set up the homepage authors as FTP guestusers, then beware of this: Let's say you disable a no-pay user by removing the home directory link. If the user is configured as an FTP guestuser, any attempt by the user to log in will fail, with this message: "Can't set guest privileges". If the user is not configured as an FTP guestuser, the user *will* be able to log in and will see this: "No directory! Logging in with home=/". This is a bad thing. You've cut them off and now they're upset. And now they are logged in to your root directory.

When you disable a homepage, you should lock the user account (in addition to removing the home directory link). Enter this shell command:

```
passwd -l jdoe
```

With the account locked, any attempt by jdoe to log in will fail with this message: "Login incorrect." When it's time to re-enable the user, reconstruct the home link with this shell command:

```
ln -s /mnt/webpub/homepages/jdoe /home/jdoe
```

replacing the directory names as appropriate for your system. And then unlock the user account with this shell command:

```
passwd -u jdoe
```

For tips on other FTP security measures, see Chapter 6: "Securing the Server, the Content, and the Connection," in the section "Securing the Server," in the subsection "Locking Down Internet Services."

Creating Virtual Domain Web Sites

Choosing a Structure

One of the key features of the Apache Web server is that it is very easy to configure and maintain virtual hosts using Apache. As far as scalability is concerned, Apache can easily support hundreds of virtual hosts on the same server on many platforms; the key constraint is generally resource allocation limits (such as allowed open file descriptors) on the server itself. There are a variety of approaches you can take when configuring Apache for virtual hosting: you can employ both name-based and IP-based virtual hosts, and you can configure them manually or *en masse* using `mod_vhost_alias`. Other critical choices include how you are going to layout your file system, how you are going to handle CGI, and how your virtual hosts will be updated.

Name-based virtual hosting is a relatively new phenomenon: it is dependent on the `Host:` header in HTTP 1.1, and some older (pre-1997) browsers may not handle it correctly. While Apache provides a workaround mechanism to try to accommodate older browsers, it requires additional configuration effort (and cooperation from domain webmasters) that is generally not cost effective when trying to support browser software obsoleted three years ago. The more traditional mechanism for virtual hosting is IP-based, but that consumes precious IP space in a voracious (and officially wasteful") manner (which could jeopardize future applications for additional IP space wherein you must show "efficient" usage of existing allocations). Thus, name-based virtual hosting is recommended in all but the most extreme instances (for example, only running your regular site and one virtual host on a box, where that extra IP address is probably worth it). Note that IP-based virtual hosting is *not* the same as some of the multiple-server-binaries/multiple-IPs (using the `BindAddr` directive) discussed in subsequent chapters: those arrangements solve a different collection of problems than virtual hosting and do, in fact, require additional IP addresses.

In the case of whether or not to use `mod_vhost_alias`, that decision is probably best made based on the number of virtual hosts you expect to configure. There is a memory cost to having the additional module in the server (see Chapter 10: "Troubleshooting," section "Tuning Apache for Performance"), and it is probably not worth paying if you are only going to have one or two virtual hosts on the machine; just configure them by hand. On the other hand, if you are setting up a Web server that is going to host dozens or hundreds of virtual hosts, `mod_vhost_alias` will feel like a godsend. It is worth noting that `mod_vhost_alias` was developed at Demon Internet, one of Britain's leading ISPs, specifically because they wanted to simplify the configuration of large numbers of virtual hosts.

When it comes to laying out the file system for the server, there are three key considerations: performance, convenience, and security. Performance issues (discussed at greater length in Chapter 10) include optimizing the speed at which documents are read and logs are written, and reducing the number of system calls (such as `stat()`) that Apache has to make. Convenience issues stem from trying to make life as easy as possible for a (potentially) diverse body of webmasters updating the individual sites. Security issues stem from the prospect of one virtual host's interfering with another's processes and/or data, or one host's being used to exploit another (or the whole system) intentionally.

CGI configuration is largely a matter of taste, but consistency is important. If you have defined a global `/cgi-bin/` directory on the server with `ScriptAlias`, then you would probably be well served to call the per-virtual host CGI directories `/cgi-local/`. There is a great deal of debate regarding whether or not to use `suexec` for CGIs on virtual hosts; for performance reasons alone (see Chapter 10) it is probably worth avoiding unless you have some reason to distrust your domain webmasters.

On a similar note, how your domain webmasters will update their sites is also generally a matter of preference; in some environments, the third-party `mod_frontpage` module to handle Microsoft's FrontPage extensions will be appropriate. In the general case, however, it is probably best to allow FTP transfers for uploading, since FTP is the standard that almost every page-generating software package supports, if it is not fully adopted. Whether or not you want domain webmasters to also be allowed to telnet into the server to make edits (using `vi`, for instance) is going to depend once again on how much trust you are willing to place in those webmasters.

Configuring the DNS

Configuring DNS for a virtual host is easy, regardless of platform. If your network uses NT-based DNS, for instance, it is simply a matter of filling in a few blanks in a configuration form. Even with `BIND` on a UNIX/Linux system, there really isn't much difficulty in creating the configuration. The example below assumes that you are setting up virtual hosting for the domain `asdfghjkl.com` (and in particular, the virtual host `www.asdfghjkl.com`) on the server whose IP address is `172.30.30.30` and whose "common" hostname is `server30.myhostingshop.net`. Then to configure `BIND8`:

- In the `named.conf` file, add a block similar to the following:

```
zone "asdfghjkl.com" in {
   type master;
   file "master/asdfghjkl.com";
};
```

- In the file specified above (in this case, `master/asdfghjkl.com`), specify:

```
$ORIGIN asdfghjkl.net.
@    in      soa     asdfghjkl.com. postmaster.asdfghjkl.com. (
                     2000012201      ; Version number
                     1800    ; Refresh time - 30min
                     300     ; Retry time - 5min
                     604800  ; Expiration time - 1 week
                     3600    ; Minimum ttl time - 1 hr
                     )

                in   ns      server30.myhostingshop.net.
                in   ns      secondary.myhostingshop.net.

asdfghjkl.com.       in   mx 10   server30.myhostingshop.net.

www.asdfghjkl.com.   in   a       172.30.30.30
```

- At this point, restart (sending a SIGHUP works beautifully) the BIND server and the entry will be in the DNS. However, be advised that it does take modifications time to propagate. Only *after* the DNS is configured properly locally should you submit the completed domain template to your domain name registrar of choice, at least in theory; in practice, given the time lag between submission and processing (usually about a day), you can first submit the template and then set up the DNS.

Creating Virtual Host Directories

As we discussed above, file system layout depends a great deal on considerations specific to your server; it is probably worth skipping ahead (if you haven't done so already) to Chapter 10 at this point to read the section on performance tuning before you try to settle on a layout. While you are doing so, keep the following things in mind:

■ It is considered a good practice to log to a file system different from that where a server's documents reside, for a variety of performance, stability, and security reasons.

■ For the sake of consistency, your webmasters' home directories should probably reside on the same partition (often called /home) as the other users on the system. The server root directories for each of their virtual hosts should be symlinked from their home directories for convenience.

■ Expect your webmasters to require at least four subdirectories off of each virtual server root:
  – A DocumentRoot directory for the virtualhost.
  – A local /cgi-bin/ directory.
  – An archive directory, to keep material that has been taken down for some reason but cannot be discarded; they should be instructed that this is not a magic bag whose contents are allowed to grow forever, but rather temporary storage for things taken offline for the short term. Failing to provide them with such a directory will invariably lead to clutter accumulating under the DocumentRoot, a bad practice all the way around.
  – A data directory, where CGIs can store data files and their ilk. Providing the users database access is inadequate: there are a number of smaller applications that (while a database could do the job), a dbm file (or "bucket," in dbm parlance) can do it better, faster, and with a lot less overhead. This is also where things like component graphics for images generated on the fly (the ubiquitous odometer-lookalike hit counter, for example) can be stored.

Once you have taken all that into account, and read the appropriate parts of Chapter 10, you should be ready to dissect the sample configuration below. Keep in mind that this is a sample configuration, designed to serve as an example to work from.

■ Three of the partitions on the system are /home, /usr/local/web, and /var. User home directories live in /home, logs, spools, and their ilk live in /var, and everything specifically pertaining to the Web server lives in /usr/local/web; for example, the Apache source code lives in /usr/local/web/src/Apache and the global ScriptAlias directory /cgi-global/ points to /usr/local/web/cgi/.

■ The server root for each virtual host lives in /usr/local/web/vhost/<server>, where <server> can be shorthand either for the server name (like asdfghjkl for www.asdfghjkl.com), or for the server name itself.

- Each server root directory has four subdirectories: /docroot, /cgi, /archival, and /data, based on the four directories outlined above.
- All the transfer logs are written to a single logfile in the /var/weblogs directory, and split and mailed to the individual domain webmasters at the end of the reporting period for that log; for an explanation why, read the section below on logging.
- Each domain webmaster has a home directory in /home; little is there to begin with, but they may accrue a few configuration files (especially if they have telnet access) such as .exrc (the vi preferences file) over time. The server root for each domain is accessible via a symlink from the home directory of the domain webmaster, for convenience.

Creating Virtual Host Webmasters

This will be an almost trivial task for most UNIX administrators; in most instances just create a user on the system for each virtual host using the system-appropriate tool, useradd, adduser, dxaccounts, or whatever. Set that user's shell to /bin/false or /bin/date or something equally innocuous that will effectively deny logins (unless you want the webmaster to be able to telnet in to make edits in vi), and drop a symlink in the user's directory pointing to the server root of the virtual host.

In many cases, this will even prove unnecessary. For instance, if only a few people on your staff will be updating all the sites on your server, the best approach is to create a group on the server, place all the appropriate users in that group, set the group owner on all the files and directories in the virtual hosts to that group, and make all those files and directories group writeable with chmod.

One key security consideration worth noting is that if you have multiple domain webmasters able to browse (via FTP or telnet) files on the server, and those users are creating nontrivial CGIs (i.e. scripts that connect to databases, handle sensitive data, etc.), their individual CGI directories must be set up (through proper group ownership and read permissions) so that users cannot read the contents of each other's CGI directories. Otherwise, users may be able to "mine" database passwords, etc. from each other's CGI scripts. In the example below, users "friskie," "trixie," and "antsie" are domain webmasters for "fdomain," "tdomain," and "adomain," respectively, "geronimo" is the user/group under which Apache runs, and the individual CGI directories live in /usr/local/web/localcgis (not necessarily a good choice, but illustrative for this example) and are `ScriptAliased` to `<virtualhost>/cgi-local/`. Then:

- In the "geronimo" group, "geronimo" should be the only member.
- Directory and file permissions for "friskie," "trixie," and "antsie"'s individual CGI directories should be as follows (this is the output of `ls -l /usr/local/web/localcgis/`:

```
total 3
drwxr-x---   2 friskie  geronimo    512 Sep  6  1999 fdomain
drwxr-x---   2 trixie   geronimo    512 Apr 18  1999 tdomain
drwxr-x---   2 antsie   geronimo    512 Jun 11  1999 adomain
```

This configuration will allow the users to view and update their own CGIs, and the Web server to access and run them, while preventing unauthorized directory browsing.

FTP and the Domain Webmaster

FTP is the *de facto* standard for updating websites. Everything from Microsoft FrontPage (where it isn't the default choice) to Netscape Composer to BBEdit to Arachnophilia supports FTP for publishing; even text-editor jockeys like your authors use FTP to push files around; it isn't called the "File Transfer Protocol" because it's used to deliver cakes to penitentiaries. This doesn't mean that FTP is the prettiest way to go about doing it, and in some environments, `mod_frontpage`, NFS, or Samba may be better choices. What it does mean is that it is hard to go wrong allowing your domain webmasters to update their sites with FTP.

That said, it is comparatively easy to go wrong with your FTP implementation; to make things worse, FTP daemons (and their configurations) vary greatly from version to version of UNIX, and from distribution to distribution of Linux; to complicate matters further, there are a number of third-party FTP daemons available as well. Consequently, it is all but impossible to write a catch-all configuration guide for FTP daemons in less than a tome in and of itself; a few critical tips and a pointer to the ftpd(8) man page will have to suffice:

- The ftpd(8) man page will contain system specifics (provided it is written correctly), such as the userid for the anonymous FTP user (FTP on many systems), where the FTP configuration files live (generally /etc), and what they are called (examples include ftpusers, ftpch-root, ftphosts, etc.).

■ Allowing anonymous FTP is discouraged, unless you specifically need to be running an anonymous FTP server on the machine. In any case, all anonymous FTP should take place within a chroot "jail"—consult your system's documentation for the particulars of creating such an environment.

■ In some instances (a large-scale public hosting operation, for example) it may be desirable to create chroot "jails" for domain webmasters as well, but as a general rule, it is security over enhancement at the expense of performance; the group-permissions technique outlined in the previous section should prove sufficient for most applications. The performance impact on a server from chrooting the domain webmasters is indirect: forcing the webmasters into a "jail" precludes the multi-spindling advantages outlined above and in Chapter 10.

■ Use TCP wrappers (**ftp://ftp.porcupine.org/pub/security/ index.html**). Live by them. If at all possible, get a list of hostnames/IP addresses/IP ranges (worst case) your domain webmasters will be FTPing from, and block out all others; in any case, log all FTP connections, block large domains (e.g. all of Uruguay, *.uy) from which it is reasonable to assume no legitimate updates will take place, and insist on successful reverse DNS lookups of the FTP client's host.

Configuring the Apache Server

This is really the easy part. Once you've identified things like local directory structures, a few minor modifications to httpd.conf are all that's required.

Configuring Virtual Hosts

There are three choices, you may recall, regarding configuring Apache to support virtual hosts, IP-based, name-based, and mod_vhost_alias (which can be configured to support either IP-based or name-based virtual hosts). We'll explore each case individually:

IP-based

In this scenario, each virtual host has a separate IP address. Requests to the server are processed based on the destination IP address of the incoming request. (Those new to network hardware should note that not only can you have more than one IP address assigned to a machine, it is generally the case that each network interface on a computer will have at least one and often more IP addresses, especially if that machine is being used as a server platform.) As was discussed above, this practice of IP-based virtual hosting is considered wasteful of precious IP addresses and should be avoided when possible.

This "traditional" configuration is the easiest to set up in Apache. To define this variety of virtual host, simply add a block similar to the following to `httpd.conf`:

```
<VirtualHost 172.30.30.30>
    ServerName www.asdfghjkl.com
    ServerAdmin webmaster@www.asdfghjkl.com
    DocumentRoot /usr/local/web/vhosts/asdfghjkl/docroot
</VirtualHost>
```

You'll notice that with the exception of the `VirtualHost` container, the directives used to configure the server for virtual hosting are exactly the same as the directives used to configure a standalone server in Chapter 3.

Name-based

The configuration of name-based virtual hosts is very similar to the above. Observe that there are only a couple of minor adjustments:

```
NameVirtualHost 172.30.30.30
<VirtualHost 172.30.30.30>
    ServerName www.asdfghjkl.com
    ServerAdmin webmaster@www.asdfghjkl.com
    DocumentRoot /usr/local/web/vhosts/asdfghjkl/docroot
    ServerAlias asdfghjkl.com w3.asdfghjkl.com
</VirtualHost>
```

The `NameVirtualHost` directive specifies that `172.30.30.30` will be used for name-based virtual hosting. The `ServerAlias` directive specifies other names (these should be valid DNS names) that may be used to request documents from this virtual host; these need to be defined because without the HTTP `Host:` header corresponding to `ServerName`, Apache would be unable to determine for which of the virtual hosts on this IP a request for one of the aliases was actually intended.

mod_vhost_alias

To borrow from part of the rich cultural heritage of Demon Internet's native England, *Monty Python's Flying Circus,* "And now for something completely different...." mod_vhost_alias was written with the (often correct) assumption that defining individual VirtualHost blocks is tedious and makes configuration changes difficult. Consequently, mod_vhost_alias is designed to greatly simplify that configuration. Assume, for the example, that we have several domains hosted on the server and that each server's DocumentRoot is set up at /usr/local/web/vhosts/www.domain.com/docroot. Then:

```
UseCanonicalName Off
VirtualDocumentRoot /usr/local/web/vhosts/%0/docroot
```

The above is literally all that is required to enable on-the-fly mass name-based virtual hosting on a server with mod_vhost_alias installed. To change from a name-based configuration to an IP-based configuration, set UseCanonicalName DNS.

Configuring Logging

It is an unfortunately all-too-typical scenario that Web server administrators, eager to get virtual hosts up and running, and contented by the fact that Apache supports using logfile directives on a per-virtual host basis, simply modify the sample VirtualHost in the distribution httpd.conf file, creating a separate CustomLog and ErrorLog for each virtual host on the server. This configuration is wasteful in a number of ways. First, it requires a pair of file descriptors (one for each logfile) for each virtual host, consuming scarce (on some systems, notably Solaris 2.x) file descriptors and imposing an artificially low ceiling on the total number of allowable virtual hosts on the server. Second, it causes the server to have many files open for append (they are logs, after all) simultaneously, which increases the number of seeks the drives have to do, reducing their overall throughput, especially if the logs all live on the same file system (a typical configuration). As if all of this were not bad enough, the extra descriptors require memory overhead in every Apache child process.

Half this wastefulness is completely unnecessary and the other half is easily avoided. There is really little use for a separate ErrorLog for each host, as long as you provide a facility where the domain webmasters can view it (while they are trying to debug CGIs, in particular); its messages are not in a format that is particularly conducive to generating reports from, so its primary purpose is debugging. As far as the CustomLog goes, it is substantially cleaner to accumulate all the logs on the server in one location, and then write a short script to split them on a host-by-host basis at the end of the reporting period (week, month, whatever, once that logfile is rotated out of production). By prepending the name of the virtual host to each log entry, you can reduce the complexity of the log-splitting task from "painfully easy" to "trivial":

```
LogFormat "%V %h %l %u %t \"%r\" %>s %b \"%{Referer}i\" \"%{User-Agent}i\"" vcomb
CustomLog /var/weblogs/access_log vcomb
```

For interactive debugging, you could supply a CGI script to extract and report a virtual host's entries in the error log. See Chapter 5: "Using Logs."

Controlling Browser Access

Just as you need to have a <Directory> block specifying options for a standalone server, you also need one for each virtual host. It doesn't have to be particularly complicated:

```
<Directory "/usr/local/web/vhosts/asdfghjkl/docroot">
    Options Includes FollowSymLinks
    AllowOverride Limit FileInfo
    Order allow,deny
    Allow from all
</Directory>
```

If you are using mod_vhost_alias, keep in mind that a little globbing goes a long way: using <Directory "/usr/local/web/vhosts/*/docroot"> is valid syntax.

Enabling CGI for Individual Virtual Hosts

It is not altogether unlikely that at least some of your virtual hosts will need their own private CGIs, even if you provide them globally with a reasonably comprehensive collection in /cgi-global/ using ScriptAlias. Fortunately, you can do that fairly easily within the context of a VirtualHost block:

```
<VirtualHost 172.30.30.30>
    ServerName www.asdfghjkl.com
    ...
    ScriptAlias /cgi-bin/ /usr/local/web/vhosts/asdfghjkl/cgi/
</VirtualHost>

<Directory "/usr/local/web/vhosts/asdfghjkl/cgi/">
    Options +ExecCGI
    AllowOverride None
```

```
     Order deny,allow
     allow from all
</Directory>
```

It is also the case that the above situation scales nicely for `mod_vhost_alias`. It turns out that the `ScriptAlias /cgi-bin/` directive in the above configuration can easily be replaced under `mod_vhost_alias` with a simple single-line entry (Note: this only works for `/cgi-bin/`, and the virtual domain server root directory has to be named `www.asdfghjkl.com`, not just `asdfghjkl`):

```
VirtualScriptAlias /usr/local/web/vhosts/%0/cgi/
```

Once again, we can use the globbing technique defined in the section on `<Directory>` directives to produce an *en masse* configuration appropriate for `VirtualScriptAlias` directories:

```
<Directory "/usr/local/web/vhosts/*/cgi/">
    Options +ExecCGI
    AllowOverride None
    Order deny,allow
    allow from all
</Directory>
```

Configuring E-mail for Virtual Domains

As a caveat, this is not intended to be a tutorial on configuring sendmail. In fact, you may find that q-mail (**www.qmail.org**) is substantially easier to configure and use; it has a rich feature set, including the ability to do certain things (mail-only users, who exist only in a database, for example) fairly simply that are either unsupported or cumbersome under sendmail.

That said, the newer (version 8) versions of sendmail provide support for a feature (configured with the m4 rule `FEATURE('virtusertable')`) that allows very elaborate mappings between domain-specific e-mail addresses and how they are to be delivered. You *must* use m4 to create your `sendmail.cf` file for this to work: in addition to adding a `Kvirtuser` line near the top of `sendmail.cf`, it also adds some rules to the "magic runes" at the bottom of `sendmail.cf` that tell sendmail how to parse addresses. Complete directions for building sendmail with the virtusertable enabled are available online at **www.sendmail.org/virtual-hosting.html**.

Once you have sendmail configured properly, it is simply a matter of creating the correct source file for your virtual user table, and using the `makemap` utility bundled with sendmail to create a hash representation that sendmail can use internally to parse the addresses. As a sample, remember our domain webmasters friskie, trixie, and antsie from earlier in the chapter? Suppose that each of their companies gets its in-house intranet connectivity from ISP `netqqom.net`, and has a generic corporate e-mail address of `company@netqqom.net`. Then the appropriate portion of the virtual user table would look like:

```
webmaster@fdomain.com    friskie
abuse@fdomain.com        root
@fdomain.com             fdomain@netqqom.net
webmaster@tdomain.com    trixie
abuse@tdomain.com        root
@tdomain.com             tdomain@netqqom.net
webmaster@adomain.com    antsie
abuse@adomain.com        root
@adomain.com             adomain@netqqom.net
```

Proxying
with Apache

Strategies

There are two different principal types of proxy servers, the "forward," or client-side proxy, and the "reverse," or server-side proxy. The two are used for radically distinct purposes and require equally distinct configurations. This chapter will cover the use of Apache in either situation.

Client-Side Proxy

The most common use for a proxy server is as a facilitator to enable, enhance, monitor and often restrict the activities of web browsers. In this role, the browser clients are configured to send all their requests for information to the proxy server, which subsequently retrieves the information from the appropriate web servers. For example, one common configuration in many offices has the desktop workstations connected to a LAN that is *not* directly addressable from the Internet. A machine may then be configured to "straddle the firewall," with a network interface on the LAN and a second interface to the outside world. A client-side proxy living on such a machine would take requests from browsers on the LAN interface, and subsequently make requests of servers via the internet interface. In fact, in this situation a proxy server is required in order to complete any requests; even if the firewall-straddling machine simply routed packets between interfaces using a technique such as IP masquerading, it would in effect be acting as a trivial client-side proxy server since it was forwarding requests it received to the appropriate web server.

Even in scenarios where client-side proxying is not required, it is often a good idea. There are numerous advantages to the deployment of a proxy server within an organization:

- **Performance**—Proxy servers often make better web clients than many browsers, in terms of their ability to formulate requests and process the results. This may seem surprising on the surface, but consider that an average web page often requires 10–15 requests to download completely, and that one common browser is only really good at handling data from about 4–6 requests at once.
- **Caching**—Proxy servers have the ability to cache results from one query (which is said to "pioneer" the cache), and serve those results in response to subsequent queries for the same page without having to retrieve the page from the original server each time. This can result in a substantial improvement in network performance; consider the

number of times in a given day your bandwidth is being used to repeatedly retrieve the same content, over and over again (Microsoft's home page, for example).

■ **Monitoring**—Proxy servers keep logs. By forcing its employees to use a proxy server to view web pages, a company can keep a record of who was retrieving what, when. This information, needless to say, is extremely valuable in today's legal climate, where companies find themselves under increasing pressure to document nearly all workplace behavior.

■ **Filtering**—Proxy servers can say "no" to requests you deem unacceptible. Want to keep employees from accessing sites with "sex" in the domain name? Forbid it by rule. Want to prevent your engineers from doing their own patent searches? Forbid `uspto.gov` and `patents.ibm.com` by rule. If you have problems with people wasting time at the office, playing online backgammon or downloading obnoxious flatulence sounds, forbid the offending sites by rule. Proxy servers give you control over what your employees view on the web while at work; again, extremely valuable in today's legal climate, in addition to helping keep employees focused and productive.

Depending on how sophisticated your organization's needs are, Apache may prove to be a more than adequate client-side proxying solution. However, if your needs include more extensive caching, you should investigate Apache's also-open-source cousin Squid (**squid.nlanr.net**). If your needs include more sophisticated filtering than Apache's `ProxyBlock` directive provides (described in detail below), consider using either a commercial filtering proxy server, or squidGuard (**info.ost.eltele.no/freeware/ squidGuard**), a filtering extension for Squid.

Server-Side Proxy

Just as there are demonstrable advantages to using a client-side proxy server, there are also some significant, though perhaps less readily apparent advantages to using a server-side, or "reverse" proxy. Such a proxy is operated at the server end of the transaction, and unlike a client-side proxy, is completely transparent to the web browser—it thinks the server-side proxy is the real web server. Among the advantages of such an arrangement:

■ **Security**—The server-side proxy acts as an additional layer of armor between the Internet and the actual web server. Thus, if the machine running the proxy server is compromised, any sensitive information residing on the machine hosting the actual web server (e.g. credit card numbers from e-commerce transactions, lists of email addresses, user profiles) is not exposed in the process.

- **Delegation, Specialization, and Load Balancing**—The server-side proxy can integrate content from multiple servers and present it as if a single server were handling all the requests. This enables, for instance, your ordering apparatus to reside on a server at your Los Angeles warehouse while the rest of your web site is served from your Indianapolis data center; end-users are none the wiser. Similarly, you may decide that all requests for images should be handled by a server running a lightweight binary optimized to handle static content. Or, you may choose to host your site on an array of small servers, with the requests load-balanced among them.

- **Caching**—The server-side proxy can also cache, servicing frequently requested documents without having to burden the underlying web server with processing the requests. Needless to say, this too can have a positive impact on performance.

While the actual configuration of server-side proxies is relatively easy, the architectural considerations are substantially more challenging: for instance, knowing when you need specialization or load-balancing, how much of it you need, and what the best strategy is for the particular situation; this sort of expertise is gained and makes a person quite valuable as a consultant. A sample configuration for a reverse proxy is included later in this chapter, along with a description of how to use mod_rewrite for load-balancing. For an alternate approach to load-balancing, investigate the module Backhand (**www.backhand.org**), recently developed at Johns Hopkins. Also see Chapter 10: "Troubleshooting," the section titled "Load Balancing."

A Sample Client-Side Proxy

Compilation

The act of building Apache as a proxy server is, in and of itself, a relatively painless task. Thanks to the APACI utility, this can be accomplished in a few simple steps. First, change to the distribution directory (/path/to/apache_1.3.9) and run the following:

```
./configure --disable-module=auth \
--disable-module=asis  --disable-module=include \
--disable-module=cgi --disable-module=actions \
--disable-module=imap --enable-module=info \
--enable-module=proxy --prefix=/usr/local/approxy
```

Note that in the above example, you will need to change /usr/local/approxy to wherever you want the proxy server installed. The --disable-module directives are there to produce a smaller binary: the modules being disabled are those that deal with specific types of content-handling that, while convenient in a web server, aren't particularly useful for a client-side proxy. The two modules added are the proxy module itself, and the info module, useful for examining the configuration of a running server. Once the build is configured, it is a matter of running make and then make install in order to have the server build completed.

Configuration

Once the build is configured and the server compiled and installed, the next step is to set the run-time configuration of the server to act as a proxy. The configuration file httpd.conf distributed by default with Apache isn't designed for this; it is designed to act as the configuration file for a web server, not a proxy server. The example below shows what the configuration file should look like for a client-side proxy server. Note that the OS-specific settings in Section 1 assume Linux; some adjustment may be needed for other systems.

```
#Proxy Server Apache httpd.conf... modified from the config files from the
#distribution, which rely on the original configs written by R. McCool

#Jeff Almeida, January 2000, for Chapter 9 of Administering Apache

#Section 1 -- generalities

#First, some stuff that doesn't change much, from the distribution
#conf file... change the path to whatever you set --prefix to at
#configure time
ServerType standalone
ServerRoot "/usr/local/approxy"
PidFile /usr/local/approxy/logs/httpd.pid
ScoreBoardFile /usr/local/approxy/logs/httpd.scoreboard
Timeout 300
KeepAlive On

#These next two deal with keep-alives.  For most proxies you can get
```

```
#away with ratcheting these substantially higher -- like 1000
#consecutive requests and a timeout of 120 (two minutes).
MaxKeepAliveRequests 100
KeepAliveTimeout 15

#Since this is a proxy, these numbers are going to vary greatly based
#on the number of users on your network.  Depending on per-person
#usage, the 11 in the following formula may need to be lowered, but in #general a
good rule-of-thumb is MaxClients = [(Users/11) * 4] * 1.3.
#These numbers come from the following:
#1. Typically, one in every eleven people with net access is online.
#This is the dialup-user-to-modem ratio for ISPs that Boardwatch
#Magazine recommends.
#2. The 4 is the number of simultaneous pieces of content (documents,
#images, etc.) a browser will retrieve by default.
#3. The 1.3 is a 30% fudge factor, to allow for spikes in traffic.
#Needless to say, round up to the nearest integer.
MinSpareServers 2
MaxSpareServers 5
StartServers 3
MaxClients 15

#See Chapter 10 on Performance Tuning for an important warning about
#this:
MaxRequestsPerChild 0

ExtendedStatus On

#Section 2 -- this server

#Pick a nice, high numbered port -- you have to configure this on
#users' workstations.
Port 8011

#There's really no reason to run a proxy as anyone else
User nobody
Group nobody

#Put your email address here
ServerAdmin spud@administeringapache.com

#Since we're using mod_info and mod_status, we have to configure some
#semblance of a web server as well
DocumentRoot "/usr/local/approxy/htdocs"

#Change the IP range in the allow directives below to correspond to
#your INTERNAL network -- you don't want the rest of the world using
#your proxy server, do you?
<Directory />
```

```
        Options FollowSymLinks
        AllowOverride None
        Order deny,allow
        deny from all
        allow from 192.168.5
</Directory>

<Directory "/usr/local/approxy/htdocs">
        Options Indexes FollowSymLinks
        AllowOverride None
        Order deny,allow
        deny from all
        allow from 192.168.5
</Directory>

DirectoryIndex index.html

#Overrides are off, this should be irrelevant
AccessFileName .htaccess
<Files ~ "^\.ht">
        Order allow,deny
        Deny from all
</Files>

#This is always a good choice
UseCanonicalName On

#MIME stuff, for the web server running by default
TypesConfig /usr/local/approxy/conf/mime.types
DefaultType text/plain

#This is ALWAYS a good idea -- see Chapter 10 for details
HostnameLookups Off

#Logfile stuff from the distribution conf file
ErrorLog /usr/local/approxy/logs/error_log
LogLevel warn
LogFormat "%h %l %u %t \"%r\" %>s %b \"%{Referer}i\" \"%{User-Agent}i\"" combined
LogFormat "%h %l %u %t \"%r\" %>s %b" common
LogFormat "%{Referer}i -> %U" referer
LogFormat "%{User-agent}i" agent

#This is particularly useful when running a proxy -- collect as much
#info as you can in the logs
CustomLog /usr/local/approxy/logs/access_log combined

#This is for error messages.  Turning it off is NEVER a good idea.
ServerSignature On
```

```
#The icons and indexing directives below are for the default web
#server described above, and come from the distribution conf files.
#Again, change the IP range.
Alias /icons/ "/usr/local/approxy/icons/"
<Directory "/usr/local/approxy/icons">
    Options Indexes MultiViews
    AllowOverride None
    Order deny,allow
    deny from all
    allow from 192.168.5
</Directory>
IndexOptions FancyIndexing
AddIconByEncoding (CMP,/icons/compressed.gif) x-compress x-gzip
AddIconByType (TXT,/icons/text.gif) text/*
AddIconByType (IMG,/icons/image2.gif) image/*
AddIconByType (SND,/icons/sound2.gif) audio/*
AddIconByType (VID,/icons/movie.gif) video/*
AddIcon /icons/binary.gif .bin .exe
AddIcon /icons/binhex.gif .hqx
AddIcon /icons/tar.gif .tar
AddIcon /icons/world2.gif .wrl .wrl.gz .vrml .vrm .iv
AddIcon /icons/compressed.gif .Z .z .tgz .gz .zip
AddIcon /icons/a.gif .ps .ai .eps
AddIcon /icons/layout.gif .html .shtml .htm .pdf
AddIcon /icons/text.gif .txt
AddIcon /icons/c.gif .c
AddIcon /icons/p.gif .pl .py
AddIcon /icons/f.gif .for
AddIcon /icons/dvi.gif .dvi
AddIcon /icons/uuencoded.gif .uu
AddIcon /icons/script.gif .conf .sh .shar .csh .ksh .tcl
AddIcon /icons/tex.gif .tex
AddIcon /icons/bomb.gif core
AddIcon /icons/back.gif ..
AddIcon /icons/hand.right.gif README
AddIcon /icons/folder.gif ^^DIRECTORY^^
AddIcon /icons/blank.gif ^^BLANKICON^^
DefaultIcon /icons/unknown.gif
ReadmeName README
HeaderName HEADER
IndexIgnore .??* *~ *# HEADER* README* RCS CVS *,v *,t
AddEncoding x-compress Z
AddEncoding x-gzip gz tgz
AddLanguage en .en
AddLanguage fr .fr
AddLanguage de .de
AddLanguage da .da
AddLanguage el .el
AddLanguage it .it
```

```
LanguagePriority en fr de
AddType application/x-tar .tgz

#More useful hacks from the distribution conf files
BrowserMatch "Mozilla/2" nokeepalive
BrowserMatch "MSIE 4\.0b2;" nokeepalive downgrade-1.0 force-response-1.0
BrowserMatch "RealPlayer 4\.0" force-response-1.0
BrowserMatch "Java/1\.0" force-response-1.0
BrowserMatch "JDK/1\.0" force-response-1.0

#Mod_status is helpful in diagnosing problems.  You may wish to further
#restrict the IP range below to just your own workstation.
<Location /status>
    SetHandler server-status
    Order deny,allow
    deny from all
    allow from 192.168.5
</Location>

#Mod_info shows the server's current running configuration.  The IP comment
#above about mod_status goes likewise here.
<Location /info>
    SetHandler server-info
    Order deny,allow
    deny from all
    allow from 192.168.5
</Location>



#Section 3 - virtual hosts - omitted (not needed for a proxy)


#Finally -- the meat of the matter -- the Proxy Configuration itself

#Enable the Proxy Server
ProxyRequests On

#Restrict Access to the INTERNAL network
<Directory proxy:*>
    Order deny,allow
    deny from all
    allow from 192.168.5
</Directory>

#Allow HTTP 1.1 Via: headers.  "On" is standards-compliant.
Anything else
#is being a bad netizen.
ProxyVia On
```

```
#Where to put documents we're caching.
CacheRoot "/usr/local/approxy/proxy"
#How big (in KB) to make the cache.  Anything less than 8 MB would be
#uncivilized.  Bigger is better.  Because of the nature of caches, this
#will tend to fragment a lot -- consider putting it on its own partition.
#The cache will outgrow this -- this is the target size for the garbage
#collector.
CacheSize 8192
#How often to run the cache garbage collector (hours between runs). The
#more often it runs, the closer the cache will remain in size to the target
#set with CacheSize above.
CacheGcInterval 8
#Retain documents without checking for freshness for this many hours.
CacheMaxExpire 48
#This is the fudge factor used to guess expiration dates on
documents when
#none is supplied -- if the last modified time is n hours ago, multiply by
#this constant to get the expiration time.  For example, if this is set to
#0.5, and the document is six hours old, it gets a 3 hour expiration. The
#higher you set this, the more likely it is that documents will get hit by
#the setting of CacheMaxExpire (which takes precedence) instead, and the
#more you are trading freshness for bandwidth.
CacheLastModifiedFactor 0.5
#If no expiry times are supported at all, use this.  It takes precedence
#over the CacheMaxExpire directive for affected
documents.  Beware setting
#this too high, these documents are often the ones that change the MOST.
CacheDefaultExpire 1
```

Directives

The following configuration directives pertain to client-side proxies, and are available in servers containing mod_proxy:

AllowCONNECT

AllowCONNECT describes which HTTPS ports the CONNECT method is allowed to permit access to. By default, HTTPS (443) and SNEWS (563) are enabled. Use this directive to replace the defaults with connections to the ports listed. For example, to allow the defaults and port 8443, use:

```
AllowCONNECT 443 563 8443
```

CacheDefaultExpire

The number of hours to use for the expiration time of documents retrieved with a protocol that doesn't include expiry information. It defaults to 1 (hour). Caution is advised when raising this value: documents retrieved in this manner are often those which change the *most*.

CacheDirLength

`CacheDirLength` sets the length (in characters) of the names of subdirectories of the cache directory. The default setting is 1, and there is very little reason to deviate in most circumstances.

CacheDirLevels

The depth below `CacheRoot` at which cached data will be stored. The default is 3. For fewer files per directory set this number higher. To reduce the amount of space in the file system taken up by directories themselves, set this number lower.

CacheForceCompletion

The percentage of downloading a document that has to be completed for the proxy to continue downloading if the request is terminated. The default is 90. Setting this lower will result in faster cache population/"pioneering" for proxies with a large number of users, but also may lead to the inadvertent caching of documents of little interest.

CacheGcInterval

The number of hours to wait between runs of the garbage collector for the cache. Lower settings of this number will result in more processor/disk consumption (as the runs will be more frequent), but will help to keep the cache close to the specified `CacheSize`. Warning: this parameter has *no* default value, and if it is left unset, the cache will continue to grow unchecked. You can specify floating-point values here to indicate fractions of an hour.

CacheLastModifiedFactor

`CacheLastModifiedFactor` specifies the "fudge-factor" by which a document's age (as given by a `Last-Modified:` header) is multiplied to generate an expire time, when explicit expiry information is *not* specified.

Regardless of how this is set, documents expired in this fashion will never be less fresh than the number of hours specified in CacheMaxExpire. This defaults to 0.1, meaning a 15-day-old document only gets 18 hours of cache life; a higher setting (0.2) is recommended as a minimum, and most installations can probably get by setting this as high as 0.5 or even 0.75.

CacheMaxExpire

CacheMaxExpire sets the longest a document can linger (in hours) in the cache before checking with the original server to verify freshness. The default is 24 hours. Since this setting will override any expiry information from the original server specifying a longer period, administrators are encouraged to let this value creep upwards gradually to the point where end-users find it intolerable, as a way of optimizing cache performance.

CacheRoot

CacheRoot is exactly what it sounds like: the directory in which the cache will be constructed. This directory must be writable by the user specified in the User directive. Failing to specify a CacheRoot will result in a proxy server that does not cache. If at all possible, try to construct the cache for a busy server in its own disk partition; because of the nature of cache population and garbage collection, caches typically experience a large amount of fragmentation.

CacheSize

The target size (in KB) for the garbage collector to leave the cache when it finishes. As such, it is *not* the maximum size the cache will grow to; to reduce the amount the cache grows beyond this number, run the garbage collector more frequently. In most circumstances, the larger the cache, the better. Anything less than 8 MB is wasteful (why bother caching at all?).

NoCache

NoCache sets a list of words/domains/hostnames that, if the requested host matches, will result in documents not being cached. This is a rather limited approach, and if you desire deeper control of caching behavior, you are strongly encouraged to investigate Squid (**squid.nlanr.net**). It is also the case that setting NoCache to * will disable caching explicitly (remember that you can implicitly disable caching by failing to specify CacheRoot).

NoProxy

NoProxy sets a list of words/domains/hostnames/addresses that, if the requested host matches, will not be forwarded on to a proxy server specified with ProxyRemote. Thus, if there are some servers on the local network and this proxy is configured to forward requests to another proxy with ProxyRemote, the local servers can be excluded with this directive.

ProxyBlock

ProxyBlock sets a list of words/domains/hostnames/addresses that, if the requested host matches, will be denied upon request. For example:

```
ProxyBlock xxxsexxxycam.com
```

will prevent anyone from accessing servers in the xxxsexxxycam.com through the proxy.

ProxyDomain

ProxyDomain sets the default domain for requests with incomplete hostnames. This domain will be appended to the incomplete hostname, and a redirect returned to the browser.

ProxyReceiveBufferSize

ProxyReceiveBufferSize sets a size for the receive buffer on outgoing requests. It defaults to the buffer size set by the system. A configuration file can explicity contain a directive to use the default by setting this to 0. Meaningful settings of this parameter are 512 or greater. Theoretically, throughput can be increased by setting this larger than the system default, but there is memory overhead associated with doing so.

ProxyRemote

ProxyRemote sets a URL-match pattern and proxy server to forward requests through. When used in conjunction with ProxyDomain and NoProxy, this can be used to set up a network of departmental proxy servers cascaded through a corporate intranet, each forwarding external requests higher up the chain.

```
ProxyRemote http://www.waupacawidgets.com http://192.168.0.12:81
```

will result in requests for the Waupaca Widgets site to be proxied through the specified server.

```
ProxyRemote * http://192.168.0.13:8011
```

will result in all requests being proxied through the specified server (except those excluded with NoProxy).

ProxyRequests

ProxyRequests defaults to Off. Setting this directive to On enables client-side proxying.

ProxyVia

ProxyVia controls how the server handles HTTP 1.1 Via: headers. It defaults to Off, which passes Via: headers through unchanged, but doesn't add one for the current proxy, which is (unless your organization meets the criteria for the exception stated in RFC 2068) standards non-compliant. To achieve compliance, set this to On, which both passes Via: headers through and adds an appropriate Via: header for this server. Another compliant option is Full, which adds version info about this server as a Via: comment field. Another option, which is even more badly behaved than the default Off, is to set this to Block, which strips all Via: headers from each request; it is highly recommended that you forget this option even exists.

Transparent Proxying

Apache does not natively support the "transparent" proxies often configured on many LANs today. Such proxies are set up so that any requests for port 80 (and potentially others; other common HTTP ports include 81, 1080, 1081, 8000, 8001, 8080, and 8081) on an external host are automatically rerouted to the network's proxy server. That proxy server, however, must know how to deal with incoming requests that aren't explicitly asking to be proxied; to do that in Apache requires an additional layer of request filtering before the proxy module can function properly.

Two common solutions exist to fulfill the required filtering function. The first is John Saunders' transproxy (**www.transproxy.nlc.net.au**) program, for which there are packages and ports to many common UNIX and Linux distributions, in addition to available source code; the chief drawback of this is that it is a separate program, and hence an additional process on the server has to handle each request. The other is Steve Kann's `mod_tproxy` (**www.stevek.com/projects/mod_tproxy/**), which compiles directly into the Apache server and handles the URL translation issues associated with transparent proxying.

Server-Side Proxies

Configuration

Configuring server-side proxies in Apache is extremely straightforward. In fact, the implementation is versatile enough to be equally of use in situations that are not server-side proxying in the traditional sense. Once again, make sure the proxy module is compiled into the server binary (though this time you may wish to include more of the content-handling modules that were excluded in the client-side proxy), but set `ProxyRequests Off` since you aren't actually forwarding requests explicitly intended for another server. Then, it is just a matter of judiciously applying the `ProxyPass`, `ProxyPassReverse`, and (possibly) `RewriteRule` directives in order to make remote documents appear local.

A Brief (de)Tour to the Apache Rewriting Engine

The intricacies of how URLs can be rewritten in Apache using `mod_rewrite` could fill an entire, lengthy chapter, if not a whole book in and of themselves. The prolific Ralf Engelschall, author of everything from GNU Portable Threads to ePerl, has produced in `mod_rewrite` an extensible regex-based text-mapping engine comparable to (though more powerful than) the one in Sendmail. Ralf has written a detailed "cookbook" to using `mod_rewrite` (**www.apache.org/docs/misc/rewriteguide.html**) that is filled with examples of solving real problems. Fundamentally, there are three key directives in `mod_rewrite`:

RewriteEngine

Set this to `On` to enable `mod_rewrite`. This presupposes that you've compiled the server with `mod_rewrite` installed.

RewriteMap

`RewriteMap` specifies an external map to use in rewriting, which, while it seems highly specialized, is actually extremely useful in many cases, including our example below. The syntax is:

```
RewriteMap     MapName   MapType:MapSource
```

where *MapName* is the name you've chosen to call your map (needed for `RewriteRule`, below), *MapType* is one of `txt`, `rnd`, `dbm`, `int`, or `prg`, to denote which variety of map it is, and the syntax for *MapSource* varies based on *MapType*. Essentially, `txt` represents an external text map, `rnd` is an external text map containing random choices, `dbm` is a dbm-hashed external text map (faster than `txt`), `int` is a call to one of the built-in text-mapping functions, and `prg` is a call to an external program which reads from `STDIN` and writes to `STDOUT`.

RewriteRule

`RewriteRule` is the guts of the rewriting engine. Essentially, this is just regex-based substitution in its rawest form; it takes as arguments a pattern to match, a replacement, and optional modifier flags.

Together, the three rules can be used to define how a particular URL mapping will occur. In the sample below, requests for content in the directory `/images/` will be handed off at random to three servers, `imsrv1`, `imsrv2`, and `imsrv3`. First, the content in the map file:

```
##rewriting mapfile - imsrvmap.txt
imserver imsrv1|imsrv2|imsrv3
```

Then, the content for `httpd.conf`:

```
RewriteEngine On
RewriteMap    imsrvs    rnd:/path/to/imsrvmap.txt
RewriteRule   ^/images/(.*) http://${imsrvs|imsrv1}.thisdom.com/$1 [R,L]
```

That's all that is required to offload image requests to a random image server.

Sample Server-Side Proxy Configuration

Unlike the rather involved configuration required to implement a client-side proxy, a server-side proxy's configuration is very simple. The proxy module does need to be compiled into the server, but `ProxyRequests` does not have to be enabled. In fact, there are only two directives of interest.

ProxyPass

`ProxyPass` is used to specify that requests for a particular local URL are to be converted into proxy requests made of some other server. It takes the appropriate local pathname, and the corresponding remote server with replacement pathname as arguments.

ProxyPassReverse

`ProxyPassReverse` is used to specify that redirects issued by the remote server are to be translated to use the proxy before being returned to the client. Its syntax is identical to `ProxyPass`, and the two directives are almost always used in concert.

In the following example, any requests for content in the `/msiss/` (more-secure internal server's scripts) directory are treated as proxy requests of the `/cgi-bin/` directory on `roosevelt`, which is accessible from the proxy server but not directly from the internet. Further, we are going to instruct the proxy to rewrite any redirects issued by `roosevelt` to point back to the proxy server instead; failing to do so in this case would cause the redirects to fail, since `roosevelt` cannot be accessed directly).

```
ProxyPass          /msiss/   http://roosevelt.int.thisdom.com/cgi-bin/
ProxyPassReverse   /msiss/   http://roosevelt.int.thisdom.com/cgi-bin/
```

Troubleshooting

Getting the Status of the Running Server

Reporting the Server Status

The Apache server can output a report describing its current status: server name and version, CPU usage, current states of the parent daemon and its children, etc. The mod_status module, which is *not* a default module, provides this report. To compile this module with the APACI utility, use the parameter --enable-module=status. The parameter --enable-module=most will also include the mod_status module. Once your server has been compiled with this module, add the following directive to the list of other AddModule directives:

```
AddModule mod_status.c
```

If the mod_status module was compiled as a dynamically shared object, then also add the following directive to the list of LoadModule directives:

```
LoadModule status_module libexec/mod_status.so
```

More information on compiling the server and configuring modules is available in Chapter 2: "Creating the Web Server."

To enable the Apache Server Status report, add the following <Location> block to the configuration file's global context:

```
<Location /server-status>
    SetHandler server-status
</Location>
```

The above <Location> block tests if the requested URL is /server-status and if it is, sends the request to the server-status handler in the mod_status module. Note that /server-status is a completely fictitious URL. There needn't be any file by that name anywhere in your Web site.

Once configured, the report can be obtained in two ways. The Apache startup script, /usr/local/apache/bin/apachectl, will output a text version of this report when passed the word status as a parameter. This text report looks like this:

```
     Apache Server Status for administeringapache.com
Server Version: Apache/1.3.9 (Unix)
Server Built: Feb 29 2000 06:31:18
```
```
Current Time: Wednesday, 01-Mar-2000 03:55:05 CST
Restart Time: Wednesday, 01-Mar-2000 03:54:22 CST
```

```
Parent Server Generation: 5
Server uptime: 43 seconds
Total accesses: 3 - Total Traffic: 7 kB
CPU Usage: u0 s.01 cu0 cs0 - .0233% CPU load
.0698 requests/sec - 166 B/second - 2389 B/request
1 requests currently being processed, 4 idle servers
_W___.................................................
......................................................
......................................................
......................................................
Scoreboard Key:
"_" Waiting for Connection, "S" Starting up, "R" Reading Request,
"W" Sending Reply, "K" Keepalive (read), "D" DNS Lookup,
"L" Logging, "G" Gracefully finishing, "." Open slot with no current
process
```

In the above report, the middle section (the section with all the dots) displays the status of up to 255 Apache child daemons. Each child daemon is given one character in the above grid. That character displays a status code for that daemon. In the report, the Scoreboard Key shows what the status codes mean. In the above output, we see that the one child daemon is sending a reply and four child daemons are waiting for a connection.

The second way to obtain the status report is to request it with a browser. Enter this URL:

```
http://administeringapache.com//server-status
```

replacing `administeringapache.com` with the name of your server. The browser should then display a screen like the one shown in Figure 10.1.

The status report can be made more verbose by setting the following directive in the Apache configuration file's global context:

```
ExtendedStatus On
```

The `ExtendedStatus` directive instructs the `mod_status` module to additionally report a detailed log of the files requested, which looks like this:

```
Srv  PID  Acc    M CPU  SS Req Conn Child Slot Client      Vhost                    Request
0-10 4785 0/1/1 W 0.00 41 0   0.0  0.00  0.00 192.168.1.7 administeringapache.com GET /server-status HTTP/1.0
3-10 4788 0/1/1 _ 0.00 41 1   0.0  0.00  0.00 127.0.0.1   administeringapache.com GET /server-status HTTP/1.0
Srv                      Child Server number - generation
PID                      OS process ID
Acc                      Number of accesses this connection / this child / this slot
M                        Mode of operation
```

CPU	CPU usage, number of seconds
SS	Seconds since beginning of most recent request
Req	Milliseconds required to process most recent request
Conn	Kilobytes transferred this connection
Child	Megabytes transferred this child
Slot	Total megabytes transferred this slot

Figure 10.1

Server status report.

Note that this extended status information is only available to the browser. It is not displayed when the report is requested through the Apache startup script—even if `ExtendedStatus` is `On`.

The information displayed on the Apache Server Status report is by no means public. You might want to restrict access to the `/server-status` URL by adding access directives to the `/server-status <Location>` block, as in

```
<Location /server-status>
    SetHandler server-status
    Order deny,allow
    Deny from all
    Allow from 192.168.1. 127.0.0.1
</Location>
```

The access directives in the above block (`Order`, `Deny`, and `Allow`) restrict access to the `/server-status` URL to browsers connecting from the local area network (`192.168.1.`) or from the localhost (`127.0.0.1`).

Note that if you don't add the localhost, you won't be able to obtain the report through the Apache startup script—which actually makes a request to the running server.

Note also that the status report is only available to a server running in `standalone` mode. The report is not available to servers whose `ServerType` directive is set to `inetd`.

For more information, see the *Apache User's Guide* page named **manual/mod/mod_status.html**.

Reporting the Server Configuration

Apache provides an Apache Server Information report along the same vein as the Apache Server Status report, except that the Apache Server Information report is available only to the browser. This report displays the values of the configuration directives in the configuration file's global scope, followed by a list of module sections displaying the values of the directives applicable to each module. The `mod_info` module, which is *not* a default module, provides this report. To compile this module with the APACI utility, use the parameter `--enable-module=info`. The parameter `--enable-module=most` will also include the `mod_info` module. Once your server has been compiled with this module, add the following directive to the list of other `AddModule` directives:

```
AddModule mod_info.c
```

If the `mod_info` module was compiled as a dynamically shared object, then also add the following directive to the list of `LoadModule` directives:

```
LoadModule info_module libexec/mod_info.so
```

More information on compiling the server and configuring modules is available in Chapter 2: "Creating the Web Server."

Once your server has been compiled with this module, the display of the Information report can be enabled with the following `<Location>` block directive in the Apache configuration file's global context:

```
<Location /server-info>
    SetHandler server-info
</Location>
```

The above `<Location>` block tests if the requested URL is `/serverinfo` and, if it is, sends the request to the server-info handler in the `mod_info` module. Note that /server-info is a completely fictitious URL. There needn't be any file by that name anywhere in your Web site.

Once configured, the report can be obtained via the browser with a URL similar to

```
http://administeringapache.com/server-info
```

replacing administeringapache.com with the name of your server. The browser should then display a screen like the one shown in Figure 10.2.

Figure 10.2

Server info report.

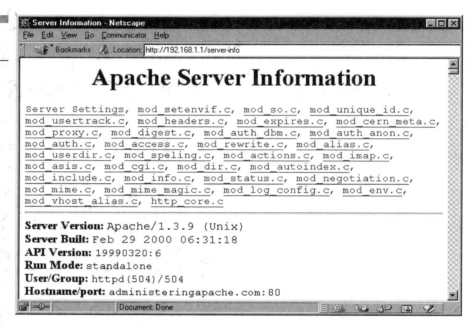

AddModuleInfo

AddModuleInfo adds the specified information to the Apache Server Information report section describing the specified module. The AddModuleInfo directive accepts two parameters: the name of a module and the text to be added to that module's report section. The added information can be in HTML format. For example, the following directive

```
AddModuleInfo mod_vhost_alias.c 'See the <A
HREF="http://administeringapache.com/manual/mod/
mod_vhost_alias.html"> Module mod_vhost_alias</A> documentation'
```

would add, to the mod_vhost alias section of the report, a link to the *Apache User's Guide* documentation on vhost_alias. The added information is displayed in the Additional Information: subsection of the module's section. The above example would display a screen like the one shown in Figure 10.3.

Figure 10.3
Please provide caption

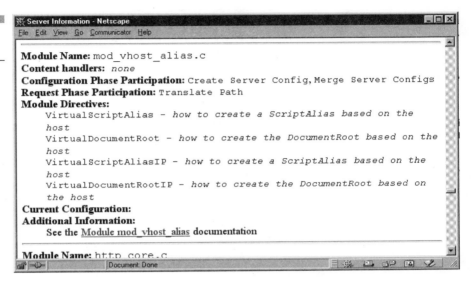

The information displayed on the Apache Server Information report is by no means public. You might want to restrict access to the /server-info URL by adding access directives to the <Location /server-info> block, as in

```
<Location /server-info>
    SetHandler server-info
    Order deny,allow
    Deny from all
    Allow from 192.168.1.
</Location>
```

The access directives in the above block (Order, Deny, and Allow) restrict access to the /server-info URL to browsers connecting from the local area network (192.168.1.)

The *Apache User's Guide* page named manual/mod/mod_info.html adds some interesting caveats and warnings worthy of reading.

Benchmarking the Server

Apache ships with a binary called ab that performs Apache benchmarking. The ab program accepts options and parameters specifying what URL to request, how many times to request it, how many concurrent requests to make, etc. Then ab calculates and reports statistics displaying how long it took to satisfy each request, how long it took to satisfy all the requests, the total number of bytes transferred, and the like. The ab program can accept a number of options. See the ab(1) manual page for a complete list. Here, we will present a short example. I entered the following shell command on my test server

```
ab -n 30 -c 3 -v 2 administeringapache.com/
```

The -n option specifies the number of requests to make. The -c option specifies the number of requests to make concurrently. The -v option sets the verbosity of the report, 2 being a very verbose report. The program output the following report:

```
Copyright (c) 1996 Adam Twiss, Zeus Technology Ltd,
http://www.zeustech.net/
Copyright (c) 1998-1999 The Apache Group, http://www.apache.org/

Benchmarking 192.168.1.1 (be patient)...INFO: POST header ==
---
GET / HTTP/1.0
User-Agent: ApacheBench/1.3a
Host: 192.168.1.1
Accept: */*


---
Server Software:      Apache/1.3.9
Server Hostname:      192.168.1.1
Server Port:   80

Document Path:/
Document Length:    1622 bytes

Concurrency Level: 3
Time taken for tests:    0.035 seconds
---
Server Software:      Apache/1.3.9
Server Hostname:      192.168.1.1
Server Port:   80

Document Path:/
Document Length:    1622 bytes

Concurrency Level: 3
Time taken for tests:    0.035 seconds
Complete requests: 30
```

```
Failed requests:   0
Total transferred: 56070 bytes
HTML transferred:  48660 bytes
Requests per second:   857.14
Transfer rate:1602.00 kb/s received

Connnection Times (ms)
            min       avg       max
Connect:     0         0         2
Processing:  3         3         1
Total:       3         3         3
```

The Apache benchmarking tool may prove handy when "Tuning Apache for Performance" (a section presented later in this chapter). Read the ab(1) man page, since there are several caveats that might produce inaccurate results.

The ab program can be found in the bin/ subdirectory of the Apache installation directory (e.g. /usr/local/apache/bin/). If a previous version of Apache was installed on your server as a package (such as a Red-Hat RPM), then an older version of the ab program may have been installed in the /usr/sbin or /sbin directory. You may wish to refresh that older version with the latest version from the Apache installation directory.

Getting the Raw HTTP with Telnet

Sometimes you need to see the response headers generated by your server—especially when debugging metafiles. The browser doesn't display these response headers in the browser window and doesn't display all of them in the View Page Info window. What you need is a non-rendering browser that shows the raw characters spewing forth from your server. Telnet can do just that. Instruct telnet to connect to your Web server using the HTTP port (port 80) instead of the telnet port (port 23). Then type in an HTTP request, just as a normal browser would. The telnet client will then display every character sent back by the Web server. Hint: For this operation, configure your telnet client to locally echo what you type; otherwise, you won't be able to see the request you are entering. The simplest valid request you can enter is

```
HEAD / HTTP/1.1
Host: administeringapache.com
```

Note that the request is followed by an empty line. The server will not respond until this empty line is transmitted. The above request asks for the default document from the root of the Web site on the administeringapache.com server. The first line is the request line. It specifies the method to use (HEAD), the document to transmit (/), and the version of the HTTP protocol in use by the browser (HTTP/1.1). The HEAD method instructs the server to deliver just the response headers without the document body. If you use the GET method, the server will deliver the response headers and the content body. The content body, more often than not, will scroll the response headers off of the top of your telnet window. If you need to see both the response headers and the content body, then use the GET method; but turn on your telnet client's logging facility before making the request (so that you can capture the request headers that scroll off of the screen). The second line in the above request specifies the name of the server that should satisfy the request. This Host: request header became available in the HTTP protocol version 1.1. The Host: request header requests a server by name and is useful for connecting to servers that host multiple Web sites through name-based virtual hosting. (That's where more than one registered domain is served by a server with only one IP address).

Given the example HEAD request, above, the server might respond with

```
HTTP/1.1 200 OK
Date: Wed, 01 Mar 2000 12:33:08 GMT
Server: Apache/1.3.9 (Unix)
Last-Modified: Wed, 20 May 1998 14:59:42 GMT
ETag: "206e4-656-3562efde"
Accept-Ranges: bytes
Content-Length: 1622
Content-Type: text/html
```

The first line in the above response is the status line. It contains the HTTP protocol version used to respond to the request (HTTP/1.1, in the above response). It also contains the status code of the request. A status of 200 OK means that the request was successfully satisfied. The subsequent lines each contain a response header as <name>:<value> pairs. For a detailed discussion of request and response headers and the conversations that go on between the server and the browser, see Chapter 4: Manipulating Content, the section "Configuring MIME." (the subsections "Configuring Content Types and Content Negotiation") and the section "Sending Metadata and Other Headers."

Responding to Error Messages

What follows is a short list of some of the most common errors that you will find in the error log and what to do about them. You can find more errors and answers in the Apache FAQ, available at **http://www.apache. org/docs/misc/FAQ.html**.

File does not exist

- the requested document is not underneath the server's DocumentRoot directory tree, or
- the document is not underneath the UserDir directory tree, or
- the document is not underneath a directory named by a <Directory> directive, or
- the document is not under the directory named in a ScriptAlias or ScriptAlias match directive, or
- the user typed the URL in wrong, or
- the file actually doesn't exist.

Premature end of script

If you are using suexec, then

> this is not the real error. It is bogus. Go look in the suexec log for the real error. Usually, the script or the environment violated one of suexec's requirements. Suexec performs 20 checks before allowing a script to run. There is a list of them in the *Apache User's Guide* in manual/suexec.html. Remember, the script is run under the user ID of the user account owning the user site and the script must be owned by that user and grouped by that user's default group. Make sure that the user has execute privileges on the script. Make sure that the Web server can search the directory for the script.

If you are *not* using suexec, then

> the script didn't output the expected data. A script must output a ContentType: response header. A script must *not* output a Date: response header. A script must output a blank line after all of the response headers.

Permission denied

File system permissions are not set correctly for the file or directory. For a non-script file, the Web server needs read permissions on the file. It also needs read and execute permissions on the directory.

client denied by server configuration

The `Order`, `Allow`, and `Deny` directives do not grant the requesting browser permission to request the file.

file permissions deny server execution

For a script (without `suexec`), the Web server needs execute permissions on the file.

Directory Index Forbidden by Rule

The browser requested a directory and that directory does not contain a file named by the `DirectoryIndex` directive and `Options Indexes` is not in effect for the directory.

Tuning Apache for Performance

Apache performance tuning is a task made complex by the huge variation in demands among servers. Physical contraints such as processor, operating system, memory, and I/O play an enormous role; the vast differences among the very ways various Apache servers are utilized create substantial distinctions among a performance-optimized configuration for one server and that for another. We can divide the different performance-tuning tips listed in this section into three categories: axiomatic (those principles generally good for nearly all servers), module-specific (things which make particular modules perform better), and site-specific (things which will make a server perform better under certain conditions).

Axiomatic

Dean Gaudet, performance guru of the ASF, maintains a site (**www.arctic.org/ ~ dgaudet/apache/perf**) containing his notes on Apache performance tuning. In it, he identifies the number one hardware issue affecting a server (RAM. Buy more. Now.), and a number of common-sense rules to follow when configuring a server; the three most important are:

1. Enable `Options FollowSymLinks`. Enable it everywhere in your `config` file. Failure to do so will result in the server's performing a system call on `/every/single/filesystem/node/above/your.doc` just to see if it is a symbolic link, every time any document is requested.
2. Turn `HostnameLookups Off`. Making the server do DNS in real time is a huge amount of extra work; if you need the hostnames for reporting purposes, write a script to do the lookups when you're generating the reports. Remember that inside `allow` and `deny` directives, you can use IP addresses/ranges instead of hostnames.
3. Set `AllowOverride None`. This may not be practical in a lot of cases (if you run a server where individual domain webmasters need to create `.htaccess` files, for instance), but it has an impact similar to the `FollowSymLinks` problem above—every node in the filesystem between the `DocumentRoot` and your document has to be checked for the presence of a `.htaccess` file.

Among his other performance tuning notes on the page, Dean also discusses some issues with respect to process creation that are probably better addressed in the context of tuning a server for specific modules or site demands.

Along a similar vein, there are other common-sense measures that can be applied. In general, anything that minimizes system calls and/or hardware demands fits into this category. In particular:

1. Only compile into the server those modules you explicitly have a need for. This will reduce both the overall size of the server's memory image, and the number of routines that need to be called in the course of servicing a particular request (investigate Chapter 12 for details on how Apache services a request if this seems elusive). Whether to link the server statically or dynamically depends greatly on your choice of platform; on some systems dynamic linking reduces memory consumption and doesn't have a negative impact on execution speed, while on others there is no significant memory savings and a huge performance penalty—it pays to know your hardware.
2. Avoid `suexec` like the plague. While this seems contrary to good security practices, usually the user Apache is configured to run as `nobody`, `http`, `apache`, etc., has fewer privileges than the regular users on your system anyway. Moreover, the performance penalty associated with

suexec'd CGIs is elephantine: while a normal CGI requires a single `fork()`, a `suexec` requires a `fork()`, a lengthy series of security checks implemented as system calls, and then a second `fork()`. It is the logical equivalent of ordering a health inspection (and waiting for it to be completed) in the course of a routine stop-for-donuts on the way to work, and about as efficient.

3. Avoid server-side includes. `mod_ssi` is (at least according to several benchmarks) significantly slower than many alternatives, not the least of which is simulating the SSI results using `mod_perl` or PHP.

4. Benchmark `MaxClients`. It doesn't do a lot of good to have `MaxClients` set at the default 150 if, when servicing more than 38 simultaneous requests, your server grinds to a near halt, mired in swap I/O, more simultaneous file reads than it can handle, etc. At the other end of the spectrum, if your OS has a relatively large penalty associated with `fork()` (AIX comes to mind), it can also be beneficial to benchmark `MinSpareServers` as well, to guarantee that request demand is met as it comes in.

5. If you're serving a lot of static content, consider caching it in memory using `mod_mmap_static`, as a way of reducing disk access; remember, by `mmap`'ing content you're trading valuable RAM space for file I/O, so use it sparingly.

Of course, there are also important hardware considerations that go into performance-tuning a server. We've already mentioned RAM. I/O is the other major issue, disk I/O in particular. Here are points to consider when designing your server's file system:

1. IDE is inadequate in a high-performance Web environment. While fast IDE interfaces like Ultra-ATA/66 provide great power-for-price results on desktop workstations, the blocking nature of the IDE protocol makes it less desirable than SCSI in a server environment, where multiple disk operations happen concurrently as a matter of course.

2. The more highly parallelized your disk activity, the better your disks will perform. In order of increasing preference, your `docroot`, server logs, and swap should be on separate partitions, spindles, SCSI channels, and (ideally) SCSI controllers.

3. In the spirit of parallelizing disk activity, consider investing in RAID. The disk redundancy of RAID will not only enable you to sleep better at night (not having to do recovery from tape at 3 a.m. is good for that), it also boosts performance by spreading the disk access across

multiple spindles. Controller features like write-back cache even help to smooth out activity caused by demand spikes.

4. When it comes to disk partitions, clutter is nobody's friend. If your docroot lives on the same partition as /usr space, users' home directories, and a RDBMS, you'll pay for it on every single seek into that partition. Be forewarned.

Module-Specific

Different modules can have tremendous impact on Apache performance tuning. As an example, MaxRequestsPerChild has optimal settings of about 10000 on a regular server, 200–400 on one with PHP installed, and 10–30 on one with mod_perl installed. These considerations make proper server and site architecture essential. Often, a single misconfigured module can lead to disastrously slow results.

mod_perl is far and away the most complicated module to use effectively. This is largely a consequence of it being both the most powerful and the most far-reaching. Vivek Khera of the ASF has written (**perl.apache.org/tuning**) a guide to performance-tuning mod_perl. He discusses primarily the most salient performance consideration of using mod_perl: mod_perl is, by its very nature, a *huge* consumer of memory. Hence, setting MaxRequestsPerChild to a comparatively low number (somewhere from 10–30 is a good choice) helps tremendously, as the bloated children die off rapidly, rather than lingering around sucking up memory.

The use of several complex rewriting rules inside mod_rewrite can also lead to an appreciable drop in performance, especially if they are called on nearly every page on the site and/or invoke an external perl script to perform the rewriting. Consider using perlcc to precompile any external rewrites written in perl, and try not to overuse it.

mod_ssi is a performance dog, as was mentioned before. If replacing SSI with mod_perl or PHP is impractical, consider one of the "sanitized" (i.e. less bloated) replacements for the stock mod_ssi that are available. Another option that is generally not considered enough is to use a preprocessor (such as cpp) to generate the pages for a site; if a global look and feel change is desired, rather than editing the SSI-based include file (and depending on SSI to generate every page on the fly with the appropriate change), edit the preprocessor include file, rerun the preprocessor on the source files for the site, and replace the site's HTML documents wholesale.

Site-Specific

Needless to say, it is hard to elaborate on installation-specific performance tuning hints, since by definition they vary greatly from installation to installation. However, some general principles may be applied:

- The advantages of running as minimal a server binary as possible have already been discussed. This can be taken even further in some instances: run several smaller, special-purpose binaries on multiple host-names bound to distinct IP addresses. For example, if a section of the site relies heavily on mod_perl, the main site is just straight HTML, and there are a number of images on each page, you might be well-served using three separate servers: one with mod_perl, one with a "standard" collection of modules, and one "stripped" server for just images.

- Another way of getting around sticky problems regarding server hardware performance is to configure your main Web server as a server-side proxy (see Chapter 9, and remember mod_proxy has to be compiled into the binary) for one or more servers which sit behind it (from a network perspective) handling the applications load. This is really just a variation on the "application server" in the often-touted three-tier server model, with Apache serving as each of the top two tiers.

- If you are serving Java classes, package them together into .jar files. This way, the server will only have to handle one transaction to serve each application, rather than a separate transaction for each class file. As a more general rule, anything that can be bundled together for easier downloading should be bundled together: if you have people downloading an application from your site, put the application, the documentation, etc. into the same archive, unless the archive becomes so large that download errors cause users to have to attempt to retrieve it multiple times before being successful (at which point any load savings from bundling has been lost).

- On a similar note, one large image is worth half a dozen smaller ones, so whenever possible, use imagemaps in your site navigation instead of single images; your designers may miss their JavaScript rollovers, but the performance savings is often well worth it.

- It pays to know your architecture. For instance, on some systems /tmp and swap share disk/memory space. Thus, when the system is not swapping, reads/writes to /tmp are often accomplished with RAMdisk-like performance; there are numerous ways crafty developers can exploit this to milk additional performance out of scripts.

■ Finally, experimentation is the mother of performance tuning. Try different things. Small changes can sometimes effect huge improvements. For example, if you find yourself serving a lot of similar-sized documents, an appropriate adjustment to the default MTU on your system's network interface could result in a huge improvement in the performance of that interface...and the only way to know is to experiment and benchmark.

Load Balancing

Load balancing becomes necessary when traffic to a single site is so heavy that a dedicated Web server can't keep up with it. This is a nice problem to have. To balance the load, two or more servers are set up to serve the same busy site and some routing mechanism distributes requests for the site to various servers. There are thus two problems to solve: 1) replicating the site to the various servers, and 2) routing requests to the various servers.

To solve the first problem, you could copy the site, mount it, cache it, or replicate it. The easiest solution is to just copy it. A commercial Web server built by a team of people will have a development cycle. At certain points along that cycle, the new or modified Web site will be deployed to the production server. Just deploy the site several times, once for each server. This is great for incremental releases. It becomes a nightmare for frequent maintenance patches.

You could keep the site on a main server and have the replica servers mount the main server's hard drive with NFS. Deploy the software once and everybody gets it. However, this creates a bottleneck. Every request hits the same hard drive. Plus, the data hits the network twice on each request: once from the main server to the replica and again from the replica to the client.

You could configure the replica servers to act as caching proxies to the main server. This reduces hits to the main server's hard drive. This is a good solution for very static content. This is a bad solution for frequently updated content. The proxies might overwhelm the main server if documents expire quickly. You could dedicate the main server to serving requests from the caching servers (and not have the main server serve client requests). For this to be effective, you will need a minimum of three servers. If you were planning on buying more than two, this might not be a bad deal. On the other hand, if documents have a long expiry period, updates to the content will take a long time to propagate (which may or may not be a big concern). For dynamic content (script or database generated), the proxy solution simply will not work. You cannot cache dynamic content.

You could have the replicas replicate the main server's site. The replicas keep a copy of the site. When a file on the main server's site is updated, the update is detected and distributed automatically. You need not deploy the site to each replica. The replicas hit the main server only when an update has occurred. Propagation doesn't have to wait out an expiry period. Dynamic content can be generated by each replica (they have the scripts and can run them locally). For directory replication, the UNIX tool of choice is slapd/slurpd. The slapd daemon implements the Lightweight Directory Access Protocol for sharing directories and files. The slurpd daemon watches the slapd logs and, when an update entry is added to the log, the slurpd daemon uses slapd to distribute the modified file to the replicas. The source code for these daemons is available at **ftp://terminator. rs.itd.umich.edu/ldap/ldap.tar.Z** though you may already have these daemons on your system (see if you have the slapd(8) and slurpd(8) man pages). You'll find the SLAPD and SLURPD Administrators Guide at **http://www.umich.edu/ ~ dirsvcs/ldap/doc/guides/slapd/**.

To solve the second problem (request distribution), a name server can round-robin requests among the replicas. All you have to do is give all the replicas the same name (but different addresses) in the name-server database. The problem is that if a replica server goes down, the name server will just keep routing requests to it.

More elegant solutions are available commercially but cost about $10,000. On Linux, a more elegant solution is available free. Linux machines can be clustered into a Linux Virtual Server. Requests to the virtual server are caught by the lvs daemon and routed to one of the real servers in the cluster. The ipvsadm program configures the cluster. The pulse and nanny daemons watch over the cluster and implement failover. With the lvs system, you can weight each replica by its abilities and schedule more requests to faster machines. Three load-balancing algorithms are available: weighted least connection, round robin, and weighted round robin. The lvs(8), ipvsadm(8), pulse(8), and nanny(8) man pages will tell you all about it.

There is an Apache module that will perform Web load balancing. It's called mod_backhand and is available at **http://www.backhand.org/ mod_backhand**/. It runs on BSDI, NetBSD, FreeBSD, OpenBSD, Linux, and Solaris.

Using Apache on
Windows NT

Installation

Installing the Apache Server in a Windows NT 4.0 Server installation is a relatively straightforward process if certain constraints are taken into consideration. First and foremost, the Apache Server will not install successfully unless the Windows NT 4.0 machine is running an Intel Processor. At this time you can forget about running Apache on an AMD or Cyrix-based machine.

Second, you must already have TCP/IP installed and configured on the Windows NT machine. Also, the Windows NT machine should have been upgraded to Service Pack 2 prior to installation. Actually, I consider this a "given" as there should be no Windows NT 4.0 Servers currently in a production environment that have not been upgraded to at least Service Pack 5, the first release that was Year 2000 compliant. For purposes of testing the release for this chapter, Windows NT Server 4.0 Service Pack 6.0A was used.

Prior to installing an Apache server on Windows NT it is advisable to check the Apache Web site, **http://www.apache.org**, and get the latest information from the Apache community. It is also a good idea to be sure you have the latest download of the software.

The Apache Server can be installed in any directory you like or you can accept the default of `C:\Program Files\Apache Group\Apache`. A Start menu entry will be set up as Apache Web Server.

There are three selections you can make for the Install process: Typical, Custom and Minimum. In reality, there is very little difference in the three choices. All the Apache Server software will be installed in each case. However, Typical also loads the manuals, and Custom loads both the manuals and the source code.

During a normal install, Apache will place all the configuration files in `C:\Program Files\Apache Group\Apache\Conf` unless an alternate path is specified. If this is a reinstall, duplicate files will not be replaced, but a second file will be put into the directory with a .default extension to indicate it is a new version of that file.

Configuration

Although the Apache Server, once installed on Windows NT Server 4.0, should run without modification, there are a number of configuration changes that can be made and can prove quite useful. Although these differ from installation to installation, certain things can be generalized and are covered here. All the files for customizing the configuration are stored in `C:\Program Files\Apache Group\Apache\Conf`.

The primary differences for Windows NT lie in just two areas. When you are using Apache directives that accept filenames as arguments, there is a little "twist" that can be very confusing. You must, in the NT environment, use Windows file names. However, the Apache server uses UNIX conventions internally, so you cannot use the backward slash but must use a forward slash instead.

The other difference comes from the fact that, when implemented in a Windows NT environment, the Apache server is multi-threaded, not single-threaded as used in the UNIX version. This means two directives need to be set accordingly. The following text is taken directly from the Apache Web site, as it most clearly states the proper use of these directives.

> "MaxRequestsPerChild—Like the Unix directive, this controls how many requests a process will serve before exiting. However, unlike Unix, a process serves all the requests at once, not just one, so if this is set, it is recommended that a very high number is used. The recommended default, MaxRequestsPerChild 0, does not cause the process to ever exit."
>
> "ThreadsPerChild—This directive is new, and tells the server how many threads it should use. This is the maximum number of connections the server can handle at once; be sure and set this number high enough for your site if you get a lot of hits. The recommended default is ThreadsPerChild 50."

The `ThreadsPerChild` directive, provided by the Apache core, is available only in the Windows flavor of Apache.

The `UNIQUE_ID` feature is not yet available on the NT version. The UNIX version creates an ID number for every request. This ID is unique among all requests. Apache assigns this number to the `UNIQUE_ID` environment variable, which is then available to CGI scripts and certain configuration directives. Certain differences between time formats and thread styles have prevented this feature from being implemented on NT. A more portable design may be currently in the works. The `mod_unique_id` module, which is *not* a default module, provides the `UNIQUE_ID` environment variable. This module provides no directives of its own, but the lack of an expected `UNIQUE_ID` variable might affect `SetEnvIf`, `CustomLog`, and other directives.

Other than the above differences, most of the Apache configuration directives should behave the same on both the UNIX and NT platforms.

Starting and Stopping the Server

The best, and really the only effective, way to run Apache Server in the Windows NT Server 4.0 environment is to set it up as an NT Service. This will allow Apache to start on Boot Up and to remain operational whether or not an administrator has the console active.

The easiest way to set up the Apache Server as an NT service is during the Install process. Select the option "Install Apache as Service" and let the install program do the rest. Unless you are an experienced NT and Apache administrator, I would strongly recommend you take this approach until you have set up a number of Apache/NT operations. Letting the Installer automatically establish the Service in NT will cause the default Service, Apache, to be set up in NT. Windows NT Server 4.0 is a multi-tasking environment, and as such can accommodate more than one consecutive Apache Service. These can be installed under any name you choose and can be placed into Windows NT at any time.

To install additional Apache Services under NT is relatively simple. Just type on the command line `apache -i -n` and the name of the new Service. Remember, the default "Apache" is already running and cannot be re-used. If you have set up a configuration other than the default, you can specify it for the new Service by typing `apache -I -n servicename -f \C:\Program Files\Apache Group\Apache\Conf\special.conf` or whatever path you used to install Apache if you did not use the defaults.

Once Apache has been installed as a Windows NT service, it can be started and stopped in two ways. First, you can go to the Control Panel by clicking START, then SETTINGS and finally CONTROL PANEL. Double click on the SERVICES icon, select Apache and then click on START. This will start the Apache Server running in the background.

To stop the Apache Server, simple repeat the same process: START, then SETTINGS, then CONTROL PANEL and double click on the SERVICES icon and select STOP.

If you don't want to bother with the control panel, and most of us don't, then you can start and stop the Apache Server from the command line. The commands are quite simple:

```
Net START Apache
Net STOP Apache
```

It's as easy as that.

After the Apache Server is running under Windows NT you will want to access it from time to time to monitor activity and so on. Doing this is extremely simple. Just launch any browser (MS Internet Explorer or Netscape are preferred) and enter the URL **http://localhost/**. This will take you to the welcome page.

Windows-Specific Considerations

The primary difference in running Apache in the Windows NT Server 4.0 environment is that you must remember that you may have multiple Apache Services running at any one time and that each is a unique entity and must be managed as such. This means that each will have its own set of directives in the configuration and will operate differently from other Apache Services. As an NT and Apache administrator you will need to devise a scheme to allow you to know *which* Apache Service is in question whenever a problem arises or someone calls with a question.

You must also remember that each Service is started and stopped individually. This will cause you to modify the START and STOP commands as follows:

```
Net START "apacheservicename"
Net STOP "apacheservicename"
```

You can also signal an Apache Service from the command line with the following commands:

```
Apache -n "apacheservicename" -k start
```

Starts the particular Apache Service.

```
Apache -n "apacheservicename" -k restart
```

Causes the Service to restart and the Configuration files to be re-read.

```
Apache -n "apacheservicename" -k shutdown
```

This is the best way to do and orderly shutdown of an Apache Service.

Module mod_so is a default module in the Windows environment; not a default module in the UNIX environment. It is used to load .dll modules at runtime and replaces mod_dll, which should now be considered obsolete. No recompile is required as the .dlls are loaded at runtime using the Dynamic Shared Object mechanism. To use this approach effectively, you must first create the appropriate .dll files from the modules you would have used for a UNIX installation. After having done this, you can load them at run time using the LoadModule directive.

Module mod_isapi is compiled in the Windows environment and allows for use of ISAPI (Internet Server Applications Program Interface) Extensions in that environment. These Internet Server applications operate within Apache when running under Windows. This ISAPI implementation conforms to all ISAPI 2.0 specifications except for the Microsoft-specific extensions dealing with Asynchronous I/O, which is not supported by Apache.

Configuration Files

The Apache server will actually read three different files for Configuration directives to use with Windows NT:

- Conf/httpd.conf—Controls operation of the server daemon.
- Conf/srm.conf—Controls the specification of documents.
- Conf/access.conf—Controls the entity for access to documents.

Log Files

Beware of the log files. Anyone who can gain access to the log files can find a means of accessing virtually all of the files on the server. DO NOT give write access to them.

- **PID File**—Another log file type that holds the process id of the parent http process.
- **Error Log**—Error message generated by Apache for tracking problems after they occur.
- **Transfer Log**—A log of requests for transfer of file.

Keep-Alive Support

It is not recommended that the KeepAlive directive be used with Windows at this time. It is known to create a number of problems and can cause the NT Server to "hang" and require a restart. Older versions of

Internet Explorer and Netscape are also known to have problems with the `KeepAlive` option.

Other differences exist, but you will run across them soon enough as you run your Apache Server from day to day. Don't forget that the Apache Web site is an excellent source of detailed information on the most current data regarding running Apache in any environment, including Windows NT Server 4.0.

Programming the Apache Server

Introduction

This chapter will help you navigate the Apache module API and some of the Apache internals. It is not meant to be an exhaustive treatment of the modules inside Apache or the Apache API but rather an overview of how Apache works, where modules fit in the Apache scheme of things, how they do their jobs, and what you need to do to write a module. In this chapter, we'll cover the following topics:

- Common questions
- The structure and contents of the Apache source tree
- The life cycle of an Apache module
- The anatomy of an Apache module
- The important structures involved in an Apache module
- The important Apache APIs including
    - Memory API
    - Configuration API
    - Logging API
    - Request Servicing API
    - Cleanup API
    - Configuration API
- Creating a module
- Writing a module
- Debugging a module.

Common Questions

What is an Apache module?

An Apache module is a library of functions that implement callbacks (function pointers stored in a `module` structure) that are called at specific points during an HTTP transaction. Modules can be invoked at any phase while servicing an HTTP request for any reason. For example, a module can be invoked based on the requested MIME type, the directory of the requested URI, or the IP address of the requesting client, etc. In fact, most of the Apache Web server itself is written using modules. It makes tremendous sense if you think about it: a core set of protocol handlers and a process loop that calls "helper functions" during each phase of the HTTP request. In this way, Apache may be extended indefinitely.

What modules are available?

There are three kinds: The standard modules included with the Apache distribution, third-party modules, and those you write yourself.

- You will find a list of the standard modules at
  http://www.apache. org/docs/mod/index.html
- You can find many third-party modules in the Apache module registry
  http://modules.apache.org/
- Your modules may be found at **http://still/in/your/head/**.

How do I find what modules are loaded at runtime?
If your server is configured with info enabled then just browse to **http://myserver/server-info/**.
Why would I want to write a module?

- If you have an expensive or time critical task to perform
- If you want to modify the fundamental behavior of your Apache server
- If you want to distribute proprietary server-based software
- If you want to implement a new protocol wrapped by HTTP
- If you want to extend HTTP
- If you have new and interesting content that needs to be served in a special way
- If you have an applet, control, or plug-in that you want to control interactively
- If you want to control a device.

The list is endless.
How do I write a module?
Read on.

The Apache Source Tree

The Apache source tree is structured like this:
The top level directory looks similar to the Apache `install` directory tree:

```
|-- cgi-bin          Where CGI programs reside
|-- conf             The apache configuration files
|-- htdocs           HTML documents
|-- icons            Images for FTP directory displays, etc
|-- logs             The access, transfer, and error logs
`-- src              The Apache source tree
```

Inside the src directory lives all the interesting stuff:

```
'-- src
    |-- ap               The apache API code. Compiles into libap.a
    |-- helpers          Scripts to help compile and link apache
    |-- include          All the apache include files
    |-- lib              External libraries
    |   `-- expat-lite   James Clark's XML parser
    |-- main             The apache core code. Compiles into libmain.a
    |-- modules          Where all modules live
    |   |-- ferret       Our example module mod_ferret
    |   |-- example      The apache example module shell
    |   |-- experimental Where experimental modules live
    |   |-- extra        Currently empty
    |   |-- php4         If you have PHP4 this is where it lives
    |   |-- proxy        The apache proxy/caching module
    |   |-- standard     Standard apache modules
    |   `-- tcod         An experimental module of mine
    |-- os               OS specific directories
    |   |-- bs2000       Siemens Open Server Dimension BS2000
    |   |-- os2          IBM's OS/2
    |   |-- tpf          IBM's Transaction Processing Facilty
    |   |   '-- samples
    |   |-- unix         Unices of almost all varieties
    |   `-- win32        Windows 32 bit versions and the endless
    |       `-- installer    minutia they require
    |           `-- installdll
    |               `-- test
    |-- regex            Henry Spencer's regular expression library
    `-- support          man pages and module compilation utilities
        `-- SHA1         Utilities to use NIST Secure Hash Alg passwords
```

The Life of a Module

How Apache Executes

How Apache works is interesting and crucial to the understanding of how a module works and what it can actually do. In some Web server APIs, the "plug-in" architecture is limited and severely restricts what you can do at various points in the HTTP transaction. This is irritating. Apache's API has no such limitations. In fact, if you haven't noticed already, most of Apache itself is implemented with the module API. With the exception of the core HTTP functions, structures, and error-handling routines, Apache is implemented with modules. Studying the standard modules is really the best way to learn how modules work. The standard modules are in the directory `src/modules/standard` if you're the curious and adventuresome sort.

When the Apache Web server starts, it initializes its variable, and allocates memory. Then it parses its command-line parameters, opens, and parses the various configuration files. When this process encounters directives in the configuration files requiring modules, each directive is parsed according to a module supplied configuration function. (Refer to the `module` structure in the `const command_rec *ferrets;` field.) Directives in the configuration files are processed linearly so be careful in editing your configuration file. A misplaced configuration directive can throw some really interesting and non-intuitive errors making the entire server exit. Errors in a `<VirtualHost … >` section will usually result in the entire server's aborting, not just that one site. So make certain that you have all your virtual hosts in order or none of your Web sites will start!

Apache starts as root then immediately forks child processes that have no, or almost no, privileges. Usually this user is "www" or "nobody" or "http". Since Apache starts as root, the child processes inherit handy and essential file handles from their parent server process. This includes file handles like `logs/error_log` and `logs/access_log`. At this point Apache begins to run the request loop, a series of decisions that must be made for each request of the server processes. At every point a module has the ability to handle each decision. Every module installed has the opportunity to handle every one of the phases described below. All the installed handlers will be executed, unless one returns an error or `DONE`. The modules are invoked in the order they loaded. This is another important detail. Some modules have dependencies on other modules, so the load order of modules can be a crucial issue.

Let's look at each phase of this loop below. The name of each phase will be followed by the function prototype that implements the callback for that phase of the request loop.

The module structure that holds the each callback looks more or less like this:

```
struct {
    ... (stuff omitted)  /* magic numbers and names and ... */
    void (*init) (server_rec *, pool *);  /* module init phase of the request loop */
    ... (stuff omitted )             /* configuration record merge callbacks */
    const command_rec ferrets;    /* List of parsers for commands in the config files */
    const handler_rec handlers;   /* List of handlers for mime types */
    int (*translate_handler) (request_rec *);  /* URI Translation phase */
    int (*ap_check_user_id) (request_rec *);   /* Authentication phase */
    int (*auth_checker) (request_rec *);       /* Authorization phase */
    int (*access_checker) (request_rec *);     /* Access Control phase */
    int (*type_checker) (request_rec *);       /* MIME type checking phase */
    int (*fixer_upper) (request_rec *);        /* fixups phase */
    int (*logger) (request_rec *);             /* log handler */
    int (*header_parser) (request_rec *);      /* header parsing phase */
    void (*child_init) (server_rec *, pool *); /* init phase */
    void (*child_exit) (server_rec *, pool *); /* exit phase */
    int (*post_read_request) (request_rec *);  /* post read request phase */
} module;
```

The order of the fields in the structure has no real relation to the order of execution inside the request loop. Refer to the module structure definition below for more details. Generally, each callback is passed a record pointer to either the server or the request. It will also be passed a memory pool pointer. Memory pools are managed memory structures Apache uses to help prevent memory management errors and maintain sanity. Memory pools and their use are described in some detail below.

What follows is a description of each phase of the request loop and the field in the module structure that contains the callback for that phase. As a module writer you may implement as many, or as few, callbacks as you wish.

Module Initialization—void (*init) (server_rec *, pool *);

After Apache starts and parses the configuration files it calls each module's initialization function in the module structure. As you can see from this prototype, this function is passed a pointer to a server record (described below) and a memory pool pointer (also described below). This memory pool is server-wide memory so it will exist until the entire server dies. Any memory object that each instance of your module may want to share should use this memory pool. The code in the init function runs as root and no child processes have spawned yet. The module src/modules/standard/mod_mime.c is a good example of using server-wide memory. This module creates a hash table in server-wide memory of each mime type for use by child instances of mod_mime.

Child Initialization—`void (*child_init) (server_rec *, pool *);`

After the module initialization, Apache forks itself into several servers (see the `MinSpareServers` and `MaxSpareServers` configuration directives usually found in `conf/httpd.conf`). Each child has the opportunity to initialize itself with this function. This is particularly handy for database handles and other resources that don't survive a fork or require a per-instance initialization. Whatever infrastructure you need to handle requests should be built during this phase. Don't initialize per-request data here though. That happens in the next phase.

Post Read Request—`int (*post_read_request) (request_rec *);`

This is the first handler called by Apache after it receives a valid HTTP request. Since it is the first handler called, it is a good place to initialize per-request data. This might be anything that subsequent handlers in the request loop might need during a particular request. A good example of this is the standard module `src/modules/standard/mod_unique_id.c`. This module generates and verifies unique IDs from client requests on a per request basis.

URI Translation—`int (*translate_handler) (request_rec *);`

This phase of the request loop concerns itself with deciding what the URI actually is. It determines where the file lives in the file system through the eyes of Apache. It could be a memory buffer or the output of an external program but the request must translate to a location in the file system (with optional material after the location) so that Apache may handle the request. This "file" will be used in access control directives. The directives

```
Alias
ScriptAlias
DocumentRoot
```

found in the configuration are examples of translation. The standard module `src/modules/standard/mod_rewrite.c` is an example of taking control at this phase. After pasting `DocumentRoot` to the beginning of the request, Apache parses the request to a location in the file system. Everything after the last valid location in the file system is regarded as extra data and can be treated as parameters to any handler that cares to parse them.

Header Parser—`int (*header_parser) (request_rec *);`

The header parser phase allows installed modules to handle the incoming request's headers. The modules may ignore, examine, modify, or entirely alter the incoming headers. The header parser phase is good for implementing proxy servers and blocking robots or implementing your own HTTP method. For example, you'll need to rewrite the headers to proxy the request, you'll want to block nasty robots before they consume any significant resources, and if you don't parse your new HTTP method yourself, the server will return `HTTP_NOT_IMPLEMENTED`. None of the modules included with Apache implements a header parser.

Access Control—`int (*access_checker) (request_rec *);`

This phase of the request loop concerns itself with whether or not access is allowed to a resource. Access can be controlled at this point, without ever knowing who is attempting to access the URI, by the time, date, requesting IP address, or some other method that doesn't require user identification. For example, if a URI requires access to another process, and that process is not running, then you would want to deny access to that URI. The standard module `src/modules/standard/mod_access.c` implements an access control function.

Authentication—`int (*ap_check_user_id) (request_rec *);`

This phase establishes who the user is. It allows the exchange of credentials such as a username and a password or some other crypto token. If you wanted to roll your own password encryption scheme, or validate users from a database, this would be the place to do it. A good example is the standard module `src/modules/standard/mod_auth.c` which implements an authentication handler.

Authorization—`int (*ap_auth_checker) (request_rec *);`

The authorization phase of the request loop concerns itself with whether or not the user (having now been authenticated during the authentication phase) has the proper authorization to access the requested URI. A good example is the standard module `src/modules/standard/mod_auth.c`, which implements an authorization handler. There are many nifty authorization and authentication modules to be found at **http://modules.apache.org/**. These include authentication via LDAP, NIS, LDAP, MySQL, mSQL, DCE, NDS, Lotus Notes, Windows NT, PostgreSQL, RADIUS, dbm, db, Samba (LAN Manager), SiteMinder, PAM,

ACE, and any random external process. As you can see, this is a very popular variety of module to write. A real-world example is a video server. Now that you know *who* is logging in, you need to find out *whether* they see what they requested.

Type checking—`int (*type_checker) (request_rec *);`

The type-checking phase of the request loop concerns itself with determining the MIME type and encoding of the requested document. The standard module `src/modules/standard/mod_mime.c` implements a MIME type handler.

Usually, the MIME type is determined by the extension of the file referenced by the requested URI. The file `conf/mime.types` is a table with record pairs delimited by white space. Each pair is composed of the MIME type and then file extension(s) associated with that type. This file of MIME types is used along with the `AddType` and `AddEncoding` directives to determine types and encodings. The MIME type checker can also perform the task of assigning a content handler based on the `SetHandler` directive.

Fixups—`int (*fixer_upper) (request_rec *);`

The fixup phase is a last chance to handle the request before the response handler is called to do its duty. The standard modules `mod_headers.c`, `mod_alias.c`, `mod_cern_meta.c`, `mod_expires.c`, `mod_headers.c`, `mod_negotiation.c`, `mod_rewrite.c`, `mod_spelling.c`, and `mod_usertrack.c` all implement the "fixer_upper" handler. All these modules may all be found in the `src/modules/standard` directory of the Apache source tree. As you can see, this is really a utility phase for any last-minute munging of the request, or the behavior of the server, before the response actually gets processed and sent back to the client. Use it at your discretion; any task appropriate for a request already passed through all the previous phases of the request loop, but not a response, is a good candidate. The best example of the group mentioned above is probably `mod_usertrack.c`. That module implements cookie-based user tracking. User tracking is not really any of the steps listed so far; nor is it a response to the client; but we know when we get called in a `fixer_upper` that the request has been validated. This is a last chance to act before you speak.

Response

This is where "content handlers" live. If you want to produce your own dynamic HTML output, this is the phase to hook. This is where your module writes back to the client, opens the pipe, and streams the data to the waiting browser. PHP4 is a great example. You will find PHP4 at **http://www.php.net/version4/downloads.php**.

A module may have as many or as few content handlers as the need. They are held in a list of structures. Each structure contains a function pointer to the handler and the MIME type that invokes the handler.

Logging—int (*logger) (request_rec *);

After the response to a request has been sent, Apache has a logging phase. Once the request has been serviced we have a complete record of the transaction. We know whether, who, from where requested, what, how, when, and how much they got. That's a perfect time to log.

Cleanup

This phase is after the entire HTTP transaction has completed, so it has some special utility. The cleanup phase is particularly handy for releasing database handles and resources not allocated from the module's special memory pool. This phase is reflexive with the POST-READ-REQUEST phase.

Child Exit—void (*child_exit) (server_rec *, pool *);

The child exit handler should tear down whatever the child init handler built. Remember, a child usually runs MaxRequestsPerChild times and then exits, so the resources released in this handler should have lived though multiple requests. Per-request data should already have been released by the time this handler is called.

The Anatomy of a Module

Important Structures

Apache has a surprisingly small number of structures that manage to run the entire web server machine. Modules only have to be concerned with a few of them and we will try to cover them here.

Module

The module from include/http_config.h holds a number of callbacks that are called at different phases of the request loop.

```
typedef struct module_struct {
    int version;                       /* API version, *not* module version;
                                        * check that module is compatible with this
                                        * version of the server. */
    int minor_version;                 /* API minor version. Provides API feature
                                        * milestones. Not checked during module init. */
    int module_index;                  /* Index to this modules structures in
                                        * config vectors. */
    const char name;                   /* The name of the module */
    void dynamic_load_handle;          /* DSO handling mechanism */
    struct module_struct next;         /* pointer to the next module installed */
    unsigned long magic;               /* Magic Cookie to identify a module structure;
                                        * It's mainly important for the DSO facility
                                        * (see also mod_so). */
/* init() occurs after config parsing, but before any children are
 * forked.
 * Modules should not rely on the order in which create_server_config
 * and create_dir_config are called. */
    void (*init) (server_rec *, pool *);
    void *(*create_dir_config) (pool *p, char *dir);
    void *(*merge_dir_config) (pool *p, void *base_conf, void *new_conf);
    void *(*create_server_config) (pool *p, server_rec *s);
    void *(*merge_server_config) (pool *p, void *base_conf, void *new_conf);
    const command_rec cmds;    /* List of parsers for commands in the config files */
    const handler_rec handlers; /* List of handlers for mime types */
    /* Hooks for getting into the middle of server ops...
     * translate_handler --- translate URI to filename
     * access_checker --- check access by host address, etc.  All of these
     *            run; if all decline, that's still OK.
     * check_user_id --- get and validate user id from the HTTP request
     * auth_checker --- see if the user (from check_user_id) is OK *here*.
     *            If all of *these* decline, the request is rejected
     *            (as a SERVER_ERROR, since the module which was
     *            supposed to handle this was configured wrong).
     * type_checker --- Determine MIME type of the requested entity;
     *            sets content_type, _encoding and _language fields.
     * logger --- log a transaction.
     * post_read_request --- run right after read_request or internal_redirect,
     *            and not run during any subrequests.
     */
    int (*translate_handler) (request_rec *);
    int (*ap_check_user_id) (request_rec *);
    int (*auth_checker) (request_rec *);
    int (*access_checker) (request_rec *);
    int (*type_checker) (request_rec *);
    int (*fixer_upper) (request_rec *);
    int (*logger) (request_rec *);
    int (*header_parser) (request_rec *);
```

```
/* Regardless of the model the server uses for managing "units of
 * execution", i.e. multi-process, multi-threaded, hybrids of those,
 * there is the concept of a "heavy weight process". That is, a
 * process with its own memory space, file spaces, etc. This method,
 * child_init, is called once for each heavy-weight process before
 * any requests are served. Note that no provision is made yet for
 * initialization per light-weight process (i.e. thread). The
 * parameters passed here are the same as those passed to the global
 * init method above.
 */
void (*child_init) (server_rec *, pool *);
void (*child_exit) (server_rec *, pool *);
int (*post_read_request) (request_rec *);
} module;
```

The `handler_rec` structure holds a response handler callback and the MIME type that invokes that response handler.

```
typedef struct {
    const char *content_type;       /* MUST be all lower case */
    int (*handler) (request_rec *);  /* The response handler */
} handler_rec;
```

The `command_rec` structure contains the name, parser, data, argument types, and error message associated with a particular directive that we would find in a configuration file.

```
typedef struct command_struct {
    const char *name;         /* Name of this command */
    const char *(*func) ();   /* Function invoked */
    void *cmd_data;           /* Extra data, for functions which
                               * implement multiple commands... */
    int req_override;         /* What overrides need to be allowed to
                               * enable this command. */
    enum cmd_how args_how;    /* What the command expects as arguments */
    const char *errmsg;       /* 'usage' message, in case of syntax errors */
} command_rec;
```

There are three other important structures that we've seen referred to here but not described. They are the `request_rec`, the `conn_rec`, and the `server_rec`. We will cover them below.

What a module returns and what it means

A module may return any valid HTTP return code (see the Appendix, the section "HTTP Status Codes").

```
#define DECLINED -1 /* Module declines to handle */

#define DONE -2        /* Module has served the response completely
                        * - it's safe to die() with no more output */
#define OK 0           /* Module has handled this stage. */


/* ----------------- HTTP Status Codes ------------------- */
/* The size of the static array in http_protocol.c for storing
 * all of the potential response status-lines (a sparse table).
 * A future version should dynamically generate the table at
startup.
 */
#define RESPONSE_CODES 55

#define HTTP_CONTINUE                            100
#define HTTP_SWITCHING_PROTOCOLS                 101
#define HTTP_PROCESSING                          102
#define HTTP_OK                                  200
#define HTTP_CREATED                             201
#define HTTP_ACCEPTED                            202
#define HTTP_NON_AUTHORITATIVE                   203
#define HTTP_NO_CONTENT                          204
#define HTTP_RESET_CONTENT                       205
#define HTTP_PARTIAL_CONTENT                     206
#define HTTP_MULTI_STATUS                        207
#define HTTP_MULTIPLE_CHOICES                    300
#define HTTP_MOVED_PERMANENTLY                   301
#define HTTP_MOVED_TEMPORARILY                   302
#define HTTP_SEE_OTHER                           303
#define HTTP_NOT_MODIFIED                        304
#define HTTP_USE_PROXY                           305
#define HTTP_TEMPORARY_REDIRECT                  307
#define HTTP_BAD_REQUEST                         400
#define HTTP_UNAUTHORIZED                        401
#define HTTP_PAYMENT_REQUIRED                    402
#define HTTP_FORBIDDEN                           403
#define HTTP_NOT_FOUND                           404
#define HTTP_METHOD_NOT_ALLOWED                  405
#define HTTP_NOT_ACCEPTABLE                      406
#define HTTP_PROXY_AUTHENTICATION_REQUIRED       407
#define HTTP_REQUEST_TIME_OUT                    408
#define HTTP_CONFLICT                            409
#define HTTP_GONE                                410
#define HTTP_LENGTH_REQUIRED                     411
#define HTTP_PRECONDITION_FAILED                 412
#define HTTP_REQUEST_ENTITY_TOO_LARGE            413
#define HTTP_REQUEST_URI_TOO_LARGE               414
```

```
#define HTTP_UNSUPPORTED_MEDIA_TYPE           415
#define HTTP_RANGE_NOT_SATISFIABLE            416
#define HTTP_EXPECTATION_FAILED               417
#define HTTP_UNPROCESSABLE_ENTITY             422
#define HTTP_LOCKED                           423
#define HTTP_FAILED_DEPENDENCY                424
#define HTTP_INTERNAL_SERVER_ERROR            500
#define HTTP_NOT_IMPLEMENTED                  501
#define HTTP_BAD_GATEWAY                      502
#define HTTP_SERVICE_UNAVAILABLE              503
#define HTTP_GATEWAY_TIME_OUT                 504
#define HTTP_VERSION_NOT_SUPPORTED            505
#define HTTP_VARIANT_ALSO_VARIES              506
#define HTTP_INSUFFICIENT_STORAGE             507
#define HTTP_NOT_EXTENDED                     510
```

The guts of a module

Let's build a simple content handler, sometimes called a response handler. A content handler is a module that creates content of some sort based on a SetHandler or AddHandler directive. At the very minimum a content handler module must contain the following items:

- Some standard headers
- A response (or content) handler
- An entry in a handler_rec
- A module record with an entry for the handler_rec

Here is a bare-bones module that handles a .ferret file type.

```
/*----------------------------------------------------------------------
 * name: mod_ferret
 * synopsis:
 * description: implements a simple Apache response handler
 * returns: OK
 * errors:
 * calls: Apache API
 * notes:
 *----------------------------------------------------------------------
/* The minimum apache includes */
#include "httpd.h"
#include "http_config.h"
#include "http_core.h"
#include "http_log.h"
#include "http_protocol.h"
```

```
/* Our content handler. This ends up being in the module record */
static int ferret_handler( request_rec *r )
{
    const char cpHostName;    /* place to store the calling hostname */

    ap_send_http_header( r );  /* send a standard HTTP header */
    cpHostname = ap_get_remore_host( r->connection,       /* this connection */
                    r->per_dir_config,                    /* for this directory */
                    REMOTE_NAME );                        /* give us the hostname */
    /* send the content body */
    ap_rputs( "<HTML>\n" , r );
    ap_rputs( "<HEAD>\n", r );
    ap_rputs( "<TITLE>This is the ferret module talking…</TITLE>\n", r );
    ap_rputs( "</HEAD>\n", r );
    ap_rputs( "<BODY>\n", r );
    ap_rprintf( r, "<H1>Hello %s!</H1>\n", cpHostName );
    ap_rputs( "</BODY>\n", r );
    ap_rputs( "</HTML>\n", r );
    return OK;
}

/* Our list of content handler records */
static handler_rec ferret_handlers =
{
    { "ferret-handler", ferret_handler },
    { NULL }
};

/* Our module structure. */
module ferret_module =
{
    STANDARD_MODULE_STUFF, /* macro containing all the non-callback members of
module */
    NULL,               /* module initializer */
    NULL,               /* per-directory config creator */
    NULL,               /* dir config merger */
    NULL,               /* server config creator */
    NULL,               /* server config merger */
    NULL,               /* command table */
    ferret_handlers,    /* [7] list of handlers */
    NULL,               /* [2] filename-to-URI translation */
    NULL,               /* [5] check/validate user_id */
    NULL,               /* [6] check user_id is valid *here* */
    NULL,               /* [4] check access by host address */
    NULL,               /* [7] MIME type checker/setter */
    NULL,               /* [8] fixups */
    NULL,               /* [10] logger */
    NULL,               /* [3] header parser */
    NULL,               /* process initializer */
```

```
    NULL,                    /* process exit/cleanup */
    NULL                     /* [1] post read_request handling */
};

                        /* end of file mod_ferret.txt */
```

Creating Your New MIME Type

In order to call your new module (if it's a content handler), you'll have to create a new MIME type. Your system may look in several places for MIME types. Usually, MIME types are kept in the `mime.type` file either in `/etc` or in your Apache `conf` subdirectory. For your Apache Web server actually to know what module to invoke when it runs across this new MIME type, you must tell it in one of the .conf files. New MIME types should go in `conf/httpd.conf`. Our new MIME type is a .`ferret` type. In we would have an entry like this:

```
AddType image/x-our-nifty-new-type .ferret
```

To add the handler, add a line (usually right under this one) that reads:

```
AddHandler ferret-handler .ferret
```

Notice the first field after the `AddHandler` directive. It is "ferret-handler". This must match the `content_type` field in the `handler_rec` structure:

```
typedef struct {
    const char *content_type;        /* MUST be all lower case */
    int (*handler) (request_rec *);  /* The response handler */
} handler_rec;
```

In our example, the `handler_rec` looks like this:

```
static handler_rec ferret_handler =
{
    { "ferret-handler", ferret_handler },
    { NULL }
};
```

Your module can also be called based on other directives. Usually, you'll include a block like this one somewhere in your `srm.conf` or (if you're more modern) in `httpd.conf`. (See Chapter 2: "Creating the Web Server," the section "Configuring the Installed Server," the subsection

"Directive Scopes." Also, see Chapter 4: Manipulating Content, the section "Configuring MIME".)

```
<Location /info-location>
    SetHandler ferret-handler
</Location>
```

In this case, any request that asks for content from the /info-location directory will call the ferret-handler function. SetHandler may be used within Location, Directory, and Files directives. Below are examples for the Directory and Files directives. For all files in the directory /info-directory the handler info-handler will be called while in the Files example all files that contain the string "-goo-" the handler goo-handler will be called.

```
<Directory /info-directory>
    SetHandler info-handler
</Directory>
```

```
<Files *-goo-*>
    SetHandler goo-handler
</Location>
```

There is no UnSetHandler directive in Apache. However, you can do essentially the same thing by setting the handler back to the default handler. For example, to reset the Files directive above we could issue the directive:

```
<Files *-goo-*>
    SetHandler default-handler
</Location>
```

This has the same effect as an UnSetHandler directive would if it existed and had the expected behavior.

Creating Your Module

Getting your module into the Apache source tree can be confusing. The best place to start is with the file src/modules/example/README. The README explains how to take the excellent example module and use it inside Apache.

The Apache source tree is managed by a configure script and Makefile. To include our module in the source tree we conduct the following steps:

Step 1: Create the source directory for you module

Create a directory under `src/modules` where our test module resides. Let's call it `src/modules/ferret`.

Step 2: Insert source code

At the very minimum we want `src/modules/ferret/mod_ferret.c` to exist.

Step 3: Configure Apache

Run `./configure` in the directory with the following command line options:

```
./Configure -activate-modle=src/modules/ferret/mod_ferret.c \
--enable-module=ferret
```

The configure scripts makes Apache aware that it has a new module in the `src/modules` directory that it needs to process. During configuration Apache will make entries in the files:

- `src/Configuration.apci`
- `src/Makefile`
- `src/modules.c`

You will need to copy the Makefile from `src/modules/` example and replace the instances of "example" with "ferret." If you have any special library or include paths for your own dependencies, put them in that makefile. The procedure above will create the module as statically linked within Apache.

The output should look something like this:

```
% ./configure --activate-module=src/modules/ferret/mod_ferret.c \
    --enable-module=ferret
Configuring for Apache, Version 1.3.9
 + using installation path layout: Apache (config.layout)
 + activated ferret module (modules/ferret/mod_ferret.c)
```

```
Creating Makefile
Creating Configuration.apaci in src
Creating Makefile in src
 + configured for Linux platform
 + setting C compiler to gcc
 + setting C pre-processor to gcc -E
 + checking for system header files
 + adding selected modules
 + checking sizeof various data types
 + doing sanity check on compiler and options
Creating Makefile in src/support
Creating Makefile in src/regex
Creating Makefile in src/os/unix
Creating Makefile in src/ap
Creating Makefile in src/main
Creating Makefile in src/lib/expat-lite
Creating Makefile in src/modules/standard
```

At this point it's time to compile.

Compiling and Linking Fineries

Apache can link with its modules in a couple of ways. Modules may be statically linked or they may dynamically linked with the main Apache HTTPD file. It is easier and faster just to compile and link a static HTTPD than to set up a dynamically linked module. However, for production servers, it is probably better to manage your modules separately from your Apache binary. That is, compile them as .so files that may be dynamically linked. That makes maintenance of both your modules and the Apache core much easier. A great example of this is the Apache distribution inside RedHat Linux. For just playing though, a statically linked Apache is fine.

Monolithic Linkage

After following the steps above to configure Apache to recognize your module, type Make in the src/ subdirectory. The result is a new httpd with your module statically linked and ready to run. There is a certainty about recompiling Apache in its entirety but it can be a hassle to reinstall every time.

Dynamically Loadable Module

Since version 1.3, Apache has had the ability to load modules dynamically at runtime. This is really one of the most attractive things about Apache. Once you build the module as a `.so` file and put it in a location known to Apache, place an `AddModule` entry in `conf/httpd.conf` and then restart the server. Voila! Your module is installed and working along side all the other Apache modules. Feel the power.

For dynamic loading to work, you must be on a system with the ability to load object code dynamically. Linux, FreeBSD, AIX, IRIX, and Solaris are systems that have dynamic loading available. You must also have enabled the module `mod_so`. `Mod_so` lives in the `src/modules/standard` subdirectory and is *not* enabled by default. You must configure Apache to use `mod_so`. To do that, the configuration process must change a bit. The new configure command would be:

```
% ./configure -enable-module=so
```

This command enables dynamic loading in Apache.

Now that we have an HTTPD that can dynamically load modules, we can include our test module in the configure process like this:

```
% ./configure --activate-module=src/modules/ferret/mod_ferret.c \
     --enable-shared=ferret
```

This instructs Apache to compile `mod_ferret.c` to `mod_ferret.so`. The happy side effect of doing this is that the `--enable-shared=ferret` automatically enables `mod_so` in Apache. Now make as usual and place the resultant `mod_ferret.so` file in the modules subdirectory. In RedHat 6.x it would live in `/etc/httpd/modules` and in a standard Apache source install it would be in `/usr/local/apache/libexec`. The configure option `-libexecdir` controls where Apache looks for its modules.

The next step is to enable the module in the `conf/httpd.conf` file. Add the entry

```
LoadModule ferret_module libexec/mod_ferret.so
```

to your `conf/httpd.conf` file.

Now start or restart your Apache server and you will run with the new, dynamically loaded, `mod_ferret.so` module!

APXS

The Apache wizards have included a nifty Perl scriptoid to aid in the building and installation of dynamically loaded modules. This script is APXS. In the source distribution it lives in `src/support/apxs`. An installed Apache server should have APXS in `bin/apxs`. APXS is an acronym for APache EXtenSion tool. You can see that the process of configuring, compiling, linking, and installing a new module can be a little daunting. APXS takes care of all that. It compiles, configures, and installs a new module. If you type `apxs` with no parameters you should see

```
Usage: apxs -g [-S <var>=<val>] -n <modname>
       apxs -q [-S <var>=<val>] <query> ...
       apxs -c [-S <var>=<val>] [-o <dsofile>] [-D <name>[=<value>]]
               [-I <incdir>] [-L <libdir>] [-l <libname>] [-Wc,<flags>]
               [-Wl,<flags>] <files> ...
       apxs -i [-S <var>=<val>] [-a] [-A] [-n <modname>] <dsofile> ...
       apxs -e [-S <var>=<val>] [-a] [-A] [-n <modname>] <dsofile> ...
```

For example, to use APXS on our test module we would type:

```
% apxs -c -i -a mod_ferret.c
```

The `-c` option will compile the module.
The `-i` option will install the module.
The `-a` option will adds a `LoadModule` directive to your `conf/httpd.conf` file.
There are several time-saving features in APXS that make it an indispensable tool for developing Apache modules:

- It allows the management of your module source outside the Apache source tree.
- It has the ability to create skeleton modules and Makefiles ready for work (`-g`).
- It checks your development environment and publishes important paths for use in your own environment and makefiles (`-q`).

A complete treatment of APXS may be found in the APXS man page.

```
% man 8 apxs
```

should do the trick. Otherwise look in the `src/support` directory in the Apache source distribution for `apxs.8`.

Debugging the Module

Now we have the module configured, compiled, and installed. It is working and we're happy but not quite totally equipped yet. We need to be able to debug. It would be nice to be able to step through your module or even the innards of Apache to see what's really going on. Since Apache is a server, this can be strange and not as straightforward as debugging CGI scripts or more pedestrian C code.

The following section concerns itself with gdb but many of the issues regarding debugging Apache are independent of the debugger.

The first thing we need to make certain of is that Apache is compiled with debugging enabled. By far the easiest way to do this is to set the CFLAGS environment variable before you run the ./configure script. For example:

```
% CFLAGS=-g ./configure --activate-
module=src/modules/ferret/mod_ferret.c \
    --enable-shared=ferret
```

Then compile Apache as usual and you're ready to debug. Beware; this command is all one line! The CFLAGS on this command line is not the CFLAGS environment variable. It is a GNU configuration.

When Apache starts, it usually forks several processes. These processes are ready and waiting to service HTTP requests. Having multiple processes running doesn't help our debugging efforts. Which process should we debug? Which will receive the request?

We can tell Apache to run in the foreground and NOT fork processes with the -X command line parameter. For example:

```
% gdb httpd
(gdb) run -X -f /home/programmerX/httpd.conf
```

The -X parameter should allow Apache to cooperate with any debugger, not just gdb.

The -f parameter tells Apache to use another configuration file. In the alternate httpd.conf file you might want to define alternate log files to confine your debugging efforts and their results. Don't forget to change the PidFile and ScoreBoardFile as well, to avoid conflicts with an already running Apache that may not be primed for debugging. We might also want to configure Apache to run on a port other than 80 for the same reasons.

At this point Apache is running and you should be able to fetch pages with any web browser.

To enable gdb to break at our ferret_handler callback, we might have a gdb session like this:

```
% gdb httpd
(gdb) b ferret_handler
(gdb) run -X -f /home/programmerX/httpd.conf
```

Now request a page from Apache with a browser and begin debugging. If we request a Location, Directory, File, or MIME type that has our function registered as a handler, the breakpoint will fire and we can step through the code.

Depending on the kind of debugging you're doing, you might not want to start Apache as a single process and debug just that single process. If your error occurs in a more "real-world" setting you might want to set up another, more powerful, way to debug. Examples of debugging targets like this are:

- Loading modules
- Interprocess communication
- Resource management

To debug like this:

1. Compile Apache with debugging enabled.
2. Use ps (or its equivalent) to get the process ID of a running HTTPD.
3. Invoke gdb with the command line % gdb httpd.
4. Once in gdb, attach to the running process with "(gdb) attach pid" where pid is the process ID from step 2.

The dialog with gdb should look something like this:

```
% ./httpd
%
% ps eax | grep httpd
17862 ?   S    0:00 ./httpd
17863 ?   S    0:00 ./httpd
17864 ?   S    0:00 ./httpd
%
% gdb ./httpd
GNU gdb 4.18
Copyright 1998 Free Software Foundation, Inc.
GDB is free software, covered by the GNU General Public License,
```

```
and you are welcome to change it and/or distribute copies of it
under certain conditions.
Type "show copying" to see the conditions.
There is absolutely no warranty for GDB. Type "show warranty" for
details.
This GDB was configured as "i386-redhat-linux"...
(gdb) attach 17864
Attaching to program:
/usr/local/src/apache/apache_1.3.9/src/httpd, Pid 17864
Reading symbols from /lib/libm.so.6...done.
Reading symbols from /lib/libcrypt.so.1...done.
Reading symbols from /lib/libdl.so.2...done.
Reading symbols from /lib/libc.so.6...done.
Reading symbols from /lib/ld-linux.so.2...done.
Reading symbols from /lib/libnss_files.so.2...done.
Reading symbols from /lib/libnss_nisplus.so.2...done.
Reading symbols from /lib/libnsl.so.1...done.
Reading symbols from /lib/libnss_nis.so.2...done.
0x40116c32 in __libc_accept () from /lib/libc.so.6
(gdb) b ferret_handler
Breakpoint 1 at 0x804fefe
(gdb) c
Continuing.
```

In this scenario, you should adjust the number of servers to start in the
conf/httpd.conf file to something small. Otherwise, you may have to
make several requests in order to get the process you've attached to service a request.

A tool to better use gdb is xgdb, emacs, or xemacs. All these tools allow
source code browsing while debugging. The emacs family of editors are
great. They have really good integration with gdb. I am especially fond of
xemacs, which can be found at **http://www.xemacs.org/**.

The Apache API

The header files are the definitive place to look for the Apache API.
Below is a description of each header file's contents.

File	Description
alloc.h	Memory allocation functions. Memory pool, array, table, and utility functions.
ap.h	Exec, kill, printf, base64 codec, and password validation functions.
ap_compat.h	Apache 1.2 to 1.3 namespace conversion and compatibility macros.
ap_config.h	System-dependant defines and includes.
ap_config_auto.h	Automatically generated configuration header.
ap_ctype.h	LIBC 8 compatibility macros.
ap_md5.h	MD5 encoding API for Apache passwords.
ap_mmn.h	Module magic number defines.
ap_sha1.h	Secure hash algorithm interface for Netscape server passwords.
buff.h	IO buffer structrures, functions, and macros.
compat.h	Legacy header.
conf.h	Legacy header.
explain.h	Logging macros.
fnmatch.h	Filename/directory matching functions.
hsregex.h	Henry Spencer's regex structures and functions.
http_conf_globals.h	Global configuration variables.
http_config.h	Configuration and module structures and headers.
http_core.h	The Apache core structures and functions.
http_log.h	Logging levels and functions.
http_main.h	Virtual server and module timeout handling functions.
http_protocol.h	HTTP protocol and content get/set and read/write functions.
http_request.h	Request redirection and processing functions.
http_vhost.h	Virtual host setup functions.
Httpd.h	Main structures, functions, and status codes.
Multithread.h	Apache threading wrapper.
rfc1413.h	Identd protocol function.
scoreboard.h	Server scoreboard structures and functions.
util_date.h	Date parsing utilities.
util_md5.h	MD5 API wrapper functions.
util_script.h	CGI environment and execution functions.
util_uri.h	URI parsing structure and functions.

The Structures

In the Apache API there are four major structures that make everything go: the module, the request_rec, the server_rec, and the conn_rec. Since we've just covered the module structure and substructures, we'll mention the rest now.

The request_rec

The request_rec structure is the "biggie" in both size and importance. It contains all the information about a request: where, when, from whom, for what, in what language, and how the request it to be performed are all in the request_rec structure. The request_rec is defined in src/include/httpd.h.

```
struct request_rec {
    ap_pool pool;            /* request specific memory pool */
    conn_rec connection;     /* the connection record for this request */
    server_rec server;       /* the server record for this request (see below) */
    request_rec *next;       /* If we wind up getting redirected,
                              * pointer to the request we redirected to. */
    request_rec *prev;       /* If this is an internal redirect,
                 pointer to where we redirected *from*.
*/
    request_rec *main;       /* If this is a sub_request (see request.h)
                              * pointer back to the main request.
                              */
    /* Info about the request itself... we begin with stuff that only
     * protocol.c should ever touch...
     */
    char *the_request;       /* First line of request, so we can log it */
    int assbackwards;        /* HTTP/0.9, "simple" request */
    int proxyreq;            /* A proxy request (calculated during
                              * post_read_request or translate_name) */
    int header_only;         /* HEAD request, as opposed to GET */
    char *protocol;          /* Protocol, as given to us, or HTTP/0.9 */
    int proto_num;           /* Number version of protocol; 1.1 = 1001 */
    const char *hostname;    /* Host, as set by full URI or Host: */
    time_t request_time;     /* When the request started */
    const char *status_line; /* Status line, if set by script */
    int status;              /* In any case */
    /* Request method, two ways; also, protocol, etc.. Outside of protocol.c,
     * look, but don't touch.
     */
    const char *method;      /* GET, HEAD, POST, etc. */
    int method_number;       /* M_GET, M_POST, etc. */
    /*
```

allowed is a bitvector of the allowed methods.

A handler must ensure that the request method is one that
it is capable of handling. Generally modules should DECLINE
any request methods they do not handle. Prior to aborting the
handler like this the handler should set r->allowed to the list
of methods that it is willing to handle. This bitvector is used
to construct the "Allow:" header required for OPTIONS requests,
and METHOD_NOT_ALLOWED and NOT_IMPLEMENTED status codes.

Since the default_handler deals with OPTIONS, all modules can
usually decline to deal with OPTIONS. TRACE is always allowed,
modules don't need to set it explicitly.

Since the default_handler will always handle a GET, a
module which does *not* implement GET should probably return
METHOD_NOT_ALLOWED. Unfortunately this means that a Script GET
handler can't be installed by mod_actions.

```c
*/
int allowed;               /* Allowed methods - for 405, OPTIONS, etc */
int sent_bodyct;           /* byte count in stream is for body */
long bytes_sent;           /* body byte count, for easy access */
time_t mtime;              /* Time the resource was last modified */
/* HTTP/1.1 connection-level features */
int chunked;               /* sending chunked transfer-coding */
int byterange;             /* number of byte ranges */
char *boundary;            /* multipart/byteranges boundary */
const char *range;         /* The Range: header */
long clength;              /* The "real" content length */
long remaining;            /* bytes left to read */
long read_length;          /* bytes that have been read */
int read_body;             /* how the request body should be read */
int read_chunked;          /* reading chunked transfer-coding */
unsigned expecting_100;    /* is client waiting for a 100 response? */
/* MIME header environments, in and out. Also, an array containing
 * environment variables to be passed to subprocesses, so people can
 * write modules to add to that environment.
 *
 * The difference between headers_out and err_headers_out is that the
 * latter are printed even on error, and persist across internal redirects
 * (so the headers printed for ErrorDocument handlers will have them).
 *
 * The 'notes' table is for notes from one module to another, with no
 * other set purpose in mind...
 */
table *headers_in;
table *headers_out;
table *err_headers_out;
table *subprocess_env;
```

```
    table *notes;
    /* content_type, handler, content_encoding, content_language, and all
     * content_languages MUST be lowercased strings. They may be pointers
     * to static strings; they should not be modified in place.
     */
    const char *content_type;        /* Break these out --- we dispatch on 'em */
    const char *handler;             /* What we *really* dispatch on         */
    const char *content_encoding;
    const char *content_language;    /* for back-compat. only -- do not use */
    array_header *content_languages; /* array of (char*) */
    char *vlist_validator;           /* variant list validator (if negotiated) */
    int no_cache;
    int no_local_copy;
    /* What object is being requested (either directly, or via include
     * or content-negotiation mapping).
     */
    char *unparsed_uri;              /* the uri without any parsing performed */
    char *uri;                       /* the path portion of the URI */
    char filename;                   /* filename of the target */
    char path_info;                  /* path to the target */
    char *args;                      /* QUERY_ARGS, if any */
    struct stat finfo;               /* ST_MODE set to zero if no such file */
    uri_components parsed_uri;       /* components of uri, dismantled */
    /* Various other config info which may change with .htaccess files
     * These are config vectors, with one void* pointer for each module
     * (the thing pointed to being the module's business).
     */
    void *per_dir_config;    /* Options set in config files, etc. */
    void *request_config;    /* Notes on *this* request */
/*
 * a linked list of the configuration directives in the .htaccess files
 * accessed by this request.
 * N.B. always add to the head of the list, _never_ to the end.
 * that way, a sub request's list can (temporarily) point to a parent's list
 */
    const struct htaccess_result *htaccess;
/* Things placed at the end of the record to avoid breaking binary
 * compatibility. It would be nice to remember to reorder the entire
 * record to improve 64bit alignment the next time we need to break
 * binary compatibility for some other reason.
 */
};
```

The server_rec

The server_rec contains the name, administrator, configuration files, per-server module configuration structures, timeout values, and UID/GID of the server among other things. Notice that each request record has a pointer to a `server_rec`. In that way you can find out which server invoked your module. This structure is defined in `src/include/httpd.h`.

```
struct server_rec {
    server_rec *next;

    /* description of where the definition came from */
    const char *defn_name;
    unsigned defn_line_number;

    /* Full locations of server config info */
    char *srm_confname;          /* where the srm.conf file lives */
    char *access_confname;       /* where the access.conf file lives */

    /* Contact information */
    char *server_admin; /* e.g. admin@your-host.com */
    char *server_hostname;       /* e.g. www.your-host.com */
    unsigned short port;         /* what port this server is listening on for
                                    redirects, etc. */

    /* Log files --- note that transfer log is now in the modules... */
    char *error_fname;
    FILE *error_log;
    int loglevel;

    /* Module-specific configuration for server, and defaults... */
    int is_virtual;         /* true if this is the virtual server */
    void *module_config;    /* Config vector containing pointers to
                             * modules' per-server config structures.
                             */
    void *lookup_defaults;  /* MIME type info, etc., before we start
                             * checking per-directory info.
                             */
    /* Transaction handling */
    server_addr_rec *addrs;
    int timeout;            /* Timeout, in seconds, before we give up */
    int keep_alive_timeout; /* Seconds we'll wait for another request */
    int keep_alive_max;     /* Maximum requests per connection */
    int keep_alive;         /* Use persistent connections? */
    int send_buffer_size;   /* size of TCP send buffer (in bytes) */

    char *path;             /* Pathname for ServerPath */
    int pathlen;            /* Length of path */

    array_header *names;       /* Normal names for ServerAlias servers */
    array_header *wild_names;  /* Wildcarded names for ServerAlias servers */

    uid_t server_uid;       /* effective user id when calling exec wrapper */
```

```
    gid_t server_gid;                 /* effective group id when calling exec wrapper */

    int limit_req_line;               /* limit on size of the HTTP request line     */
    int limit_req_fieldsize;          /* limit on size of any request header field */
    int limit_req_fields;             /* limit on number of request header fields   */
};
```

The conn_rec

The conn_rec structure contains information regarding a specific connection between a client and a server. It is defined in src/include/httpd.h.

```
struct conn_rec {

    ap_pool pool;                     /* connection specific memory pool */
    server_rec *server;               /* the server this connection belongs to */
    server_rec *base_server;          /* Physical host this conn come in on */
    void *vhost_lookup_data;          /* used by http_vhost.c */

    /* Information about the connection itself */
    int child_num;                    /* The number of the child handling conn_rec */
    BUFF *client;                      /* Connection to the client */

    /* Who is the client? */
    struct sockaddr_in local_addr;    /* local address of connection */
    struct sockaddr_in remote_addr;   /* remote address of connection */
    char *remote_ip;                  /* Client's IP address */
    char *remote_host;                /* Client's DNS name, if known.
                                       * NULL if DNS hasn't been checked,
                                       * "" if it has and no address was found.
                                       * N.B. Only access this through
                                       * get_remote_host() */
    char *remote_logname;             /* Only ever set if doing rfc1413 lookups.
                                       * N.B. Only access this through
                                         get_remote_logname() */
    char *user;                       /* If an authentication check was made,
                                       * this gets set to the user name. We assume
                                       * that there's only one user per connection(!)
                                       */
    char *ap_auth_type; /* Ditto. */

    unsigned aborted:1;               /* Are we still talking? */
    signed int keepalive:2;           /* Are we using HTTP Keep-Alive?
                                       * -1 fatal error, 0 undecided, 1 yes */
    unsigned keptalive:1;             /* Did we use HTTP Keep-Alive? */
    signed int double_reverse:2;      /* have we done double-reverse DNS?
                                       * -1 yes/failure, 0 not yet, 1 yes/success */
    int keepalives;                   /* How many times have we used it? */
```

```
        char *local_ip;        /* server IP address */
        char *local_host;      /* used for ap_get_server_name when
                                * UseCanonicalName is set to DNS
                                * (ignores setting of HostnameLookups) */
};
```

Managing Memory

Managing memory in C is notoriously problematic. Languages like Perl and Java have gained enormous popularity largely due to their memory-handling facilities. Memory allocation and deallocation in C must be done explicitly and in a complex program. This can be tedious and fraught with nasty problems. Multiple deallocations of the same memory block usually result in segmentation faults. Not deallocating at all can result in memory leaks that may eventually bring the server to its knees or worse. In order to get around the problems inherent in managing memory in large and complex C programs, the Apache developers have created a memory management scheme. Like many of the APIs we will see here, the memory API is a wrapper around standard library functions couched in the Apache Server framework.

The framework for memory allocation is called *resource pools*. Each module's memory pool is accounted for in a structure that can release allocated memory automatically when the pool is no longer needed. When is the pool no longer needed? Apache takes care of that by passing the appropriate pool pointer to your callback depending on the phase of module execution. At the end of a particular phase of execution, the appropriate resource pool will be released. There are also pool pointers inside the request_rec and the conn_rec. These memory pools exist as long as the request and connection exist.

Pool memory allocation is somewhat inflexible. Once memory is allocated in a pool, it's best just to leave it to be automatically deallocated at the end of the request handling phase. However, if your module has a lot of allocation and deallocation to do during its processing, it is best to use sub_pools. These may be easily deallocated at will. However, only the *entire subpool* may be deallocated so use accordingly.

Memory Pool API

Allocating Pools

The memory pool API has a consistent mapping to the standard C library allocation routines. The general form of allocation routines follows.

```
void *ap_xalloc( struct pool *p, int number_of_bytes );
```

Where `void *` is the returned pointer and the `pool *` is the memory pool with the scope you need for the task at hand; server, request, connection, module, etc.

```
ap_palloc() and ap_pcalloc()
```

These functions allocate from the pool parameter. Cast them to the structure of your choice.

```
void *ap_palloc(struct pool *p, int nbytes);
void *ap_pcalloc(struct pool *p, int nbytes);
```

```
ap_pstrdup() and ap_pstrndup()
```

Duplicate null terminated strings, `char *s`, from `pool *p` and return them as character pointers. `ap_pstrndup()` duplicates at most `int n` characters.

```
char *ap_pstrdup(struct pool *p, const char *s);
char *ap_pstrndup(struct pool *p, const char *s, int n);
```

```
ap_pstrcat()
```

Concatenates strings.

```
char *ap_pstrcat(struct pool *,...);
```

```
ap_psprintf() and ap_pvsprintf()
```

`Printf`-like string producers.

```
char *ap_psprintf(struct pool *, const char *fmt, ...)
    __attribute__((format(printf,2,3)));
char *ap_pvsprintf(struct pool *, const char *fmt, va_list);
```

Managing Subpools

To manage subpools of memory use the functions below. You may create a subpool, destroy an entire subpool, or clear the subpool without destroying it.

```
ap_make_sub_pool()
```

Makes a sub pool of from `pool *p` and returns a pointer to the new subpool;

```
pool *ap_make_sub_pool(pool *p);

ap_destroy_pool()
```

Destroys `pool *p` and all its contents.

```
void ap_destroy_pool(pool *p);

ap_clear_pool()
```

Clears the contents of `pool *p` without deallocating the pool.

```
void ap_clear_pool(struct pool *p);
```

Getting Pool Information

To get information about a pool and its relationship with other memory pools use the functions below.

```
ap_pool_join()
```

Make a subpool have the same lifetime as a parent pool. Once you join two pools like this, the subpool will be destroyed when the parent pool is destroyed.

```
void ap_pool_join(pool *p, pool *sub);

ap_pool_is_ancestor()
```

Is one pool contained within another?

```
int ap_pool_is_ancestor(pool *a, pool *b);

ap_find_pool()
```

Find a pool.

```
pool *ap_find_pool(const void *ts);
```

```
ap_bytes_in_pool()
```

Query a pool for the number of bytes consumed.

```
long ap_bytes_in_pool(pool *p);
```

```
ap_bytes_in_free_blocks()
```

Queries a pool for the number of bytes free out of the currently allocated blocks in the memory pool.

```
long ap_bytes_in_free_blocks(void);
```

Array API

The array API is in `src/include/alloc.h`. It is handy for quick lookups and stacklike affairs.

The array_header structure

```
typedef struct {
    ap_pool *pool; /* the pool involved with this array */
    int elt_size; /* the size of each element */
    int nelts;    /* the number of elements */
    int nalloc;   /* number allocated */
    char *elts;   /* elements. Cast appropriately before use */
} array_header;
```

Creating and Operating on Arrays

```
ap_make_array()
```

Creates an array `nelts` long each of `elt_size` size. The array API will resize your array if it needs to do so to complete a `cat`, `push`, etc.

```
array_header *ap_make_array(pool *p, int nelts, int elt_size);
```

```
ap_push_array()
```

Adds an element (as defined in the `array_header`) to the end of the array and passes back a pointer to the allocated element. To get your data into the array, write it into the element passed back.

```
void *ap_push_array(array_header *);
```

`ap_array_cat()`

Concatenates on array onto the end of another array. Make sure that the element size is the same inside each `array_header`.

```
void ap_array_cat(array_header *dst, const array_header *src);
```

`ap_append_arrays()`

Creates a whole new array from `pool`; its contents are the elements of the two array arguments.

```
array_header *ap_append_arrays(pool *, const array_header *,
    const array_header *);
```

`ap_array_pstrcat()`

Creates a character string allocated from `pool` comprised of the elements of the array `arr`. If `sep` is non-null it will be used as a separator between each element.

```
char *ap_array_pstrcat( pool *p, const array_header *arr,
    const char sep);
```

`ap_copy_array()`

Copies the entire array to the returned array allocated from `pool *p`.

```
array_header *ap_copy_array(pool *p, const array_header *src);
```

`ap_copy_array_hdr()`

Just copies the `array_header` and prepares the contents for copying only if the next array operation is a `push` or `arraycat`.

```
array_header *ap_copy_array_hdr(pool *p, const array_header *src);
```

Table API

The table API uses the array API to implement a key/value pair table. It's like most key/value pair-type tables you've seen and used like in TCL and Perl with a couple of exceptions:

- It can only store character strings
- It is case insensitive
- A key may have multiple values in a list.

The table_entry and table structs

```
typedef struct {
    char *key;      /* maybe NULL in future;
                     * check when iterating thru table_elts
                     */
    char *val;
} table_entry;

struct table {
     array_header a;      /* the table is really an array */
#ifdef MAKE_TABLE_PROFILE  /* for debugging only */
     void *creator;
#endif
};
```

Creating Tables

The functions below create and clear tables:

ap_make_table()

Creates a table from pool *p that is nelts long.

```
table *ap_make_table(pool *p, int nelts);
```

ap_copy_table()

Makes a copy of const table * from pool *p and returns a pointer to the new table.

```
table *ap_copy_table(pool *p, const table *);
```

ap_clear_table()

Clears the elements from a table without deallocating the table.

```
void ap_clear_table(table *);
```

Getting and Setting Tables

The functions below perform a number of get/set functions on tables:

```
ap_table_get()
```

Given a table and a key returns the value at that key.

```
const char *ap_table_get(const table *, const char *);
```

```
ap_table_set()
```

Sets the key name to value val in table. If the key already exists, the current value is replaced and if the key does not exist it is created. This function actually copies the values into the table.

```
void ap_table_set(table *, const char *name, const char *val);
```

```
ap_table_setn()
```

Performs the same function as ap_table_set() except that it does not copy the values into the table. The strings in the function must remain valid for the lifetime of the target table.

```
void ap_table_setn(table *, const char *name, const char *val);
```

```
ap_table_merge()
```

Copies the value more_val into the table at key name. Use this function to insert multiple values into a single key.

```
void ap_table_merge(table *, const char *name, const char *more_val);
```

```
ap_table_mergen()
```

Does the same job as ap-table_merge() except that it does not copy the values from the parameter list. It uses the actual pointers, so make sure those values stay valid.

```
void ap_table_mergen(table *, const char *name, const char *more_val);
```

```
ap_table_unset()
```

Deletes all entries in a table with the indicated key.

```
void ap_table_unset(table *, const char *key);
```

ap_table_add()

Adds the value val to the table at the indicated key. If the key already exists the value is added to the list associatead with the key.

```
void ap_table_add(table *, const char *name, const char *val);
```

ap_table_addn()

Is like all the other ap_table_xn() functions. It performs an add, creating a multi-valued key if the key already exists but does not copy the strings into the table. It uses the pointers passed to the function instead.

```
void ap_table_addn(table *, const char *name, const char *val);
```

ap_table_do()

Iterates through a multi-valued key. This function takes a function pointer as an argument. The callback function takes three arguments:

- void *—Any data you like
- const char *—The key you're looking for
- const char *—The value you're looking for.

The callback function is called when the value in the key matches a value in the last parameter of the ap_table_do() function. If no values are passed into ap_table_do() the callback function is called for every key. ap_table_do() iterates through the entire table. If you want to abort this process from inside the callback, return 0 from the callback function.

```
void ap_table_do(int (*comp) (void *, const char *,
                              const char *), void *rec,
                              const table *t,...);
```

For example, here is a simple callback:

```
static int sample_callback( void *data, const char *key, const
char *value )
{
    request_rec *r = (request_rec *)data;
    ap_printf( r, "Field: %s = %s\n", key, value );
```

```
        return TRUE;
    }
```

Here is how we would call `ap_table_do()` with our callback printing out the "Content-language" key and all its associated values in the request headers:

```
ap_table_do( sample_callback, (void *)r, r->headers_out,
                "Content-language", NULL );
```

`ap_overlay_tables()`

Updates the table `base` with the table `overlay`. Any values in both tables are replaced by those in `overlay`. Any entries in the table `overlay` that don't exist in the table `base` are added to `base`.

```
table *ap_overlay_tables(pool *p, const table *overlay,
                            const table *base);
```

Configuring the Module

There are two important configuration activities you'll perform inside an Apache module: reading configuration items and merging configuration records.

We can read configuration items by filling in the `command_rec` array in the `module_rec` structure and implementing certain command parser callback functions. Merging configuration records takes place by calling callbacks in the `module_rec` structure.

Reading Module Directives

Before we can merge configurations, we must be able to read configuration items. Filling in the `command_rec` structure provides command information. Multiple commands are implemented by creating an array of `command_rec` structures. This array of `command_rec` structures is the `const command_rec *cmds;` field in the `module_rec` structure.

The `command_rec` structure:

```
typedef struct command_struct {
    const char *name;               /* Name of this command */
    const char *(*func) ();         /* Function invoked */
    void *cmd_data;                 /* Extra data, for functions which
```

```
                                       * implement multiple commands... */
    int req_override;                  /* What overrides need to be allowed to
                                        * enable this command. */
    enum cmd_how args_how;             /* What the command expects as arguments */
    const char *errmsg;                /* 'usage' message, in case of syntax errors */
} command_rec;
```

The first two fields are almost self-explanatory: the name of the command and the function that parses the command. The cmd_data field is usually cast to an int that is used as a switch in a case statement to process multiple commands with one function (Don't worry, there's an example below). The override is a field where we may OR together flags to allow different combinations of over ride options.

Constants for configuration override (req_override) field:

The args_how field instructs the command parser how many and what kind of arguments to expect.

Constants for the args_how field are:

FLAG	If this flag is present then the command may appear...
OR_LIMIT	Inside <Directory> or <Location> and .htaccess when AllowOverride Limit exists on a directory
OR_OPTIONS	In *.conf files and .htaccess when AllowOverride Options exist for a directory
OR_FILEINFO	Anywhere and in .htaccess when AllowOverride FileInfo exists
OR_AUTHCFG	Inside <Directory> or <Location> and .htaccess when AllowOverride AuthConfig exists
OR_INDEXES	Anywhere and in .htaccess when AllowOverride Indexes exists
OR_UNSET	Unsets all other OR_* argument flags
ACCESS_CONF	Inside <Directory> or <Location> and *.conf files but not in .htaccess
RSRC_CONF	Outside <Directory>, <Location>. Or and in *.conf files but not in .htaccess
OR_ALL	(OR_LIMIT|OR_OPTIONS|OR_FILEINFO|OR_AUTHCFG|OR_INDEXES) anywhere it pleases
OR_NONE	This command may not be overridden.

FLAG	The cmd_fun function will...
RAW_ARGS	Parse the argument(s) itself
TAKE1	Take 1 argument
TAKE2	Take 2 arguments
ITERATE	Execute once for each argument in a list
ITERATE2	Iterate on the second argument after a mandatory first argument
FLAG	Interpret the argument as an "On" or "Off"
NO_ARGS	Not take any arguments
TAKE12	Take 1 or 2 arguments
TAKE3	Take 3 arguments
TAKE23	Take 2 or three arguments
TAKE123	Take 1, 2, or 3 arguments
TAKE13	Take 1 or 3 arguments

Example Configuration

Like other modules in Apache, `mod_ferret` may need its own directives. In order to parse directives in Apache, use the configuration API. Let's add some directives to `mod_ferret.c`.

- `ferret_debug`—is a value to set a debug level
- `ferret_cache_size`—sets the cache in our module
- `ferret_track_errors`—is a flag to turn some special tracking widget on and off

We'll need a structure to hold our module configuration.

```
typedef struct {
    int debug;
    int cache_size;
    int track_errors;
} ferret_conf;
```

If we declare a variable of type `ferret_conf` global to `mod_ferret.c` then we'll have module-wide configuration. It is possible to create configuration records for different virtual servers, directories, and file groups, but we'll get into that later. Our global configuration variable is

```
ferret_conf *conf;
```

In the module `init` we should allocate the memory for this structure and remember to free it during the cleanup phase. The cleanup API is covered below.

The command syntax and usage are defined in the `command_rec` data structure (covered above in the `module_rec` section). These `command_rec` structures are processed by callbacks in the `mod_ferret` module.

To add commands to the `mod_ferret` module, first we add the configuration structure array:

```
static const command_rec ferret_cmds[] =
{
  /* take one directives */
    {
        "ferret_debug",          /* directive name */
        ferrettake1handler,      /* module configuration callback */
        ( void * )0,             /* argument to include in call */
        OR_OPTIONS,              /* where available */
        TAKE1,                   /* how many arguments? */
        "ferret_debug directive - 1 argument: flags" /* directive description */
    },
    {
        "ferret_cache_size",     /* directive name */
        ferrettake1handler,      /* module configuration callback */
        ( void * )1,             /* argument passed to callback */
        OR_OPTIONS,              /* where overrides apply */
        TAKE1,                   /* how many arguments? */
      "ferret_cache_size - 1 argument: size in bytes" /* usage message */
    },
    /* flag directives */
    {
        "ferret_track_errors",   /* directive name */
        ferretflaghandler,       /* configuration callback */
        ( void * )0,             /* argument to callback */
        OR_OPTIONS,              /* where it can appear */
        FLAG,                    /* argument type */
        "on|off"                 /* usage message */
    },
    {NULL}
};
```

In the previouse structures we have defined three directives that help control `mod_ferret`. You can see that `ferret_debug` and `ferret_cache_size` both have the same configuration callback, `ferrettake1handler`. The function `ferrettake1handler` takes one argument. Notice that the third field in the `command_rec` structure is the value of that parameter. In this way, `ferrettakelhandler` can parse similar directives.

Handling Commands

```
/*-------------------------------------------------------------------------
 * name: ferretflaghandler
 * synopsis: const char *tcodflaghandler( cmd_parms *cmd,
 *                          ferret_conf *conf,
 *                          int val );
 * description: This function takes
 * returns: NULL
 * errors:
 * calls: none
 * notes:
 *-----------------------------------------------------------------------*/
const char *ferretflaghandler( cmd_parms *cmd,
                               ferret_conf *conf,
                               int val )
{
  int c = (int) cmd->info;

  switch (c)
    {
    case 0: /* track errors */
      conf->track_errors = val;
      break;
    }
  return NULL;
}
/*-------------------------------------------------------------------------
 * name: ferrettakelhandler
 * synopsis: const char *ferrettakelhandler( cmd_parms *cmd,
 *                          ferret_conf *conf,
 *                          char *arg );
 * description: takes 1 argument from a command in an Apache conf file
 *
 * returns: NULL
 * errors: no error handling
 * calls: none
 * notes:
 *-----------------------------------------------------------------------*/
const char *ferrettakelhandler( cmd_parms *cmd,
                                ferret_conf *conf,
                                char *arg )
{
  int c = (int) cmd->info;
```

```
  switch (c)
    {
    case 0: /* debug-message flags */
      conf->debug = atoi(arg);
      break;
    case 1: /* cache size */
      conf->cache_size = atoi( arg );
      break;
    }
  return NULL;
};
```

Now we add the command handler to our module structure:

```
/* Our module structure. */
module ferret_module =
{
    STANDARD_MODULE_STUFF,
    NULL,                 /* module initializer */
    NULL,                 /* per-directory config creator */
    NULL,                 /* dir config merger */
    NULL,                 /* server config creator */
    NULL,                 /* server config merger */
    ferret_cmds,          /* command table */
    ferret_handler,       /* [7] list of handlers */
    NULL,                 /* [2] filename-to-URI translation */
    NULL,                 /* [5] check/validate user_id */
    NULL,                 /* [6] check user_id is valid *here* */
    NULL,                 /* [4] check access by host address */
    NULL,                 /* [7] MIME type checker/setter */
    NULL,                 /* [8] fixups */
    NULL,                 /* [10] logger */
    NULL,                 /* [3] header parser */
    NULL,                 /* process initializer */
    NULL,                 /* process exit/cleanup */
    NULL                  /* [1] post read_request handling */
};
/* end of file mod_ferret.c */
```

Configurations

Somewhere in the conf/*.conf files we can put:

```
ferret_cache_size = 2048
ferret_track_errors = On
ferret_debug = 4
```

This example keeps module-wide configuration across all servers and directories. Access the values in the global `conf` variable.

Different Types of Configuration

As you know, Apache may run several virtual servers (i.e. `<VirtualHost>`s, see Chapter 8: "Creating Multiple Domain Web Sites On One Server"), each with different directory structures and access restrictions on the content served. This means that your module will need different configuration records depending on which Web site was requested by a particular client. Apache provides four API functions for dealing with creating and merging these configurations. Merging is an opportunity to take care of conflicting and overriding options that might occur between the directory and server configurations.

The term "merging" is somewhat confusing. What these functions actually do is process the configurations for the server and directory requested. Imagine that an Apache server has two virtual servers that may access the same files. One virtual server has access to the files and the other does not because of an override directive on the directory itself. This is the kind of case where we would want to merge server and directory configurations to determine access privileges.

These functions are in `src/include/http_config.h` in the `module_rec` structure.

Per Directory Configuration Functions

```
void *(*create_dir_config) (pool *p, char *dir);
void *(*merge_dir_config) (pool *p, void *base_conf,
                           void *new_conf);
```

Per Server Configuration Functions

```
void *(*create_server_config) (pool *p, server_rec *s);
void *(*merge_server_config) (pool *p, void *base_conf, void
*new_conf);
```

If your module implements a `create_server_config()` function each virtual server will have its own configuration record. Likewise, if your module implements a `create_dir_config()` function, each module-specific directive will produce a configuration record. A typical `create server_config()` function looks like this:

```
static void * ferret_create_server_config( pool *p, server_rec *s )
{
  /* create space for the new configuration record */
  ferret_conf *config = (ferret_conf *)ap_pcalloc( p,
                        sizeof( ferret_conf ));
  /* set any default values you like */
  config->debug = 0;
  config->track_errors = 0;
  config->cache_size = 1024;
  /* return the new configuration record */
  return ( void * )config;
}
```

The directory configuration creation function looks essentially the same.

To reconcile two sets of configurations (say two servers) with a merge routine, we could write something much like this:

```
static void *ferret_merge_server_config( pool *p, void *basecfg,
void *newcfg )
{
  /* create space for the new configuration record */
  ferret_conf *merged_conf = ( ferret_conf * )ap_pcalloc( p,
                          sizeof( ferret_conf ));
  /* put the base and new configurations into variables
     so we may deal with them */
  ferret_conf *base_conf = ( ferret_conf * )basecfg;
  ferret_conf *new_conf = ( ferret_conf * )newcfg;

  /* adjust the configuration items to taste ... */
  /*
  merged_conf->debug = new_conf->debug;
  merged_conf->cache_size = max( base_conf->cache_size,
     new_conf->cache_size );
  /* return the new record */
  return ( void * )merged_conf;
};
```

Other Configuration Goodies

There are a great number of things you can do with the configuration API. All the configuration structures and functions may be found in src/include/http_config.h. Among them are things like:

Configuration Streams

These allow you to create your own configuration read and write functions. The `configfile_t` structure and all its friends are in `src/include/httpd.h`.

Querying and Setting Configuration Options in Other Modules

```
void *ap_get_module_config(void *conf_vector, module *m);
void ap_set_module_config(void *conf_vector,
                          module *m, void *val);
```

Loading and Unloading Other Modules

```
void ap_add_module(module *m);
void ap_remove_module(module *m);
void ap_add_loaded_module(module *mod);
void ap_remove_loaded_module(module *mod);
int ap_add_named_module(const char *name);
void ap_clear_module_list(void);
const char *ap_find_module_name(module *m);
module *ap_find_linked_module(const char *name);
```

Built-in Directive Handlers

```
const char *ap_set_string_slot(cmd_parms *, char *, char *);
const char *ap_set_string_slot_lower(cmd_parms *, char *, char *);
const char *ap_set_flag_slot(cmd_parms *, char *, int);
const char *ap_set_file_slot(cmd_parms *, char *, char *);
```

Writing the Log Files

The Apache log files are replete with detailed information (see Chapter 5: Using Logs). How do we reproduce all that when we want to log an event? We don't have to go digging inside the `server_rec` and `request_rec` for all the pertinent information to print in the log file (unless we want to); the Apache logging API does all that for us.

If you wish, you can send all your errors to `stderr` and they will appear in the appropriate Apache log file. Apache has this behavior because when it starts, it reopens `stderr` to the `ErrorLog` file descriptor. This is fine but lacks the nice messages that come with the logging API. It is good to keep the format provided by the API level logging functions, rather than rolling your own, because then the logs are easier to parse and run reports on.

The logging API may be found in `src/include/http_log.h`.

Log API

Various logging API functions include:

ap_log_error() and ap_log_rerror()

These are the workhorse functions of the Apache log API. The `file` and `line` arguments are like the C language `__FILE__` and `__LINE__` tokens. There is a macro, `APLOG_MARK`, that will fill in the first two parameters for you. The third parameter is the log level. The log levels are detailed in a table below. Those familiar with the `*nix` `SYSLOG` levels will feel right at home with the Apache API log levels.

```
void ap_log_error(const char *file, int line, int level,
            const server_rec *s, const char *fmt, ...)
            __attribute__((format(printf,5,6)));

void ap_log_rerror(const char *file, int line, int level,
        const request_rec *s, const char *fmt,
        ...)__attribute__((format(printf,5,6)));
```

ap_log_reason()

`ap_log_reason()` is a wrapper around the `ap_log_error()` function. It pastes a character string that is the reason for the error into an `ap_log_error()` call:

```
void ap_log_reason(const char *reason, const char *fname,
    request_rec *r);
```

Logging Severity Levels

The log levels in the table below should look familiar to anyone familiar with the `*nix` `SYSLOG` facility. These flags may be `ORed` with the flag `APLOG_NOERRNO`. Or-ing the log level with the `APLOG_NOERRNO` flag prevents the system variable `ERRNO` from appearing in the log messages.

The log levels below are passed to the logging API in the level parameter. For example:

```
ap_log_error( APLOG_MARK,
    APLOG_DEBUG | APLOG_NOERRNO,
    r->server,
    "This is a test error message…\n" );
```

Log Level	Meaning
APLOG_EMERG	System is unusable
APLOG_ALERT	Action must be taken immediately
APLOG_CRIT	Critical conditions
APLOG_ERR	Error conditions
APLOG_WARNING	Warning conditions
APLOG_NOTICE	Normal but significant condition
APLOG_INFO	Informational
APLOG_DEBUG	Debug-level messages
APLOG_NOERRNO	Do not include system level errno in error messages

Piped Log API

The piped log API allows you to pipe your logged information to a running program. The piped logging is already a part of Apache as a convenience in the built in logging facility. If any of your logging directives start with a | symbol, then Apache treats everything after the | symbol as a program to run. However, in some modules you may wish to log to a custom logging facility. You may use these functions to log to an external process independent of the Apache logging facility. You may also use this API to read from the logging program.

ap_open_piped_log()

`ap_open_piped_log()` opens a pipe to the program in the program parameter. It does this by starting the program specified and opening a bidirectional pipe to it. If starting the process and opening a pipe is successful, the function will return a `piped_log *`. The output of the logging will appear at the standard input of the logging process.

```
piped_log *ap_open_piped_log (pool *p, const char *program);
```

```
ap_close_piped_log()
```

closes a previously opened piped log.

```
void ap_close_piped_log (piped_log *pl);
```

ap_piped_log_write_fd( )

`ap_piped_log_write_fd(   )` returns a regular file descriptor you may use with the standard C library `write()` routine to write to the piped log.

```
int ap_piped_log_write_fd (piped_log *pl);
```

ap_piped_log_read_fd()

`ap_piped_log_read_fd()` reads from the logging processes standard out.

```
int ap_piped_log_read_fd (piped_log *);
```

Handling the Request

We've gone through the steps Apache uses to service a HTTP request. Now let's rehearse the steps to actually handle a request in the response handler. In our simple example, `mod_ferret.c`, the response handler did-n't really do anything except spew HTML. In order effectively to service a HTTP request with a response handler, we must be aware of several other activities we probably need to do:

- Reading the request
- Getting server level information
- Writing the response
- Timing out
- Emitting return codes

For the most part, the following functions and constants may be found in `src/include/http_protocol.h`.

Reading the Request

Conveniently, Apache parses header information from the client and places it all very neatly into the `request_rec` structure and its friends `server_rec` and `connect_rec`. The body of the request is left up to the response handler. The body is usually the data portion of a POST, PUT, or other method of your own invention. This part of the transaction (after the CR/LF terminating the HTTP header) may contain binary data, form information, documents, etc. If you are implementing a new MIME type you may be particularly interested in this part of the transaction as this is where your type specific commands and data reside. If you're just serving up straight data with no special content and no special negotiation you may have everything you need in the `request_rec` already and may never need to read the body after the headers.

Reading data from the client means that we need to cooperate with the client. Sometimes we have to deal with a broken client or a broken network. Sometimes the data sent from the client will come in chunks rather than in one nice big piece.

If the client or the network is broken, you don't want your server just hanging forever on a dead connection. You need to tell the handler how and when to time out. (See the timeout API below.) You also need to set a read policy with the client that defines how to read the data from the client.

The read policies are:

REQUEST_NO_BODY

This actually does what it says; it accepts no body at all. If the content has any body at all, it returns a HTTP error code of `HTTP_REQUEST_ENTITY_TOO_LARGE` (413).

REQUEST_CHUNKED_ERROR

This policy requests that the content be in one big chunk. If the data are not in one big chunk, it will return the error `HTTP_LENGTH_REQUIRED` (411). The client may send chunked data if it's using the HTTP/1.1 protocol. If the client is HTTP/1.1-compliant then it will resubmit the data as non-chunked.

REQUEST_CHUNKED_DECHUNK

This policy accepts both chunked and non-chunked data. The Apache read routine `ap_get_client_block()` will buffer the chunked data and return the number of bytes read. There is an example below.

REQUEST_CHUNKED_PASS

This read policy is exactly as above except that the Apache read routines will not buffer the chunked data. You must manage buffers that are set up to read exactly the number of bytes specified in the content length parameter sent by the client with each chunk.

In order to apply these read policies and read data from the client you'll need to use the client read API:

```
int ap_setup_client_block(request_rec *r, int read_policy);
int ap_should_client_block(request_rec *r);
long ap_get_client_block(request_rec *r, char *buffer, int bufsiz);
int ap_discard_request_body(request_rec *r);
```

Below is a example that reads a chunk of data:

```
static int read_body( request_rec *r, const char **read_buffer )
{
    int ccode;

    /* this sets up the read policy and bails if it fails */
    if (( ccode = ap_setup_client_block( r, REQUEST_CHUNKED_ERROR )) != OK )
        return ccode;

    if (ap_should_client_block( r ))
    {
        char in_buff[ HUGE_STRING_LEN ];    /* input data buffer */
        int num_read, len_read, buf_pos = 0; /* position accounting for the data */
        long remaining = r->remaining;      /* the number of bytes yet to read */
        *read_buffer = ap_pcalloc( r->pool,
                    remaining + 1 );        /* allocate a read buffer */
        ap_hard_timeout( "read_body", r );  /* starts a hard timeout in case the
                                                client or the network fails */
        /* now, while there is data to read… */
        while (( len_read = ap_get_client_block( r, sizeof( in_buff ))) >= 0 )
        {
            ap_reset_timeout( r );              /* reset the timer since we're reading */
            num_read = len_read;
            memcpy(( char *)*read_buffer + buf_pos, in_buff, num_read );
            buf_pos += num_read;
        }
        /* we're done reading now to let's nuke the timeout */
        ap_kill_timeout( r );
    }
    return ccode;
}
```

Your content will be returned in the buffer passed in as read_buffer. What you do to process the data from the client is now up to you.

Getting Server Level Information

While servicing requests, we may need to get specific information about the server: things like the server version, default types, which server we're running, etc. These routines may be found in `src/include/http_core.h`, `src/include/httpd.h`, and `src/include/http_config.h`.

ap_default_type()

This returns the default MIME type of the current server. Usually this is `text/plain`.

```
const char *ap_default_type (request_rec *);
```

ap_server_root_relative()

Returns the server root, relative to the path passed in as `fname`. If you pass in no relative path, the server root itself is returned. This is very handy.

```
char *ap_server_root_relative(pool *p, char *fname);
```

ap_get_server_name()

Given the request, returns the server name.

```
const char *ap_get_server_name(request_rec *r);
```

ap_get_server_port()

Returns the port the current server is listening on.

```
unsigned ap_get_server_port(const request_rec *r);
```

ap_get_server_version()

Returns the version string for the HTTPD running.

```
const char * ap_get_server_version(void);
```

ap_add_version_component()

Adds a module's version information to the Apache version information returned from `ap_get_server_version()`. For example: `add_version_component("mod_ferret/0.01");`

```
void ap_add_version_component(const char *component);
```

ap_get_server_built()

Returns the time and date the server was built.

```
const char *ap_get_server_built(void);
```

Getting Transaction Level Information

Most of the information regarding the HTTP transaction comes from the `request_rec`. These are some of the functions you can use to access that information without accessing the `request_rec` directly.

ap_get_remote_host()

Returns the IP address in dotted quad format or the DNS hostname of the requesting client.

```
const char *ap_get_remote_host(conn_rec *conn, void *dir_config,
                               int type);
```

The first parameter is the connection record. The second parameter is the per-dir-configuration record of the request, and the third is the type of name lookup. The types of name lookups are in the table below.

For example:

```
char *requesting_host = ap_get_remote_host(r->connection,
    r->per_dir_config, REMOTE_NAME );
```

Value of int type	Meaning
REMOTE_HOST	REMOTE_HOST returns the hostname, or NULL if the hostname lookup fails. It will force a DNS lookup according to the HostnameLookups setting.
REMOTE_NAME	REMOTE_NAME returns the hostname, or the dotted quad if the hostname lookup fails. It will force a DNS lookup according to the HostnameLookups setting.
REMOTE_NOLOOKUP	REMOTE_NOLOOKUP is like REMOTE_NAME except that a DNS lookup is never forced.
REMOTE_DOUBLE_REV	REMOTE_DOUBLE_REV will always force a DNS lookup, and also force a double reverse lookup, regardless of the HostnameLookups setting. The result is the (double reverse checked) hostname, or NULL if any of the lookups fail.

ap_get_remote_logname()

Returns the login name of the remote user via RFC 1413. If you're on a *nix system RFC 1413 is implemented as `identd`.

```
const char *ap_get_remote_logname(request_rec *r);
ap_method_number_of()
```

Lurking in `src/include/http_protocol.h`, `ap_method_number_of()` returns the method number as an integer.

```
int ap_method_number_of(const char *method);
```

For example:

```
int method = ap_method_number_of( r->method );
case (method)
{
  M_GET:
  ...
```

Writing the Response

So far we've discussed interpreting, validating, finding the target, and discovering who is sending the request. We've mentioned almost nothing about sending data back to the client.

Because we're writing to the client through a TCP connection, we need to make certain that we constrain these calls inside `ap_hard_timeout()` or `ap_soft_timeout()`. Please refer to the reading data example above and the timeout API below.

Apache accounts for data we write back to the client. You may find the number of bytes written to the client in the `bytes_sent` field in the `request_rec` structure.

Below are functions that write data back to the client. They all return the number of bytes written or EOF (-1) if the connection closed prematurely. They may be found in `src/include/http_protocol.h`.

ap_send_http_header()

Sends the HTTP headers and status back to the requesting client. All the information here can be retrieved from the `request_rec` by hand. The headers may be assembled from the `content_type`, `content_encoding`, `headers_out`, and `err_headers_out` tables inside the `request_rec` structure.

```
void ap_send_http_header(request_rec *l);
```

ap_send_fd()

Sends a file to the client. Returns the number of bytes sent.

```
long ap_send_fd(FILE *f, request_rec *r);
```

ap_send_fd_length()

Sends length bytes of file to the requesting client. If the length parameter is less than 0 the entire file is sent.

```
long ap_send_fd_length(FILE *f, request_rec *r, long length);
```

ap_send_fb()

Sends a buffer to the client.

```
long ap_send_fb(BUFF *f, request_rec *r);
```

ap_send_fb_length()

Sends only length bytes of a buffer to the client.

```
long ap_send_fb_length(BUFF *f, request_rec *r, long length);
```

ap_send_mmap()

Sends the contents of a memory buffer to the client.

```
size_t ap_send_mmap(void *mm, request_rec *r, size_t offset,
    size_t length);
```

ap_rputc()

Sends a single character to the client just like the standard C function putc().

```
int ap_rputc(int c, request_rec *r);
```

ap_rputs()

Sends a string to the client.

```
int ap_rputs(const char *str, request_rec *r);
```

ap_rvputs()

Is just like `ap_rputs()` except that it sends a variable number of strings the last of which must be null.

```
int ap_rvputs(request_rec *r,...);
```

For example:

```
ap_rvputs( r, "first string", "second string", NULL );
ap_rwrite()--Sends nbytes of a buffer to the client .
int ap_rwrite(const void *buf, int nbyte, request_rec *r);
```

ap_vrprintf() and ap_rprintf()

These functions are standard C style `printf()`-like functions. The string resulting from these functions is sent to the client. They return the number of bytes sent or –1 if an error occurs.

```
int ap_vrprintf(request_rec *r, const char *fmt, va_list vlist);
int ap_rprintf(request_rec *r, const char *fmt,...)
        __attribute__((format(printf,2,3)));
```

For example:

```
ap_vrprintf( r, "This server was built on %s", ap_get_server_built());
```

ap_rflush()

Flushes the Apache output buffer. Use this function to force data to the client.

```
int ap_rflush(request_rec *r);
```

Below are some functions that don't really write to the client but do set important information in the HTTP headers.

ap_set_content_length()

Sets the HTTP Content-length header information from the length parameter.

```
int ap_set_content_length( request_rec *r, long length );
```

ap_set_etag()

Sets the ETag header information. This is useful if you're serving up static files because the entity tag allows the client to do HTTP/1.1 smart caching.

```
void ap_set_etag( request_rec *r );
```

ap_update_mtime()

Updates the modification time of the requested document.

```
time_t ap_update_mtime( request_rec *r,
    time_t dependency_mtime );
```

Timing Out

The timeout API may be found in src/include/http_main.h. The timeout functions are a critical part of communicating successfully with the requesting client. During any network I/O almost anything can and will go wrong. The network may stop working, the client software may crash, hang, or stop the request. If any of this happens, we need to make certain that we're not waiting for an event that may never occur.

Calls to the timeout API usually frame sections of code that have to perform IO with the requesting client. For example:

```
ap_soft_timeout( "ferret handler", r );

while ( … )
{
    … /* do stuff… */
    ap_puts( r, "Hello from the ferret handler!" ); /* perform IO */
    ap_reset_timeout( r ); /* we've succeeded so reset the timeout */
}
ap_kill_timeout( r ); /* we're done with IO so kill the timeout */
```

ap_hard_timeout()

Begins a timeout alarm. The first parameter is merely a character string to identify the timeout. This character string is the one that will appear in logged messages. The timeout takes the value set in the timeout configuration directive. If this alarm fires, the request will immediately abort the content handling phase of the transaction and enter the logging phase of the transaction.

```
void ap_hard_timeout(char *, request_rec *);
```

ap_soft_timeout()

Like `ap_hard_timeout()` but does not abort the content handler. All I/O with the client is disabled but the control is returned to the content handler. This enables the content handler to continue what it needs to do, such as close files or log appropriately.

```
void ap_soft_timeout(char *, request_rec *);
```

ap_kill_timeout()

Cancels a pending timeout alarm. Be sure to call this function before you exit the content handler to cancel any pending timeouts, otherwise a timeout may fire during a subsequent phase of the response handling.

```
void ap_kill_timeout(request_rec *);
```

ap_reset_timeout()

Resets the timeout alarm. If an I/O block protected by a timeout call succeeds, you should call this function to reset the pending timeout.

```
void ap_reset_timeout(request_rec *);
```

ap_block_alarms() and ap_unblock_alarms()

These two functions protect a section of code from having an alarm fire within the particular section of code. Use this to protect blocks of code from interruption.

```
void ap_block_alarms(void);
void ap_unblock_alarms(void);
```

Cleaning Up

The `cleanup` API is different from the other HTTP request handling phases in that these functions don't appear in the `module_rec` structure even though they are callback functions. The cleanup functions should take care of deallocating resources that don't fit neatly into the Apache memory pool paradigm. The `cleanup` API can be found in `src/include/alloc.h`.

ap_register_cleanup()

To be able to use a cleanup handler, you must first register the handler. The registration takes four arguments. The first parameter is a pool pointer and is usually the pool pointer from the request record (e.g. r->pool). The second parameter is any module or request-specific data the cleanup handler needs access to. This can be the request record itself or any other data you require. The third parameter is a function pointer. This implements the cleanup callback called for your module. The forth parameter is also a function pointer but is only called if your module forks a child. Usually, you won't need to implement a child_cleanup() function since most modules won't fork children that need resource management. To indicate to ap_register_cleanup() that you have no child_cleanup() function pass in the Apache convenience function ap_null_cleanup. Don't pass in NULL as the cleanup API will try to execute NULL.

```
void ap_register_cleanup( pool *p, void *data,
    void (*plain_cleanup) (void *),
    void (*child_cleanup) (void *));
```

ap_kill_cleanup()

To unregister a cleanup callback function, call ap_kill_cleanup() with the data and function pointer address. Make certain that all the data match the ap_register_cleanup() call or the cleanup function will not be removed.

```
void ap_kill_cleanup( pool *p, void *data,
    void (*plain_cleanup) (void *));
```

ap_run_cleanup()

To run a cleanup function before its appointed time, call ap_run_cleanup(). The cleanup function will be unregistered after it executes so that it may not be run again.

```
void ap_run_cleanup(pool *p, void *data,
    void (*cleanup) (void *));
```

Handling URIs

The URI API can deconstruct a URI into its component parts and reconstruct it again. The data structure used by these routines is the uri_components struct. The URI manipulation routines and the definition of the uri_components struct can be found in src/include/util_uri.h.

The structure is:

```
typedef struct {
    char *scheme;                /* scheme. HTTP, HTTPS, FTP, FILE */
    char *hostinfo;              /* host information including user info
                                    [user[:password]@]host[:port] */
    char *user;                  /* user name, as in http://user:passwd@host:port/ */
    char *password;              /* password, as in http://user:passwd@host:port/ */
    char *hostname;              /* hostname from URI (or from Host: header) */
    char *port_str;              /* port string (integer representation is in "port") */
    char *path;                  /* the request path (or "/" if only scheme://host was given) */
    char *query;                 /* Everything after a '?' in the path, if present */
    char *fragment;              /* Trailing "#fragment" string, if present */
    struct hostent *hostent;
    unsigned short port;         /* The port number, numeric, valid only if port_str != NULL */
                                 /* don't use these fields. They are internal to Apache */
    unsigned is_initialized:1;
    unsigned dns_looked_up:1;
    unsigned dns_resolved:1;
} uri_components;
```

ap_is_url()

Returns TRUE if its argument is a fully qualified URI. Returns FALSE if not.

```
int ap_is_url(const char *u);
```

ap_unescape_url()

Unescapes URI hex character escapes. It will return OK if it succeeds or HTTP_BAD_REQUEST if the argument contains a bad escape sequence or it will return HTTP_NOT_FOUND if the unescaped URI contains \0. The process of unescaping the string is performed in place.

```
int ap_unescape_url(char *url);
```

ap_os_escape_path()

Returns an escaped URI when passed a file system path. If the partial flag is TRUE then the returned URI will not start with the / character. If it is FALSE then the returned string will begin with /.

```
char *ap_os_escape_path(pool *p, const char *path, int partial);
```

ap_construct_server()

Contructs the hostname:port section of the URI and returns that as a
character string. It will only return the port section if the port passed as
an argument is different from the default port for the current server.

```
char *ap_construct_server(pool *p, const char *hostname,
    unsigned port, const request_rec *r);
```

ap_construct_url()

Builds a fully qualified URL from the contents of the request record and
the second argument URI. The pool *p should be the request pool (e.g.
r->pool).

```
char *ap_construct_url(pool *p, const char *uri,
    const request_rec *r );
```

ap_default_port_for_scheme()

Returns the port number for any of the schemes (HTTP, FTP, HTTPS,
FILE). The scheme passed in as an argument is case insensitive.

```
unsigned short ap_default_port_for_scheme(const char *scheme_str);
```

ap_default_port_for_request()

Returns the default port for the current request. The port will be the same
as the ports returned by ap_default_port_for_scheme() but all you
must pass as an argument is the request rather than the scheme. This
function will determine the scheme for you.

```
unsigned short ap_default_port_for_request(const request_rec *r);
```

ap_pgethostbyname()

Returns a hostent structure (see below) with the host name and address
information filled in.

```
struct hostent *ap_pgethostbyname(pool *p, const char *hostname);
struct hostent {
    char *h_name;                    /* official name of host */
    char **h_aliases;                /* alias list */
```

```
      int h_addrtype;                /* host address type */
      int h_length;                  /* length of address */
      char **h_addr_list;            /* list of addresses */
};
```

ap_parse_uri_components()

Pass this function a memory pool pointer, a URI, and a pointer to a `uri_components` structure and it will return either `HTTP_OK` or `HTTP_BAD_REQUEST`. If the function succeeds the `uri_components` structure will be filled in with the parsed URI information.

```
int ap_parse_uri_components(pool *p, const char *uri,
    uri_components *uptr);
```

ap_unparse_uri_components()

This function takes a populated `uri_components` structure and returns a string that is the reconstructed URI. The information contained in the URI will depend on the value of the `flags` parameter.

```
char *ap_unparse_uri_components(pool *p,
    const uri_components *uptr,
    unsigned flags);
```

ap_unparse_uri_components Flags	Meaning
UNP_OMITSITEPART	Suppress "scheme://user@site:port"
UNP_OMITUSER	Just omit user
UNP_OMITPASSWORD	Just omit password
UNP_OMITUSERINFO	Omit "user:password@" part
UNP_REVEALPASSWORD	Show plain text password (default: show XXXXXXXX)
UNP_OMITPATHINFO	Show "scheme://user@site:port" only
UNP_OMITQUERY	Omit the "?queryarg" from the path

Creating Subprocesses

Because of the complex environment that is the Apache Web server, creating new external processes is not automatic because we really can't use the standard C library functions to do it. The Apache API provides facilities for creating new processes. These functions are scattered through `alloc.h`, `buff.h`, `util_script.h`, `http_main.h`, `http_log.h`, and `httpd.h`.

ap_add_cgi_vars() and ap_add_common_vars()

These functions populate the `subprocess_env` structure inside the `request_rec` structure with environment variables. These environment variables are passed to your new process.

```
void ap_add_cgi_vars(request_rec *r);
void ap_add_common_vars(request_rec *r);
```

ap_create_environment()

Returns a list of environment variables from an Apache key/value pair table suitable for creating a child process. The `subprocess_env` table is such a table.

```
char **ap_create_environment(pool *p, table *t);
```

For example:

```
char **env_list = ap_create_environment( r->pool, r->subprocess_env );
```

ap_can_exec()

This function returns `TRUE` if the file inside the `stat` structure is executable by the current UID/GID. It returns `FALSE` otherwise. The single parameter is usually the `info` field inside the `request_rec` structure.

```
int ap_can_exec(const struct stat *);
```

For example:

```
int runnable = ap_can_exec( &r->info );
```

ap_bspawn_child()

This function forks a child and can also open pipes to a child.

```
int ap_bspawn_child(pool *p,
    int (*)(void *data, child_info *pinfo),
    void *data, enum kill_conditions,
    BUFF **pipe_in, BUFF **pipe_out,
```

```
    BUFF **pipe_err);
```

The first argument is a memory pool. It is usually the pool in the request record.

The second argument is a function pointer with a prototype of `int child_routine( void *data, child_info *pinfo );`

This child routine is the first function called after the new process forks. The data argument is the same as the third argument to `ap_bspawn_child()`.

The third argument is a void pointer that may be whatever you wish. In most cases you're going to want to send the request record to the child.

The fourth parameter is an enumerated type that determines how Apache treats the spawned child during startup and shutdown.

kill_conditions	Meaning
kill_always	The child process is sent SIGKILL on pool cleanup
kill_after_timeout	Send the child SIGTERM, then wait 3 seconds then send SIGKILL
just_wait	Wait forever for the child process to complete
kill_only_once	Send SIGTERM and then wait forever

The last three arguments are for reading from and writing to the child. Pass NULL here if you do not intend to communicate with the child. If you do want to communicate pass BUFF pointers in each argument and the function will pass back structures connected to the child process's standard in, standard out, and error files.

```
ap_spawn_child()
```

This function is essentially the same as `ap_bspawn_child()` except it uses FILE pointers to communicate with the child rather than the Apache BUFF structures.

```
int ap_spawn_child(pool *,
    int (*)(void *, child_info *),
    void *, enum kill_conditions,
    FILE **pipe_in, FILE **pipe_out,
    FILE **pipe_err);
```

ap_error_log2strderr()

This nifty function will reconnect the standard error of the new child process to the server error log of the server that spawned it. Call `ap_error_log2strderr()` after `ap_bspawn_child()` and before `ap_call_exec()` to get child log messages in the parent error log.

```
void ap_error_log2strderr( server-rec *s );
```

ap_cleanup_for_exec()

This function cleans up all the resource pools and subpools just prior to a call to `ap_call_exec()`.

```
void ap_cleanup_for_exec(void);
```

ap_call_exec()

Call this function after `ap_spawn_child()` to replace your running process with the new process. The command that will try to run is in `r->filename` and its arguments are in `r->args`. The first argument is the `request_rec` which has the file to run and the arguments in it. The second argument is the `child_info` used in `ap_spawn_child()`.

```
int ap_call_exec(request_rec *r, child_info *pinfo,
    char *argv0, char **env, int shellcmd);
```

ap_child_terminate()

Cleanly terminates the running child process.

```
void ap_child_terminate(request_rec *r);
```

ap_scan_script_header_err()

This function scans the file for HTTP headers. If the headers are valid HTTP headers they will be added to the requests `headers_out` table. If the headers are valid the function will return `OK`. Any other return is an error. The third parameter is a buffer that should be at least `MAX_STRING_LENGTH` in size. If an error occurs, this buffer will contain the data that caused the error.

```
int ap_scan_script_header_err(request_rec *r, FILE *f,
    char *buffer);
```

ap_scan_script_header_err_buff()

This function does just what `ap_scan_script_header_err()` does but with BUFF structures rather than files. You would use this function if you used `ap_bspawn_child()`.

```
int ap_scan_script_header_err_buff(request_rec *r,
    BUFF *f, char *buffer);
```

Other APIs

There are varieties of Apache APIs that perform a number of useful tasks not directly related to handling the series of module callbacks. They are scattered over all the Apache header files. There are a great number of API functions in the Apache environment. Below is a list of tasks and where you may look to the API to supply functionality:

- Handling Strings—Apache has a very full-featured set of string matching and regular expression functions. These may be found in `httpd.h` and `fnmatch.h`.
- Checking Types—The standard C type checking and conversion functions are declared in `ap_ctype.h`.
- Handling Files and Directories—`alloc.h` contains all the file and directory open and close functions you'll ever need. `httpd.h` contains declarations for routines to manipulate path names, count directories, change directories, etc.
- Using the Time and Date—Date and time functions can be found in both `util_date.h` and `httpd.h`.
- Getting User and Group Information—`ap_uname2id()` and `ap_gname2id()` allow access to user and group information and are declared in `httpd.h`.
- Locking Data—Data mutex locking is implemented in a cross-platform way in `multithread.h`.
- Checking Authenticity with MDA5—The Apache MD5 API can be found in `ap_md5.h`. This API implements the MD5 Message Digest agorithm.

Conclusion

To extend a base functionality (like a new HTTP command) or embed an expensive task (like a search engine, language interpreter, command parser, etc.), a module is the sure-fire way to get it done. While this chapter has concerned itself with the C interface, there exists a Perl interface called `mod_perl`. `mod_perl` wraps the Apache API quite nicely. The `mod_perl` interface contains all the functionality of the C interface with the convenience of Perl.

References and Further Reading

The Apache example readme is found in the Apache source distribution `src/modules/example/README`.

Find the Apache API Notes in **http://www.apache.org/docs/misc/ API.html**.

The Apache Web Server API Dictionary is at **http://dev.apache.org/ apidoc/**.

Stein, L. and MacEachern *Writing Apache Modules with Perl and C,* O'Reilly & Associates, Inc., 1999.

Also, see the section "Where in the Web," in the Appendix.

Appendix

Using the vi Editor

Generalities

Users inexperienced with UNIX often find the vi editor (and its cousins, vim, nvi, and elvis, among them) one of the most foreign applications to learn; unlike word-processor-like text editors, which are continuously in what we will come to call "insert mode," always ready to accept text and using control characters or function keys to invoke commands, vi lives in what can be called "command mode," using the keyboard as a large control panel from which commands to find, manipulate, and even insert text are invoked with a minimal number of keystrokes. While this distinction perhaps makes vi less well-suited for use in composing lengthy mail missives to Aunt Sally, it makes it particularly well-suited for editing existing configuration files.

Insert Mode

This is the mode most word-processors are in all the time. Characters that you type are treated as new components of the body text of the document. In vi, you enter this mode by using one of several command mode commands, and remain in it until you exit back to command mode with the escape key.

Command Mode

This is the business end of the vi editor. It is here that functions such as text navigation, deletion, change, insertion, and file-handling are invoked. Understanding command mode is thus the key to understanding vi.

Commands

There are a number of commands used in vi, but only a small group of them are needed to use it effectively. They are typically broken down into two groups: commands that act at the current cursor position, and commands that take additional input (which occurs on the bottom line of the window; these commands are generally preceded by a colon [:]).

- h, j, k, and l move the cursor back a character, up a line, down a line, and forward a character, respectively. While vi will respect the arrow keys on most keyboards, often systems attached to KVM switches, etc., do not send the arrow keys properly.

- G (shift-g) takes you to the end of the document.
- J (shift-j) joins the current and following lines together.
- I and i insert text. I inserts at the beginning of the current line, while i inserts at the current cursor position. Use the aforementioned [esc] to return to command mode.
- A and a append text. A appends to the end of the current line, whereas a appends after the current cursor position.
- Cs change text. cc changes the current line, cw changes the current word, and C changes from the cursor position to the end of the current line. Replaced text is stored in the "cut buffer" from which it can be subsequently pasted. Similarly, the letter r may be used to "replace" the character at the current cursor position with another single character.
- Ds delete text. dd deletes the current line, dw deletes the balance of the current word (after the cursor position), and D deletes the balance of the current line. Deleted text is stored in the cut buffer.
- Lines may be copied to the cut buffer using yy. Think "y" as in "yank."
- Ps paste text. P pastes before the current line, p pastes after.
- ~ will reverse the case of the alphabetic character at the current cursor position.
- /word will take you to the next occurrence of "word" in the document. /[enter] will take you to the next occurrence of the last searched word.
- . will repeat the last command.
- The u key will undo the last command.
- :[number][enter] will take you to that line of the document. Thus, to go to the beginning, use :1.
- :w [filename] will write out the current file to disk. If you supply a filename, it will use that filename, otherwise it defaults to overwriting the file originally opened (if there was one).
- :r [filename] will import the contents of another textfile, beginning on the line after the current cursor position. Think of r as "read."
- :q will quit. :q! is used to quit abandoning changes. :wq is used to write out the file and then quit.
- :%s/stuff/newstuff/g will replace all occurrences of "stuff" with "newstuff;" the syntax is a compromise byproduct of the command syntax of older UNIX editors.
- Many commands may be prefaced by a number to indicate "act on this many lines." For example, 5yy copies 5 lines to the cut buffer, and 7u undoes the last 7 commands. Obviously, one should exercise caution with commands like "100dd."

While dozens of other commands in vi exist, these are the basics a person needs to know to use it effectively. Other commands allow for such things as copying to multiple buffers, editing multiple files simultaneously, and other power-user applications.

Using Regular Expressions

This text will give the briefest introduction to regular expressions. Maybe it will be enough to get you going on using them in Apache configuration directives. For a lengthy discussion, consult the regex(7) man page.

Regular expressions are used to determine if a given string of characters conforms to a specified pattern. The pattern may be a literal string (in which case, you are trying to determine if the given string is exactly the same as the pattern, verbatim). The pattern may be reasonably complex (e.g. you are looking in the given string for a particular substring at the end of the given string). The pattern may be insanely complex (e.g. you are looking for a series of substrings and the second substring must begin with one of four specified characters and the third substring can be one or more numeric characters, and the fourth substring can be anything but empty, etc.). Regular expressions are powerful.

Many of the Apache configuration directives use regular expressions. The <LocationMatch> block directive uses a regular expression to recognize particular URL requests. The <FilesMatch> block directive uses a regular expression to determine if a particular file has been requested. The SetEnvIf directive uses a regular expression to test if a response header or a request header or an environment variable contains a particular value.

The <DirectoryMatch> block directive uses a regular expression to determine if the requested directory is a particular subdirectory—if it is, the directives within the block are evaluated. The following example, taken from Chapter 7: "Creating Multiple User Sites On One Server," uses the <DirectoryMatch> block directive to determine if a requested directory is a user home directory or a subdirectory thereof:

```
<DirectoryMatch ^/home/[A-Za-z0-9]+/html/.*>
    Options Indexes FollowSymLinks
    AllowOverride None
</DirectoryMatch>
```

In the above example, the regular expression

```
^/home/[A-Za-z0-9]+/html/.*
```

means: "Match any directory that begins with `/home/`, followed by one or more alphanumeric characters (which we take to be the username), followed by `/html/`, followed by zero or more characters of any type (which we take to be the requested subdirectory)". This regular expression matches strings like this

```
/home/jdoe/
```

and this

```
/home/jdoe/scrapbook
```

Regular expressions use special characters to describe special patterns. All other character (i.e. all non-special characters) match verbatim. Here are some of the more relevant `regex` special characters:

^   matches the beginning of the string.
    `^/home`   matches   "/home";
                     but not   "/ahome"
                     and not   "home"
                     (because those strings do not begin with `/home`).

$ matches the end of the string
    `gif$`   matches   "gif"
                     but not   "gif.bak"
                     (because the gif does not appear at the end of the stirng).

.   matches any character
    `./.`   matches   "j/d"
                     and even   "@/ = ";
                     but not   "jjd"
                     (because the middle character is not a slash).

*   matches zero or more occurrences of the previous character.
    `a*`   matches   ""
                     and   "a"
                     and   "aaaaaaaaaa"

    `/~.*/cgi-bin` matches   "/ ~jdoe/cgi-bin"
                     and   "/ ~patg/cgi-bin";
                     and even   "/ ~ /cgi-bin"

+   matches one or more occurrences of the previous character.

`/~.+/cgi-bin` matches   "/ ~jdoe/cgi-bin"

                   and   "/ ~patg/cgi-bin";

                   but not   "/ ~/cgi-bin"

                   (because there are no characters between the tilde and the slash. The + requires that there be at least one character in that position)

[]   matches any of the characters listed within the brackets.

`[ab]cd`   matches either the letter a or the letter b, followed by the letters c and d;

                   matches   "abc"

                   and   "bbc";

                   but not   "ccd"

                   (because cd is not preceeded by either an a or a b).

`[A-Z]`   matches any capital letter

`[0-9]`   matches any numeric character

`[A-Za-z0-9]+` matches one or more alphanumeric characters;

                   matches   "ab3";

                   and   "5";

                   but not   ""

                   (because the + requires at least one character)

                   and not   "___"

                   (because those characters are not alphanumeric)

Now look again at the example `<DirectoryMatch>` directive, above, and see if it makes more sense.

In regular expressions, parentheses store back, or "remember," the enclosed substring in the search pattern in order to reuse that substring later in a replacement pattern. In the following example (also taken from Chapter 7: "Creating Multiple User Web Sites On One Server"), the ScriptAliasMatch directive uses a regular expression to determine if a requested URL resides in a user site's CGI scripts directory. If it does, the directive translates the virtual URL into a physical filename—using substrings saved back from the regular expression.

```
ScriptAliasMatch ^/~([A-Za-z0-9]+)/cgi-bin/(.*) /home/$1/cgi-bin/$2
```

The above directive would recognize this request

```
/~jdoe/cgi-bin/cgitest
```

and translate it to this filename

```
/home/jdoe/cgi-bin/cgitest
```

The first parenthesized expression, ([A-Za-z0-9]+), matches one or more alphanumeric characters—which we take to be the username. The $1 variable in the replacement string is replaced by this first saved-back substring. The second parenthesized expression, (.*), matches zero or more characters of any type—which we take to be the requested file (which may be an empty substring if the user site's "document root" was requested). The $2 variable in the replacement string is replaced by this second saved-back substring.

Here is one of my favorite examples (which we didn't get to use, because large ISPs don't provide CGI to homepages):

```
ScriptAliasMatch ^/~([A-Za-z0-9])([A-Za-z0-9])([A-Za-z0-9]+)
/cgi-bin/(.*) /home/$1/$2/$1$2$3/cgi-bin/$4
```

The above directive translates a request like this:

```
/~jdoe/cgi-bin/cgitest
```

and translates it into this filename:

```
/home/j/d/jdoe/cgi-bin/cgitest
```

It works, really. I tested it.

Relevant RFCs

RFC Number	Title
791	INTERNET PROTOCOL
	DARPA INTERNET PROGRAM
	PROTOCOL SPECIFICATION
792	INTERNET CONTROL MESSAGE PROTOCOL
	DARPA INTERNET PROGRAM
	PROTOCOL SPECIFICATION
796	ADDRESS MAPPING

continued on next page

RFC Number	Title
1591	Domain Name System Structure and Delegation
1883	Internet Protocol, Version 6 (IPv6) Specification
1918	Address Allocation for Private Internets
2616	Hypertext Transfer Protocol—HTTP/1.1
2487	SMTP Service Extension for Secure SMTP over TLS
1186	The MD4 Message Digest Algorithm
1319	The MD2 Message Digest Algorithm
1321	The MD5 Message Digest Algorithm
1421	Privacy Enhancement for Internet Electronic Mail: Part I: Message Encryption and Authentication Procedures
1422	Privacy Enhancement for Internet Electronic Mail: Part II: Certificate-Based Key Management
1423	Privacy Enhancement for Internet Electronic Mail: Part III: Algorithms, Modes, and Identifiers
1424	Privacy Enhancement for Internet Electronic Mail: Part IV: Key Certification and Related Services

HTTP Status Codes[1]

The first digit of the Status Code defines the class of response. The last two digits do not have any categorization role. There are five values for the first digit:

1xx: Informational—Request received, continuing process.

2xx: Success—The action was successfully received, understood, and accepted.

3xx: Redirection—Further action must be taken in order to complete the request.

4xx: Client Error—The request contains bad syntax or cannot be fulfilled.

5xx: Server Error—The server failed to fulfill an apparently valid request.

---

1 RFC 2616 Hypertext Transfer Protocol—HTTP/1.1, section 6.1.1 **ftp://ftp.isi.edu/in-notes/ rfc2616.txt**. The text is quoted from the RFC document. The table of status codes is a reformatting of the BNF grammar from the RFC.

The individual values of the numeric status codes defined for HTTP/1.1, and an example set of corresponding reason-phrase's, are presented below. The reason phrases listed here are only recommendations—they MAY be replaced by local equivalents without affecting the protocol.

Status Codes

Status Code =	Section	Reason-Phrase
100	10.1.1	Continue
101	10.1.2	Switching Protocols
200	10.2.1	OK
201	10.2.2	Created
202	10.2.3	Accepted
203	10.2.4	Non-Authoritative Information
204	10.2.5	No Content
205	10.2.6	Reset Content
206	10.2.7	Partial Content
300	10.3.1	Multiple Choices
301	10.3.2	Moved Permanently
302	10.3.3	Found
303	10.3.4	See Other
304	10.3.5	Not Modified
305	10.3.6	Use Proxy
307	10.3.8	Temporary Redirect
400	10.4.1	Bad Request
401	10.4.2	Unauthorized
402	10.4.3	Payment Required
403	10.4.4	Forbidden
404	10.4.5	Not Found
405	10.4.6	Method Not Allowed
406	10.4.7	Not Acceptable
407	10.4.8	Proxy Authentication Required
408	10.4.9	Request Time-out
409	10.4.10	Conflict
410	10.4.11	Gone

continued on next page

Status Code =	Section	Reason-Phrase
411	10.4.12	Length Required
412	10.4.13	Precondition Failed
413	10.4.14	Request Entity Too Large
414	10.4.15	Request-URI Too Large
415	10.4.16	Unsupported Media Type
416	10.4.17	Requested Range Not Satisfiable
417	10.4.18	Expectation Failed
500	10.5.1	Internal Server Error
501	10.5.2	Not Implemented
502	10.5.3	Bad Gateway
503	10.5.4	Service Unavailable
504	10.5.5	Gateway Time-out
505	10.5.6	HTTP Version Not Supported

HTTP status codes are extensible. HTTP applications are not required to understand the meaning of all registered status codes, though such understanding is obviously desirable. However, applications MUST understand the class of any status code, as indicated by the first digit, and treat any unrecognized response as being equivalent to the x00 status code of that class, with the exception that an unrecognized response must not be cached. For example: if an unrecognized status code of 431 is received by the client, it can safely assume that there was something wrong with its request and treat the response as if it had received a 400 status code. In such cases, user agents SHOULD present to the user the entity returned with the response, since that entity is likely to include human-readable information which will explain the unusual status.

Where in the Web[2]

Apache Server

Apache Web Server
http://www.apache.org

---

2 Descriptions and links quoted from their respective URLs (sometimes paraphrased).

Apache for the BS2000/OSD
http://www.siemens.com/servers/apache_osd/apache_us.htm

Apache Projects

Apache Module Registry
http://modules.apache.org/
The Apache Module Registry offers a broad assortment of contributed works from developers around the globe. The registry includes a searchable database, which can be used to find modules and assorted patches that have been found useful, but have not been officially included as part of the standard Apache distribution.

Apache Server Project

http://www.apache.org/httpd.html
A collaborative software development effort, the Apache Server Project is aimed at creating a robust, commercial-grade, freely available source code implementation of an HTTP server.

Apache XML Project

http://xml.apache.org/
A focus for XML-related activities within Apache projects, the Apache XML Project currently consists of four subprojects, each focusing on a different aspect of XML.

1. Xerces—XML parsers in Java, C + +, and Perl
   a. Xerces Java—**http://xml.apache.org/xerces-j/index.html**
      The Xerces-J 1.0.0 release contains advanced parser functionality, such as XML Schema, DOM Level 2, and SAX version 2, in addition to supporting the industry-standard DOM Level 1 and SAX version 1 APIs.
   b. Xerces C + + Parser—**http://xml.apache.org/xerces-c/index.html**
      A validating XML parser written in a portable subset of C + +.
   c. Xerces Perl—**http://xml.apache.org/xerces-p/index.html**
      XML4P delivers the benefits of the XML4C DOM Parser in Perl5. XML4P includes a collection of Perl5 wrapper objects that internally use their XML4C counterparts for high-performance, scalable and localizable XML DOM parsing.

2. Xalan —XSLT stylesheet processors, in Java and C + +
   a. Xalan-Java—**http://xml.apache.org/xalan/overview.html**
      Xalan-Java provides high-performance XSL stylesheet processing, and
      fully implements the W3C XSLT recommendation.
   b. Xalan - C + + —**http://xml.apache.org/xalan/xslt4c.html**
      Xalan-C + + implements W3C Recommendation 16 November 1999
      XSL Transformations (XSLT) Version 1.0. Version 0.19.0 is the first
      release, including a build for Win32; other builds are to follow.

3. FOP: **http://xml.apache.org/fop/index.html**
   A print formatter driven by XSL formatting objects, FOP is a Java 1.1
   application that reads a formatting object tree and then turns it into a
   PDF document.

4. Cocoon—**http://xml.apache.org/cocoon/index.html**
   A Java publishing framework that relies on new W3C technologies
   (such as DOM, XML, and XSL) to provide web content, allowing the
   three layers (creation, rendering, and serving) to be independently
   designed, created and managed.

Jakarta Project

http://jakarta.apache.org/
The Jakarta Project's aim is to provide commercial-quality server solutions, based on the Java Platform, which are developed in an open and
cooperative fashion.

Java Apache Project

http://java.apache.org/
The Java-Apache Project is home to various other server-side Java projects.

Apache/Perl Integration Project

http://perl.apache.org/
Mod-perl brings together the full power of the Perl programming language, and the Apache HTTP Server.

Mod PHP:

http://php.apache.org
PHP is a server-side, cross-platform, HTML embedded scripting language.

Security

Introduction to SSL

http://developer.netscape.com/docs/manuals/security/sslin/contents.htm

Using Encryption and SSL

http://developer.netscape.com/docs/manuals/enterprise/admnunix/encrypt.htm

SSLeay and SSLapps FAQ

http://www2.psy.uq.edu.au/ ~ ftp/Crypto/

Information on Cryptography

http://HTTP.CS.Berkeley.EDU/ ~ daw/crypto.html

National Institute of Standards and Technology (NIST) Computer Security Resource Clearinghouse

http://csrc.ncsl.nist.gov/

Computer Incident Advisory Capability (CIAC)

http://ciac.llnl.gov/

National Information Assurance Partnership (NIAP)

http://niap.nist.gov/
The NIAP is a collaboration between National Institute of Standards and Technology (NIST) and National Security Agency (NSA).

Center for Education and Research in Information Assurance and Security (CERIAS)

http://www.cerias.purdue.edu/

Information on Computer Security

http://HTTP.CS.Berkeley.EDU/ ~ daw/compsec.html

RFC Information

RFC Editor

http://www.rfc-editor.org/
The RFC Editor includes search options.

Index of RFCs

http://www.ietf.org/rfc/
RFC Frequently Asked Questions (FAQ)—**http://www.faqs.org/rfcs/**

Standardization Organizations

Internet Engineering Task Force (IETF)

http://www.ietf.org/
The IETF is the protocol engineering and development arm of the Internet.

World Wide Web Consortium (W3C)

http://www.w3c.org/
This international industry consortium is jointly hosted by the Massachusetts Institute of Technology Laboratory for Computer Science [MIT/LCS] in the United States (**http://www.lcs.mit.edu/**); the Institut National de Recherche en Informatique et en Automatique [INRIA] in Europe (**http://www.inria.fr/**); and the Keio University Shonan Fujisawa Campus in Japan (**http://www.keio.ac.jp/**). The W3C was founded in 1994, to lead the World Wide Web to its full potential by developing common protocols which promote evolution and ensure interoperability.

International Organization for Standardization (ISO)

http://www.iso.ch/
ISO is a non-governmental organization established to promote the development of standardization and related activities in the world. This worldwide federation of national standards bodies works towards facilitating the international exchange of goods and services, and to developing cooperation in the areas of scientific, technological, intellectual, and economic activity.

Internet Society (ISOC)

http://www.isoc.org/
The Internet Society (ISOC) is the organization home for the groups responsible for Internet infrastructure standards, including the Internet Engineering Task Force (IETF) and the Internet Architecture Board (IAB).

The Internet Corporation for Assigned Names and Numbers (ICANN)

http://www.icann.org/

A non-profit corporation was formed to assume responsibility for the IP address space allocation, protocol parameter assignment, domain name system management, and root server system management functions now performed under U.S. Government contract by IANA and other entities.

Internet Assigned Numbers Authority (IANA)

http://www.iana.org/

IANA is in charge of all "unique parameters" on the Internet, including IP (Internet Protocol) addresses.

Internet Architecture Board (IAB)

http://www.iab.org/iab/

Overseeing a number of critical activities, the IAB is responsible for defining the overall architecture of the Internet.

International Telecommunication Union (ITU)

http://www.itu.int/

ITU is an international organization within which goverment and the private sector coordinate global telecom networks and services.

European Telecommunication Standards Institute (ETSI)

http://www.etsi.org/

ETSI is an open forum with members from 50 countries, representing administrations, network operators, manufacturers, service providers, and users. Their goal is to determine and produce telecommunications standards.

International Trademark Association (INTA)

http://www.inta.org/

INTA is dedicated to promoting the role of trademarks, worldwide.

World Intellectual Property Organization (WIPO)

http://www.wipo.int/

Responsible for the promotion of the protection of intellectual property throughout the world, the WIPO is one of the 16 specialized agencies of the United Nations system of organizations.

Firewalls

Brimstone and FreeStone

SOS CORPORATION
SunOS, Sun 4s, BSDI, IRIX
http://www.soscorp.com/

FireWall-1

CHECK POINT SOFTWARE TECHNOLOGIES LTD.
Solaris, HPUX, AIX, 95, 98, NT
http://www.checkpoint.com/products/firewall-1/index.html

Gauntlet Firewall

NETWORK ASSOCIATES
UNIX, NT
http://www.nai.com/asp_set/products/tns/gauntlet.asp

Guardian Firewall

NETGUARD
NT
http://www.ntguard.com

Raptor Firewall

RAPTOR SYSTEMS, INC.
Solaris , NT
http://www.raptor.com/products/datasheets/prodsheet.html

SecureWay Firewall

IBM
NT, AIX
http://www4.ibm.com/software/security/firewall/

SecurIT Firewall

AXENT TECHNOLOGIES
Sun OS, Solaris, NT
http://www.milkyway.com/prod/info.html

TIS Internet Firewall Toolkit

TRUSTED INFORMATION SYSTEMS, INC.
UNIX using Berkeley sockets
http://www.tis.com/research/software/fwtk/index.html

Shopping Cart Software

Electronic Commerce Cart

http://www.ecomcart.com/

PerlShop

http://www.arpanet.com/PerlShop/perlshop.html

Titanium Commerce Server

http://www.bluemoney.com/comprod/products/BlueMoney/

Web+Shop

http://www.talentsoft.com/new/products/webplusshop.wml/

Commerce.cgi

http://www.careyinternet.com/cgi-bin/demo/store/commerce.cgi

Credit Card Verification Services

Authorize.Net

http://www.authorizenet.com/

ITransact.com

http://www.itransact.com/

CCVS (Credit Card Verification System)

http://www.hks.net/

CyberCash

http://www.cybercash.com/

General Information

Unix vs. NT Organization

http://www.unix-vs-nt.org/

Cern's WebOffice

http://www.cern.ch/WebOffice/

This site officially ceased to exist on February 1, 1999. This page covers the old group. The new group is under two different divisions:

- Web Services section inside the Internet Applications group of IT Division: **http://www.cern.ch/CERN/Divisions/IT/IA/**
- Web Communications unit inside DSU: **http://www.cern.ch/CERN/Divisions/DSU/dsuwcome.html**

Webopedia

http://webopedia.internet.com/

Webopedia is an online computer dictionary for Internet terms, and technical support.

Acronym Finder

http://www.acronymfinder.com/

The Perl Archive

http://www.perlarchive.com/

Tech-NIC.net

http://www.tech-nic.net/

Tech-NIC is a non-profit site, meant to provide technical information on the technical part of working with and on the Internet.

Apache Week

http://www.apacheweek.com

This weekly e-zine is full of Apache articles and useful information.

Userfriendly

http://www.userfriendly.org/

This site offers comic relief from the everyday drudgery of life. Be sure to check out the archives!

Mailing Lists and Discussion Groups

Geocrawler

http://www.geocrawler.com/

Apache Discussion

http://www.topica.com/lists/apache/

Java-Apache-framework

http://www.topica.com/lists/java-apache-framework@list.
working-dogs.com/

MODPERL

http://www.topica.com/lists/MODPERL@listproc.itribe.net/

mod_java

http://www.topica.com/lists/mod_java@list.working-dogs.com/

stronghold-announce

http://www.topica.com/lists/stronghold-announce@c2.net/

stronghold-users

http://www.topica.com/lists/stronghold-users@c2.net/?cid = 2782

apacheweek

http://www.topica.com/lists/apacheweek@www.ukweb.com/

mu-apache list

http://www.topica.com/lists/mu-apache@nicar.org/

SecurePoint Apache Discussion

http://msgs.SecurePoint.com/cgi-bin/get/apache-current.html

A search of your news server should turn up several newsgroups related
to Apache and HTTP server administration.

Index

Note: Boldface numbers indicate illustrations.

About the Author

Mark Arnold is a general partner with Auxentropic, a firm specializing in the creation of shopping cart packages for Web commerce.